The
U.S. Army
in a
New Security Era

The
U.S. Army
in a
New Security Era

edited by
Sam C. Sarkesian
John Allen Williams

Lynne Rienner Publishers   Boulder & London

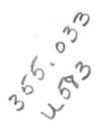

Published in the United States of America in 1990 by
Lynne Rienner Publishers, Inc.
1800 30th Street, Boulder, Colorado 80301

and in the United Kingdom by
Lynne Rienner Publishers, Inc.
3 Henrietta Street, Covent Garden, London WC2E 8LU

© 1990 by Lynne Rienner Publishers, Inc. All rights reserved

Library of Congress Cataloging-in-Publication Data
The U.S. Army in a new security era / Sam C. Sarkesian, John Allen
  Williams, editors.
  Includes bibliographical references.
  ISBN 1-55587-191-7 (alk. paper)
  1. United States. Army. 2. United States—National security.
I. Sarkesian, Sam Charles. II. Williams, John Allen.
UA25.U46 1990
355'.033073—dc20   90-8052
                                                                  CIP

British Cataloguing in Publication Data
A Cataloguing in Publication record for this book
is available from the British Library.

Printed and bound in the United States of America

The paper used in this publication meets the requirements
of the American National Standard for Permanence of
paper for Printed Library Materials Z39.48-1984.

Contents

List of Tables and Figures vii
Preface ix

PART 1 INTRODUCTION

1 U.S. National Security Strategy: The Next Decade
  Sam C. Sarkesian 1
2 The U.S. Army: A Strategic Force for a New Security Era
  Gen. Carl E. Vuono, U.S. Army 19

PART 2 U. S. DOMESTIC POLITICS AND SECURITY ISSUES

3 The Public and National Security Douglas Kinnard 33
4 Congress and the Defense Budget Robert F. Hale 51

PART 3 EUROPE AND THE UNITED STATES

5 Gorbachev's Gambit: Soviet Military Doctrine and Conventional
  Arms Control in an Era of Reform Jacob W. Kipp 83
6 NATO in a New Strategic Environment Edward A. Kolodziej 121
7 Forces and Politics in Europe Arthur Cyr 139
8 Force Structures: The United States and Europe in the
  Coming Decade Col. David E. Shaver, U.S. Army 152

PART 4 BEYOND EUROPE

9 Conventional Conflicts Beyond Europe David W. Tarr 177

10 U.S. Strategy and Unconventional Conflicts:
   The Elusive Goal *Sam C. Sarkesian*   195

PART 5 NAVAL AND AIR STRATEGIES

11 The Maritime Strategy in a New Security Era
   John Allen Williams   217
12 New Dimensions in Air Strategy *Lt. Col. David MacIsaac,
   U.S. Air Force (Ret.)*   236

PART 6 EDUCATION AND TRAINING OF THE U.S. ARMY

13 Education of U.S. Army Officers *Lt. Gen. Howard D. Graves,
   U.S. Army*   249
14 Challenges of U.S. Army Reserve Force Readiness
   *Lt. Gen. Frederic J. Brown, U.S. Army (Ret.) and
   Col. Aubrey R. Merrill, Jr., U.S. Army (Ret.)*   258

PART 7 CONCLUSIONS

15 Challenges and Requirements for the Future
   John Allen Williams   285

   About the Contributors   298
   Index   302
   About the Book   314

Tables and Figures

Tables

4.1	Key Steps in the Congressional Defense Budget Process	54
4.2	1987 Defense Expenditures as a Percentage of Gross Domestic Product	68
4.3	Percentage of Adults in Various Countries Who Believe the Chance of World War Within the Next 10 Years Is 50 Percent or Greater	68
4.4	Trends in Public Attitudes Toward Defense Spending	70
14.1	Relative Manpower Standing of NATO Countries	260
14.2	Profile of U.S. Army Officers and Enlisted Personnel	280

Figures

4.1	National Defense Budget Authority	64
4.2	Federal Deficit as a Percentage of GNP	64
4.3	Government Outlays as a Percentage of GNP	65
13.1	Military Education Related to the Levels of War Planning and Conduct	251
14.1	Active and Reserve Components of the Federal Republic of Germany	260
14.2	Manpower Quality of U.S. Army Reserve Components	263
14.3	U.S. Army Defense Commands	266

Preface

The dramatic changes that took place in Eastern Europe in 1989 and early 1990 as a result of glasnost and perestroika seemed to confirm earlier signs that the grip of Moscow was easing. Mikhail Gorbachev, recognizing the internal problems facing the Soviet Union, not only in terms of economics, but of political cohesion, is apparently trying to reshape the Soviet Union's external power relationships in order to devote more energy and resources to revitalizing the Soviet domestic political-economic system. Part of this reshaping includes a changed Soviet military posture in Europe and a more accommodating relationship with the United States. As a result, the perception regarding the Soviet military threat has receded in the minds of most Europeans and many Americans. Additionally, most believe that there is now an arms control momentum, including a drive to reduce conventional forces in Europe. These developments have serious implications for the U.S. military.

Setting the stage for all of these security issues was the INF (Intermediate-range Nuclear Forces) Treaty between the United States and the USSR. Signed in 1987, this treaty not only is intended to destroy an entire class of weapons, but it established procedures for inspections and provided a precedent for a multitude of contacts and exchanges between U.S. and Soviet military officers and defense specialists. At the same time, it changed the security equation between the United States and the Soviet Union, with implications for U.S. military force posture. With critical elements of its operational forces stationed in Europe, the U.S. Army is perhaps the branch of service that is most directly affected by these emerging strategic changes.

In an attempt to come to grips with these issues, General Carl E. Vuono, Chief of Staff, U.S. Army, sought the views of a variety of specialists and defense authorities in government and academia. Equally important, the U.S. Army reached beyond the "beltway" to tap the resources in the U.S. Midwest. The result was a workshop entitled, "U.S. National Security Strategy: New Challenges and Opportunities." The focus of the workshop was to explore the implications for U.S. national security of the changing strategic landscape, with particular emphasis on how it affected the U.S. Army. Additionally, the workshop was intended to stimulate public discussion and awareness of the important issues evolving from these strategic changes. The workshop, sponsored jointly by the Inter-University Seminar on Armed Forces and Society and the U.S. Army, with support from the National Strategy Forum, was held between September 30 and October 2, 1988, in Chicago. George Washington University, Washington, D.C., provided invaluable administrative support.

The final report of the workshop was submitted to General Vuono in August 1989. It included copies of all the papers and an executive summary. These papers have been extensively revised by their authors and are included in this book. In addition, three other contributions are included herein that were not part of the workshop: Chapters 1, 12, and 15. The need for introductory and concluding chapters is self-evident. The addition of an Air Force perspective is important for a more comprehensive view of the post-INF era. However, the workshop and this book are not intended as final words on the changing strategic environment and U.S. military posture. Rather, the intent is to generate serious thinking on the emerging security issues, to develop a research agenda, and to help identify the shape of the strategic environment in which the U.S. Army will operate in the 1990s.

All of the answers are not here, but we believe that many of the most important questions are. Workshop participants and contributors to this book struggled with these questions in their search for answers. We believe that they have set out directions and an agenda critical in responding to the changing strategic landscape. This is particularly important for policymakers and strategists, as well as scholars. We also believe that this book provides important insights for professional military officers and those involved in national security studies at the graduate level.

This study was undertaken during a period of uncertainty and transition in Europe (particularly in divided Germany) and the Soviet Union. The fluidity of the political environment and the nature of the changes taking place make it extremely difficult to predict the precise contours of the strategic landscape. Yet even in such circumstances, force structures must be designed and strategic options thought out completely. Those concerned with such issues do not have the luxury of waiting until political directions are clear. Fortunately, the focus of this study is primarily on long-range strategic issues and force structures, regardless of the politics of the moment, since it is likely that changes in the European environment will continue even as this book is being published.

At the same time, U.S. military operations in Panama have highlighted a possible future role of the U.S. Army as a quick-reaction crisis intervention force that can augment friendly forces and draw upon a strategic reserve of resources positioned in the continental United States. These operations have also highlighted the political and military difficulties inherent in Third World intervention operations and demonstrated anew the need for sound planning and effective interservice cooperation. These difficulties were apparent even in Panama, despite some thirteen thousand U.S. Army forces already in place, a domestically and internationally unpopular leader to be overthrown, and a treaty that could be construed as permitting U.S. intervention.

Part 1, "Introduction," consists of two selections, one of which is written by General Carl E. Vuono; both provide a broad overview of the changing strategic landscape and how the U.S. Army intends to respond. Part 2 focuses on the domestic environment and security issues with two selections, one addressing public opinion and the other on Congress and the defense budget. These chapters examine the constraints on responding to security issues and the reshaping of military posture imposed by a democratic system. Part 3 shifts the direction to specific issues in Europe. The selections range from an examination of the Gorbachev phenomenon and the changing dynamics within NATO to the conventional force balance and U.S. and European force structures. Part 4 extends the view beyond Europe, examining conventional conflicts in non-European areas and unconventional conflicts. Part 5 comes to grips with the impact of the new landscape on maritime strategy and the changing dimensions of air strategy. Part 6 focuses on the new challenges posed to the education and training of U.S. Army officers and Army reserve forces. The last part, "Conclusions," summarizes the major points made in the book, draws conclusions regarding the strategic landscape in the 1990s, and raises critical questions regarding national security strategy and U.S. Army force posture.

We are indebted to General Carl E. Vuono, U.S. Army, for the strategic vision that inspired this project, and to Lieutenant Colonel Kenneth Allard and Lieutenant Colonel Rolland Dessert, U.S. Army, for their critical role in bringing together various administrative and logistical elements that made for a successful workshop and publication. We wish to convey our special appreciation to Colonel Raul H. ("Roy") Alcala, U.S. Army, for his innumerable contributions to our project and, more generally, to Army strategic thought.

Robert L. Vitas, once our student and now our colleague, rendered invaluable assistance in organizing the workshop and preparing the final report. We appreciate the continuing interest of Eugene P. Visco, Department of the Army, in our project, and note with gratitude the contribution of resources and expertise of the National Strategy Forum. Also, we wish to thank the Institute for Technology and Strategic Research of the School of Engineering and Applied Science, George Washington University, whose fiscal guidance and administration contributed greatly to the success of this project. Finally, and very importantly, without the support and assistance of the Inter-University Seminar on Armed Forces and Society, especially its chairman, Charles C. Moskos, we could not have undertaken this project.

Despite the considerable assistance in organizing and conducting the workshop just noted, the final responsibility for material included and omitted and for strategic judgments expressed rests with the editors. This is particularly true of the assessments and conclusions that appear in Chapter 1, "U.S. National Security Strategy: The Next Decade," and Chapter 15, "Challenges and Requirements for the Future."

Sam C. Sarkesian
John Allen Williams

PART 1
Introduction

CHAPTER 1

U.S. National Security Strategy: The Next Decade

SAM C. SARKESIAN

Historians are likely to depict the 1980s as a decade of important changes that signaled an end to one era and the beginning of another. The decade began with a resurgence of U.S. power and ended with glasnost and perestroika promising to unravel the Soviet empire and change the political and strategic landscape. During the course of the decade, important changes began to take place in the European strategic environment and in U.S. domestic politics that will likely have a long-range impact on U.S. defense posture. Equally important, the political dynamics resulting from Gorbachev's glasnost and perestroika unleashed forces that appear irreversible.

While acknowledging these political changes, few agree where they will lead. The most that can be said at this time is that the superpower concept and political alignments resulting from these changes are eroding. In the process, the international order has moved to a multidimensional power alignment. The most visible change is in U.S. relations with Europe and involvement in NATO, and the Soviet Union's relationship with Eastern Europe, particularly in terms of the unraveling of the Eastern bloc. Simultaneously, Soviet internal politics have been affected by the surfacing of deep-seated nationalistic forces and the exacerbation of historical nationalistic animosities within the Soviet state. But, again, it is not clear where all of this will lead. Thus, the 1980s ended amid a number of uncertainties and a fluidity in the strategic arena that make it difficult for the United States to come to grips with strategic directions and relevant military posture.

Yet, no major state and its military system have the luxury of deferring strategic guidelines and appropriate military posture while awaiting political developments. Thus, the more compelling question for the United States that has arisen from the decade of transition has to do with its military posture and strategic capabilities.

The purpose of this chapter is to assess the changing political character of the international environment, paint a broad picture focusing on its critical features, and identify some of the major strategic signposts that have emerged or are likely to do so. From this, conclusions will be drawn as to how these factors impact on the U.S. military, with specific reference to the U.S. Army. This overview will lay the groundwork for the more detailed discussions in subsequent chapters.

The Gorbachev Era: Glasnost and Perestroika

It is generally acknowledged that as a result of glasnost and perestroika, the strategic landscape in Europe is changing, with important implications for the international security environment. To be sure, all of this is not simply a result of the newfound truths by Mikhail Gorbachev and the new leadership in the Soviet Union. Much also can be traced to the persistence of NATO and the United States regarding security policies and strategies, as well as to serious internal problems in the Soviet Union. But the fact remains that Gorbachev's arrival on the scene has precipitated an array of new political forces, energized a new set of Soviet political actors, and muddled existing relationships between the Soviet Union, Europe, and the United States. In the process, Gorbachev has transformed the Russian terms *glasnost* and *perestroika* into a universal language.

It is safe to presume that few in the USSR or elsewhere could have predicted the impact of Gorbachev's policies or of the man himself. Some also argue that Gorbachev could hardly have known the kind of Pandora's box that glasnost and perestroika have precipitated. There is a body of Western opinion that is convinced that the "genie is out of the bottle" and that what has been unleashed is irreversible. The independence drive in the Baltic states, the nationalistic fervor in the Caucasus, and the unraveling of the Eastern European Communist bloc have not only had a disquieting effect (to say the least) on the Soviet Communist leadership, these events have had consequences on the Western power base and alliance system. Further, these developments have awakened a public sensitivity in Eastern Europe that makes a military response by the Soviets very problematic for them. In this respect, the emergence of political opposition within the Soviet Union and the loosening of Soviet control have narrowed the freedom of action associated with earlier governments.

As one observer concludes:

> The increasing intensity of ethnonationalism among Russians and non-Russians alike, sometimes taking extreme and chauvinistic forms, has not only provoked increasing alarm among Soviet citizens and leaders, it has also precipitated a sharp controversy over Soviet policy toward the "nationalities question" and over the nature and future of the Soviet federal system itself.[1]

In the final analysis, care must be taken in analyzing these Soviet problems. "All this underscores the complexity as well as the volatility of the Soviet scene and the difficulties in assessing—let alone predicting or influencing—political developments there."[2] In this respect, "the new thinking provides a general framework for policy rather than a detailed plan of action. Hence, there is much that is still unclear about it and its implications for Soviet policy."[3]

Although many of the problems now surfacing have their roots in the pre-Gorbachev era, glasnost and perestroika have provided the framework and precipitating mechanism for public discussions of these problems. In turn, the public airing has offered Gorbachev an opportunity to plan and implement political and economic reforms. The dilemma is that the public airing exacerbates the difficulty of these problems by broadening public awareness and feeding the drive for resolution.

For example, part of the nationalities problem is related to the demographic patterns within the Soviet state—patterns that have been evolving for many years. Not only will the Great Russian population be a minority in its own state in the very near future, but the growth rate of non-European populations is four to five times that of the European population. The demographic developments give impetus to the nationalities pressures, particularly since questions have been raised about sharing power at the central level between Great Russians and others. Problems of ethnicity and nationality have also plagued the composition of the Soviet armed forces. These problems are likely to continue and become acute as time goes on.

The problems facing the Soviet leadership are compounded by the inability of the economic system to meet the needs of the people. The most visible area of failure of the Marxist-Leninist system is in economic organization and productivity. After seventy years of effort, the Soviet economic system remains embedded in problems normally associated with many Third World states. While a number of Gorbachev's proponents argue that this is a result of the efforts of previous leaders to maintain a large military establishment, others argue that it is a result of the inefficient economic structure itself. The difficulties encountered in economic reform and the potential for social unrest they create have prompted some to conclude that the Gorbachev reforms are in real trouble.[4]

A number of Soviet military men and academicians have also argued that the Gorbachev era has not spared the Soviet military. Internally, efforts are in progress to assure party control over the military. As one scholar noted, "Indications that the effort to reassert party control over the military would continue or even intensify were visible almost from the moment Gorbachev took over as general secretary."[5] Among other things, Gorbachev was able to reshuffle much of the top military leadership and reduce the military's role in some aspects of the security and defense policymaking process. Additionally, "while the main emphasis has been on increasing discipline and raising troop morale, the military has also been called upon to admit previous shortcomings."[6]

In the external sphere, the strategy put into place in 1987 is based on parity with the West, reliance on arms control, and reshaping the Soviet military into a defensive posture, while abandoning the earlier "dual track" strategy. Marshal Sergei Akhromeyev emphasized in a July 1989 visit to Chicago that the reductions in force taking place in the Soviet Union and the emergence of a Soviet defensive posture are based on defensive defense and sufficiency. The Marshal argued strongly that there is now a reduced Soviet military threat to the West. In brief, the Soviets have projected the notion that their new doctrine of "defensive defense" and "sufficiency" offers no threat to the West. However, based on available intelligence, such declaratory policies have yet to take effect on the Soviet national security posture.[7]

Finally, the fundamental problem facing the Gorbachev leadership stems from the system of government that has evolved over the past decades, a system that has become bloated by bureaucracy and rigidity masked by Marxist-Leninist ideology. Some important steps have been taken to change this. For example, the Supreme Soviet has been reduced in size and based on the election of deputies, who now number 542. Election to that body was a new phenomenon in the Soviet Union and laid the groundwork for what many hoped would be the basis for an effective legislative system. Moreover, the debates that have occurred within the body suggest that glasnost has had a positive effect. Yet, it is also clear that much disagreement remains regarding the long-range implications of these new structures. For example, Gorbachev seems to have drawn most of the executive power (President of the USSR, General Secretary of the Communist Party, and Chairman of the Defense Council) into his own hands, prompting some to argue that he may well become another Stalin.[8] Thus, serious questions remain regarding the effectiveness of the Supreme Soviet as a legislative body and the final shape of the governing system in the Soviet state.

In sum, the declaratory policies of the Soviet Union and the leadership style of Mikhail Gorbachev, combined with the visible changes taking place in the USSR and Eastern Europe, have drastically altered the popular perception of the Soviet Union and its leadership. Especially in Europe (both East and West), Gorbachev is perceived as a reformer and peacemaker, and the image of the Soviet Union is less threatening. Even in the West, the Soviets are seen as concerned with internal problems and developing into a more acceptable international actor.

Further, the Gorbachev leadership has managed to develop a coherent strategy to reflect the "new" Soviet Union:

> Mikhail Gorbachev and his lieutenants appear to have an integrated global view, at least as articulated in the General Secretary's book and UN address, in which politics, economics, arms control, foreign

policy, development and even the world environment are related. Within the Soviet Union, the radical evolution which is unfolding does seem to depend for success upon the inter-linkage of perestroika, glasnost, new thinking, and demokratizatsiya.[9]

In the process, however, these efforts have divided Western scholars, policymakers, and military officers regarding the intentions of the Soviet Union and the long-range goal of Mikhail Gorbachev. On the one hand, there are those who argue that this is the right path for a more open and less threatening Soviet Union. Thus, Gorbachev should be helped by the West. On the other hand, there are those who argue that Gorbachev has certainly not abandoned the basic tenets of Marxism-Leninism and that he is intent on strengthening the Soviet Union economically, politically, and militarily to ensure dominance over the West in the long run. In the meantime, according to this view, he is engaged in a historical Marxist-Leninist tactic of taking steps backward in order to move forward. Regardless of which view or combination of views one adopts, there is little question that the new leadership in the Soviet Union has made a significant impact within the Soviet homeland as well as on Europe and the European landscape.

The European Landscape

The Gorbachev effort has, in no small measure, led to the reshaping of the European landscape, manifesting itself in at least three major areas: security posture, public opinion, and evolution of a European entity. At the same time, these changes have also been felt in some Third World areas.

In the past, the major fear has been a Soviet attack into the heartland of Europe. This has now become an improbable scenario for many Europeans. "The Soviet threat seemed especially acute to West Germans in the 1950s and 1960s, [and] the current perception that it has declined takes on a special importance. A recent opinion poll showed that 75 percent of the respondents saw no major military threat; most West Germans want to believe that Gorbachev will succeed."[10]

But there is disagreement among Western scholars regarding the extent and reality of changes in the Soviet military and its security posture. One expert writes, "A wide range of senior Soviet military officers and civilian academic specialists have made bold claims about the 'strictly defensive' nature of Soviet current and future military policy." But, he concludes, "the deeply entrenched offensive tradition in the military-technical (operational) side of Soviet military doctrine . . . remains largely unaltered."[11] Another argues, however, that:

> The Soviet military is undergoing a process of change greater than anything it has faced at least since the introduction of nuclear weapons, and perhaps since the purges of the late 1930s. These changes, if fully implemented and supported by a more viable economic infrastructure, will over the long run produce a more efficient and effective military force.[12]

Regardless of the various scholarly views, the perceived Soviet initiative, combined with announced unilateral reductions in Soviet forces in Europe and the follow-through with the INF agreement, have given considerable impetus to the peace environment in Europe, particularly in the Federal Republic of Germany. This has come at a time when the projected decrease in West Germany's population and resultant 30 percent decrease in military manpower cohorts have raised concerns about the future of the Federal Republic's defense postures and its ability to maintain twelve active divisions in NATO.

In a recent French poll, almost 40 percent of the West German respondents believed that "the policy of the Soviet Union aims at achieving peace and disarmament. There is nearly no risk of war today."[13] Interestingly enough, in the same poll, 53 percent of the Italians responded positively to that statement, the British and French polled responded with 31 percent and 29 percent, respectively. The results of the poll also showed that:

> By wide majorities . . . French and Italians (and the British, to a lesser extent) feel that the creation of a common European nuclear force is a better guarantor of future security than the US' pledge to use nuclear weapons in the face of Soviet invasion.[14]

Finally, the poll also indicated changing views in Europe regarding defense spending and the U.S. role in Europe:

> West Germans voiced the most confidence in promised Soviet defense policy changes. . . . While in favor of seeing a continuing presence of US forces in Europe, in the event of a partial US withdrawal they would be willing to devote more of their national budget to defense spending.[15]

In combination with these changing views, the rise of a new generation of Germans, who have not experienced World War II, may help create a momentum to reshape Germany's military posture—one that is based on a more pointed European (and West German?) perspective rather than on the purposes of NATO. The surfacing of such views may already have had some impact in influencing the Federal Republic to defer plans to lengthen conscription from fifteen to eighteen months. Equally important, the emerging German consciousness has caused some difficulty in U.S.–West

German security relations. Modernization of ground-launched missiles remains a quarrelsome question, as does the concept of air strikes on Soviet follow-on forces. Low-level NATO air rehearsals are a considerable disturbance to the German countryside, and many see them as a useless exercise and a provocation to a nonthreatening Soviet Union, especially since the advent of the Soviet "peace offensive." Finally, the concept of U.S. Airland battle doctrine has been brought into further question by the West Germans who are critical of deep strikes into East Germany that would expose West Germany to similar Warsaw Pact/Soviet tactics. In sum, what the Gorbachev offensive seems to have accomplished in Europe in general (and West Germany in particular) is to shift the peace initiative to the Soviet Union and place the United States and NATO in a politically defensive posture, with similar implications for its military.

A number of other developments reinforce the evolution of a European perspective on security issues and enhance the nonthreatening image of the Soviet Union. The proposed integration of the European economy in 1992 is a case in point. Such an integration is likely to develop a European economic entity and a distinctive European perspective. Indeed, it may establish the foundations for a European political entity in the long term. Although a stronger Europe is surely an advantage to open societies and democratic systems, many Americans see it as an economic challenge that is likely to favor major European trade relationships with the Soviet Union. With this, some fear a transfer of important technologies and hard currency to help the Gorbachev agenda, a transfer that would have long-term implications for U.S.-USSR-European security relationships.

According to a former civil servant with the German Ministry of Defense, "For many years the United States has called for a united Europe. Now that 'European Community 1992' is imminent, Washington is worried . . . in this case, the unknown represents a potentially mighty economic entity."[16] If Gorbachev's intent was to delink the United States from Europe, he certainly has had some initial successes.

The more serious security implications have to do with NATO. If the original purpose of NATO was to provide a defensive alliance against the Soviet threat, how valid is the organization if a number of members feel that the threat is now minimal? The new political structures in Poland and the apparent unraveling of the Eastern European bloc seem to have eroded the idea of a concerted Pact attack on Europe. Moreover, many Europeans are becoming more concerned about ecological issues, further mitigating concerns about military threats and defense matters. For these and other reasons, the military raison d'être of NATO may have diminished. This is prompting suggestions by some that NATO turn its attention to developing into a political alliance, while still others suggest that NATO may be obsolete in the current security environment. For many strategists in the United States, however, the Soviet threat remains real and, for some, even more ominous than in the past. Accordingly, one argument concludes, "There are no visible changes in Soviet military doctrine or force structure that offer any comfort to NATO, or offset the adverse impact of the INF Treaty."[17] Nevertheless, the consensus of most knowledgeable observers is that the Soviet military threat to NATO has, in fact, decreased.

Adding significant turmoil to the strategic world is the emerging issue on German reunification. The constitution of the Federal Republic has as one goal the reunification of Germany. The economic resurgence of the Federal Republic, combined with the new European landscape and the flow of East Germans in 1989 into West Germany (where they are granted automatic citizenship) has given credence to the view that there may be a "Fourth Reich" emerging. According to one view, "The resultant German economic giant will deserve the label 'Fourth Reich.' This will not be brought about by Bundeswehr bayonets, but by a gradual, even stealthy, penetration of the Eastern half of Europe and achievement of competitive preeminence in the Western half."[18]

While it may be a while before any West-East German political reunification occurs, the surfacing of such views is sure to have some chilling effects on concepts of Western alliance. Such views are part of the new political forces being generated within Europe. Combined with the move toward economic integration, the strengthening of the European parliament, and a number of other measures that seem to be drawing the Europeans into an interlocking web of political and defense directions, political forces seem to be coalescing into a European point of view that has its own distinctive rationale. "The future U.S. role in European security will also be shaped by the rapid rise of Western Europe as such—as a single market, certainly, but also as a defence entity with enough political authority to be taken seriously within Europe as well as elsewhere in the world."[19] And in terms of relationships with Eastern Europe, the author states, "The Washington role, while important, will be secondary. Europe is first of all an issue for the Europeans."[20]

For the Soviet Union, the hint of a European nationalism with a sharper perspective on political, military, and economic policy and strategy than in the past is likely to be a welcome development, at least initially. Such a European entity is in the best possible position to distance itself from the United States while looking more favorably to the Soviet Union. This could be the forerunner for accepting the Soviet Union as a major actor in Western European affairs.

Finally, what is taking place in Europe may have an important spillover effect in the peripheral areas—the Third World. While there is little question that the Soviet Union is rethinking its role and strategy in Third World areas, it is unlikely to give up its outposts there because of glasnost and perestroika. Withdrawing from Afghanistan is one thing, but retreating from other parts of the Third World is quite another. The more likely scenario is consolidation and retrenchment, with no new military adventures unless there is a decided Soviet advantage and where a power vacuum exists. Even then, it is likely that indirect measures will be used rather than overt military involvement. For example, there is little evidence to suggest that Soviet aid to the Kabul government or to Nicaragua has been significantly reduced since the new U.S.-USSR "détente" or the evolution of a new European strategic environment.

According to one view:

> Soviet leaders can no longer escape the realization that their "central" relations are endangered by their "peripheral" adventures. Both this realization and the clear re-evaluation of the risks, costs and potential advantages of expansion outside Europe do not mean that Gorbachev's Russia will simply turn its back on the opportunities for power and influence in the Third World. It may mean, however, that in the foreseeable future the Soviet Union will not start any new military adventures abroad, and that its overall level of activity and material support for allies in the Third World will continue to decline.[21]

The United States: Strategic Challenges and Military Posture

All of the political forces and strategic changes evolving from the Gorbachev leadership within the Soviet Union and in Europe have had an equally important impact on the United States. In retrospect, it can be argued that many of these forces were set into motion when the United States and the Soviet Union signed the INF Agreement. Although the political and military posturing of the Soviet Union began earlier, the signing of this treaty formalized the new U.S.-Soviet defense posture and opened the door for a new set of relationships between the United States and USSR. For example, procedures for on-site inspections were established, setting the stage for cooperative efforts between U.S. and Soviet experts and military officers. Further, the treaty triggered an arms control momentum and with it a variety of institutional efforts aimed at perpetuating the momentum. In late 1989, this momentum promised to include conventional force reductions in Europe.

Somewhat lost in all of the optimism associated with the INF Treaty and the impetus given to other arms control efforts are the long-range strategic challenges posed to the U.S. military. Many of these challenges are a result of the arms control momentum and a perception that "peace is at hand." In the view of many, the Cold War has ended and the Soviet Union no longer poses a realistic military threat. The Soviet threat has been transformed into the Soviet challenge, with all this suggests with respect to strategy and military posture.[22] But there remains serious disagreement regarding the long-term strategy of the "new" Soviet Union.

As a British scholar concludes, "What is clear . . . is that the American strategic debate itself is deeply divided. In a very real sense there has been a major breakdown in the strategic consensus, and nowhere has that been more obvious than in the debate over strategic defences."[23]

With no firm grasp of where all this will lead, the U.S. military is still faced with the need to redefine its strategic role and reshape its posture in response to the changed strategic landscape. And these changes demand a capability to respond across the conflict spectrum. This has become more complicated because U.S. policy and strategy must encompass the Pacific Rim in a more realistic way. As the European landscape is increasingly placed into the hands of Europeans, U.S. influence may decrease accordingly. At the same time, however, U.S. interests and security issues are becoming increasingly affected by the politics and challenges of the Pacific Rim.

To fully understand the implications of and linkages between the opportunites and challenges facing the U.S. military, one must first place the changing external situation into the context of the changed U.S. domestic political environment. The combination of external events, erosion of an earlier American consensus on defense, and the increasing concern with domestic social issues have considerably lessened the U.S. perceptions of threat and muted the concern about Soviet military expansion. Domestic, institutional, and professional pressures have coincided with those evolving from the new strategic realities. This is complicated by the policies of the United States in response to many of these security issues—policies that in 1990 were not yet fixed, coherent, or with clearly stated purposes. Again, while all the services may have similar problems, it appears that the U.S. Army is in the most difficult position. Its numbers and equipment generally give it an operational visibility more pronounced on foreign soil than other services, and the very nature of combat missions and purposes places the army in a more difficult strategic position than other services.

From all of these problems, three appear particularly pronounced: budgetary constraints, the changing "military culture," and the effectiveness of the total force system. It is a generally accepted view that the U.S. Congress is reluctant to increase defense spending, with the federal budget deficit seemingly providing the justification. Moreover, the defense consensus created during the early Reagan years (1981–1984) has virtually disappeared. According to some, the Reagan defense buildup may have been too successful, convincing many Americans that the United States had overcome the defense weaknesses of the late 1970s. Also disturbing to some strategists is congressional micromanagement of defense issues and the apparent "politicization" of procurement and weapons development. This is nothing new, of course, but congressional assertiveness, the perception of a less-threatening Soviet Union, and budgetary constraints have placed the Department of Defense clearly on the defensive in the defense budget debate, requiring it to justify research and weapons procurement even for some of its most basic requirements.

But as retiring Chairman of the Joint Chiefs of Staff Admiral William Crowe stated in 1989, "The popular view of the Soviet Union may be too rosy, and the public's attitude toward the U.S. defense budget may not be bleak enough."[24] Further, the lack of a defense consensus, which requires policy and strategy coherency and some well-defined antagonists, has placed the military and its budget requirements in a position susceptible to "pop" strategists and advocates of a variety of domestic programs resting on a reduction in defense spending. Without addressing the wisdom of one or the other position, it seems clear that the U.S. military is placed in a position in which it must defend its political-military rationale, strategic design, and force requirements within the parameters of budgetary constraints, fiscal reality, and cost-effective domestic momentum. All of this must be done in a politically convincing, yet professionally considered, manner. This is particularly difficult to do in addressing unconventional conflict contingencies, not only because of the variety of political views in Congress on the utility and desire of becoming involved in such conflicts, but also because of the nontraditional and nonconventional nature of such conflicts. Ironically, it seems that part of the lack of consensus regarding defense in the legislative and, to a certain degree, executive branch, is what was intended, consciously or otherwise, by Mikhail Gorbachev as he reshapes the Soviet security posture to deny the United States an enemy.

The second major challenge facing the military is institutional and professional. Admiral Crowe has termed these "military culture":

> Crowe found the greatest change of all in what he terms the "culture" of military operations, a concept that describes the increasingly stressful interplay between soldiers, sailors and airmen, the sophisticated weapons they crew and the delicate political environment in which they discharge their missions.[25]

The key to this military culture is the development of doctrine and its necessary intellectual and practical underpinnings that come to grips with the changed nature of threats and the realities of the threat environment. In turn, those in the military must be educated and trained to undertake contingencies in an environment that will rarely offer clearly defined adversaries, postured in a conventional military mode. These difficulties are compounded when contingencies require personnel to be visibly engaged in the contingency area, where the quality of those on the ground remains critical to successful operations. This is particularly characteristic of U.S. Army contingencies, of course. Yet, the political environment; the skill demands for operating sophisticated weapons; the need to be prepared for a variety of contingencies, combined with defense budgetary constraints; and the constant need for quality men and women are difficult propositions to synthesize into an effective military posture and coherent professional ethos.

Relevant and coherent strategies, as well as the political-military capability for effective response to these issues with clarity and purpose, require an "intellectualized" military profession that still retains its basic motivation and skills for success in battle. In short, the military profession must expand its intellectual horizons, revitalize serious strategic thinking, and develop professional and institutional astuteness in assessing and dealing with the political environment. To do all of this, traditional notions of battlefield skills and leadership must be realistically integrated with a broader view encompassing the political-psychological dimension beyond the battlefield.

But these matters do not rest solely with the active military. The "total force" concept is critical to the military posture and strategic capability of the United States. In addition to providing follow-on forces and the core of mobilization forces, reserves provide the majority of units in certain contingencies, such as the psychological warfare and civic action elements in the Special Forces organization. Also, many active Army divisions depend on reserve units to complement active operational elements in responding to various contingencies. Of all the services, the Marine Corps depends least on reserves. Although increasing efforts have been made by the military to develop a more proficient total force structure, much remains to be done. For example, "Army reserve training and readiness have fallen far behind that of the regular Army, according to congressional investigators. Some legislators and Army experts say the problem is so bad that it threatens the integrity of the Army's Total Force policy."[26] While this criticism is aimed at the U.S. Army, there is a degree of truth in it with respect to all services, with the possible exception of the U.S. Air Force.

All of the challenges and opportunities facing the U.S. military, however, must be placed in the broader context of the American way of war. Although there are a number of factors that shape the American view on war, according to one authority, three stand out. "These . . . are the essential American lack of sense of history, the unique American geographical endowment, and the nation's Anglo-Saxon heritage."[27] While this "way" has a historical continuity that dates back to the Revolutionary War, its contemporary interpretation takes on special importance. In light of the nature of the U.S. political system and its heavy reliance on "people power," the attitudes and opinions of the American people underpin major policy and strategic options and are critical components in determining the commitment of U.S. military forces. This is particularly important in contingencies that encompass conflicts short of major war. The values, norms, and quality of political life characteristic of U.S. democracy establish a special linkage between the people and their military. The well-known adage that the military reflects society is especially apt in the U.S. system. Without public support and acceptance of military involvement in various contingencies, it is unlikely that the military can effectively perform its role.

In this respect, the American way of war presumes, among other things, that military operations must be against a clearly defined "enemy" in which American moral good is arrayed against evil. Further, it is expected that U.S. military behavior on the battlefield will conform to accepted moral and ethical norms of democracy, including such things as fair play, justice, and humane behavior. Equally important, most Americans presume their moral and ethical standards and values are equally applicable in the international environment.

Almost twenty years ago, Charles Burton Marshall aptly commented on the notion of good arrayed against evil:

> For some people, it is hard to affirm commitment to a military cause except on a premise of unequivocal good arrayed against unmitigated evil. In combined efforts, this notion requires postulating an immaculate ally. The trouble is that immaculate allies are fabled rather than real.[28]

What does all of this mean with respect to strategy and contingencies for the U.S. military? If the American people believe that the Gorbachev era has produced a less-threatening world and if this is translated into a world view, then the concerns about projecting U.S. military power may not be major in the minds of many Americans. Indeed, in 1990 the major issues troubling Americans was not external threats, but drugs, crime on the streets, and the environment. Denied a clearly defined external enemy, and with many Americans (including members of Congress) convinced that there is a diminished Soviet threat, attention is likely to remain focused on domestic social issues and drug wars. While the U.S. military may play a role in such matters, by and large doing so may be a secondary effort in support of law-enforcement agencies.

In sum, U.S. attitudes and expectations establish the boundaries and the moral and ethical substance that shape the context within which the military must operate. This was well stated by General Fred Weyand, the commander who supervised the withdrawal of U.S. forces from Vietnam.

> Vietnam was a reaffirmation of the peculiar relationship between the American Army and the American people. The American Army really is a people's Army in the sense that it belongs to the American people who take a jealous and proprietary interest in its involvement. When the Army is committed the American people are committed, when the American people lose their commitment, it is futile to try to keep the Army committed. In the final analysis, the American Army is not so much an arm of the Executive Branch as it is an arm of the American people. The Army, therefore, cannot be committed lightly.[29]

Conclusions

The combination of new political and economic forces emerging in Europe, the new Soviet leadership, the impact of glasnost and perestroika on defense and security issues, and a whole range of arms control initiatives have combined to change the political and strategic landscape. Coming at a time when U.S. domestic political forces, budgetary constraints, and congressional caution over defense expenditures are in the process of reshaping U.S. military posture, these external forces have created a strategically muddled arena, posing challenges as well as opportunities to the U.S. military. Not only is the U.S. military faced with rethinking strategies, but it must come to grips with reshaping U.S. military forces in order to make them more adaptable, flexible, and strategically relevant to the new strategic landscape.[30]

While the final outcome of these new directions remains unclear, the fact is that the 1990s will require a new set of strategic options and a force posture increasingly concentrated in the continental United States. Even with the presumed changes in the Soviet threat posture, the United States will need to maintain sufficient forces for credible deterrence, as well as a capability to respond across the conflict spectrum. And this must be done with reduced financial resources and in the face of domestic opinion reluctant to accept the commitment of U.S. forces into contingencies that are unclear in terms of purpose, and in an environment shaped by foreign cultures and likely to be engulfed in local conflicts.

In addition to intellectual demands, strategic rethinking, and force restructuring, there are other challenges to the U.S. political-military system that need to be emphasized. First, there must be a centralized and cohesive strategic study and planning effort that integrates the responsibilities of all the services and is institutionalized in a joint command structure. From this should evolve a coherent strategy, feasible in implementation and relevant to the various contingencies the military is likely to face. Indeed, in late 1989, there were arguments made for changing the National Defense University into the University of National Strategy and establishing a think tank for the Joint Chiefs of Staff called the National Center for Strategic Study.[31]

Second, the U.S. military must become more astute and proficient in functioning in a budget-constrained domestic political atmosphere that is likely to continue into the foreseeable future. This does not mean it should become actively involved in partisan politics. It does mean, however, developing the kind of political wisdom and astuteness that can clearly define defense needs and strategic options, outlining the costs and consequences of each, and translating these into effective input into the policy- and strategy-making process.[32]

Third, the challenge of special operations and low-intensity conflicts (unconventional conflicts) are likely to demand a higher level of commitment and a more relevant operational structure. This is important in light of the continuing conflicts in Third World areas and the continuing, if reduced, role of the Soviet Union in support of its outposts in the Third World. Further, regional conflicts, both intrastate and interstate, are likely to be continuing characteristics of Third World areas, some of which may demand U.S. involvement. Conventionally postured forces are not the best instrument for such contingencies. Thus, light, mobile forces, with the adaptability to provide a variety of mixes, need to be strengthened and fashioned for Third World contingencies. At the core of this strategic rethinking and force reshaping is the need to develop a more coherent conceptual framework regarding characteristics of unconventional conflicts and the demands they pose to forces involved. This conceptual clarity must be based, among other things, on making clear distinctions between conventional and unconventional conflicts. And, in this respect, clear operational responsibilities must be spelled out for light infantry forces, special operations units, and Special Forces.

Fourth, the U.S. military must be prepared to play a secondary but important role in a variety of contingencies, ranging from drug abatement and border control to peacekeeping missions. In most of these contingencies, the military will not be the lead agency. Development of procedures, doctrines, operational guidelines, and a deep professional understanding of the role and responsibilities of other agencies with which the military must deal are essential.

Fifth, a more realistic integration of the reserves and national guard into active force operations and strategic planning is needed. It follows that a more concerted and effective effort must be made to develop the necessary combat-effective reserve forces and national guard to engage in the variety of contingencies expected in the 1990s. It is obvious that the strategic capability of the U.S. military depends to a great extent on the ability of the reserves and national guard to carry out active-duty missions.

Sixth, and finally, the education and training of professional military officers must encompass the broader and more complex strategic landscape that is likely to characterize the 1990s if the profession and the military institution are to retain their ability to serve society and effectively carry out their military missions in the new environment. Professional military education must go beyond traditional boundaries and narrow battlefield orientation. Some of these efforts are already in place. It is difficult, however, to engage the profession and the institution in the political-psychological dimension of the new strategic landscape since this dimension often goes beyond mainstream military thought and conventional force posture. Moreover, many Americans perceive this dimension in purely nonmilitary terms, as do many military professionals. Yet, to neglect the military perspective is to invite policymaking based on incomplete and inadequate input.

In sum, the combination of challenges and opportunities created by the new landscape are sure to severely test the U.S. military. Moving from the Cold War to cold peace will not be an easy transition, nor are there well-established policies and strategic guidelines for doing so. This transition period will require not only astute political leaders, but military professionals who understand the character and function of political systems and the nature of U.S. politics, and who are able to assess and understand the strategic landscape, determine what should and can be accomplished, and bring to bear keen judgment regarding appropriate military posture. And, finally, this judgment must be conveyed to the American people and to the executive and Congress in the spirit of General Weyand's view:

> As military professionals we must speak out, we must counsel our political leaders and alert the American public that there is no such thing as a "splendid little war." . . . The Army must make the price of involvement clear before we get involved, so that America can weigh the probable costs of involvement against the dangers of noninvolvement.[33]

Finally, the challenges and opportunities created by the new strategic landscape do not rest solely with the U.S. military. The policy framework must be clearly established by the political leadership, the wherewithal provided by the governing bodies, and, perhaps most important, a more realistic understanding and appreciation of professional military life and the demands of the military profession must develop within the U.S. body politic, the mass media, and political leadership circles. Without such an understanding, all of the strategic rethinking and reshaping of the U.S. military posture will be futile.

Notes

1. Gail W. Lapidus, "Gorbachev's Nationalities Problem, *Foreign Affairs*, Vol. 68, No. 4, 1989, p. 92.
2. Ibid., p. 108.
3. David Holloway, "Gorbachev's New Thinking," *America and the World 1988/89*, *Foreign Affairs*, Vol. 68, No. 1, p. 80.
4. "Soviet Reforms Faltering," *Chicago Tribune*, Sept. 3, 1989, p. 1.
5. F. Stephen Larrabee, "Gorbachev and the Soviet Military," *Foreign Affairs*, Vol. 6, No. 5, Summer 1988, p. 1006.
6. Ibid., pp. 1008–1009.
7. See, for example, Steven Rosefielde, "Military Modernization and 'New Thinking': Economic Determinants of Soviet National Security Policy in the Nineties," in *Assessing Change in the U.S.S.R.* (Washington, D.C.: International Security Council, May 1989), pp. 56–69. See also Francis Fukuyama, "Gorbachev and the Third World," *Foreign Affairs*, Vol. 64, No. 4, Spring 1986, pp. 715–731, in which the author concludes, "Kremlinological evidence notwithstanding, early indications suggest that Gorbachev is, if

anything, trying to stake out a more combative position in the Third World" (p. 725).

8. Albert L. Weeks, "Soviet Political and Constitutional Reform," in *Assessing Change in the USSR*, note 7, pp. 70–88.

9. John P. Hardt and Timothy W. Stanley, "Indicators of Change in Soviet Security Policies," Occasional Paper (Washington, D.C.: The Atlantic Council of the United States, April 1989), p. 28.

10. Henry Owen and Edward C. Meyer, "Central European Security," *Foreign Affairs*, Vol. 68, No. 3, Summer 1989, p. 23.

11. Edward L. Warner III, "New Thinking and Old Realities in Soviet Defence Policy," *Survival*, Vol. XXXI, No. 1, January/February 1989, p. 13.

12. Dale Herspring, "The Soviet Military and Change," *Survival*, Vol. XXXI, No. 4, July/August 1989, p. 321.

13. John G. Roos, "Europeans Trust US Conventional Shield but Would Favor 'Euro-Nuclear' Force," *Armed Forces Journal International*, Vol. 127, No. 2, September 1989, p. 24.

14. Ibid.

15. Ibid., p. 28.

16. Rolf Roesler, "Europe 1992—A German View," *Armed Forces Journal International*, Vol. 127, No. 2, September 1989, p. 48.

17. Jeffrey Record and David B. Rivkin, Jr., "Defending Post-INF Europe," *Foreign Affairs*, Vol. 66, No. 4, Spring 1988, p. 751. See also John Borawski, "The INF Treaty and Beyond," *Parameters*, Vol. XVIII, No. 2, June 1988, pp. 63–73.

18. Richard W. Judy, "The 'Fourth Reich': Commerce Gains Where Bayonet Lost," *Wall Street Journal/Europe*, March 23, 1989, as reprinted in *Hudson Opinion*, April 1989.

19. Robert F. Ellsworth, "The Future of US-European Relations," in *Survival*, Vol. XXXI, No. 3, May/June 1989, p. 197.

20. Ibid., p. 198.

21. Seweryn Bialer, "'New Thinking' and Soviet Foreign Policy," *Survival*, Vol. XXX, No. 4, July/August 1988, p. 305.

22. Peter Almond, "Latest Pentagon Assessment Deflates Soviet 'Threat,'" *Washington Times*, September 18, 1989, p. A3.

23. Stuart Croft, *The Impact of Strategic Defences on European-American Relations in the 1990's*, Adelphi Papers (London: The International Institute for Strategic Studies, 1989), p. 39.

24. "Move with Caution on Arms Control; Beware Budget," *Army Times*, September 11, 1989, p. 4. See also Scott D. Dean, "Galvin to Lawmakers: Soviet Plans for Europe Unchanged by *Perestroika*," *Armed Forces Journal International*, Vol. 126, No. 1, August 1988, p. 22.

25. P. J. Budan, "The Thoughts of Chairman Crowe," *Army Times*, September 11, 1989, p. 4.

26. Petr Koch, "New Questions Raised About Reservists' Readiness Training," *Army Times*, August 14, 1989, p. 24. See also "The Sad State of Weekend Warriors," *U.S. News and World Report*, September 25, 1989, pp. 28–30. See also Delbert L. Spurlock, Jr., "Reserve Forces: Crucially Important but Unknown," Standing Committee on Law and National Security *Intelligence Report*, American Bar Association, Vol. 9, No. 12, December 1987, pp. 1–2, 4.

27. Donald M. Snow, *National Security: Enduring Problems of U.S. Defense Policy* (New York: St. Martin's Press, 1987), p. 21.

28. Charles Burton Marshall, "Morality and National Liberation Wars," *Southeast Asian Perspectives*, No. 4, December 1971.

29. Gen. Fred C. Weyand, "Vietnam Myths and American Realities," Commanders Call (July–August 1976), as quoted in Harry G. Summers, Jr., *On Strategy: The Vietnam War in Context* (Carlisle Barracks, PA: U.S. Army War College, 1981), p. 7.

30. Responding to an interview, Gen. Robert W. RisCassi had this to say, in part, about the future: "Probably the most difficult question is, What do you envision the Army ought to look like in the 21st century? That will depend primarily on the Vienna talks and the recasting of the environment in the European theater." See Benjamin F. Schemmer, "An Exclusive *AFJI* Interview with General Robert W. RisCassi, USA, Vice Chief of Staff, United States Army," *Armed Forces Journal International*, Vol. 127, No. 3, October 1989, p. 72.

31. Grant Willis, "New National Security Studies Center Probable," *Army Times*, September 18, 1989, p. 10. See also *Report of the Panel on Military Education*, Committee on Armed Services, House of Representatives, 101st Congress, 1st session, April 21, 1989, particularly pp. 4–6. This report is commonly referred to as the "Skelton Report," after the chairman of the committee, Representative Ike Skelton.

32. See, for example, Richard Thomas Mattingly, Jr., and Wallace Earl Walker, "The Military Professional as Successful Politician," *Parameters*, Vol. XVIII, No. 1, March 1988, pp. 37–51.

33. As quoted in Summers, note 29, p. 25.

CHAPTER 2

The U.S. Army: A Strategic Force for a New Security Era

GEN. CARL E. VUONO, U.S. Army

On the threshold of a new century, the United States is confronted by a world in the throes of fundamental and unprecedented change. While some threats to U.S. security appear to be abating, other complex and dangerous challenges are emerging. These include terrorism, trafficking in illicit drugs, proliferation of sophisticated weaponry in potentially hostile developing nations, and regional instability that threatens democratic regimes. At the same time, the United States is seeking to reduce its reliance on nuclear arms. Together, these developments underscore the importance of conventional, and in particular, ground forces.

Because of its vital roles in all aspects of our national security strategy, the Army will play an increasingly important part in our nation's response to those challenges. The Army will still, of course, have to maintain the broad range of land-force capabilities needed to support U.S. joint commands and country teams around the world. But the Army will also have to adapt its structure to carry out the new responsibilities that the American people and our civilian leaders will expect us to perform.

The success of U.S. post–World War II strategy, in which forward-deployed forces have had a key role, is self-evident. This strategy undoubtedly will continue to guide us for some time. Consequently, forward deployment of combat-ready forces in places where U.S. interests require them will remain a key Army responsibility. The scope of this responsibility, however, may be reduced in the near future as a result of improved security and new arms control agreements. Our challenge will be to ensure that deterrence, stability, and ongoing arms control negotiations are not undermined by premature or excessive reductions of forces or capabilities.

Another enduring Army role will be that of maintaining a strategic reserve in the United States able to deploy immediately to trouble spots around the world in response to crises. These contingency forces must have a full range of military capabilities, because they furnish our nation with flexible options that provide the most appropriate response to meet any challenge to U.S. national interests. The strategic reserve must also be able to reinforce forward-deployed and previously committed contingency forces, ultimately backing them by the full mobilization of the military and industrial potential of the United States should that ever be required.

Support to allies and other partners around the world, in the form of peacekeeping operations, security assistance, and nation-building activities, has been a historical Army role. Recently, this role has acquired new meaning in view of the challenges to, and opportunities for, democracy seen in the developing world. The Army has also continued to perform its historical responsibility of providing support to civil authorities, including disaster relief and emergency assistance; and it has received new tasks in the war on drugs.

The Army's roles fulfill vital U.S. defense needs in a complex and continually evolving international environment. These roles must be our focus as we shape the Army of the future.

Today's Army: Trained and Ready Foundation for the Future

Today's Army is the best trained, most ready peacetime force in our nation's history. Over the past decade, we have undergone an extensive transformation that has prepared us well for the changes ahead. This transformation is evident in our soldiers, doctrine, force structure, training, materiel, and leaders—a transformation produced by uncompromising adherence to six fundamental imperatives that guide the Army today and serve as a beacon for the future.

The first of these imperatives, and the most important, can be summed up in a single word—quality. It is this characteristic that enables the Army to fulfill its worldwide strategic roles in spite of our relatively small size. The high quality of the American soldier—a combination of intelligence, initiative, combat skill, tenacity, and physical toughness—has been a traditional source of victory in battle. The experiences of recent years have reaffirmed that quality produces the versatility needed to respond rapidly to unforeseen situations. The high quality of our soldiers has been essential in many of our recent successes, including protection of shipping in the Persian Gulf, rapid deployment of forces for operations in Panama and exercises in Honduras, interdiction of illicit drug traffic, fighting forest fires, and assisting in the recovery from natural disasters. These experiences have strengthened our conviction that recruiting and retaining talented men and women must continue to be our top priority in the Army of the 1990s and beyond. Therefore, if we are to attract the best our nation has to offer, we must continue to offer them the personal and professional challenges, and quality of life, equal to those of the citizens they are sworn to defend.

The rise in the quality of our soldiers has been accompanied by a renaissance in our thinking about war. The second imperative focuses on sustaining our momentum in this area by maintaining a forward-looking warfighting doctrine. AirLand Battle, the Army's contemporary doctrine, provides the basic rationale for designing forces, determining materiel needs, conducting training, and developing leaders. This doctrine recognizes the need to integrate the capabilities of Army units with those of the other services and of our allies to achieve maximum combat power and effectiveness. It establishes the foundation for the Army's disciplined evolution to the future, ensuring the Army's preparedness for the battlefield challenges of the 1990s and beyond.

As our doctrine and the security environment have evolved, so too has the composition of Army forces. That evolution must continue. Thus our third imperative is to maintain the appropriate mix of heavy, light, and special operations forces in our Active and Reserve Components. While our present force structure does not meet the current needs of all U.S. commands worldwide, the Army can meet the highest priority U.S. strategic requirements. As we shape the forces needed for the future, we will take into account the U.S. need for a sustained land combat capability worldwide, other land force roles, and ongoing East-West negotiations for reducing conventional forces in Europe.

The conduct of tough, realistic training—our fourth imperative—has set a standard for armies everywhere. The investment we have made in training over the past decade has produced the readiness for war that is the basis for credible deterrence and capable defense. The exercises conducted at our Combat Training Centers in California, Germany, and Arkansas, as well as our recent operations around the world, stand as evidence of our training achievements. And lest we forget, tough, meaningful, and fulfilling training is a key element in encouraging the very best soldiers to stay in our ranks. Demanding training, accomplished to standard today, is one of the best investments we can make in the Army of tomorrow.

Another dramatic improvement over the past decade has been modernization, particularly in the combat equipment of our forces. Our fifth imperative is to continue to modernize our warfighting capability. The Abrams tank, the Bradley fighting vehicle, and the Apache helicopter are three examples of weapon systems fielded in the 1980s that have served this end. They, and other systems like them, are the products of a continuous process that reflects our strategy, doctrine, technological advantages, and overarching commitment to providing our soldiers the best equipment possible. Modernization enables Army forces to win rapidly on the battlefield while preserving our most valuable asset, the lives of our soldiers. Because our dollars have always been limited, Army modernization plans ensure that units likely to be the first to fight—including selected Army Reserve and National Guard units—are modernized first. To develop needed future capabilities on time, the Army will continue to emphasize aggressive research and development in the key areas of operational concepts, unit designs, materiel, and training innovations.

In the final analysis, the capabilities of the Army depend not only on the quality of our soldiers, but also on the competence of our leaders. Thus, our sixth imperative is to continue development of Army leaders. We have pioneered many joint and Army initiatives in this area, to include enhancements in formal education and training, successive operational-level experiences, and continuous self-development opportunities. Leader development for soldiers and civilians is our most important and lasting contribution to shaping the Army of the future.

By adhering to these imperatives, today's trained and ready Army is positioned to meet the challenges of tomorrow. The Army of the 1990s and beyond will continue to be an Army that reflects the values and ingenuity of our nation.

The World Tomorrow: Challenges and Opportunities

The world is changing in a number of profound ways, and the U.S. will have to adapt to those changes. Nonetheless, many elements of our present national security strategy will remain important in the future. The post–World War II Western strategy of containment and flexible response, in particular, has achieved unprecedented success. We have enjoyed four decades of peace between the superpowers. Our NATO allies have developed strong economies, and vast regions of the Americas, Africa, Asia, and the Middle East, are now advancing politically and economically as well. Success should not, however, cause us to discard the basic elements that have made this strategy work. Rather, we must adapt them to the demands of the future because, undoubtedly, the years ahead will present traditional challenges as well as new threats and unique opportunities.

Allies and Coalition Strategy

Because of its geographic and political position in the world, the United States must rely on a coalition strategy, working in cooperation with allies and other friendly nations to protect mutual interests. The unprecedented periods of peace in Europe and Northeast Asia demonstrate this strategy's success. Cooperation with other nations has also characterized U.S. actions in the Persian Gulf, the Middle East, Central America, and elsewhere.

Past successes, however, do not guarantee future peace. Alliance relations are becoming more complex, with several close allies emerging as leading economic powers in their own right. While our nation cannot allow the combined stresses of economic competition and budget constraints to compromise shared interests, it is clear that changing political and economic conditions will affect allied security arrangements. The years ahead will witness an evolution in the sharing of defense burdens and risks among coalition partners.

But as the complexity of the adjustments facing our alliances grows, there will be no substitute for the leadership that the United States has provided to the West. No other allied or friendly nation has, or is likely to develop, the necessary economic, political, and military power to replace the United States in that role. Nonetheless, the United States is not so independent that it can routinely act alone. We will continue to depend on the cooperation and support of our allies and other friends, just as they will continue to expect from us the leadership that we have provided since World War II.

The Soviet Union

The changes taking place in the Soviet Union and throughout Eastern Europe are, in large measure, a testament to the success of NATO's strategy and to the inescapable attraction of democracy and market-oriented economic systems. Containment is not only succeeding militarily and politically, it is also providing time for the rebirth of the forces of democracy now sweeping across the Warsaw Pact. There is reason for optimism that the Soviet Union will become a more open and pluralistic society, reduce the size of its excessively large land forces, and more clearly embrace the concepts of human rights and democratic political institutions.

History suggests, however, that there are equal grounds for caution. There is a potential in the Soviet regime for a retreat from reform and openness, and regression to a closed society that again confronts the external world. Nor is this potential limited to the U.S.SR. The domestic turmoil that often accompanies vast social restructuring is aggravated throughout the Warsaw Pact by ethnic conflict, economic inefficiency, and political instability. This turmoil alone creates uncertainties about the future intentions of the Soviet Union toward its neighbors and the West.

Moreover, despite the Soviet Union's announced unilateral cuts, the United States and its NATO allies still face a severe force imbalance. Meanwhile, advances in Soviet military technology and overall force modernization continue. Even if the Soviets reduce the size of their Army and the quantity of their defense production in the 1990s, NATO will face a higher-quality Soviet army with more powerful individual units designed for flexible offensive and defensive operations. A major lesson of the successful Intermediate-range Nuclear Forces (INF) treaty negotiations is that U.S. and NATO force deployments and modernization provide irreplaceable incentives for the Soviets to negotiate in good faith. The United States and its allies must continue to apply this lesson to the negotiations on reducing conventional forces in Europe.

For the foreseeable future, therefore, deterrence and defense against potential Soviet and Soviet-supported military action in Europe and Asia will remain the most demanding challenges for the United States and its allies. In the years ahead, the West must be patient and vigilant, carefully examining Warsaw Pact military developments and bearing in mind that capabilities, not intentions, decide the outcome in battle and determine the fate of nations. Given the situation in the East, NATO clearly will remain an essential instrument for promoting stability while Warsaw Pact countries attempt to reform their political and economic structures. A strong NATO will be a fundamental guarantor of U.S. interests, European stability, and continued peaceful relations between East and West.

The Developing World

The developing world presents new challenges to the United States. Conflicts there can pose clear threats to U.S. security interests, and the precise time and location of these occurrences are largely unpredictable. The underlying causes of these conflicts exist within the developing nations themselves and will not necessarily diminish even if Soviet international behavior continues to moderate. Indeed, as more developing countries gain significant military capabilities, they may resort more readily to force in settling local disputes.

The proliferation of sophisticated weapons in the developing world vastly complicates U.S. defense planning. At least a dozen developing countries have more than 1,000 main battle tanks, and several of these nations have more tanks than our Army has in its active units in Europe. Portable antiaircraft and antitank missiles are widespread and have been used with great effectiveness in Afghanistan and Africa. A number of developing states are acquiring modern fighter and attack aircraft, giving them significant long-range strike capabilities.

Ballistic and cruise missiles also are being exported to many parts of the world, and a number of developing countries could have them in the next ten years. Even more disturbing, chemical weapons are entering the arsenals of several of these nations. The result of this proliferation of advanced military capabilities is an increasing number of countries with the ability to engage in sustained, mechanized land campaigns.

The Iran-Iraq war illustrated the intensity with which the developing world can now wage war. These two countries fought for nearly a decade, using sophisticated weapons, long-range missiles, chemical agents, heavy armored formations, and a large amount of artillery. The casualties exceeded one million. We cannot rule out future wars of this type. The United States must maintain the capability of protecting vital interests wherever they are threatened. That could mean confronting a fully equipped army in the developing world.

But the obvious challenges in the developing world should not lead us to ignore the opportunities that also are present. Not only does the United States have a wide range of economic and political interests it can pursue with developing countries, it also has a considerable potential for enhancing mutual security. Security assistance and army-to-army initiatives provide ideal vehicles for advancing host country and U.S. interests. The continuing challenge will be the need to reconcile economic and defense concerns.

Low-Intensity Conflict

A growing challenge to U.S. interests and national security strategy is so-called low-intensity conflict. International drug trafficking, terrorism, insurgency, and subversion of legitimate democratic regimes pose serious threats. Low-intensity conflict can undermine important allies and other friendly nations, impede the development of democratic institutions, and hamper essential U.S. economic and military ties. Nor are these problems limited to the developing world; as Americans know well, terrorism and drug trafficking can plague even a superpower. Clearly, low-intensity conflict is the security challenge most likely to demand a U.S. military response with little or no warning.

The dangers of low-intensity conflict, and particularly of terrorism, are magnified by the increasing worldwide availability of sophisticated explosives and weapons. Precision-guided munitions are becoming available through illegal arms markets or from states supporting international terrorist organizations. Terrorist use of the ultimate weapons of terror—chemical, biological, and nuclear arms—is not inconceivable.

We must not forget, however, that the causes of low-intensity conflict generally are political and economic rather than military. Although the military aspects may be crucial, the solutions to low-intensity conflict go far beyond the military dimension. Military action can only be a shield against violent opponents and a source of assistance to the civil authorities responsible for political, economic, and social development. Recent history demonstrates that military might cannot substitute for effective nation building and legitimate political institutions that meet citizens' needs.

Considering this array of challenges, the world of the future will not be any simpler nor necessarily any safer than it is today. Indeed, as the Army moves into the 1990s, we will confront a security environment that is demanding and dangerous, and we will have to do so in an era of limited defense resources.

The Army of the Future: Versatile, Deployable, Lethal

The Army of the future will have to be versatile, deployable, and lethal. In view of the rapidly changing international environment, the precise time, location, and nature of the threat will always be uncertain. Consequently, the exact composition of the Army element needed to overcome any specific threat will best be determined on a case-by-case basis. In the near future as well, the Army will be smaller as a result of changes in the domestic and international environments. It will rely on its ability to expand again should circumstances require it. Nevertheless, there is no doubt about the general characteristics of versatility, deployability, and lethality that Army forces will need to fulfill their strategic roles. Guided by the six fundamental imperatives, and exploiting our society's many advantages, tomorrow's Army will have unprecedented capabilities.

A Versatile Army

Versatility will be an essential characteristic of the Army of the 1990s and beyond. We must be able to defend and advance U.S. security interests around the world against a wide array of potential threats with a relatively small force. It would be wasteful to maintain large forces uniquely specialized for every conceivable geographical area and type of combat. Therefore, a highly capable, versatile Army will be the most effective solution to worldwide requirements for ground forces. Versatility will require the right proportions of Active and Reserve Components, the correct mix of forces (heavy, light, and special operations), adequate sustainment stocks, and, above all, high quality in all aspects of the force.

The Army of the future, consequently, will require an Active Component sufficiently large and capable of providing both the forward-deployed elements and the U.S.-based forces needed for immediate contingencies and rapid reinforcement of forward-deployed units. We will maintain and possibly expand today's already substantial active force capabilities available for immediate contingency response. In the Army Reserve and National Guard, we will maintain those combat and support units required to sustain the operations of the active forces beyond a prudently defined initial period. Army National Guard units, backed when necessary by the rest of the Total Army, will also be needed to fulfill traditional support responsibilities to civil authorities.

The armies of many of our potential adversaries are becoming increasingly capable and sophisticated. Combat at any level of intensity would place great demands on our force structure. The Army must, therefore, maintain sufficient numbers and the correct mix of all types of units. Whether for operations in the developing world or in Europe, we would need a combination of heavy, light, and special operations units. The difference would be in the proportions of the different types of forces committed.

The ability to tailor force packages for specific missions without delays for retraining or mobilization, thus, will be essential. Versatility, therefore, demands intensive training and frequent exercises. For the Army of the future, training programs and worldwide deployment exercises will have to demonstrate the ability to configure elements from battalion to corps in size, to deploy them within anticipated contingency warning times, and to employ and sustain them as necessary to assure success.

Wherever employed, the combat power of the Army's forces must be sustainable. The need to support our forces in peacetime operations or in combat will directly affect the mix of units in the force structure of the future. We must ensure, therefore, that we have in being, or can mobilize in the necessary time, the type and quantity of support needed to execute our plans. Contingency operations, in particular, will demand a higher level of sustainment stocks than we currently maintain for that purpose.

Versatility will also be essential in enabling our Army to meet other challenges. We anticipate the need to support national efforts to combat drug trafficking and terrorist organizations. Assisting civil authorities in disaster relief and during other unforeseen emergencies will similarly demand adaptive and responsive Army civilians, soldiers, units, and leaders. The same will be true of the Army elements that will carry out our security assistance efforts in the future. Our focus in this area will be on programs that yield a multiplier effect in host nation armies. Leader development initiatives, training enhancements, joint exercises, and exchange programs—more than equipment transfers—frequently shape how friendly armies address their needs and help defend our mutual interests. Such activities will be given new emphasis. In addition, U.S. offers of materiel under security assistance will be tailored to match needed military capabilities with available resources.

More than any other characteristic, the quality of our people—soldiers and civilians—will determine the versatility of the future Army. With our volunteer force, we must provide incentives to attract and retain the highest caliber men and women. This means that we will have to provide not only adequate compensation, but also a living and working environment that meets the standards of American society. Only by caring for our soldiers and their families will we be able to meet our most essential imperative, that of attracting and retaining high quality men and women.

A Deployable Army

The nature of the United States' interests around the world, and its coalition-based strategy, will require that U.S. forces be globally deployable, often with little or no warning, from the United States or from forward bases. While operational circumstances will determine which deployment mode is best in each case, the Army must have forces prepared to execute either option.

The Army's ability to deploy units rapidly—to reinforce our forward-deployed forces in maintaining deterrence, to support allies in defusing a crisis, and to fight—has been tested repeatedly around the world. Recent events in Panama and current trends in the international environment make it abundantly clear that rapid deployment will become even more important in the future. The conduct of exercises with allies and other friendly armies around the world has long provided a very visible demonstration of this capability. But no amount of commitment and political will to defend vital interests around the world can substitute for timely deployment of sustainable land forces capable of countering a miscalculation or deliberate aggression by an opponent.

Forward-deployed ground forces will continue to be essential although their specific numbers will change to reflect contemporary circumstances. Soviet acceptance of the President's proposal for achieving parity in conventional forces in Europe, for instance, would lead to reductions in the size of our forces based there. The locations of our bases abroad, moreover, are likely to be limited to those areas where deterrence and regional stability cannot otherwise be assured.

In the future, the United States will also have to maintain an unquestionable ability to conduct an opposed entry into combat in defense of vital interests anywhere. In many contingencies, a forced entry will only be possible, or will best be achieved, by air. As they demonstrated in Panama, Army airborne and Ranger forces, supported by strategic airlift, are uniquely capable of performing this function, and they will remain a key element in the Army of the future.

Even the most deployable and combat-ready land force, however, cannot be employed without adequate strategic lift. The United States cannot afford to risk the effectiveness and credibility of its overall defense strategy by failing to develop and field adequate worldwide lift assets. Airlift and sealift assets currently available or approved for acquisition are inadequate. This deficiency will have to be addressed in the years ahead. Of particular importance will be the further development of sufficient fast sealift capacity to support contingency requirements.

In the 1990s and beyond, the United States will have to rely even more heavily on the rapid deployment of Army forces from the United States to guarantee its security. Thus, despite reductions in the defense budget, it is vital that sufficient resources be allocated to correcting the serious shortfalls in U.S. sealift and airlift.

A Lethal Army

Lethality is the assured capability to defeat an opponent, winning as quickly as possible while preserving our most valued asset—the lives of our soldiers. Lethality depends on the capabilities of units and the overall size of the force structure. Assuring the lethality of Army forces will demand a disciplined, continuous modernization effort. This will mean maintaining the capability to counter the forces of the Soviet Union, which for the foreseeable future will remain our most capable potential adversary, while at the same time fielding capabilities that can defeat other threats around the world.

Army modernization will capitalize on U.S. advantages and strengths—particularly the qualities of our soldiers, leaders, and technology—and exploit vulnerabilities and weaknesses in our adversaries. This approach will guide all aspects of our modernization process, including the development of doctrine, force design and structure, materiel, training, and leaders.

In the 1990s and beyond, as in the present, concepts and doctrine must guide our efforts to field combat-ready forces. For the near term, AirLand Battle doctrine provides this foundation. Projecting ahead, the Army has launched the AirLand Battle-Future initiative, which is designed to update all our warfighting concepts for the early twenty-first century. The Army also will continue to participate in the development of joint and combined doctrine and warfighting concepts for operations at all levels of intensity.

Future budgets are likely to be tight, so we must assign appropriate priorities and levels of effort to all aspects of modernization. We should, concomitantly, maintain an adequate investment in our technology base in order to identify promising new technologies and make the best use of our resources. Additionally, we must avoid mortgaging the future for useful but noncritical near-term capabilities. While we will strive to ensure that our soldiers have every technological advantage, we nonetheless will need to impose appropriate procurement criteria to get the most overall value from our resources.

Modern, short-range nuclear forces will be an essential element in maintaining deterrence, as well as in assuring the lethality of the future Army. The Army's nuclear capabilities will remain an irreplaceable link between conventional forces and U.S. intercontinental nuclear forces. To be credible, they must be visible and militarily effective, and in sufficient numbers. The Army's chemical defense and retaliatory capabilities also must be modern and effective if they are to continue their contribution to deterrence, at least until the President's announced objective for the global, phased elimination of chemical weapons is realized.

The Army's modernization strategy guides the development and fielding of future equipment, placing priority on those units whose missions require them to be first in combat, whether active or reserve. It also guides the development of long-range plans for all major functional areas. These plans promote a continuous, disciplined sequence of development, fielding, and replacement of materiel over a 30-year period. They enable the Army to take advantage of the entire range of technological advances and to allocate resources according to national priorities. Finally, these plans also help us to align resource levels with budget and program changes and to avoid the "bow waves" that have caused programs in the past to become unaffordable.

Continuous modernization also applies to the Army's facilities. The resources allocated to facilities must reflect the priority accorded to the functions they support. We cannot afford to take a short-sighted view, deferring indefinitely the development of new facilities or the maintenance of those we need for the present and future. On the other hand, we must divest ourselves of marginal or unneeded facilities in order to conserve resources. Furthermore, to the maximum extent, the Army must plan for full use of all facilities and avoid inefficient single-purpose uses whenever possible.

The accelerating pace of technological change will continue to offer significant opportunities to enhance the lethality and effectiveness of all types of Army forces. Indeed, the array of potentially useful emerging technologies will exceed our ability to fund their exploitation. Therefore, the greatest challenge in this area lies in selecting those key technologies that will provide the greatest increase in warfighting capability for each dollar spent.

Technologies that apply across several functional areas and enable us to develop efficient, integrated "systems of systems" will receive high priority. Especially promising are sensor and automation technologies that facilitate "seeing" the battlefield and collecting, analyzing, disseminating, and acting on battlefield information. Similarly, the Army's work on rockets and missiles, which provided the foundation for the current U.S. space program, continues to support the Strategic Defense Initiative and other developments for Army and joint operations. In sum, high-technology research and development is, and will remain, a central feature of the Army's modernization strategy. The Army of the 1990s and beyond will reflect significant increases in battlefield effectiveness as a result of the application of advanced technologies.

The lethality of the Army of the future will be determined, above all else, by the actual combat readiness of the force—which, in turn, is a product of training. That is why training will continue to be the cornerstone of readiness. Combat training centers will remain the key to developing the maximum lethality of Army units. These centers not only hone combat skills, they also enable us to assess the validity of our combat doctrine and to develop our officer and noncommissioned officer leaders. The Army will continue to provide tough, realistic training to the highest standards so that our soldiers, units, and leaders have the best possible chance of accomplishing their missions and surviving should they be committed to combat.

Conclusion

The nature of our vital interests and the growing complexity of the international environment will demand that the Army of the future be versatile, deployable, and lethal—qualities essential to the defense of our nation in the years ahead. Moreover, as the Army reduces its size in the coming decade, it must remain trained and ready and able to expand again should circumstances change.

We must never forget that, in the final analysis, the Army and the nation depend upon the soldiers, civilians, and families who dedicate their lives to the service of their country. Everything we do to build the trained and ready Army of the future must have, as its primary focus, the men and women of the Total Army.

As we enter the 1990s and position ourselves for the twenty-first century, the Army is assuming increased prominence in U.S. national security strategy. The measure of our success as a strategic force will be the extent to which we protect the survival, freedom, and prosperity of the United States. By uncompromising adherence to our fundamental imperatives, and by exploiting the aggressive imagination and daring that characterize our society, we will maintain the trained and ready Army our country requires. This is the collective task of the Army, as well as our moral commitment to the nation.

PART 2
U.S. Domestic Politics and Security Issues

CHAPTER 3

The Public and National Security

DOUGLAS KINNARD

The purposes of this chapter are, first, to set in perspective the role of the public in the national security policymaking process; second, using available polling data, to summarize the substance of public attitudes toward major national security issues just prior to the Bush presidency; and finally, to draw together process and substance in the form of observations and unanswered questions as we view an uncertain future.

We begin by summarizing the diverse elements involved in the process of national security policymaking.[1] Then we can examine a relevant historical case: the Eisenhower Administration and the New Look. Granted that all historical analogies are unique, they still give a bedrock of reality on which to discuss the present and to conjecture as to the future.

There are, moreover, other compelling reasons for using the Eisenhower period in discussing the process of policymaking. The case is comparatively recent (the 1950s); yet, it is well documented, much more so than the Reagan period will be for years to come. It is also more applicable than are comparable cases in the 1960s and 1970s, which were driven by the Vietnam War. Most important, the case is concerned explicitly with national security policy formulation that emphasizes budgetary constraints, a vital consideration for military and civilian policymakers alike in the 1990s.

A discussion of the changing role of Congress in national security policymaking then follows. It is dramatically different from what it was during the Eisenhower period—and it is still changing. The way that Congress, beginning in the 1970s, resurged in the policymaking process is stunning, both in pace and breadth. Whether viewed as good or ill, this aggressive function raises important issues as to the future role of the public because of the public's symbiotic relationship with Congress.

An Overview

In the process of national security policymaking, there are four participating elements: presidential, bureaucratic, congressional, and nonelected. The latter includes the media, special-interest groups, and the public or, more precisely, the publics.

Responsibility and authority for formulating and implementing national security policy begins with the President. This stems, of course, from his constitutional authority, whether explicit, implied, or prerogative. Other sources of presidential power depend in degree on the President himself and the times in which he serves—for example, his participation in the legislative process, his political skills, and his ability to capture public attention and support through the media.

The President's immediate staff and advisors constitute another power center. Though their power is derived from the President and depends on his support, they obviously exercise power in their own right. Of particular interest for our purposes are the Assistant for National Security Affairs and the Director of the Office of Management and Budget.

In the area of national security policy, the key presidential appointees are the Secretaries of Defense and State and, in a different way, the Director of the Central Intelligence Agency. These officials are both presidential and cabinet officers in the sense that they simultaneously represent the president and their departments or agencies. Their power, though again derived from the President, also exists by virtue of the offices they hold and the bureaucracies over which they preside. If they are able to win over their own fiefdoms, their power will be commensurately greater. The bureaucracies themselves also wield power by making policy—for example, they interpret legislation as well as assist the President in formulating and proposing legislation.

The struggle between the President and Congress over who has the dominant position in determining policy and conducting foreign and national security affairs is as old as the Constitution. There have been periods when one or the other branch was dominant. During the Eisenhower Administration (to be discussed below) one would conclude after analysis that Congress had only a negligible role in forming national security policy. Hence, a section relevant to present political realities, entitled "A Changing Congressional Role," follows the description of the Eisenhower case.

As for nonelected participants in the policymaking process, comments in this chapter are focused on the media and the public itself.[2] We are primarily concerned with only that news media, such as the *New York Times*, that both select the news to be reported and comment upon it. Such media play a significant role by first defining the agenda of the political process and then helping to form public attitudes. Besides forming public opinion, the news media play other roles with regard to the executive branch: They carry its message to the public, and they keep the President in public view.[3]

The public itself is an element in national security policy formulation. Everyday citizens influence and are influenced by the President, Congress, and the media. Although public opinion tends to be tentative and defers to the judgment of government leaders in national security affairs more than in domestic issues, it does react to international events and sometimes even leads policymakers, as in the case of Vietnam.

There are, in fact, many publics in the area of national security; in increasing size and decreasing knowledge, they can be described as the influential public, the knowledgeable public, and the general public. Presumably, the influential and knowledgeable publics are of greatest influence.

A Historical Case: The Eisenhower Administration

During his 1952 presidential campaign, Eisenhower made two major promises: to end the Korean War and to reduce the budget. The two were related because ending the war, which he did within six months of taking office, was a prerequisite for reducing the budget. But he needed to do more. To reduce the overall budget from $74 billion the fiscal year of his taking office to $70 billion the next year and then to $60 billion the following year, he had to pare the defense budget further. This meant taking a close look at the kind of strategy the United States was going to pursue in the post–Korean War period.

In his memoirs, Eisenhower reveals his thoughts on strategy when he came to the Oval Office. In brief, he wanted to rely on deterrence and to rule out preventive war; to stress the role of nuclear technology, reducing reliance on U.S. conventional force; to place heavy reliance on Allied land forces around the Soviet periphery; to stress economic strength, especially through reduced defense budgets; and to be prepared to continue the struggle with the USSR over a period of decades.[4] His problem was to blend these strategic views into a credible strategy that could be implemented at a fairly low cost and be sold both to the American public and America's allies. To accomplish this, the President used organizational means, careful selection of key appointees, his long experience in handling bureaucracies, and his great rapport with the American people—a rapport on which he depended during major challenges to his policies.

At the apex of the defense and foreign policy process, Eisenhower restructured the National Security Council, transforming it into a formal organization with formal procedures, balancing this with informal organization and procedure. In practice, he placed even more emphasis on informal meetings and briefings on defense-related matters. The number of such meetings was rather substantial.

By July 1953, Eisenhower felt that it was time for his newly appointed

Service Chiefs to take a look at U.S. strategic policy. He asked them to come up with an agreed-upon paper regarding overall defense policy for the indefinite future. This paper was the first step toward what subsequently became known as the New Look, which the President later defined as "first a reallocation of resources among the five categories of forces, and second, the placing of greater emphasis than formerly on the deterrent and destructive power of improved nuclear weapons, better means of delivery, and effective air-defense units."[5]

The Chiefs of Staff were able to agree on a basic paper of strategic premises and guidelines, but translating these generalities into specifics for the fiscal year 1955 defense budget was another matter. Reasoning that there was no change in the perceived threat or in alliance commitments, and no new guidance on the employment of nuclear weapons, they decided that no substantial changes could be made in the defense budget of $42 billion.

It fell to the Chairman of the Joint Chiefs of Staff (JCS), Admiral Arthur W. Radford, to defend the Service Chief's premises before the National Security Council (NSC). Radford centered his presentation at the October 13, 1953, NSC meeting on the nature of presidential guidance for employment of nuclear weapons. His message, which was to have very significant results, was that if the use of nuclear weapons from the outset of a conflict was accepted as a planning premise, then a less costly force structure could be developed.

Admiral Radford's premise led to a subsequent NSC session on October 29, at which the President approved NSC-162/2, the policy basis of the New Look. The paper placed maximum reliance on nuclear weapons from the outset of a conflict. Radford's talk of October 13 had been entirely on his own; neither the Army nor the Navy had agreed with the new NSC policy on nuclear war. Nevertheless, Secretary of Defense Charles Wilson, with Radford's help, was able to get qualified agreement from Army Chief Matthew B. Ridgway and Navy Chief Robert B. Carney, and to use the new policy to get the defense budget down to a level acceptable to Eisenhower and the Secretary of the Treasury.

Congress examined the New Look during hearings on the fiscal year 1955 defense budget. Members offered no challenge to the concept and almost none to the particulars. The administration's image of unanimity on the Eisenhower strategy remained intact during the hearings, despite the misgivings voiced by Army Chief Ridgway concerning the administration's lack of emphasis on land forces. Floor debate was neither systematic nor informed. With the defense appropriation cleared, Eisenhower had his strategic policy.[6]

By early 1956, Congress was pressuring the administration to raise the level of defense expenditures in fiscal year 1957. No extraordinary event had occurred, but 1956 was an election year and some members of Congress wanted to impress the voters with their zeal for a greater defense effort.

Pressures also came from the Air Force in an effort to secure additional funds for its strategic bomber force. That spring, Senator Stuart Symington, an Air Force proponent, obliged with airpower hearings held by his subcommittee of the Senate Armed Services Committee.

It was in this atmosphere that Eisenhower met with Defense Secretary Charles Wilson and Chairman Radford concerning congressional probes and possible Air Force testimony. Ike's message to the senior military went beyond the immediate question of the Air Force budget, however. The President maintained that "a Chief of Staff of one service should not present just the picture of his own service . . . each man testifying must think of what other services contribute. If he can't bring himself to do this, he doesn't belong in the position he holds."[7]

In early October 1957, the Soviets orbited Sputnik. Its psychological and strategic impact brought on congressional and, to some extent, public pressure to increase the size of the fiscal year 1959 defense budget. The President, however, was not one to overreact, especially when it came to defense spending. To help counter public anxiety over the Soviet launching and the attendant public commentary, the President decided to give three "confidence" speeches to the American public. His major points were that the overall military strength of the free world was greater than that of the communist countries and that the United States must be selective in expending its resources. In the end, Ike's wide public support was key, and his views on the defense budget prevailed.

As the executive preparation of the fiscal year 1960 defense budget reached its final stages, the President met in late November 1958 with his civilian defense advisors and the Chairman of the Joint Chiefs. His new Secretary of Defense, Neil McElroy, developed the major issues and pointed out that he had reduced the service estimates by almost a billion dollars in recent months. The director of the Bureau of the Budget, Maurice Stans, agreed that the Defense Department had made substantial cuts, but said more cuts (in the vicinity of $3 to $4 billion) were needed. The President asked McElroy to look over the budget again to make additional cuts, which he did.[8]

However, by that time, the climate was right for Congress to try to intervene more forcefully in defense matters. Technology was in a state of flux, raising many technical and strategic questions, and few people seemed certain of the answers. The goals of the services were sufficiently far apart so that it was not difficult for Congress to find points of conflict between the services or between a service and administration. Finally, the political climate created by the congressional elections just passed, and the presidential election on the horizon encouraged Congress to take on the administration.

Committees in the House and Senate asked the usual questions about hardware and strategy, as well as the unusual question about who had played what part in the development of the defense budget, including the guidelines on which it was based. In these hearings, the senior military began showing publicly its lack of consensus regarding the particulars of the defense budget. The most spectacular hearings that spring, though, were not those related directly to the appropriations process, but rather those conducted by Senator Lyndon B. Johnson's Senate Preparedness Subcommittee.

Under the heading "Four Military Chiefs List Objections to Budget Limits," the *New York Times* of March 9, 1959, carried the story of the Chiefs' testimony before Johnson's subcommittee, as well as the written texts of their memoranda. "General Maxwell D. Taylor, the Army's Chief of Staff," it reported, "was most vehement in his comments." Meeting the same morning with JCS Chairman Nathan Twining, President Eisenhower brought up the article, which he had read. The President instructed Twining "to caution the Joint Chiefs that the military in this country is a tool and not a policy-making body; the Joint Chiefs are not responsible for high-level political decision."[9]

Undoubtedly, these hearings were designed to be politically embarrassing to the administration, and they were. Nor is there any question of the breakdown in consensus within the administration. In retrospect, however, the effect of these hearings on the Eisenhower strategy and defense budget were negligible. The 1960 presidential campaign was probably the primary motivation for the hearings and from that perspective, perhaps, they were successful in setting the stage for the defense debate during the approaching national electoral struggle.

Eisenhower's basic power lay in his wide public support and, as it pertained to defense issues, the American public's perception that he was the most important military figure of that time. His successes in making this power effective lay in part in the considerable time he spent as President on military matters, not because they interested him, which they did, but because he perceived them to be a vital element in carrying out his overall presidential goals. Moreover, he was willing and able to carry his argument to the American public over the heads of Congress.

One of Eisenhower's successful leadership techniques was exemplified in his dealings with the Joint Chiefs: the avoidance of public confrontation. Specifically, he sought prior agreement on issues to prevent their becoming matters of debate among the general public. In particular, his key political and military appointees had to undergo a kind of loyalty test to convince him of their willingness to support his policies.

This is one reason why Eisenhower was able to permit vigorous debate in the NSC forum and still expect support for his decisions. In many cases, his decisions had already been made in smaller, informal meetings. However, the NSC served both to widen the base of support for Eisenhower's decisions and clarify his rationale to his key appointees. His employment of organizational process can be understood only in the context of an interplay between formal and small, informal groups.

One of the principal issues was the distribution of influence over the policy-fiscal dialogue between the senior military and key civilian appointees. Eisenhower solved this problem through his predilection to be his own Secretary of Defense. He accomplished this operationally by dealing directly with the chairman of the Joint Chiefs of Staff on strategic matters and, as is normal procedure, directly with the Secretary of Defense on budgetary matters. Thus, the President became the first civilian official who dealt with all aspects of strategy and management. This is usually seen to be one of the roles of the Secretary of Defense.

In sum, Presidential-Pentagon relations in the Eisenhower administration had these characteristics: a President superbly equipped both in fact and in his public image to deal with military matters; a chief executive who thoroughly dominated the relationship; a continuing strengthening of the civilian hand through reorganization and practice, which set the stage for an all-powerful Secretary of Defense in the next administration; and a lessening influence of the senior military on major policy decisions, which began a trend that was to continue during the next decade and beyond.

From the Eisenhower case, we can infer the following conclusions that still have relevance today.

1. The defense budget drives national security policy formulation, not vice versa.
2. In developing the defense budget, the domestic context is more important than the external context in time of peace.
3. Process is more important in developing national security policies than are the rational arguments for the policies. In this process, the President is the prime mover and is the key to mobilizing public opinion on national security issues.

A Changing Congressional Role[10]

The Founding Fathers envisioned a Congress deeply involved in foreign and national security problems, although they left the precise nature of this involvement to be decided by events. The cyclical nature of congressional participation vis-à-vis the President has been an interesting matter to observers and historians ever since. For example, the neutralist stance of Congress in foreign affairs during the 1930s frustrated Roosevelt's inclination toward greater U.S. involvement in world affairs. Then, following World War II, the powers of the President in national security affairs swelled significantly with relatively little challenge by Congress.

Executive power expanded well into the period of U.S. involvement in Vietnam. The high point was undoubtedly the Tonkin Gulf Resolution of August 7, 1964, in which Congress voted 502 to 2 to approve and support the determination of the President as Commander-in-Chief to take all necessary steps, including the use of armed force, to prevent further aggression in that area. This congressional support gradually waned until May 1970, when the tide reversed as a result of President Nixon's Cambodian incursion. Then the war became the impetus for congressional resurgence in national security affairs.

Combined with Nixon's Watergate-related problems, public alienation and congressional frustration over the war led to a large number of statutes, such as the War Powers Resolution of 1973 and the Budget and Impoundment Control Act of 1974. Their net effect was to inject Congress into national security affairs, curtailing some of the previously accepted presidential hegemony.

At the same time, other developments contributed to this congressional resurgence and its resulting complexity. For a variety of reasons, a new generation had arrived, especially in the House of Representatives. They were unimpressed by established procedures that emphasized party discipline and members' seniority. There was also an enormous enlargement in congressional staffs, permitting Congress to intrude into details in a way that had not been possible previously.[11]

All this occurred at a time when détente between the United States and the Soviet Union seemed to be wiping away the previous public consensus of the Cold War. The questions of what national security goals to pursue and of how to allot resources were now left open for debate.

The implications of all this for the role of Congress in national security policymaking were many and led to as yet unanswered questions. Because this body has disaggregated into a member-centered organization with a concomitant loss of party loyalty and committee leadership, and the individual members have become the recipients of enhanced resources and influence, the question of who really represents Congress and can arrive at understandings in its name vis-à-vis the executive is moot.

Through legislation that began in the 1970s, the chief processes of Congress—authorization, appropriation, and oversight—have become much more detailed and more intrusive into heretofore strictly executive procedures. Now the White House is much more accountable to Capitol Hill. The reaction of the executive has created problems of coordination that are often uncomfortable. On the other hand, the question of who is responsible for given actions can be obscured. When results are less than desired, the public cannot be sure which branch should be held accountable. Each side can insist, "We didn't do it; they did."

As for the relationship of the public and Congress in national security policymaking, it is acknowledged that public opinion does from time to time play an important role. In keeping with the concept that Congress is the most representative branch of our government, many legislators believe that, by virtue of their continuous contact with the people, they have "served not only to ensure democratic control over the foreign policy-making process, but have also been the conveyors of sometimes ambivalent and occasionally vociferous public opinion."[12]

Since the public has traditionally given highest priority to internal matters, while frequently displaying a lack of consensus about external goals, Congress has been provided both an opportunity and an incentive to intrude in national security affairs on the behalf of the public. Given today's resurgent Congress, the chief executive needs all the more to stay in touch with the public and should not be impressed by the congressional belief that its viewpoints are more authoritative than his on matters of public opinion.

A New Security Environment

Having looked at process, we now turn to substance. Before considering current attitudes of the American public on security issues, it is useful to consider the national security environment as it might be viewed by executive and legislative decisionmakers in the early days of the Bush Administration.

Because Moscow has achieved nuclear parity with the United States, a balance exists that makes a nuclear arms race unattractive and counterproductive. While the Soviet Union continues to pose a serious military threat, it cannot compete seriously with the West in other areas, such as economic ones.

The American people are gradually becoming aware that communism is not the root of all the nation's external problems. In this regard, the containment strategy has stopped being a unifying force in domestic politics. Replacing it is a desire for a peaceful end to the Cold War, including, if possible, the solution of long-standing problems, such as reuniting a divided Germany.

While the USSR remains the chief military rival of the United States, the diffusion of military technology is a growing threat to U.S. interests. It comes from several directions; China and, perhaps in time, Japan will become major military powers. Even smaller countries acquire advanced weapons and so decrease the relative military advantage of the major powers.

The postwar American economic hegemony has been replaced by a much more competitive world economy in which the U.S. position is in relative decline. Americans see this economic competition, which is primarily from their allies, as more threatening than communist ideology.

Perhaps the most important issue on the present national security agenda is NATO. Though strains and uncertainties are not unusual for that alliance, such recent events as the INF Treaty and Gorbachev's troop reduction initiatives make current tensions in the alliance unprecedented. These events have set countervailing forces in motion, even though the basic goals of the alliance remain. Gorbachev's announced cuts will put NATO leaders under increased pressure from their home fronts to make cuts in their own forces and will accelerate Western Europe's interest in détente over deterrence.

From the U.S. point of view, the current serious budgetary crisis and worldwide security commitments, combined with the trends in NATO, will understandably bring domestic pressure to reduce the large number of U.S. military forces in Western Europe. Such a condition would allow continued support of Navy and Air Force deployments on a flexible, worldwide basis while not diminishing U.S. interest in NATO; rather, it changes the way in which NATO obligations are met as one element of the worldwide global commitments of the United States.

Public Attitudes on National Security in an Uncertain Environment

At the beginning of the Bush Administration, the American public appears to tie in U.S. national security objectives with its economic strength and competitiveness. Furthermore, this perception is one that seems to focus less than previously upon the Soviet Union and its threat to the United States. The changing domestic and international environments have influenced these modifications. Public opinion in the United States regarding national security issues, however, is frequently ambivalent, highly fluid, and often contradictory.[13]

The Economy

The American public is concerned about the "economic well-being" of the United States and expresses serious doubts about the future "competitiveness" of the United States in a perceived hostile international economic environment. In November 1988, when asked to identify how important it was to make the United States more "competitive" in the world economy, 35 percent of those polled felt that this was "extremely important," 48 percent felt that it was "very important," and 12 percent felt that it was "somewhat important."[14] Only 3 percent felt that it was not important. Americans see the U.S. economy as basically healthy, but not competitive enough with other, more vigorous economies, especially those of West Germany and Japan. One survey found that a full 50 percent of the respondents felt that the U.S. economy was "slipping dangerously" when compared to the economies of other industrialized nations.[15]

The public has a somewhat skeptical view of continued good economic relations between the United States and our "economic competitors." In a March 1988 survey, 68 percent felt that Japan was a "strong competitor," whereas only 36 percent felt that the United States could be described as such an economic competitor.[16] When Americans were asked whether competition from West Germany and Japan represented more of a "threat" to our future than did "communism," 45 percent of the respondents felt that it did, while only 48 percent continued to view "communism" as the main threat to U.S. national security.[17] Looking specifically at the Japanese-U.S. relationship, a May 1988 survey found that 57 percent of the respondents felt that Japan would become the "preeminent" economic power in the world.[18]

The public increasingly defines a strong and dynamic economy as an essential element of national security. A November 1988 survey found that 72 percent of the respondents "strongly approved" of the notion that the United States should "devote as much attention to America's economic strength as to its military strength."[19] Americans also seem to view the heavy emphasis upon the military component of national security, as demonstrated in the Reagan era, as harmful to the economic side. Economic vitality is viewed as having been "sacrificed" by the public. In 1983, 41 percent of the respondents of one survey felt that defense spending hurt the economy, whereas in March 1988, 53 percent felt that this was true.[20] This same 1988 survey showed that large numbers of Americans associated military spending with budget deficits, tax increases, and lower spending on health and social programs.

The Military

The public appears to be having a difficult time justifying high defense spending in a "hostile" international economic environment. The public seems to be asking both the President and Congress to use shortcuts where possible, in order to keep military costs down without hurting U.S. military preparedness. Approving of the buildup of the Reagan era, Americans seem to believe, nevertheless, that this buildup to date is sufficient. It is noteworthy that, though more aware of the economic imperative, the public is not yet demanding decreases in defense spending.

There is a feeling that the United States pays too much for the defense of its allies and that the reliance of allies upon U.S. support is simply "not just." There is also a corollary to this feeling: Because of "inadequate" efforts by U.S. allies on their own behalf, they are reaping substantial economic benefits from their low level of spending. This, in turn, hurts the economic national security interest of the United States by giving the "economic competitor" an additional advantage. In terms of persuading U.S. allies to pay a greater share of their own defense, a November 1988 survey found that 35 percent of the respondents felt that this was "extremely important," 44 percent felt that it was "very important," and 15 percent felt that this was only "somewhat important."[21]

Negotiations and arms control agreements, according to the American public, may afford an acceptable means of reducing the size of the defense budget. With certain qualifications, arms control is a very popular issue with the American public. One qualification is that such agreements be "testing exercises," allowing the United States to judge Soviet intentions over the course of time.[22] Success or failure of these testing agreements would play strongly in the success of future agreements. These testing agreements should be cautious in their nature; that is, they are not to be built upon "trust," but rather upon a direct and unambiguous "verification," such as could be obtained by having American inspectors working within Soviet territory.[23] With this in mind, Americans seem to expect substantial gains from this process. A recent survey found that 61 percent of the respondents strongly approved of a U.S. effort to "negotiate with (the) Soviets to eliminate all nuclear weapons," 21 percent "somewhat approved" of this effort, while only 14 percent expressed negative attitudes toward such an effort.[24] One survey found that, by a margin of 81 to 12 percent, the respondents wanted the strategic nuclear forces of both superpowers to be cut in half.[25]

The Soviet Union

It is perhaps the U.S.-USSR relationship that will most fundamentally affect U.S. national security. The American public appears to be increasingly aware of the changing nature of the Soviet threat, while also expressing great caution regarding another détente. Americans do not want to be fooled again, and any new "détente" must be based upon a more secure foundation. Although continuing to express distrust of the Soviet system, Americans seem to have an increasingly positive impression of the leader of that system, General Secretary and President Mikhail Gorbachev. Changes occurring in the Soviet Union under Gorbachev have not gone unnoticed by the American public, which sees them as positive developments that, if continued, could lead to a "fundamentally" new relationship between the two nations.

Central to this continued warming of superpower relations is Gorbachev himself. His unprecedented popularity within the United States has generated significant public optimism concerning the Soviet-U.S. relationship, and this popularity grows with time. A 1988 survey conducted in late June and early July found that 31 percent of the respondents had a "very favorable" opinion of Gorbachev, with an additional 52 percent having a "somewhat favorable" opinion. Only 11 percent had an unfavorable opinion of him.[26] Gorbachev is seen as primarily responsible for the changes that have occurred in the Soviet system. He is also frequently viewed as somehow at odds with this system; his struggle with it seems to increase his popularity with Americans. Significantly, a March 1988 survey found that 52 percent of the respondents felt that Soviet-U.S. relations would be adversely affected were Gorbachev to lose power within the Soviet Union.[27]

Nevertheless, the American public still mistrusts the Soviet system itself and continues to believe that the Reagan military buildup was critical in improving superpower relations and in protecting the United States from potential Soviet attacks. In one survey, conducted in February 1988, 65 percent of the respondents felt that the Soviet Union "continues aggressively in pursuit of furthering the cause of communism."[28]

For many Americans, however, the nature of the Soviet threat has changed significantly from what it was in the early 1980s. The U.S. military buildup, the superpower summits, and the Gorbachev initiatives have brought about much of this change in the public's mind. The Soviet threat seems to have decreased significantly in the eyes of the American public. ATS 5, a survey conducted between April 25 and May 1, 1988, found that 17 percent viewed the Soviet Union as a "very serious" threat to the United States, 36 percent as a "serious" threat, 32 percent as a "minor" threat, and 12 percent as "not a threat." In contrast, ATS 12, which was conducted in December 1988, found that only 9 percent viewed the Soviet Union as a "very serious" threat.[29]

The new relationship may be based upon certain common efforts made jointly by both nations to resolve common problems; certain efforts have particularly strong public support. Three such areas are environmental pollution, the illicit drug trade, and international terrorism. Additional areas in which both nations could also cooperate include regional trouble spots (such as the Middle East), cultural exchange programs, and the elimination of excess nuclear weapons.[30] With time and other positive accomplishments, joint cooperation in these areas could provide a more secure foundation upon which to build a new superpower relationship.

Some Observations and Questions

In considering the public and national security policy, the approach has been to first examine the policy process itself and then the substance of relevant public views in the present environment. It is now time to bring these two strands together.

In doing so, the conclusions regarding the Eisenhower case are restated as hypotheses for the present national security policymaking environment. Each conclusion will be examined in terms of process and substance, as appropriate. It will be useful to begin by summarizing the attitudes of the American public at the end of the Reagan period concerning national security issues.

1. The American public recognizes that important changes are occurring in U.S.-USSR relations, but their outlook remains cautious on this development.

2. The public approves of the defense buildup accomplished during the Reagan period, but considers it sufficient.
3. The public is of the opinion that nuclear weapons are more likely to be used by terrorists or Third World states than by the superpowers.
4. There is increasing public concern over U.S. economic competitiveness.
5. Finally, the American public no longer thinks primarily in terms of East-West problems, but rather of global, diffuse problems involving such matters as the demise of U.S. economic hegemony, the deterioration of the environment, and random terrorist activities.

Hypothesis One

The defense budget drives national security policy formulation, not vice versa. This presumes that the means (the defense budget) determines the ends (national security policy). While this should evoke no great surprise on the part of any student of the subject, it is at variance with the established process model.

Theoretically, the President and his senior advisors begin the process of the budget cycle by deciding national security policy. This policy is then translated into military requirements and budgets by the executive branch and, after approval by the President, is sent to Congress for its action and eventual appropriation of funds. In actual practice, the size of the executive budget request is not related to policy directly but to budgetary ceilings approved by the President. This process is not wholly without logic. National security policy is rarely defined with such precision that there can be only one interpretation of the means needed to carry it out.

Thus, in the initial Bush defense budget, the debate was not over strategy but over whether the defense budget should reflect a 2 percent real growth (after inflation), as President Reagan proposed, or a zero real growth (after inflation), as President Bush proposed, or some lesser figure.

When the military chiefs present their case for continued real growth, they do so in two ways: They make the case for forces meeting their interpretation of policy goals and to the political arena in which the budget is really decided.

Hypothesis Two

In developing the defense budget, the domestic context is more important than the external context in time of peace. The notion that the domestic context influences policies directed toward external events is not a new one. Thucydides noted how the external behavior of the Greek city states was frequently shaped more by what was happening at home than by actions of the other city states. This concept is particularly relevant to the United States, whose form of government encourages open debate among officials and active involvement of the people.

The present views of the American people give little reason to believe that external matters will take precedence over domestic problems. In fact, Americans today seem worried whether too great attention to national security may be hurting the economy itself. In 1983, 53 percent of Americans polled felt that the Reagan defense buildup had been good for the overall economy; in contrast, by 1988, the same number felt that the buildup had harmed the economy.

How does all of this relate to the forty years of Cold War vigilance the United States has been through? While it would be premature to say that the public feels that the Cold War is over, there is little question that most Americans think a growth in defense spending is unnecessary.

However, Air Force Chief of Staff General Larry D. Welch challenges the public views on defense issues. In a public statement, he assailed "the unwarranted but still pervasive belief that defense spending is a major cause of the budget deficit." He lamented what he saw in the United States as two changing perceptions: that "economic competitors pose a greater threat to U.S. national security than do military adversaries" and that "the military and expansionist policies of the Soviet Union have been moderated."[31]

Whether Service Chiefs have enough political clout today to be effective in swaying the public on defense budgets is debatable. They do, however, have their bureaucratic forums with the President and the Congress. Their effectiveness is a question of process.

Hypothesis Three

Process is more important in developing national security policies than are the rational arguments for the policies. In this process, the President is the prime mover and is the key to mobilizing public opinion on national security issues. It is acknowledged that, given the differences in personalities and the times, and resurgent role of Congress, no President in the foreseeable future is going to play the role on national security policy and defense budgets that Eisenhower did in the 1950s. In particular, it is unlikely that any President will have the public image or support on defense issues that General/President Eisenhower did during his White House years.

Any President, however, is pivotal in the defense process. It is he who must, if he is convinced, make the policy and budgetary case with the Congress and, more importantly, with the public, if it is to be made.

Effective process will require a desire by the Bush Administration for a genuine dialogue with Congress regarding the assumptions and analyses of defense issues, as well as upon the policies and budgets themselves. Not an easy task, it involves restructuring the national security process at the most basic level—for example, to move economic and security decisions onto the same track.

How this will be accomplished depends, at the present, on George Bush himself. His speeches make clear that he considers Congress to have eroded presidential authority, especially on the national security process. Whether he has the political power and will to change this situation or accommodate it remains to be seen. This is an even more difficult challenge in light of the changing strategic landscape.

Notes

1. The policymaking process for national security, as used here, involves the functioning and relationships of governmental authorities and agencies responsible for national security policy formulation. It includes the participation of nongovernmental groups as well, such as the media, special interests, and the public itself. The process has intellectual, interpersonal, and bureaucratic components. A representative sampling of current publications summarizing the process of defense and foreign policymaking, and which contain detailed references, include the following: Charles W. Kegley, Jr., and Eugene R. Wittkopf, eds. *The Domestic Sources of American Foreign Policy* (New York: St. Martin's Press, 1988); Roger Hilsman, *The Politics of Policy-Making in Defense and Foreign Affairs* (Englewood Cliffs, NJ: Prentice-Hall, 1987); and John P. Lovell, *The Challenge of American Foreign Policy* (New York: Macmillan, 1985).

2. Space does not allow developing the role of special-interest groups in formulating national security policy. Such groups can be defined as "any organization or coalition of organizations that attempts to influence public policy at any of the branches or levels of government," (Hilsman, note 1, p. 204).

3. Doris A. Graber, *Mass Media and American Politics* (Washington, D.C.: Congressional Quarterly Press, 1989), p. 238. Considering the tremendous influence wielded by the media as agenda-setters—and to some extent judges—of the political process, it is interesting to note that the really influential members constitute only nine organizations: three national television network news organizations, ABC, CBS, and NBC; two national magazines, *Newsweek* and *Time*; the Associated Press; and three major newspapers, *New York Times, Washington Post,* and *Wall Street Journal.*

4. Dwight D. Eisenhower, *The White House Years*, Vol. I, *Mandate for Change* (Garden City, NY: Doubleday, 1963), pp. 445–447.

5. Ibid., p. 457.

6. NATO was brought on board at the December 1954 ministerial meeting when the NATO Council approved MC 48, making NATO's primary strategy dependent upon nuclear weapons.

7. Memorandum of Conference with the President (MCP), April 5, 1956. See Douglas Kinnard, *President Eisenhower and Strategy Management: A Study in Defense Politics*, 2d Edition (Washington, D.C.: Pergamon-Brassey's, 1989). Pressure by the Air Force and its supporters had some success in securing an increase in the Air Force budget for fiscal year 1957 that was

above the President's request. The Army's efforts, the so-called "revolt of the colonels," involved press releases of position papers critical of the Air Force. Largely because of Wilson's response, this attempt to give a greater role to the Army was abortive, and Army tactics of this sort ceased with the reassignment of the principals outside Washington. See E. Bruce Geolhoed, *Charles E. Wilson and Controversy at the Pentagon* (Detroit: Wayne State University Press, 1979), pp. 136–138.

8. MCP, November 28, 1958.
9. MCP, March 9, 1959.
10. For representative literature on this subject, see Cecil V. Crabb, Jr., and Pat M. Holt, *Invitation to Struggle: Congress, the President, and Foreign Policy* (Washington, D.C.: Congressional Quarterly Press, 1989); James M. Lindsay, "Congress and Defense Policy: 1961 to 1986" *Armed Forces and Society*, No. 13, pp. 371–401; and Wallace Earl Walker, "Congressional Resurgence and the Destabilization of U.S. Foreign Policy," *Parameters*, September 1988, pp. 54–67.
11. Representative Les Aspin, Chairman of the House Armed Services Committee, is particularly prone to lecture the executive on both the process and substance of national security policy. See his *Searching for a Defense Strategy*, House of Representatives, September 1987, and *What the Next President Should Know about National Defense*, remarks delivered at the Science Applications International Corporation, December 8, 1988, in Washington, D.C.
12. House Committee on International Relations, *Congress and Foreign Policy*, 94th Congress, 2d session, 1976, p. 19.
13. The explication and analysis of public attitudes in this section were done by Brent Lollis of the University of Oklahoma. He used as a basis twelve surveys done by the Americans Talk Security (ATS) project between October 1987 and December 1988. The ATS surveys were conducted by telephone and usually included about one thousand respondents. The surveys were conducted by four organizations: Market Opinion Research, Marttila and Kiley, Inc., the Daniel Yankelovich Group, Inc., and the Public Agenda Foundation. Each survey was conducted by one of the organizations and reviewed by the others. The ATS surveys are available at the ATS office, 83 Church St., Winchester, MA 01890.
14. Americans Talk Security (ATS) 11, this survey was conducted between November 4 and 7, 1988, and was published in December 1988, p. 232.
15. ATS 3, this survey was conducted between February 17 and 24, 1988, and published in March 1988, p. 82.
16. ATS 4, this survey was conducted between March 22 and 27, 1988, and published in April 1988, p. 82.
17. ATS 6, this survey was conducted between May 24 and 27, 1988, and published in June 1988, p. 143.
18. Ibid., p. 142.
19. ATS 11, p. 266.
20. ATS 3, pp. 21–53.
21. ATS 11, p. 238.
22. Daniel Yankelovich and Richard Smoke, "America's New Thinking," *Foreign Affairs*, Fall 1988, p. 16. This article is based upon the ATS project and a joint project by the Public Agenda Foundation (PAF) and Center for Foreign Policy Development, Brown University. This latter project was conducted in five U.S. cities in "laboratories" that brought together about two hundred people per city, subjecting them to about three hours of

professionally moderated exposure to four broad "futures" for U.S. national security policy.

23. Ibid., pp. 14, 15.
24. ATS 11, p. 262.
25. ATS 2, this survey was conducted between January 7 and 14, 1988, and was published in January 1988, p. 19.
26. ATS 7, this survey was conducted between June 25 and July 7, 1988, and published in July 1988, p. 115.
27. ATS 4, p. 99.
28. ATS 3, p. 25.
29. ATS 5, this survey was conducted between April 25 and May 1, 1988, and was published in May 1988, p. 90. ATS 12, which was conducted between December 10 and 13, 1988, and published in January 1989, also includes related information.
30. Yankelovich and Smoke, p. 3; and ATS 7, p. 25.
31. *New York Times*, November 30, 1988, p. 13.

CHAPTER 4

Congress and the Defense Budget

ROBERT F. HALE

During the first half of the 1980s, Congress approved sharp growth in defense budgets that brought improvements in many indicators of military capability. More recently, Congress has legislated four consecutive years of real decline in budgets for defense, resulting in plans to reduce numbers of military forces and in the possibility that overall military capability will also decline. Moreover, many believe that large federal deficits and other factors make additional cuts in military budgets and capability inevitable. These reductions come at a time when some analysts believe that the military capability of the Soviet Union and its allies exceeds that of the United States and its allies, unless the Soviets commit themselves to reductions in military forces well beyond those announced thus far.

Concern over the substance of the defense budget debate is exacerbated by frustration with the way it is conducted. The congressional defense budget process is almost universally criticized for producing late budgets, thereby fostering instability in defense planning, requiring too much time and work, and resulting in overly detailed legislation. In recent years, these criticisms have led to some revisions in the process, though not to the revolutionary changes advocated by some critics, and further modifications in congressional procedures seem likely in the future. An assessment of the defense budget process is the first task of this chapter.

Changes in that process, however, are not likely to alter substantially the decisions by Congress regarding the budget—especially decisions about how much to spend for defense. Those decisions reflect the attitudes of the public, which are in turn shaped by a variety of factors, ranging from concern over U.S. security on the one hand to worries over large budget deficits on the other. This chapter discusses these key factors and the effect they are likely to have on defense budgets in the early 1990s. It concludes with a brief discussion of the implications of leaner defense budgets for the Army and the other military services.

The Defense Budget Process

Congressional procedures for establishing a defense budget are lengthy and complex. The process begins with receipt of the President's budget recommendations, usually in January. Three steps follow:

The Concurrent Resolution

First, Congress establishes a three-year budget plan in what is known as the concurrent resolution on the budget. This resolution sets targets for spending in such broad areas as national defense; the targets are enforceable in the first of the three years. It also sets a target for revenues. Budget committees in the House and Senate recommend a budget resolution, which must be ratified by both houses of Congress. Since the resolution is not legislation, it does not require the signature of the President.

Authorizing Legislation

Congress next establishes defense policy in the authorization bill. This bill does not provide any funds for defense programs, but it does establish ceilings in key areas, including the numbers of weapons that can be bought, numbers of persons that can be employed, and dollars that can be spent for day-to-day operations. The authorization bill also deals with such issues as arms control and procurement policy. The armed services committees in each house recommend an authorization bill, which must be passed by Congress and signed by the President.

Appropriations Legislation

Finally, Congress makes money available for defense programs in an appropriations bill. This legislation is recommended to each house by its appropriations committee, with most of the defense work being accomplished by a subcommittee on defense. Since it is legislation, it requires the President's signature.

While sequential in concept, these three steps often take place concurrently, and repeatedly address the same key issues. This produces a complex, redundant debate. Moreover, a second budget process, separate from the regular one, goes on at the same time. The procedures of the Balanced Budget and Emergency Deficit Control Reaffirmation Act of 1987 (better known as Gramm-Rudman-Hollings) mandate automatic cuts in defense and other parts of the federal budget if deficits exceed thresholds established in the act. These deficit thresholds become important targets that govern actions in the regular budget process. The details of the Gramm-Rudman-Hollings process are beyond the scope of this chapter, but they add substantially to the complexity of the budget debate.

Recent Changes

The defense budget process has changed in recent years in significant ways. Some changes affected the entire budget debate. For one thing, the executive branch has become much more involved in the budget debate; indeed, in the early 1980s, President Reagan used the budget process extensively as a means to enact his agenda. In 1985, revisions in the governing law made spending targets in the budget resolution more readily enforceable. It is now easier to ensure that agreements about the total level of defense spending are followed during the authorizing and appropriating steps of the budget process.[1] In addition, in 1987, the administration and the Congress reached a two-year agreement on spending totals for defense and other areas of the budget. This agreement had an important effect on the debate in the second of the two years.

Other changes apply only to the defense budget debate. In the early 1980s, Congress allowed the administration to enter into more and larger multiyear contracts, which bind the government to buy weapons for more than one year. In 1987, Congress also debated a two-year budget, though it was not fully enacted.

Major Criticisms of the Budget Process

Despite these changes, frustration with the current budget process remains high. Trent Lott, the former Mississippi congressman (now a senator) who served as minority whip, likened the budget process to a sacred cow that wanders through the gardens of powerful people, munching on their flowers. Lott contends that more than one member has secretly vowed to turn the sacred cow into steaks![2]

Late Budgets

Slowness is one reason the knife is out for the defense budget process. Since fiscal year 1976, when Congress began operating under new budget procedures, ten out of thirteen budgets have been enacted after the beginning of the fiscal year. Those ten budgets were late by an average of about fifty-five days. Six of the ten were not enacted until some time in December, more than two months after the beginning of the fiscal year. The Department of Defense contends that this tardiness prevents orderly planning, and the public may share the department's concern.

Table 4.1 Key Steps in the Congressional Defense Budget Process

Step 1	Committees	Target Date for Completion
Concurrent Resolution	Budget	April 15
Authorization	Armed Services	Summer
Appropriation	Appropriations	October 1

Instability

Critics contend that the Congressional process fosters instability in defense planning by failing to provide reliable guidance about future funding. Development of a defense capability, particularly the development of experienced personnel and the procurement of complex weapons, requires stable programs over many years. Yet, the last two steps of the congressional budget process (the authorization and appropriation steps) focus almost entirely on the upcoming budget year. The first step in the congressional budget process, which results in the concurrent budget resolution, does provide guidance about the total level of defense spending for the budget year and the two following years. However, the levels in the following years are often trimmed. In every budget resolution since 1980, Congress has provided the Pentagon with a target for defense spending in the two years after the budget year. When time came to appropriate the funds, however, Congress altered its second-year targets by an average of about 6 percent and its third-year targets by an average of about 12 percent.[3]

How important is budget stability? Very important, according to former Secretary of Defense Caspar Weinberger. Between 1950 and 1987, the defense budget increased about $190 billion *after* adjustment for inflation. Yet in 1987, Weinberger told the Congress that, if defense had received steady zero growth since 1950, with no ups and downs, it would be "vastly ahead of where we are now."[4]

Congress is certainly not alone in fostering instability. In the past, the Pentagon's five-year spending plans have significantly exceeded both the Congressional spending targets and the funds that most observers felt would be appropriated.[5] But the lack of firm long-term guidance from Congress certainly does not help.

Lengthy, Heavy Workloads

From the time Congress begins formal work in January until it adjourns, often not until the following December, much of the workload revolves around the budget. Wags have suggested that when Congress created the new budget process in 1974, it thought it was voting for motherhood. Instead, it got a mother-in-law!

How heavy is the workload? The volume of information requested and received by Congress is one indication. In fiscal year 1987, Congress received 25,306 pages of material in support of that year's defense budget. It asked 555 witnesses to testify concerning the defense budget, resulting in 1,434 hours of testimony. Congress also generated 123,130 written inquiries and made 599,000 telephone calls concerning defense issues.[6] Clearly, it takes a great deal of everybody's time to prepare and assimilate this mass of information.

Congress also devotes a large amount of its own time to debate over the defense budget. In 1985, the House and Senate together spent eighteen days debating the annual authorization bill and considered 247 amendments. Ten years earlier, the two houses spent just nine days and considered only 44 amendments.[7] Only a few of these many amendments have far-reaching effects on defense; many deal with minor issues.[8] Nonetheless, they all consume time.

Overly Detailed Review

One result of spending so much time on the defense budget may be an overly detailed review. Key members of Congress have expressed concern about this congressional "micromanagement." In 1987, Senator Sam Nunn described the review process as "excessively detailed."[9] Several years earlier, then-Senator Dan Quayle criticized Congress for focusing on relatively small problems rather than more fundamental issues.[10]

The growing size of congressional budget documents attests to this detailed involvement. In 1970, the defense authorization act consumed 9 pages; by 1985, it required 169 pages. Additional limitations and requirements are found in the reports accompanying legislation. Growing professional staffs also suggest greater congressional involvement in details. The professional staffs of the committees most involved in defense matters grew from 28 in 1960 to 109 in 1987, or by almost 300 percent during a period when the real size of the defense budget grew by about 40 percent.[11]

Some Proposed Changes in the Process

Congress is awash in proposals to reform its budget procedures. But, as one keen observer has put it, if you want to change Congress, first examine the changes Congress has made.[12] This section examines some key proposals in light of past efforts at procedural reform.

Critics have suggested a wide variety of changes in the defense budget process, some of which would affect much more than defense. Examples include amending the Constitution to require a balanced budget, or enacting legislation that would allow the President to veto specific parts of spending bills (the line-item veto). Other proposals would affect only defense. Critics have suggested, for example, that the defense budget be debated in mission packages to minimize congressional involvement in detail, or that Congress set up an agency to prepare independent assessments of defense issues.[13] But two types of proposals have received the greatest attention in Congress: enactment of some type of multiyear budget, and restructuring congressional committees.

Multiyear Budgeting

A widely recommended change would have defense budgets approved for more than one year at a time. Various forms of multiyear budgets have been recommended by defense experts in Congress (including Senator Sam Nunn, Senator Ted Stevens, former Senator John Stennis, and Representative Bill Dickinson), budget experts outside Congress (including Alice Rivlin, former Director of the Congressional Budget Office), several former Secretaries of Defense (Caspar Weinberger, Harold Brown, James Schlesinger), and various study groups (including the Center for Strategic and International Studies and the Heritage Foundation).[14]

Multiyear budgeting seems most likely to take one or more of three forms: a two-year agreement about all the details of the defense budget (termed a biennial budget), a two-year agreement about the total level of defense spending, or multiyear agreements to purchase specific weapons. Recent history suggests that a biennial budget is less likely to win Congressional favor than the other two approaches.

Biennial budgeting. Under biennial budgeting, Congress would approve two budgets in the first year and make no major budget changes in the second year. In 1987, Congress passed a law requiring the Pentagon to submit a biennial defense budget—that is, two one-year budgets covering 1988 and 1989. The Defense Department strongly urged Congress to approve both budgets during the 1988 review and then avoid major changes during the 1989 review.

Biennial budgeting won strong verbal support in and out of Congress. Former Secretary Weinberger called the two-year proposal an "historic opportunity" that has "my strong support." The biennial budget was also strongly endorsed by key members of Congress who are defense experts, particularly Senator Nunn.[15] Supporters hoped that a biennial budget would address several of the key criticisms of the defense budget process. If left unchanged, a biennial budget would provide stable funding over two years. A biennial budget could also reduce the workload related to budget formulation in both the executive branch and the Congress, especially in the second year, and guarantee timely budget enactment.

But the biennial budget proposed for 1988–1989 did not win congressional approval. Congress authorized about 60 percent of the 1989 budget during the 1988 review, largely at the urging of the Senate. But that authorization was contingent on a two-year appropriation that did not occur, so that during the 1989 review the Congress was not bound by its earlier authorization. Indeed, aside from verbal praise, biennial budgeting garnered only limited support during the congressional review process. It was strongly supported by the Senate authorizing committee, particularly by Committee Chairman Sam Nunn, but support in the authorizing committee of the House was less strong. In 1987, the House committee authorized only about 7 percent of the second year of the biennial request. Its chairman, Les Aspin, called biennial budgeting a "nice idea" but one that would work well only if the entire federal budget were on a two-year basis—a requirement that would make biennial budgeting much harder to implement.[16] Moreover, at least in 1988, there was virtually no support for biennial budgeting in the appropriating committees. In their reports, those committees completely ignored the two-year budget request except to note that their appropriation covered only the first year. Nor were there many questions about the two-year budget during hearings before those committees.

The lack of success of biennial budgeting in part reflects congressional tradition. For years, Congress has focused on budgets one year at a time, and change does not come easily. Change may be especially difficult in the appropriating committees, which have showed no enthusiasm for giving up their traditional prerogative to make detailed changes in each year's defense budget.

The experiment with a biennial budget also came at a bad time. Pressure to reduce the federal deficit, coupled with growing congressional sentiment that defense spending should be reduced, led the administration to agree to large reductions in the fiscal year 1989 proposal for total defense spending after its two-year budget had been submitted. This concession led the administration to make many changes in the second year of its two-year proposal, effectively ensuring that Congress would revisit it the second year.

Finally, though not emphasized during the debate, there may be some concern about the desirability of approving the entire defense budget for two years. Fiscal conditions sometimes mandate defense spending changes, as was the case with the fiscal 1989 request. Also, some defense programs, especially new procurement and research programs, undergo substantial technical changes that make annual review desirable. Even former Senator John Stennis, who supported the principle of greater stability, said that Defense could not expect to receive two-year approval for its entire budget.[17]

The congressional experiment with biennial budgeting will continue. In 1989, the President recommended another two-year budget covering fiscal years 1990 and 1991. A recent study commission headed by former Defense Secretaries Brown and Schlesinger reiterated its firm support for biennial budgeting, and proposed a specific procedure to facilitate needed changes in the second year of the two-year budget and to handle changes in assumptions about inflation.[18] But lukewarm congressional support for two-year approval of the entire budget, especially on the part of the appropriating committees, makes biennial budgeting a congressional long shot.

Multiyear budget totals. Congress is more likely to favor approving limited aspects of the defense budget for more than one year. For example, it could agree to set total dollar levels of defense spending for two years at a time. This approach seems plausible in light of negotiations that occurred in November 1987 between Congress and the President. The talks resulted in a two-year agreement on the amount of spending for defense and for several nondefense areas of the budget, as well as agreement on revenue increases. Thus, in 1989, the administration and Congress avoided a continuation of the prolonged, heated debate over the level of defense spending that characterized most of the 1980s. For the first time in several years, Congress did not make any significant changes in the total dollars requested for defense, and the two-year budget agreement helped achieve stability in total defense spending.

Multiyear contracts. The Department of Defense could further enhance budget stability by making increased use of its existing authority to buy weapons under contracts covering more than one year. These multiyear contracts are legally binding, and hence virtually guarantee stable production. Changes in procurement laws made in 1982, coupled with revisions since that time, allow the department to enter into more of these contracts, though there are numerous restrictions, including a requirement that large multiyear contracts be approved by Congress in advance.

An analysis of forty multiyear contracts signed between 1982 and 1986 suggests that these agreements fulfilled their promises. They did confer stability; though a few were altered, none was ever abrogated. The multiyear approach also saved money: Savings between 1982 and 1987 ranged from 9 percent to 16 percent relative to the costs of purchasing the same number of weapons under annual contracts.[19] Moreover, Congress decided in 1986 to experiment with another multiyear procedure—milestone budgeting—that extends many of the provisions of multiyear contracting to research and development programs as well as procurement programs.[20]

Increased use of multiyear contracts would offer several advantages. Multiyear contracting has the approval of Congress, including the appropriating committees. If coupled with milestone budgeting, the technique would focus on research and procurement programs, which would benefit most from increased stability. Also, despite its promise, multiyear contracting has been used sparingly so far. The portion of the total defense procurement budget under multiyear contracts rose as high as about 12 percent in the mid 1980s, but will amount to only about 7 percent in 1989. Thus, multiyear contracting, along with its cousin milestone budgeting, have a lot of potential as the means to increase stability in the defense budget process.

Restructuring Congressional Committees

If multiyear budgeting would have the Congress budget less often, another proposed reform—restructuring congressional committees—would have it spend less time during each budget review. In its most far-reaching form, a restructuring of congressional committees would eliminate one of the three types of committees—budget, authorizing, or appropriation—that deal most with defense. Such a step would reduce the workload involved in the congressional review of the budget since there would be one less review. It might also reduce congressional involvement in the details of the defense budget because fewer members and staff would be directly involved.

While eliminating one type of committee would address several of the criticisms leveled at the defense budget process, Congress is nowhere near agreeing on such a step. Someone would have to give up power. But who? During discussions of the subject in 1984, Senator Ted Stevens, of the appropriations committee, favored eliminating the authorizing committee. Senator Sam Nunn, of the authorizing committee, favored combining budget and appropriations into one money committee. Representative Bill Dickinson, of the authorizing committee, supported elimination of the budget committee. Then-Senator John Tower summed it up nicely when he said, "It is a rare Senator who will support any type of reorganization plan which he perceives diminishes in any respect his role or authority."[21]

History suggests that combining committees could also create problems. Senator Pete Domenici, ranking minority member of the budget committee, noted in the same hearings in 1984 that the House and Senate appropriating committees were created to control spending. The authorizing committees, which predate the appropriators, were ineffective at controlling spending because their members strongly supported the programs they authorized.[22]

If eliminating one of the three types of committees seems unlikely, other changes are more feasible. One proposal would have major committees agree to focus their reviews more closely on their specific areas of expertise. The budget committees, for example, would focus only on total dollar levels for defense spending, the authorizing committees on broader defense policy issues and oversight, and the appropriators on dollar issues. The prospects for reducing workload under such an approach would be increased if other congressional committees that deal with aspects of defense would minimize their involvement. John Tower argued that as many as eight of these "other" committees are involved in the defense debate.[23]

The proposal to have committees focus their work on specific areas has won the endorsement of the group headed by former Defense Secretaries Harold Brown and James Schlesinger that is monitoring defense reform. More important, it has gotten some support in Congress. Senator Pete Domenici and former Senator Lawton Chiles have supported it verbally.[24] Several committees have taken steps toward focusing their reviews. In recent years, for example, the budget committees have looked mainly at total levels of defense spending, eschewing the more detailed involvement (especially in the House) of the late 1970s and early 1980s. In 1987, Senator Nunn stated that he wanted to move the Armed Services Committee "away from an excessively detailed line item review and scrub of the defense budget and more toward consideration of the fundamental issues of national defense."[25] By at least one measure, Nunn has made a beginning. During the first two years of his chairmanship, the pages of the committee report devoted to describing the authorization step of the budget process were less than half the number consumed during the previous two years.

What Lies Ahead?

The defense budget process will almost certainly continue to change in the 1990s. Far-reaching reforms, such as the elimination of some congressional committees and the approval of the entire defense budget for two years at a time, are not very likely. Change will probably be evolutionary rather than revolutionary. For example, Congress may come to make more regular use of a two-year budget agreement (though it has not done so during the debate over the budgets for fiscal years 1990 and 1991) and may make greater use of techniques like multiyear contracting. Some of its committees may decide to focus more selectively on specific aspects of the defense budget process.

A two-year agreement on budget totals, coupled with more use of multiyear contracting, would provide greater stability for some defense programs and could lead to more efficient use of defense resources. Greater focus by committees could modestly reduce the workload involved in formulating the defense budget, freeing both Congress and the executive branch to oversee spending more carefully.

On the other hand, many of the problems associated with the defense budget debate are not primarily procedural. Rather, they often reflect an inability to agree on how to allocate budget resources, which in turn reflects the country's lack of consensus in these matters. Congressional involvement in defense detail also stems from the conviction that Congress cannot rely on the executive branch to settle such issues. Until there is more trust of the executive, and more of a consensus on national priorities, agreement will be difficult. No procedural changes can (or should) force a freely elected Congress to take actions the majority do not support.

For these reasons, changes in the budget process do not seem likely to alter significantly the key outcomes of the defense budget debate, particularly the total dollars Congress decides to devote to national security. Decisions about dollars available for national defense will be determined by underlying factors that shape congressional attitudes toward defense spending. The remainder of this chapter focuses on these factors.

Factors Tending to Increase Defense Spending

Recent reductions in real defense spending seem to imply that the defense budget is headed downward for a long period. But there are several factors working to increase defense spending during the 1990s.

Concern over U.S. Security

Perhaps the most important of these factors is the strong public concern over national security. In December 1986, the Gallup organization reported results of a poll that asked people what they thought was the likelihood of a world war occurring sometime within the next ten years.[26] Fully 49 percent of the sample of U.S. adults indicated that they thought the chances were one out of two or greater. Gallup has asked this question only once, so there is no way to assess the stability of responses over time. However, a 1989 poll by Media General–Associated Press reached similar conclusions about U.S. public opinion.[27] Moreover, another national survey taken in 1988 found that 56 percent of U.S. adults agreed (either "somewhat" or "strongly") that the Soviet Union would attack this country or its allies if the United States became weak militarily. Sixty-two percent felt that the best way for the United States to strengthen its national security would be to achieve military superiority over the Soviet Union.[28]

Another reason the public is concerned about security is that Soviet capabilities have been increasing. According to the Department of Defense, the 1980s production of most categories of major weapons by the Soviet Union and its allies has exceeded production by the United States and its allies.[29] The Department of Defense has also noted other important areas of Soviet military strength. While analysts differ widely in their assessment of the balance of military forces between this country and its primary potential adversary, Americans have good reason to perceive a substantial military threat.

Not surprisingly, then, the public favors a strong military. A poll taken in 1986 for the Packard Commission on defense management found that 92 percent of those questioned agreed (either strongly or somewhat strongly) that strong and effective U.S. armed forces are essential to the preservation of freedom.[30] This huge percentage would seemingly translate into support for substantial defense budgets. Other factors, of course, weigh against increases in defense spending, and these are discussed below. But if Americans should ever feel their security threatened, they are likely to respond with strong support for higher defense spending—as they did, for example, in the late

1970s and early 1980s following such events as the Soviet invasion of Afghanistan and the Iranian detention of American citizens.

Growth in the Economy

Another factor that may favor increased defense spending is economic growth. Historically, there has not been much correlation between growth in the gross national product and the proportion of GNP devoted to defense; the latter seems to vary more with concern about security and other factors than with changes in the economy. But for any fraction of GNP devoted to defense, a larger economy means more money available to the military.

If history is a guide, the U.S. economy will continue to grow in the 1990s, though probably not steadily. The year 1989 marks the seventh consecutive year of real growth in the economy, a record exceeded only once since World War II. The economy may well experience a recession sometime during the early 1990s, but, in the long run, the course should be upward. In none of the three complete decades since the end of World War II has the economy grown by less than 32 percent in real terms. Thus, it seems reasonable to expect growth in the 1990s. That expectation is shared by forecasters at Data Resources Incorporated.[31] Their long-term economic forecast made in October 1988 calls for average real growth of 2.2 percent a year during the 1990s, which would add 25 percent to the size of the economy by the turn of the century. If defense spending maintains its present share of U.S. GNP, or nearly so, the resources available for defense will increase substantially.

Budget History

Finally, those who see many years of decline in the defense budget cannot draw much support from history. Since 1950, there have been seven periods of real decline in the budget (see Figure 4.1). Only one of those declines (that following the end of the Vietnam War) exceeded four years. Fiscal year 1989 marks the fourth consecutive year of real decline in the current period. There is certainly no guarantee that the historical pattern will hold this time, but in the past the public has been willing to support increases after short periods of declining defense budgets, perhaps because of concern over U.S. security.

Downward Influences on Defense Spending

Arrayed against these forces favoring an increase in the defense budget is a formidable list of pressures for lower defense spending that includes concern over the federal deficit, perceptions that the Soviet threat may be easing, and a desire for U.S. allies to bear a larger portion of the defense burden.

Fiscal Tightness

In the next few years, all federal spending, including defense, will likely be affected by attempts to reduce the size of the budget deficit. The deficit has decreased in recent years but remains high by historical standards (see Figure 4.2). Baseline estimates by the Congressional Budget Office (CBO) put the 1989 deficit at about $161 billion, or 3.1 percent of the GNP.[32] This is substantially less than in recent years, when deficits sometimes exceeded 5 percent and even 6 percent of the GNP, but still well above levels in the 1970s (when deficits averaged 2.1 percent of the GNP) or the 1960s (when they averaged 0.8 percent of the GNP). Though economists disagree over the short-run effects of deficits, they generally agree that over the long run, large deficits adversely affect the formation of private capital and, hence, economic growth and standards of living.[33]

Deficits could remain high for some years to come. CBO's baseline projections show the deficit declining to 2.6 percent of the GNP in 1990, with further declines thereafter. These baseline projections, however, assume no changes in current tax laws and adjust most spending programs only for inflation. Substantial increases in spending—perhaps for the cleanup of nuclear waste, aid for troubled savings and loan associations, improvements in education, aid for the homeless, or long-term medical care—could push up these baseline estimates unless the increases were offset by real cuts elsewhere in the budget. Moreover, the baseline estimates depend critically on assumptions about the future course of the economy. Since the CBO does not attempt to forecast the path of the economy for more than a year or so in advance, the projections *assume* continued moderate economic growth in accordance with long-term historical averages. More rapid economic growth, perhaps spurred by a restoration of growth in productivity, would mean lower deficits. By the same token, if the economy underwent a serious recession sometime in the next five years, then deficits could rise sharply.[34]

The deficit problem could be solved, of course, but only by enacting painful policy changes. One such change would be a substantial tax increase, but this might well not be acceptable to the public. Though marginal income tax rates are lower, total federal taxes in 1988 amounted to 19 percent of the GNP, almost equal to their level in 1980, when candidate Reagan successfully condemned them as too high. They are not far below their postwar high of 20.1 percent in 1969 and 1981. Alternatively, nondefense spending could be reduced. But nondefense spending, though higher as a percentage of GNP than in any year before 1975, has been reduced from its 1980 level (see Figure 4.3, which defines nondefense spending as all government outlays except for defense and interest on the federal debt). Selected areas of nondefense spending have been cut sharply; indeed, there is likely to be pressure to increase some types of nondefense spending.

Efforts will continue to reduce the deficit. But, because they are painful, further reductions may come only gradually. That would mean continued

Figure 4.1 National Defense Budget Authority (constant 1989 dollars)

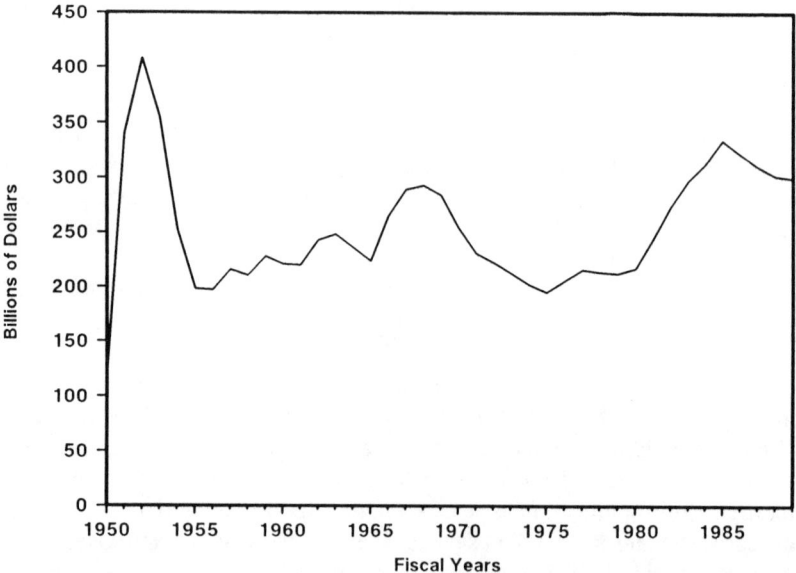

Figure 4.2 Federal Deficit as a Percentage of GNP

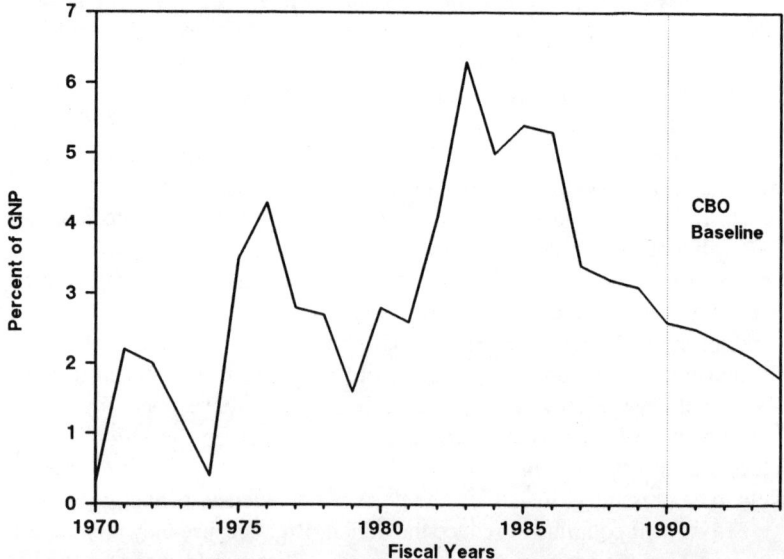

Figure 4.3 Government Outlays as a Percentage of GNP

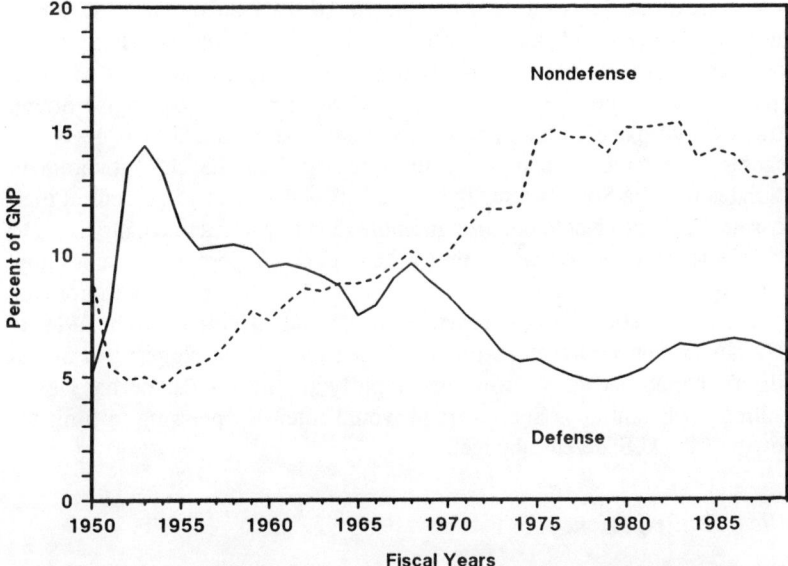

fiscal restraint, which tends to hold down all spending, including defense spending. For the next few years, this concern over the federal deficit looms as the largest single factor holding down defense spending.

Perceptions of a Lessening Security Threat

Downward pressure on defense spending caused by efforts to reduce the deficit could be intensified if foreign threats to U.S. security appear to decrease. The Soviet military challenge has a major effect on U.S. defense budgets because it provides the rationale for most military force levels.

Proposed arms control agreements involving the Soviet Union could lead to just such a decrease in the military threat. In 1989, President Bush called for arms limitations that would result in large reductions in weapons held by the Soviet Union and its Warsaw Pact allies. Under the President's proposals, the Soviets would have to withdraw and demobilize 325,000 troops from European areas outside their borders. The Warsaw Pact would have to destroy about 32,000 tanks, 18,000 armored personnel carriers, and other weapons. Many of these proposals do not differ markedly from proposals made earlier by Gorbachev.

Far-reaching arms limitation agreements may seem more plausible in view of the Soviet Union's economic problems. Those problems are summed up well by an analysis recently completed for the Department of Defense. The analysis projected that, between 1990 and 2010, the Soviet economy would grow in real terms by about 40 percent compared to about 65 to 70 percent for the United States and Japan.[35] Such relatively sluggish Soviet growth would place limits on defense spending unless the Soviets devoted a larger share of their resources to the military. Yet, the U.S. government estimates that the Soviets already devote between 15 and 17 percent of their gross domestic product to defense, far more than any Western country.

It is too soon to know whether we can expect a permanent, substantial slowdown in the arms race. Several earlier periods that promised improved superpower relations—most recently the period of détente from 1969 to 1972—were not permanent. Nonetheless, current trends suggest that Soviet military capability may grow less rapidly in the 1990s, perhaps even declining substantially. Such a trend would intensify pressure to limit the growth of the U.S. defense budget.

Allied Contributions

Yet another factor exerting downward pressure on U.S. defense spending is the conviction among some leaders that U.S. allies should bear a larger share of the burden of the common defense. Most Americans—55 percent—already believe the allies should do more, according to a survey made by Abt Associates in 1984. A Harris survey showed similar results in 1983.[36] Various trends may strengthen this feeling. For example, the GNP of the United States in 1950 made up 54 percent of the total GNP of the NATO allies. By 1985 that proportion had fallen to 38 percent.

Relatively low defense spending by some allies may allow them to spend more on nondefense research and development, thereby affording them advantages in nondefense production that seem increasingly unfair as those allies become more prosperous. According to data compiled by the National Science Foundation, the United States invests roughly the same proportion of its total GNP in research and development (about 2.7 percent in 1986) as its major allies, including Japan. But about 30 percent of the total U.S. funds for research and development (including both public and private funds) goes to defense. The United Kingdom devotes a similar percentage to defense, and France about 20 percent. But research in the Federal Republic of Germany and Japan is almost wholly civilian. These allies, while not devoting more of their total resources to research and development, are able to invest more heavily in civilian research, which may enhance their ability to compete in world markets.

While the allies have become more economically competitive with the United States in recent decades, they have not devoted more of their resources to defense. In 1987, the United States devoted 6.4 percent of its gross domestic product (GDP) to defense, compared to an average of 3.3 percent for other NATO allies and about 1 percent for Japan (see Table 4.2). That same general relationship between the U.S. and allied burdens has prevailed for the last three decades. While many other measures are used to assess defense burdens, almost all of them suggest that, relative to GDP or population, the United States is contributing its fair share and often more.[37] Nor do these comparisons change markedly when estimates of some important "hidden" costs, which make allied defense budgets appear relatively smaller than U.S. budgets, are included. Examples of hidden costs include conscription, which holds down recruit wages; provision of free land to foreign troops; and support of foreign forces.[38]

Not all inputs to the common defense can be quantified. More important, measures that can be quantified do not reflect the value to each country of alliances, nor do they take into account such factors as the willingness of the United States to bear a higher proportion of the defense spending burden in order to retain its leadership role. So, the measures discussed here do not provide a basis for a final judgment about the fairness of burdensharing. They do, however, suggest that the United States devotes more resources to the common defense than its allies at the same time that its share of allied GNP, as well as its economic competitiveness, may be declining.[39]

Public perception of these relationships could increase pressure to hold down U.S. budget and perhaps to reduce overseas commitments. If such reductions were made, the effects on Western security would depend on the extent to which they were offset by increased allied spending. It seems unlikely, though, that they would be offset. Public opinion in allied countries appears less concerned about the threat of a major war than is the case in the United States. The 1986 Gallup poll cited above, which found that 49 percent of U.S. adults polled believed there was at least one chance in two of a world war occurring within ten years, asked the same question of people in other countries. Among countries that are major U.S. allies, the percentages of respondents expressing the same degree of concern ranged from 14 percent to 38 percent, with most being under 25 percent (see Table 4.3).

Public Opinion

Public opinion exerts a tangible influence on defense spending. Gallup polls taken between 1970 and 1987 show a statistically significant correlation between the proportion of the population that tells pollsters that defense spending is too high and changes in the real level of the defense budget ($r = .73$).[40]

How does public opinion influence defense spending? Perhaps through Congress. Members of Congress regularly ask constituents, in person and in writing, for their opinions on spending issues. If large numbers of

Table 4.2 1987 Defense Expenditures as a Percentage of Gross Domestic Product (GDP)

United States	6.4
Non-U.S. NATO Average	3.3
Belgium	2.9
Canada	2.1
Denmark	2.1
France	4.0
Germany	3.1
Greece	6.2
Italy	2.4
Luxembourg	1.0
Netherlands	3.1
Norway	3.4
Portugal	3.1
Spain	2.4
Turkey	4.3
United Kingdom	4.7
Japan[a]	1.0

Sources: Congressional Budget Office computations using data from NATO Press Service, "Financial and Economic Data Related to NATO Defense," December 1988, for defense expenditures; and data for gross domestic product from International Monetary Fund, *International Financial Statistics*, December 1988.

Note: Defense expenditures are measured for the fiscal year that most closely overlaps calendar year 1987; GDP data are for calendar year 1987. The non-U.S. NATO average is weighted by each country's GDP.

[a]Defense expenditures for Japan use the national, not NATO, definition, as reported in Defense Agency, *Defense of Japan* (Tokyo: Foreign Press Center, 1987).

Table 4.3 Percentage of Adults in Various Countries Who Believe the Chance of World War Within Next 10 Years Is 50 Percent or Greater

Country	Percentage
United States	49
Australia	38
Canada	34
Portugal	25
Belgium	24
France	24
Italy	22
Spain	22
Norway	21
Austria	20
Great Britain	20
Denmark	18
Greece	18
West Germany	18
Japan	15
Sweden	15
Turkey	15
Netherlands	14

Source: *The Gallup Report* (December 1986).

constituents were to urge less defense spending, their answers would certainly influence Congress. What shapes public opinion about defense spending? One would expect public opinion to reflect concern over high federal deficits, popular perceptions of the Soviet threat, and similar factors. However, some research shows no discernible relationship between systematic measures of events and opinions about military spending, though it finds a close relationship between the treatment of events on national television networks and opinions about military spending.[41] Thus another factor—media attention—apparently influences defense spending.

Currently, public opinion is exerting downward pressure on defense spending. Polls by Gallup, Harris, and others show that a substantial portion of the population feels that the United States is spending too much on defense (see Table 4.4 for Gallup polls).

Because researchers have had limited success in identifying what shapes public attitudes toward defense spending, it is difficult to know how attitudes may vary in the future. Nonetheless, it seems likely that public opinion will work against higher defense budgets for at least the next few years. The public and Congress seem deeply concerned about waste in the Pentagon, a factor that could depress public willingness to spend on defense. Key members of Congress, including the current chairmen of the armed services committees in both the House and the Senate, have expressed strong concern.[42] Several polls suggest strong public feeling on the subject, and even indicate that a slight majority of the public thinks that waste in the Pentagon exceeds that in welfare spending.[43] These attitudes may explain the public's seemingly contradictory attitudes about defense spending: Many people appear concerned about threats to national security, but relatively few favor increases in defense budgets.

To the extent that media attention plays a major role in shaping public opinion about defense, it may have a negative or, at best, neutral influence on defense budgets in future years. Good news about defense achievements rarely makes good copy—be it a successful weapons system or the commendable job the military has done managing the all-volunteer force since 1980. Overpriced hammers and procurement scandals often create headlines.

Likely Budgets in the 1990s

How will these numerous influences combine to affect defense budgets in the 1990s? Only a soothsayer would claim confidence in an answer, especially in view of the history of U.S. defense spending since 1950 (see Figure 4.1). Real changes in spending have been dominated by two wars and the peacetime buildup of the early 1980s, all events that would have been difficult to foresee. In the other years, including the late 1950s, early 1960s,

Table 4.4 Trends in Public Attitudes Toward Defense Spending

Date	Spending Too Little	Spending Too Much	About Right
January/February 1976	22	36	32
December 1979	34	21	33
January/February 1981	51	15	22
March 1982	19	36	36
August 1983	14	42	35
September 1983	21	37	36
March 1986	13	47	36
April 1987	14	44	36
July 1988[a]	17	35	42

Sources: *The Gallup Report* various issues.
[a]Question asked as part of a larger question about federal spending rather than separately as in previous years.

and late 1970s, defense spending tended to oscillate rather than follow a simple pattern that would provide a basis for accurate predictions. Despite the cloudiness of the crystal ball, one can attempt to rank likely budget outcomes in the 1990s. Four such outcomes are discussed here, with the author's sense of their probability.

Substantial Increases: Least Likely

It is possible that defense budgets will grow sharply in the 1990s. Assume, for illustration, that they repeat the sharp growth in the 1990s that occurred between 1980 and 1985—when defense spending increased by 54 percent—but avoid the declines of the late 1980s. Growth of 54 percent in a decade would leave budget authority in 1999 at about $460 billion compared to about $300 billion in 1989. (All estimates in this section represent budget authority for the national defense function, expressed in 1989 dollars.) If the economy grows in the 1990s as Data Resources Incorporated projects (an average of 2.2 percent a year), then under these assumptions defense would claim 7.2 percent of GNP in 1999 compared to 5.8 percent in 1989. Shifts in resources to or from defense could, of course, affect the rate of economic growth. Such effects are ignored here and in subsequent calculations.[44] This share of GNP would not be without historical precedent. By 1999, defense's resource share would be at its highest level since the early 1970s but still substantially lower than defense shares in the late 1950s (see Figure 4.3).

Nonetheless, this scenario seems improbable. Sharp growth in defense would add substantially to federal deficits unless there were offsetting reductions in nondefense spending or increases in taxes, both of which seem politically unlikely. Sharp growth in U.S. defense spending would exacerbate the gap between U.S. and allied budgets, since there are no indications that allied spending will increase substantially. Indeed, the only plausible circumstances leading to substantial growth in U.S. spending would be a war or a major increase in threat to U.S. security, also improbable in view of current political trends in the Soviet Union.

Moderate Growth: More Likely

Defense spending could grow by moderate amounts, which seems more likely than a large decline. Assume, for example, that defense spending increases just enough to maintain the same share of the GNP that it is likely to have in 1989. If the economy grows at a rate of 2.2 percent a year, growth in the defense budget would average 2.2 percent a year in the 1990s. By 1999, defense budget authority would amount to about $370 billion. By definition, defense's share of the GNP would remain at about 5.8 percent.

Unless allied spending rose substantially, this scenario would not reduce the gap between U.S. and allied spending. Nor, in the absence of higher taxes, would it make much room in the federal budget for new nondefense initiatives or deficit reduction since growth in defense budgets would be similar to the growth in revenues that occurs as the economy expands.

This pattern of moderate growth, however, would have the advantage of preserving the status quo even if current arms limitation proposals do not bear fruit. Moderate growth would not add to the federal deficit measured as a share of GNP. Moderate budget growth should allow continued modernization of weapons without major reductions in numbers of U.S. forces. That would permit this country to maintain its current military commitments. This may be perceived as prudent if arms limitation agreements with the Soviets produce only modest reductions in the military threat to the United States.

Substantial Decline: A Possibility with Arms Agreement

Instead of growing, defense spending could decline substantially in the 1990s. Assume, for the sake of illustration, that the decline parallels the one that occurred after the peak of spending on the Vietnam War. In the ten years after 1968, defense spending declined by 27 percent. If repeated in the 1990s, such a decline, coupled with reductions already experienced in the defense budget, would leave budget authority at about $220 billion in 1999, not far above the average level of peacetime spending in the pre-Reagan years. Assuming annual GNP growth averaging 2.2 percent, defense's share of resources would fall to 3.4 percent by 1999.

Such a substantial decline would leave defense's share of U.S. resources well below its previous post-1950 low of 4.8 percent. More important, it would require a major reduction in U.S. military commitments. Coupled with the seemingly inexorable growth in the cost of weapons, a sharp cut in spending would leave military forces too small to support current U.S.

deployments. As yet, there are few signs that Americans are ready to support such retrenchment. A 1986 Gallup poll showed that 62 percent of U.S. adults still believe this country should maintain its commitment to NATO.[45] These results are not much changed from polls taken in 1978 and 1982. Moreover, a 1988 poll found that most Americans believe this country could best strengthen its security by maintaining military superiority over the Soviets.

But a far-reaching arms limitation agreement could cause the public to accept major reductions in U.S. defense spending. The conventional arms agreements proposed by President Bush are potentially far-reaching. If the United States only makes the minimum reductions in its military forces required by the President's arms limitations proposals, then savings would be modest: about $2 billion a year in operating costs, with another $6 billion in procurement savings that could be realized over a long period of time.[46] However, the President's proposals require that the Warsaw Pact and NATO achieve equality in numbers of selected weapons based in Europe, a step that would require highly disproportionate reductions in Warsaw Pact weapons. The Pact, for example, would have to destroy 32,000 tanks compared to NATO's 2,000. If such disproportionate reductions actually come to pass, the United States may decide that it could reduce its military capability, and hence its military budgets, by much more than the minimum required amount. Additional savings could be achieved if the United States reached a strategic arms agreement with the Soviet Union.

No Growth: Likely Without Arms Agreements

Lacking a major agreement to limit arms, a likely outcome is an oscillation of the defense budget during the 1990s, growing in some years and declining in others, but averaging no real growth over the decade as a whole. This would leave defense budget authority in 1999 at about $300 billion in today's dollars. Assuming growth in the economy as a whole averaging 2.2 percent a year, defense's share of resources would decline to about 4.7 percent of the GNP by 1999.

Zero growth over an entire decade would be unusual given the history of variation in U.S. defense budgets. An examination of moving ten-year averages beginning in 1951 shows that budgets have grown or declined by less than 1 percent in only three of the twenty-eight ten-year periods that have been completed since 1951. By 1999, under these assumptions, defense's share of total U.S. resources would be roughly at its post-1950 low. Some considerations lend plausibility to this scenario, however. Zero growth would help close the gap between U.S. and allied defense spending by reducing the U.S. level. If the U.S. economy grew but defense spending did not, the extra revenues engendered by growth would allow reductions in the deficit or make room for new nondefense programs.

Moreover, no-growth budgets might be accommodated by an acceptable retrenchment in U.S. defense commitments. Higher costs for new weapons would probably force reductions in numbers of U.S. forces or their readiness. Budget pressure caused by higher-cost weapons, however, could be minimized by keeping older weapons longer or by buying more less expensive weapons (see below). Cutbacks in forces or readiness that would be needed to finance new weapons might be achieved in part through reductions in overseas commitments, perhaps including some made at the request of U.S. allies. In some respects, this pattern of cutbacks would be similar to the one proposed by the Defense Department in its 1989 budget plan. The seemingly favorable response to that budget plan suggests that certain reductions in U.S. capability would be acceptable even to a public concerned with threats to U.S. security, the more so if, as seems possible, the Soviets also held down growth in their defense budgets.

Of the possible outcomes discussed in this chapter, this one is closest to the forecast made by the Electronic Industries Association. Each year, the association predicts defense budgets ten years in advance, based on a compendium of opinions from defense experts in government, industry, and academia. The latest forecast sees a decline averaging 0.5 percent a year between 1989 and 1998. Declines are estimated to be largest in the early 1990s and are partially offset by modest real increases later in the decade.[47]

Budgets and Military Capability

A detailed discussion of how much military capability can be bought at likely budget levels is beyond the scope of this chapter. So, too, is any extensive analysis of the effects that arms limitation agreements could have on military requirements and budgets. Nonetheless, because of public concern about national security, the purchasing power of any given budget will influence the likelihood that budget will be adopted. Therefore, it behooves anyone considering future budget outcomes to assess the implications of those budgets. This chapter makes that assessment, assuming that arms limitation agreements do not fundamentally alter military requirements.

Large New Programs Will Be Difficult

Unless there is a substantial increase in defense budgets in the 1990s, which seems the least likely outcome, major new military programs will be difficult to implement. That could spell trouble for several widely discussed initiatives. One such initiative is the improvement of NATO's conventional military capability, both in response to perceived current disadvantages and to make up for reductions in nuclear weapons. Analysis by the Congressional Budget Office showed that one plan to bolster those defenses—deployment of high-technology weapons associated with the Army's Forward Area Defense system (Follow-on Forces Attack, or FOFA)—could cost a total of about $50 billion in today's dollars over the next two decades. The cost and capability of FOFA compared favorably with other approaches to improving conventional capability, such as the addition of more troops.[48] But budget limitations would make any major addition to capability difficult to achieve. Similar considerations may apply to other initiatives, such as plans to deploy a system of strategic defenses—the Strategic Defense Initiative, or SDI.

Modernizing Weapons Will Be Difficult

Unless military budgets rise, the cost of new weapons will also be difficult to absorb. New weapons almost always cost more than their predecessors. Studies by the Congressional Budget Office compared the cost of new generations of tactical aircraft bought by the Air Force and Navy with those of previous generations. Compared to aircraft of the previous generation, costs of aircraft beginning production in the 1950s through the 1970s commonly increased in real terms in amounts averaging from about 2.5 percent a year to well over 10 percent a year.[49] That growth apparently continued in the early 1980s because percentage increases in spending for most types of weapons substantially exceeded growth in numbers of weapons.[50] Nor is there any obvious reversal of the trend. Weapons like the Air Force's new stealth bomber (the B-2) and the Navy's new Seawolf attack submarine (the SSN-21) are likely to cost substantially more than the systems they will replace.

The budget effects of more expensive weapons may be compounded by the influence of higher-cost weapons on operating and support costs. Between 1975 and 1987, total Department of Defense operating and support costs—defined as appropriations for military personnel, operation and maintenance, and the operating portion of family housing—increased roughly in proportion to increases in the dollar value of major weapons.[51] If that relationship continues, more expensive weapons will push up the costs of operating military forces.

Some of these higher costs of modernization may be offset by greater efficiency. There are proposals to achieve efficiencies in defense budgets through such actions as closing or consolidating military bases, reducing numbers of officers in relation to enlisted personnel, and stabilizing production of weapons by using multiyear contracts. These and other actions may be desirable and should reduce costs. Most such initiatives, though, save hundreds of millions of dollars (or sometimes a few billion); rarely, if ever, do they save the tens of billions of dollars needed to pay the added costs of modernizing major weapons.

Costs of modernization will have to be held down by heavier reliance on relatively cheaper weapons. For example, the relatively less expensive F-16 aircraft will have to make up the bulk of Air Force combat aircraft if the advanced tactical fighter proves to be very expensive. The Navy, while still hoping to deploy six hundred ships, will have to accept a less modern 600-ship Navy by the year 2000 than it planned in the early 1980s. The Army has implicitly decided to rely on a mix heavier in the older M60 tank by virtue of its recent proposal to slow production of the new M1 tank. Another way to minimize costs of modernization is to keep older weapons longer. For example, to minimize shortages of combat aircraft, the Navy is seeking ways to extend the life of its existing planes. The Army has always kept support equipment (trucks, for example) for long periods; its combat weapons may join them in achieving venerable ages while still in active service. While the costs of modernization may be held down, the U.S. military clearly believes that the best way to defend the country is to rely on sophisticated, and expensive weapons. Thus the costs of weapons will continue to grow.

Forces Will Be Reduced

If military budgets do not grow by much, then either the readiness of U.S. forces must be reduced or the forces themselves must be reduced in number. Since 1980, both the administration and Congress have resisted disproportionate cuts in readiness-related spending. That resistance seems likely to continue, reinforced by memories of readiness problems in the late 1970s and 1980. If so, the only way to accommodate sluggish growth in defense budgets is to reduce numbers of forces. That, indeed, was the recommendation of the recent report by the Commission on Integrated Long-Term Strategy.[52] The commission advocated higher defense budgets but, in their absence, recommended fewer forces rather than curtailment of technological improvements.

In the absence of a major arms limitation agreement, reductions in forces could conflict with the desire of the public to maintain defense commitments. But, if the reductions are modest in size and are coupled with decisions by allies (including those in the Pacific) to shoulder more of the local defense burden, they may win public acceptance.

Summary and Conclusion

The process Congress uses to debate defense budgets will undoubtedly be altered in coming years, as it has been in the 1980s, but changes are more likely to be evolutionary than revolutionary. Changes may include continued use of multiyear agreements that set the total dollars available for defense, along with more use of techniques like multiyear contracting to ensure stability for selected programs.

Whatever the changes in process, they will not play a major role in determining the outcome of the defense budget debate, especially the debate over total dollars for defense. Spending decisions will reflect many influences, including events that cannot be foreseen. It seems clear, however, that in the absence of far-reaching agreements to limit arms, the public is concerned about national security and is not yet eager to decrease U.S. military commitments, such as that to NATO. This public attitude could lead to increases in defense spending in the 1990s. Working in the other direction is the problem of the federal deficit, coupled with perceptions of a lessening Soviet threat, concern over whether U.S. allies are pulling their weight, and the perception of waste in the Pentagon. These latter influences may tend to hold down defense budgets. Taken together, the various influences suggest that large increases are not likely. Absent major arms limitation agreements, which could lead to substantial declines in the defense budget, the most likely trend would mean little or no growth in the budget.

Sluggish growth would make it difficult to undertake large new programs. Given the Pentagon's preference for buying highly capable weapons, which are inevitably costly, sluggish growth might also mean smaller U.S. military forces. That, in turn, could require reductions in U.S. military commitments. But any move toward substantial reductions might engender counteracting pressure for larger defense budgets since Americans as yet show no sign of favoring major military retrenchment. Retrenchment could gain favor if the Soviet Union undertook substantial military cutbacks, but Soviet promises would have to be followed by action before Americans would be likely to change their views.

Military strategy, then, must be planned within an uncertain environment. History suggests it would be foolhardy to expect either a steady growth or a steady decline in defense budgets, since such phenomena are determined by complex interactions of foreign events and domestic concerns that are not stable. Instead, it would be wise to assume that some minimum amount of resources is almost certain to be made available and would then be used to meet key commitments. Growth above that level can be expected to occur only periodically. One must anticipate fluctuations by planning systems that capitalize on periods of growth, and avoid becoming committed to so many projects that periods of decline or sluggish growth produce chaos.

Notes

This chapter reflects the opinions of the author, and not necessarily those of the Congressional Budget Office or any member or employee of Congress.

1. In the original budget act, a point of order (which can be used to halt legislative activity) could be raised only if total federal spending agreed to by the Congress exceeded the level set forth in the budget resolution. If proposed legislation in a particular budget area exceeded the target for that area, a point

of order usually could not be raised. The revised act allows a point of order to be raised if budget authority associated with any legislation exceeds the budget authority allocated to the cognizant subcommittee.

2. Trent Lott, "The Need to Improve the Budget Process: A Republican's View," in Allen Schick, *Crisis in the Budget Process: Exercising Political Choice* (Washington, D.C.: The American Enterprise Institute, 1986), p. 72.

3. This calculation is based on budget resolutions passed for fiscal years 1982 through 1989. The calculation compares the budget authority actually appropriated for the national defense function (function 050) in a particular year with the budget authority provided for that year in the budget resolution passed one year earlier (or two years earlier). The calculation first determined the percentage differences between actual appropriations and budget authority in the resolutions. The numbers in the text are arithmetic averages of the absolute values of those percentage differences.

4. House Committee on Armed Services (hereafter HASC), *Defense Department Authorization and Oversight: Hearing on National Defense Authorization Act for Fiscal Years 1988/1989*, 100th Congress, 1st session, March 24, 1987, p. 65.

5. Paul Bedard, "Military Programs to Cost More than Pentagon Is Claiming: Weicker," *Defense Week*, February 9, 1987, p. 16.

6. Senate Committee on Armed Services (hereafter SASC), *Hearings before the Committee on Armed Services on the Reorganization of the Department of Defense*, 99th Congress, 1st session, various dates in October, November, and December 1985, p. 82.

7. SASC, *Staff Report to the Senate Committee on Armed Services on Defense Organization: The Need for Change*, 99th Congress, 1st session, October 16, 1985, p. 589.

8. *Congressional Record*, September 12, 1984, pp. S-10957 to S-10960.

9. SASC, *Hearings before the Senate Armed Services Committee on National Security Strategy*, 100th Congress, 1st session, various dates in January, February, March, and April 1987, p. 2.

10. *Congressional Record*, September 27, 1984, p. S-12102.

11. These numbers include professional staff personnel on the armed services committees, the defense and military construction subcommittees of the appropriations committees, and the budget committees (defense staff only). Staff personnel are identified under varying titles. Numbers here *exclude* personnel with such titles as secretary, clerical aide, bill clerk, calendar clerk, assistant to the chairman, administrative aide, and receptionist. Numbers are derived from various versions of the *Congressional Staff Directory* (Mount Vernon, VA: Congressional Staff Directory, Ltd.).

12. Schick, note 2, p. 50.

13. SASC, *Hearings on Reorganization of the Department of Defense*, p. 598; and Mark Rovner, *Defense Dollars and Sense* (Common Cause, 1983), p. 76.

14. For remarks by Senators Stevens and Nunn, see *Hearing of the Temporary Committee to Study the Senate Committee System*, 98th Congress, 2d session, Part 2, August 2, 1984, pp. 11–12 and 66; for remarks by Senator Stennis, see *Hearings before a Subcommittee of the Senate Committee on Appropriations on Department of Defense Appropriations for Fiscal Year 1988*, 100th Congress, 1st session, Part 1, 1987, p. 48; for remarks by Representative Dickinson, see Brian Green, "Dickinson on Defense," *Air Force Magazine* (August 1988), p. 102; for remarks by Ms. Rivlin, see "The Need for

a Better Budget Process," *Brookings Review* (Summer 1986), p. 8; for remarks by Mr. Weinberger, see HASC, *Hearing on National Defense Authorization Act for Fiscal Years 1988/1989*, 100th Congress, 1st session, March 24, 1987, pp. 3–4; for remarks by Messrs. Brown and Schlesinger, see *Making Defense Reform Work* (Washington, D.C.: The Center for Strategic and International Studies, November 1988), pp. 19–22; for remarks by The Center for Strategic and International Studies (CSIS), see *Toward a More Effective Defense* (Washington, D.C.: CSIS, February 1985), p. 34; and for remarks by the Heritage Foundation, see Theodore Crackel, "Pentagon Management Problems: Congress Shares the Blame" (unpublished background paper, The Heritage Foundation, January 22, 1985), p. 8.

15. See note 14 for references.
16. *Defense Week*, October 11, 1988, p. 9.
17. See reference to Senator Stennis's remarks in note 14.
18. See reference to remarks by Brown and Schlesinger in note 14.
19. Congressional Budget Office, *Alternative Strategies for Increasing Multiyear Procurement* (unpublished staff working paper, July 1986), p. 17.
20. Congressional Budget Office, *Assessing the Effectiveness of Milestone Budgeting*, July 1987, pp. vii–xiv.
21. For remarks by Senators Stevens, Tower, and Nunn, see *Hearing of the Temporary Committee to Study the Senate Committee System*, note 14, pp. 4, 41, 66; for remarks by Representative Dickinson, see "Dickinson on Defense," *Air Force Magazine*, August 1988, p. 102.
22. *Hearing of the Temporary Committee to Study the Senate Committee System*, note 14, pp. 53–54.
23. *Staff Report to the Senate Armed Services Committee on Defense Organization: The Need for Change*, October 16, 1985, pp. 578–579.
24. *Hearing of the Temporary Committee to Study the Senate Committee System*, note 14, pp. 23, 47.
25. SASC, *Hearings before the Senate Committee on Armed Services on National Security Strategy*, 100th Congress, 1st session, various dates in January, February, March, and April 1987, p. 2.
26. *The Gallup Report* (Gallup: Princeton, NJ, December 1986), pp. 6–7. Gallup asked: "I'd like your opinion of the chances of a world war breaking out in the next 10 years. If 10 means it is absolutely certain that a world war will break out and zero means there is no chance of a world war breaking out, where on this scale of 10 to zero would you rate the chances of a world war breaking out in the next 10 years?"
27. "Half of all Americans expect another global war, poll says," *Baltimore Evening Sun*, August 28, 1989, p. 4.
28. *Americans Talk Security* (The Daniel Yankelovich Group, National Survey No. 7, July 1988), pp. 90, 135.
29. Department of Defense, *Annual Report to the Congress for Fiscal Year 1989*, February 1988, p. 29.
30. *A Quest for Excellence: Final Report by the President's Blue Ribbon Commission on Defense Management*, July 1986, Appendix L (Washington, D.C.: U.S. Government Printing Office), p. 194.
31. Data Resources Incorporated, *U.S. Cost Forecasting Service: Long-Term Review*, Vol. 14, No. 7 (Washington, D.C.: McGraw-Hill, October 1988), p. 87.
32. Congressional Budget Office, *The Economic and Budget Outlook: An Update* (August 1989), p. 47. Baseline estimates adjust all programs for anticipated inflation; entitlement programs are also adjusted to reflect changes

in numbers and types of beneficiaries. Baseline estimates assume no changes in current tax laws. Most estimates of the deficit in this chapter are expressed as a percent of the GNP for perspective and to facilitate comparisons over a number of years.

33. For a discussion of this complex subject, see Congressional Budget Office, *The Economic and Budget Outlook: Fiscal Years 1988–1992*, January 1987, pp. 97–106.

34. A serious recession (similar in depth to the one between 1973 and 1975) could add over $100 billion to the federal deficit, increasing the deficit as a percent of the GNP by more than two points. For details on this estimate, see Congressional Budget Office, note 33, pp. 50–52.

35. The Commission on Integrated Long-Term Strategy, *Discriminate Deterrence* (Washington, D.C.: U.S. Government Printing Office, January 1988), p. 7.

36. Abt Associates, *Survey on National Defense and Economic Issues: October 4–10, 1984*, unpublished, p. 15. The survey covered 1,002 people age eighteen or over who were selected by random-digit dialing. The margin of error is plus or minus 3 percent.

37. For a more thorough review of the data, see testimony of Robert F. Hale before the Committee on the Budget, United States Senate, March 1, 1988.

38. Congressional Budget Office, *Alliance Burdensharing: A Review of the Data*, unpublished staff working paper, June 1987, pp. 12–13.

39. Paul Kennedy, author of the best-selling book, *The Rise and Fall of Great Powers*, has noted historical precedents for these various trends. In a hotly debated analysis, Kennedy cites examples of former world powers that have declined in influence and argues that their decline was hastened by adherence to far-reaching, expensive defense commitments. He dubs this phenomenon "imperial overstretch." Kennedy also offers no firm prescriptions for how much of its resources the United States should devote to defense. See Paul Kennedy, "The (Relative) Decline of America," *The Atlantic Monthly*, August 1987, p. 33.

40. The regression relates the percentage of U.S. adults who told pollsters that the United States is spending too much on defense in a particular fiscal year to the real percentage change in defense budget authority in that year. Poll results are from Gallup for fiscal years 1970 to 1987. Gallup asked: "There is much discussion as to the amount of money the government in Washington should spend for national defense and military purposes. How do you feel about this? Do you think we are spending too little, too much, or about the right amount?" This particular question was asked in thirteen of the years between 1970 and 1987 (multiple polls in a single year were arithmetically averaged). Real percentage changes are for the Department of Defense budget (function 051) and are taken from the May 1987 report of the DoD comptroller. Correlations of budget changes with those who told pollsters that the United States is spending "too little" on defense were slightly lower ($r = .68$). Correlations were slightly higher if the poll for a particular year was correlated to the budget change one year later ($r = .75$) for "too much" and $r = .78$ for "too little".

41. Research by Mark Mellman quoted in Bruce Russett and Donald DeLuca, "'Don't Tread on Me': Public Opinion and Foreign Policy in the Eighties," *Political Science Quarterly*, Fall 1981, pp. 397–398.

42. Democratic Leadership Council, *Defending America* (Washington, D.C., September 1986), p. 18; Les Aspin, press release accompanying study

entitled *Defense Budgets Up—Whither Security*? (Washington, D.C.: House Armed Services Committee, October 7, 1985), p. 1.

43. *The Harris Survey Press Release*, July 22, 1985, p. 3; *A Quest for Excellence*, Appendix L, pp. 195, 211; CBS/*New York Times* Poll, *Before the Democratic Convention*, July 11, 1988, p. 20. (The CBS/*New York Times* Poll asked, "Where is there more government waste—in defense spending or in welfare spending?" Forty percent of respondents chose defense, 34 percent chose welfare, 15 percent said both were equal, and 11 percent said they did not know.)

44. Shifts in resources to or from defense could, of course, affect the rate of economic growth. Such effects are ignored here and in subsequent calculations.

45. The Chicago Council on Foreign Relations, *American Public Opinion and Foreign Policy 1987* (Chicago: 1987), p. 21.

46. Congressional Budget Office, *The Budgetary Effects of the President's Conventional Arms Proposal* (unpublished staff working paper, June 1989), p. 1.

47. Electronic Industries Association, *Defense Electronics Market: Ten-Year Forecast of U.S. Department of Defense Budgets FY 1989–1998* (Washington, D.C., unpublished, October 11, 1988), p. 57.

48. Congressional Budget Office, *U.S. Ground Forces and the Conventional Balance in Europe*, June 1988 (Washington, D.C.: U.S. Government Printing Office), pp. xvii–xxi.

49. Congressional Budget Office, *Tactical Combat of the United States Air Force: Issues and Alternatives*, April 1985, pp. 56–57, and *Naval Combat Aircraft: Issues and Options*, November 1987 (Washington, D.C.: U.S. Government Printing Office), pp. 63–64.

50. Statement of Robert F. Hale of the Congressional Budget Office before the Defense and International Affairs Task Force, Committee on the Budget, U.S. House of Representatives, September 14, 1987, pp. 14–17.

51. Congressional Budget Office, *Operation and Support Costs for the Department of Defense*, July 1988 (Washington, D.C.: U.S. Government Printing Office), pp. 16–20.

52. The Commission on Integrated Long-Term Strategy, *Discriminate Deterrence*, January 1988 (Washington, D.C.: U.S. Government Printing Office), pp. 59–60.

PART 3

Europe and the United States

CHAPTER 5

Gorbachev's Gambit: Soviet Military Doctrine and Conventional Arms Control in an Era of Reform

— JACOB W. KIPP

As the 1990s begin, Western military analysts have had to face a process of proclaimed changes and objective circumstances, which, taken together, have made analyzing the political and military dimensions of the Soviet threat much more complex. This chapter will address recent political and military-technical developments in Soviet military doctrine and arms control in order to provide a context for current changes in Soviet military art (strategy, operational art, and acts) and force structure and posture. The objective of this chapter is to provide a broad introductory overview of current trends and future prospects regarding Soviet military doctrine. The focus is upon recent Soviet initiatives in the areas of doctrine and arms control.

On December 7, 1988, before the General Assembly of the United Nations, General Secretary Mikhail Gorbachev announced a series of unilateral reductions to take place over the next two years in the Soviet Armed Forces, beginning with a cut of 500,000 men and including an overall reduction of 10,000 tanks, 8,500 artillery systems, and 800 combat aircraft. Furthermore, he announced cuts of 50,000 men and 5,000 tanks from among those deployed with Soviet forces and the removal of air assault and river-crossing units in Eastern Europe. In addition, he noted that Soviet combat formations were undergoing a reorganization that make their "defensive" nature evident to all. This announcement brought into sharp relief the connections between military doctrine and conventional forces in Soviet "new thinking" on international security issues and arms control.[1]

These proposed unilateral cuts, which are organically tied to recent Soviet and Warsaw Treaty Organization (WTO) doctrinal pronouncements, and arms control initiatives, stand at the core of Gorbachev's "gambit." Together, they represent elements of a very sophisticated game plan, involving the reconstruction of the international security system and a relaxation of tensions. This would permit a profound recasting of the Soviet society to meet the requirements of great power status into the next century.[2]

Gorbachev's particular combination of measures and pronouncements have brought the novelty of this approach into full relief.

Until recently, military doctrine and a military-technical revolution affecting conventional forces have figured only tangentially in arms control issues. Arms control has focused primarily on deterrence management and nuclear arms reduction. U.S. and other Western policymakers and negotiators have tended to treat the former as a phenomenon distinct from warfighting capabilities. Indeed, during the last two decades, much of the polemic over various arms control proposals has concerned their proponent's interpretation of each agreement's contribution to enhanced deterrence and their critics' skepticism over each agreement's contribution to an erosion of warfighting capabilities. The issue has been at once narrowly technical, regarding specific features of strategic systems, and broadly ideological, revealing much about the basic assumptions of advocates and opponents alike regarding the nature of the international system, the character of the Soviet-U.S. competition, and the role of force in protecting the national interest and achieving objectives. Neither military doctrine nor conventional military forces figured prominently in arms control discussions.[3]

This inattention to doctrinal and conventional force considerations in the larger arms control process has been all the more curious because the perception of the USSR's conventional superiority in Europe, along with Soviet force posture and military art, has for more than four decades been a fundamental influence on U. S. and NATO strategic posture. Such concepts as extended deterrence and flexible response owe much of their origins to a single persistent reality: the threat posed by the Soviet Union's potential capability, using conventional forces, to overrun Western Europe.[4]

A new series of multilateral negotiations on conventional forces has begun in Vienna, involving twenty-three states and encompassing the entire continent from the Atlantic to the Urals. As a senior U.S. official observed, "For the first time in the postwar period, negotiated reductions of conventional forces in Europe have emerged in public discourse as a real possiblity."[5] In the months preceding these negotiations, NATO and the Warsaw Treaty Organization (WTO) have been preparing their positions and maneuvering to influence public opinion. In November 1988 NATO published its own assessment of the status of conventional forces in Europe, emphasizing Soviet/WTO superiority in manpower, tanks, armored personnel carriers, and artillery. President Gorbachev's December 7 announcement of unilateral troop reductions over the next two years followed in short order. The Soviet government also announced the resignation of the Chief of the Soviet General Staff, Marshal Sergei Akhromeyev, and then his replacement by General Colonel M. A. Moiseyev.[6] During this period Deputy Foreign Minister Viktor Karpov announced that Akhromeyev had been appointed as a "civilian" advisor to Gorbachev on defense policy.[7] In January 1989 the Soviets published their own figures on the current conventional balance of forces in Europe and announced that these figures established a "rough parity" between NATO and the WTO forces.[8]

As of early 1990, such comparative figures on the current balance reveal a number of salient points relating to the current status of conventional arms control. First, there has been a shift in assessing that balance from manpower, which had been the mainstay of MBFR (the Mutual and Balanced Force Reduction talks), to combat systems. Second, the two sides have very different ways of calculating combat power. The WTO figures count all personnel, not just ground forces. NATO emphasizes main battle tanks to the exclusion of light tanks. The WTO emphasis is upon combined arms combat power as it might be applied within theater, whereas NATO has emphasized those forces that constitute a direct threat for immediate invasion. For example, the WTO treats interceptors as defensive systems as opposed to fighter-bombers that can be employed in direct ground support or in interdiction. While by mutual agreement naval systems have been excluded from the current Conventional Arms Talks, the WTO intends to depict NATO advantages in naval forces as effecting strategic stability in preparation for some future naval limitation talks, perhaps beyond the framework of the Atlantic to the Urals formula to embrace the Atlantic and Pacific oceanic theaters of operation (TVDS). This certainly has been a subtext and theme in some recent Soviet writings, including those by naval analysts and senior members of the Soviet General Staff.[9]

Despite the conflicts over the numbers in separate categories, the NATO and WTO figures represent substantial progress in the area of conventional arms talks. They provide quantitative parameters for serious negotiations.[10] Each side has come forward with a set of initial proposals based upon its data. The Soviet proposals introduced on March 5, 1989, at the first session of the Vienna talks used the WTO figures as the basis for a three-stage process for eliminating asymmetries and reducing the risks of surprise attack. The proposal called for first-stage reductions over two years to equal collective ceilings for both NATO and the WTO, based upon initial force reductions 10 to 15 percent lower than the levels of the weaker side in each weapons category. The second-stage cuts would reduce force levels an additional 25 percent and bring about the removal of offensive forces, including tactical nuclear weapons. A third stage would follow in which the military forces of both alliances would be restructured in keeping with the needs of nonprovocative defense. These proposals are based upon the assumption of major progress in strategic nuclear arms talks.[11]

On the other hand, such figures say very little about the military art that would direct the employment of such forces in case of war; how the respective alliances would employ their forces to get maximum combat power; or the crucial questions of the nature of initial operations, and the mobilization, concentration, and deployment of forces in case of war. Herein lies the challenge of conventional arms control, where the linkage between conventional warfighting capabilities and various deterrent theories must be reconciled. This chapter will discuss the progress that has brought the two alliances to address military doctrine as a key element in this process.

The Doctrine–Arms Control Connection

The years 1987, 1988, and 1989 saw a surge of interest in nuclear and conventional arms control and substantial movement on the Soviet side. In the early 1980s, in the face of NATO's announced intention to deploy Pershing II and ground-launched cruise missile (GLCM) theater-nuclear systems, the Soviets had refused further neogiations, relying upon domestic political pressure to force concessions from the various governments that had agreed to accept such weapons systems. Recently, Soviet civilian analysts have addressed the entire backdrop of the decision to deploy SS-20 missiles, NATO's response, and the negotiating process that brought about the INF Treaty of 1987. While these authors disagree about whether the initial decision to deploy was a mistake—they present it as a calculated move to counter U.S. strategic modernization after SALT I, especially the process of MIRVing U.S. ICBMs and SLBMs, and the anticipated deployment of new U.S. theater-nuclear systems—they are agreed that the decision to break off negotiations was a terrible mistake because it isolated the USSR, undercut its international position, and set back the Soviet program to reduce and eliminate nuclear weapons.[12]

These Soviet authors consider the Soviet reponse to have been narrow and exclusively military-technical, failing to take into account the political dimension of the question. Lev Semeyko, a senior researcher at the Institute for the Study of the United States and Canada and former officer with expertise in military foresight (*voyenoye predvideniye*), has written:

> The conclusion from this is evident: a political approach to military confrontation is more rational than a military-technical [approach]. Precisely by timely political measures one can and must prevent the jumps in the arms race and at the same time reduce the level of military confrontation to such a degree, under which both sides feel themselves really secure. The optimal variant is not a one-sided gamble on political measures.[13]

The stalemate over an INF agreement was broken, thanks in part to NATO deployments of Pershing II and GLCM systems, and a Soviet recognition that stonewalling had been counterproductive and that a political solution carried major advantages.[14] As Semeyko points out in the conclusion of his article on the decision to deploy the SS-20s in the first place, "a political approach to military confrontation is more rational than a military-technical [one]."[15] During the final INF negotiations, such a line of analysis led to Soviet concessions in three areas: the acceptance of asymmetrical reductions in forces, the geographic generalization of the agreement to include global removal of such systems, and the establishment of a verification regime that includes both national technical means and intrusive inspection.

Evidence of some change in the Soviet position along these lines was already noted during the Stockholm Conference (1984–1986) on "Confidence and Security Building Measures in Europe." At that time, a subtle shift in emphasis took place concerning conventional force arms control. While early negotiations, such as the SALT, MBFR, INF, and START talks, had all concentrated on reducing capabilities for war, the Stockholm negotiations focused on the reduction of the possibilities of a surprise attack without warning.[16]

Contemporary NATO Concerns

During this same period, reports concerning the content of the Soviet exercise *Zapad-81* raised serious issues regarding Soviet interest in a high-speed, theater-strategic operation.[17] During that exercise, the Soviet armed forces demonstrated the modern version of the theater-strategic operation in all its components, including a number of innovations. A particular concept, the Operational Maneuver Group (a large, combined arms force designed for deep-raiding and exploitation operations in the enemy rear), appeared to represent a further articulation of Soviet operational art, which since the 1930s had incorporated mobile groups for the conduct of operational maneuver in the course of deep operations.[18] The 1981 version went much further in its use of rotary-wing aviation and air assault forces to support large-scale (division size) raiding forces.[19]

The political context of *Zapad-81*, coming as it did during the Polish crisis, underscored the problem that such a Soviet "lightning operation" (a theater-strategic operation relying upon conventional military power) posed for NATO. It presented both a political and military threat to the very viability of the Western alliance by calling into question the alliance's reliance upon early escalation to nuclear weapons in case of attack and placed additional strain upon the linkage between a deteriorating theater situation and strategic nuclear deterrence.[20] This realization prompted a revival of interest in enhanced conventional deterrence.

Revival culminated in a set of proposals designed to use emerging technologies to counter the threat, notably General Bernard Rogers' plan that employed Follow-on Forces Attack (FOFA). Rogers' plan sought to improve conventional capabilities in order to raise the nuclear threshold in theater while maintaining the viability of flexible response and forward defense, the cornerstones of NATO strategy since the 1960s. The plan's principal contribution to NATO warfighting capabilities was to place the Soviet/Warsaw Pact second operational echelon at risk. The role of conventional forces in deterrence, the impact of new technologies upon the conventional battlefield, and conventional arms control emerged as major topics for consideration.

In the wake of these developments and NATO's program for the modernization of theater-nuclear forces, a range of alternative responses has emerged within NATO regarding the primacy of disarmament/arms control initiatives, confidence-building measures, and warfighting capabilities. Since the early 1970s, some German defense intellectuals in particular have manifested a growing interest in "controlling the armaments process." These authors have revived an academic critique of the U.S. military-industrial complex and applied it to conventional forces.[21] They advocate a new approach to European security based upon "defensive" defense, a defense eschewing reliance upon "offensive" weapons systems while relying upon enhanced defensive weapons systems. Fears of nuclear weapons, concern over the costs of a viable conventional deterrence, and a popular desire to reduce the risks of war made such concepts particularly appealing. Attempts to get political endorsement of such views did not meet with any success while the West German Social Democratic Party (SPD) governed. However, after it went into opposition, the party's attitude changed. At their Party Conference in 1984, Social Democrats called for denuclearization of the alliance systems and a defensive strategy based upon "sufficiency" (*Hinlaenglichkeit*). The fifth point of the SPD's statement addressed the problem of conventional deterrence:

> The conventional stability between NATO and the Warsaw Pact is to be brought down to the lowest possible level. This is to be done on the basis of a realistic threat analysis which takes into account qualitative factors of armament, economic and technological capabilities, as well as social and political conditions. The *Bundeswehr's* military force structure and armaments must unquestionably be defensive. No one should doubt the will and ability for self-defense based upon the Alliance. This is why there is a need for restructuring [*Umstrukturierung*] rather than expanding conventional armaments.[22]

Soviet Concepts

Soviet scholars have been quick to pick up on such themes to address salient features of Western security policy that they describe as reflecting both a U.S. drive for global hegemony and a commitment to nuclear warfighting capabilities. A. N. Yakovlev, former director of the Institute of International Economics and Foreign Relations (IMEMO) and Ambassador to Canada, has depicted the United States as a society dominated by its military-industrial complex, committed to global hegemony, and willing to use nuclear weapons to conduct an anti-Soviet crusade. Writing during the renewed Cold War and after the initial deployment of U.S. Pershing II and GLCMs to Europe, he characterized the United States as prone to violence, governed by deception, fixed on global hegemony and domination, and in which "the population is a blind instrument of forces pursuing only their own narrow interests."[23] Genrikh Trofimenko, Chief of the Foreign Policy Department of the Institute for the Study of the United States and Canada, also described U.S. military doctrine as the result of the interactions and interconnections of its militarized capitalism, bourgeois ideology, and an aggressive, offensive military posture. He characterizes the United States as a nation guided by "a national military doctrine and strategy serving the extravagant goals of world hegemony."[24] As he had in earlier works, Trofimenko acknowledges contradictions that limited U.S. military initiatives and gave birth to certain elements within the society that were more realistic in their approach to international affairs. The Strategic Defense Initiative was only the latest attempt to regain U.S. invulnerability to attack while retaining for the United States the ability to use nuclear weapons as an instrument of political leverage. The debate within the United States over the SDI research initiative confirmed both the general direction of U.S. military doctrine and the contradictions that served to check its most adventuristic proponents.[25] Military doctrine emerged as a major ideological battleground in which the target was the U.S. military-industrial complex and the objective was to reduce confidence in the U.S. government among its own population and as an alliance partner.

By 1985, knowledgeable observers considered the Stockholm Conference a vital test of whether confidence-building measures could be agreed to that might reduce East-West ambiguity. Thus, the conference witnessed a shift to reducing the possibilities of surprise attack. They involved reducing the threat of a surprise initiation of hostilities and creating an inspection and verification system.

During this period, a new Soviet leadership was just beginning to show vitality after the drift of the last Brezhnev years and the paralysis of a prolonged interregnum. Beginning with the XXVII Party Congress in February 1986, the new Soviet leadership under Mikhail Gorbachev came forward with a host of disarmament and confidence-building measures—some old, some new, with most simply recasting previous positions. These have included General Secretary Gorbachev's statement of a long-range goal to eliminate all nuclear weapons by the year 2000. Between April 1986 and February 1987, Gorbachev added conventional arms control to this "new thinking." He agreed to the French formulation that European conventional disarmament measures would apply "from the Atlantic to the Urals." In Budapest in June 1986, the Warsaw Pact proposed the elimination of those elimination of those weapons considered most useful for surprise attacks. In July, during French President Mitterrand's visit to Moscow, Gorbachev spoke of the need to eliminate any surplus weapons that might give either the Warsaw Pact or NATO conventional superiority. Arms control and maintenance of military parity were to be achieved by a build-down rather than a buildup. Gorbachev proposed the removal of the most dangerous kinds of offensive weapons from the zone of contact. In August 1986, Chief of the Soviet General Staff, Marshal Sergei Akhromeyev, visited the Stockholm Conference and instructed the Soviet delegation to accept as legally binding an inspection regime for exercises employing more than 17,000 troops, to provide two years' advance notification for exercises involving more than 40,000 troops, to pledge not to interfere with national technical means of verification, and to acknowledge a linkage between conventional arms control and confidence- and security-building measures.[26]

Soviet Military Doctrine

During the XXVII Party Congress, Gorbachev had linked "new thinking" on questions of international security to the question of averting nuclear war and world war by eliminating nuclear weapons while keeping the respective military potentials of the opposing sides within the confines of a "rational, sufficient defense" (*razumnaia dostatochnaia oborona*). This concept, which emphasized the continuing competition and mutual dependency of the superpowers and their alliance systems, in turn was tied to the creation of an "integrated global security system."[27]

In April 1987, A. N. Yakovlev, Head of the Propaganda Department of the Central Committee of the Communist Party of the Soviet Union (CPSU), and close advisor to Gorbachev on international issues (shortly to become a Full Member of the Politburo), addressed the Academy of Sciences and called upon Soviet political scientists to make their contribution to the "formulation of a security system" based on mutual trust to replace nuclear deterrence and military means in general. Yakovlev stated:

> The formulation of a universal system of international security presupposes the development of a *preventive diplomacy*, which is called up to prevent the escalation of conflicts. These questions demand close scientific research.[28]

In a slightly different version of the same talk published in *Kommunist*, the Party's leading theoretical journal, Yakovlev formulated two additional tasks in the field of international security policy for Soviet social scientists. First, he asked them to address "the conception of *sufficiency* of military potentials including that under conditions of the complete liquidation of nuclear weapons." Second, he charged them to work jointly with military specialists on "our military doctrine, which in its strategic content is based upon the policy of *averting nuclear war*."[29]

The Berlin Communiqué of the Political Consultative Committee of the Warsaw Treaty Organization of May 26, 1987, which articulated six general proposals addressing a range of security issues, proclaimed that the Warsaw Pact had a "strictly defensive" military doctrine. The "Rust Affair," which immediately followed the Berlin meeting, allowed the General Secretary to begin reshaping the leadership of the Ministry of Defense, removing the Chief of the Air Defense Forces and accepting the resignation of Minister of Defense Marshal S. L. Sokolov.[30] The newly appointed Minister of Defense, Army General D. T. Yazov, in his first publication after becoming Defense Minister in June 1987, repeated the Berlin formula, while relating it to perestroika in military affairs.[31]

In these and other formulations, the word *defensive* has attracted most of the attention from foreign analysts. There has been much discussion of what is new in this defensiveness and how it relates to past doctrine.[32] Yet, as Soviet spokesmen have stated repeatedly in the past, Soviet military doctrine—and by extension, that of the Warsaw Pact—has always proceeded "from the principle of retaliatory, that is defensive actions."[33]

In fact, the Soviets have presented to the world an apparent shift in the political side of their military doctrine by stressing a shift from punitive deterrence in conventional war toward prevention. Soviet political leaders, analysts, and commentators have emphasized this shift from conducting wars to preventing them.[34] This "new military doctrine" is defined as "a system of fundamental views officially accepted in the Warsaw Treaty Organization on the prevention of war, on military construction, on the preparation of their countries and armed forces to ward off aggression, and on the modes of conducting armed struggle in defense of socialism."[35] This formula was repeated by Minister of Defense Yazov in his definition of Soviet military doctrine.[36]

The "new thinking" in this formulation is best grasped when this definition of Soviet military doctrine is compared with that found in earlier Soviet works devoted to military matters. During the late 1970s, Soviet military doctrine was defined as:

> the nation's officially accepted system of scientifically founded views on the nature of modern wars and the use of the armed forces in them, as well as the requirements arising from these views regarding the preparation of the country and its armed forces for war.[37]

As recently as 1986, Soviet military writers were emphasizing the fact that such official views focused upon "the essence, aims, and nature of a possible future war."[38]

The central problem for Western analysts in dealing with this new formulation is to understand precisely the relationship among war prevention, deterrence, and warfighting capabilities. In the past, the Soviets have openly declared that their combat readiness and increased combat capabilities were forms of deterrence (*sderzhivanie*). At the same time, the Soviets have been bitter critics of U.S. nuclear strategy because, as they see it, U.S. deterrence theory separates the political and military sides of the question and seeks a mechanistic, technologically determined application of strategic nuclear power outside of and independent from political goals and objectives. The Soviet armed forces are maintained at the requisite levels of preparedness, according to Defense Minister Yazov, "which will allow them in case of attack to give a crushing repulse to any aggressor." That crushing blow involved mounting offensive operations to carry the war to the opponent's territory as rapidly and decisively as possible. Citing the formula of the XXVII Party Congress, General Yazov emphasized the following formula: "greater security the Soviet Union does not claim, less it cannot accept."[39] Should deterrence fail and a general conflict between socialism and capitalism lead to world war, such a definition of sufficient defense encompasses possession of means to fight a war of annihilation:

> If a new world war begins, it will manifest itself by its unprecedented ferocious global confrontation of the multi-million man armed forces of the coalitions and will be conducted for the most decisive political and military objectives. In it there would not be a possibility of any sort of compromise.[40]

The point of recent Soviet works has been to seek means that would reduce tensions and prevent the outbreak of such a conflict.

If sufficient defense encompasses a traditional emphasis on the ability to fight and win a war of annihilation, then what is new within Soviet military doctrine must turn on the central issues of war prevention, reduction of the risk of surprise, and the reconfiguration and redeployment of forces to reduce the ability of both sides to engage in preemptive general offensives. In the 1970s, the concept of sufficiency in defense was articulated in the West, especially by the Nixon Administration, under the rubric of "sufficient deterrence." This concept relied in the end upon the use of strategic nuclear systems to provide assured destruction, which, under the conditions of strategic nuclear parity, assumed a certain "mutuality." As Gerhard Wettig has pointed out, Soviet pronouncements about the elimination of nuclear weapons make it quite clear that the Soviets have not accepted such a definition of "sufficiency" as the foundation for their concept of "rational, sufficient defense."

Military Doctrine and Arms Control

The conclusion of the INF Treaty, with its elimination of several types of theater-nuclear forces, and the provisions for verification by national technical means and an intrusive inspection regime, underscores the Soviet willingness to eliminate nuclear weapons, even on an asymmetrical basis. It should be pointed out that this elimination of several classes of theater-nuclear weapons is dialectically asymmetrical: The Soviets are willing to give up more weapons in exchange for removing a direct threat to the Soviet homeland. Since the Soviets define all weapons of mass destruction that can reach the USSR as strategic, they can rationally assume that they got the better end of the deal. This is particularly true because of the centrality of theater systems to NATO's concept of flexible response. By reducing the options open to the NATO high command in case of deterrence failure, they increase alliance uncertainty, focus the nuclear center of gravity upon the two Germanies, and make the exercise of the theater-nuclear option more difficult. The 50-percent reduction in strategic systems, which has become the basis for START, likewise fits within this framework. The INF Treaty and progress at the START talks make the issue of conventional arms control within the European context all the more pressing. The West cannot afford to run the risk of making Europe safe for the execution of the theater-strategic operation by conventional means.

Progress in this area of arms control faced serious obstacles. The Soviets were well aware of NATO's concerns regarding Soviet/Warsaw Pact conventional force numerical superiority in certain types of weapons, most notably tanks and artillery. General Woijiech Jaruzelski's proposal to reduce Warsaw Pact tanks and artillery forces in exchange for reductions in NATO theater-aviation assets suggested one line of approach to this problem. Unilateral Soviet reductions in support of negotiating leverage—small in scale and of symbolic importance only—would be an important means of creating a climate for future NATO concessions in anticipation of actual negotiations. However, the most crucial issue remains the doctrinal context of such reductions.

From the Soviet/Warsaw Pact perspective, military doctrine has and will always have two sides: political and military-technical. The political side, which at least one Western commentator would dismiss as "the foggier and more hortatory concept of political-military doctrine," has in fact undergone important and substantive changes during the last few years, if recent Soviet writings on the political content of future war provide any indication.[41] These writings have been quite consistent with Yakovlev's call for Soviet political scientists to make their contribution to an articulation of the political and ideological context for the creation of that system of preventive diplomacy. The target of these efforts is the U.S. "military-industrial complex," which Soviet authors describe as "the true source of evil on the planet . . . which includes the monopolies who make the weapons, the generals connected with them, government bureaucracy, the ideological complex and militarized science."[42] This protracted struggle with the U.S. military-industrial complex and its allies has been presented as a central feature of ideological struggle in the modern world. Major General Iu. Ia. Kirshin of the Institute of Military History described it in the following terms: "The fate of humanity now very much depends on the outcome of the ideological struggle over questions of war and peace. To defend peace today—that means to block the forces of war with a reliable military and ideological barrier."[43]

In February 1987, Gorbachev called into question one verity of Soviet military doctrine when he observed, "After Hiroshima and Nagasaki world war ceased to be a continuation of politics by other means."[44] In their attempts to deal with this formulation, Soviet writers have polemicized among themselves over the relevance of Lenin's interpretation of Clausewitz's dictum on "war as a continuation of politics by other, i.e, violent, means." In these articles, class struggle remains the central manifestation of such politics. And recourse to war as a capitalist-imperialist response to the challenges of socialism and national liberation is still accepted as the greatest, although not the only, source of war in the modern world.[45] What has changed is the Soviet perception of the "rationality" of world war in the nuclear-space era. In D. Proektor's view, world war must lead to nuclear war and this, in turn, evokes the specter of "ecological catastrophe" and an end of human civilization.[46] In the wake of these developments, Soviet authors have rejected strategic "victory" as a term appropriate to war termination in a global, nuclear war. In its stead, they emphasize operational and tactical victories, which would still apply in a nuclear war.[47]

Soviet authors now place greater stress upon the problem of congruence between political objectives and the military means chosen to achieve those objectives. The test of congruence when applied to a systemic world war, involving the use of nuclear weapons, emerges as an invitation to mutual suicide and ecological disaster. In the case of local wars, especially those between liberated countries themselves and between socialist-oriented states and the major capitalist powers, the great risk is their escalation into general war. Typically, Soviet authors emphasize a broad range of factors that act to limit warfare by area, means, and war aims. They also stress the interconnections linking the political side of military doctrine with specifically military-technical issues. As S. A. Tiushkevich has noted:

> The realities of the nuclear age demand a new approach to the working out of political goals and the possibility of using military force to achieve them. This is explained, above all, by the fact that the contemporary revolution in military affairs has made the incongruity of military means to political objectives especially

dangerous not only for separate countries and peoples but for all of humanity. The leap in the development of military technology, the appearance of the most destructive means, has led to a distinct devaluation of these means, to a narrowing of the sphere of the employment of military force towards rational political objectives.[48]

It is precisely at the juncture between the political and military-technical aspects of military doctrine where conventional military power poses its most serious dilemma. On the one hand, the Soviets have for over two decades been moving toward a posture that emphasized the utility of conventional forces in a theater-strategic operation as the most appropriate application of military power to achieve a rational, political end should war between the European military blocs prove inevitable. At the same time, however, the Soviets have seen the political necessity of such an option decline as they have perceived the threat from the West and East (NATO and the People's Republic of China) become less imminent.

Soviet authors emphasize the fact that objective conditions in the past have led the Soviet Union to recast the political side of its military doctrine. Since the time of Lenin, the Communist Party has responded to new sets of international circumstances. During the dark years of capitalist encirclement and economic backwardness, the threat assumed a stark character, demanding rapid and often painful adjustments in international relations, military posture, and domestic policy. At the same time, Soviet academic analysts argue that incorrect assessments in the past have led to foreign policy miscalculations, the undermining of national security, and the senseless waste of resources and political capital.[49]

The same authors now emphasize the current, relative invulnerability of the USSR and the socialist camp to overt military pressure—excluding, of course, recourse to nuclear means with its risk of destruction for all of humanity, capitalist, socialist, and other. They also stress the relative freedom of maneuver that the Soviet Union now enjoys both in terms of domestic policy and international opportunities. While the political-ideological struggle with capitalism continues under many guises, the recourse to the military instrument does not represent the optimal means to resolve such issues.

> Today in relations between East and West there is not a single conflict for the sake of whose solution there would appear the temptation to resort to war. Remaining on the grounds of common sense, it is difficult to imagine what purpose would be served for Western armies to invade the territory of Socialist states. The problems of modern capitalism are not small and quite unhealthy. But these problems—the problems of capitalism at the end of the XX century—cannot, in principle, be resolved with the help of military aggression against [S]ocialism. This is one of the main reasons why

there are today neither in Western Europe nor in the USA influential political forces [that] would place before themselves such tasks.[50]

Since World War II, Soviet political and military-technical analysis has viewed Western Europe as the primary beachhead from which a crusade against the USSR might be launched. Western Europe was also seen as the most important political and economic bastion of capitalism outside of the United States. Therefore, it has been both threat and political-military objective. Whether by political-ideological or military means, Europe was the most important area of contest for influence among the superpowers. Since the beginning of the Cold War, the Soviets have consistently sought denuclearization and removal of U.S. military power from Western Europe, while recognizing those objective sociopolitical conditions that sustained the Western European bond with its trans-Atlantic ally. Recently, however, Soviet authors have stressed the socioeconomic vulnerability of Western Europe in the event of general war:

> Even a non-nuclear war on the European continent, saturated with atomic power stations, chemical plants, and large fuel depots would, for all practical purposes, mean the death of all civilization on this continent. This above all applies namely to Western Europe, where the population density and degree of urbanization is higher and the territory is less than in Eastern Europe. The very nature of a highly industrialized society here appears as a factor which deters war. In addition to that, it is impossible to imagine how one could keep a war in Europe at the non-nuclear level.[51]

The emphasis is upon a community of European interest that is conditioned by a shared vulnerability between Eastern and Western Europe.

Implied in this sobering realization is the possibility and, indeed, the necessity of "rethinking many traditional postulates of military strategy and operational art," including a reassessment of numerical requirements for various weapons systems and the nature of maneuvers carried out.[52] Soviet authors argue that:

> The guaranteed prevention of war in Europe requires the successive reduction here of the level of military confrontation, and, in the ultimate summation, the surmounting of the system of military bloc opposition [that] aggravates the military threat, and the creation of another stable, humanitarian system of security on the continent [that] precludes hostility and an arms race.[53]

At the same time, while Soviet authors stress the sufficiency of current Soviet defense capabilities to repulse an attack, they also emphasize the decline in the prospects for long-term strategic nuclear stability based upon ever-higher levels of parity, given the pace and direction of strategic weapons development and the very size of the arsenals possessed by both sides. They call attention to current U.S. efforts to shift the nature of the military competition from warfighting capabilities into the military-economic realm, a development they consider arms-racing through research and development. Soviet analysts stress current sufficiency in both conventional and strategic arms and point to long-term problems unless the Soviet economy is radically recast toward greater productivity and a higher pace of scientific-technical innovation. They envision the current challenge as embodied in a Western effort to use the arms race to bring about Soviet economic exhaustion and decline. They describe "competitive strategies" as:

> the U.S. Defense Department's strategy of forcing the Soviet Union into an intensive arms race on a maximum number of directions. By using the leading position of the U.S. in a scientific-technical field, they are counting on continually and purposefully devaluing Soviet military assets ("to bring into obsolescence Soviet investments in defense which have already been made") and forcing the USSR to expend new resources and then once again devaluing them.[54]

These authors thus place conventional arms control measures in Europe within the context of the struggle to negate politically the advantages that the United States seeks to derive from the military-economic competition at the heart of competitive strategies. The logic is quite clear. By reducing the level of forces on the European continent, the Soviets manage Western perceptions of the conventional threat in order to keep low both the level of new systems and the will to consider deploying them. At the same time, the USSR would gain time for its own breathing space (*peredyshka*), which would permit perestroika to go forward in those areas contributing to the overall strength of the Soviet economy and to the restructuring of Soviet defense industries to take into account newly emerging technologies. In this manner, the USSR might maintain its relative position in the international system while facing minimum risk during a period of reform.

The Soviet assessment of the status of U.S. defense capabilities now emphasizes a wide range of objective and subjective constraints that have emerged during the Reagan Administration to shift the thrust of U.S. policy away from seeking military superiority over the USSR toward "technological arms-racing," based upon Soviet adoption of costly symmetrical responses to these initiatives. They express major reservations regarding the American will and resources to continue such a course of action under the next administration.[55]

At the same time, the Soviets would like to use reduced tensions to manage their overextended position in the Third World. Unwilling to make unilateral concessions for fear of what that would imply in other vulnerable areas, the USSR is seeking some modus vivendi for managing regional conflicts to ensure that Soviet losses do not translate into Western gains. Evidence of shifts in Soviet policy are to be seen in Angola and Afghanistan. It remains to be seen what the final outcomes will be. One major line of Soviet discussions regarding preventive diplomacy has been the creation of international guarantees as part of the resolution of such regional conflicts.

Some Western analysts see disagreement between a reform-minded Communist Party elite and the military over "new thinking" in the area of "sufficient defense" and military doctrine. In other words, observers perceive conflict drawn along lines that pit those responsible for the "political" side of Soviet military doctrine against those who are charged with articulating the "military-technical" side. There is, however, compelling evidence pointing to some congruence of interest and symmetry of positions on these issues. The military-technical side of military doctrine addresses a whole range of questions associated with force structure, combat readiness, and military art. The last category embraces strategy, operational art, and tactics. Military art is explicitly evolutionary in that it responds to socioeconomic and technological changes. The pace of change can sometimes be quite gradual, with an emphasis only on quantitative factors; at other times, it can make qualitative leaps. The Soviet General Staff sees the present era as one dominated by such qualitative leaps, affecting both the form and content of military art. While this raises a host of difficult issues relating to the composition and structure of Soviet conventional forces and the manner in which they are raised, trained, and equipped, such leaps must be addressed in all their revolutionary aspects.

Military Art and Scientific-Technical Change

Military art evolves and is conditioned by the level of economic development of a given state and by the dominant sociopolitical structure under which it operates. Military art, which is the essential expression of the military-technical side of military doctrine, is itself shaped by military science. Soviet military science, based upon Marxism-Leninism, seeks the law-governed patterns of development that will shape future combat requirements. As Colonel General I. E. Shavrov and Colonel M. I. Galkin have asserted: "In its essence, *military science is the science of future war.*"[56] The study of future war is an exercise in foresight (*predvidenie*) and embraces both the forecasting of changes in the correlation of forces and the forecasting of trends in three areas relating to scientific-technical developments:

> The first is the determination of the direction of military-technical progress, of the ways of modernizing existing weapons systems and the appearance of qualitatively new types of armaments. The second is the searching for ways of further changes in the structure of the

armed forces, of the correlation of the branches of the services, of the means of attack and defense. The third is the determination of future tasks, which are directed towards raising the combat readiness of the troops to correspond with the nature of future war. The resolution of these tasks are the theoretical pre-conditions for the long-range planning for the development of the armed forces.[57]

In such forecasting, Soviet military analysts emphasize the need for a high correlation between military science and the natural sciences. As Colonel General Shavrov noted in his lecture on military strategy to the students at the Voroshilov Academy of the General Staff in 1973:

> Military strategy explains, in theory, the direction of development and future trends in armaments and combat equipment. [It] prepares the necessary recommendations about weapons systems determined by the development of science and technology and the economic capabilities of the nation, the missions of the Armed Forces in war, and the need to establish military and technological superiority over the potential enemy.[58]

In the past, Soviet officers have seen military science developing new requirements from the experience of military art and then counting upon a research and development process following the lines "from military affairs to science and from science to practical application." Now, however, the pace of scientific-technical development has assumed such proportions that a new relationship is required. That relationship has been described by V. M. Bondarenko, one of the Soviet Union's leading authorities in the application of cybernetics to problems of troop control, in the following terms:

> . . . from science to military affairs. This has become possible because modern science is able to find fundamentally new paths of developing military affairs, not directly growing out of traditional forms of its existence. To accomplish this with the help of scientific-research institutes and design bureaus is impossible. We need the effort of science in its totality, of the nation's various scientific-research organizations.[59]

The issue is not about the military budget or even guns or butter, but the question of whether the Soviet Union will attempt to maintain military capabilities into the next century that would retain both deterrence and war-fighting capabilities. The impact of the answer to that question will be felt in successive five-year plans. Domestic reform and economic rejuvenation in this case are the foundations of future military power. It is a question of restating national economic objectives so that socialism and its defenders can reap the full benefits of the information revolution. Given the nature of the Soviet military economy and the real fear of falling further and further behind the more dynamic economies of the West, this problem has rightly been defined by Abraham S. Becker as "Gorbachev's dilemma" as he assumed power in 1985.[60] This economic problem manifested itself in the Politburo's refusal to accept three successive variants of target data and resource allocations for the twelfth Five-Year Plan in 1985.[61]

Military spokesmen were very explicit about the linkage between the expansion of Soviet economic-technological potential and long-term military capabilities. Major General M. Yasiukov noted this linkage in 1985 when he wrote:

> In the matter of strengthening military-economic potential, it is difficult today to overestimate the Party's concern for the cardinal acceleration of scientific-technical progress. After all, the leading directions of scientific-technical progress—the further priority development of machine-building, particularly machine-tool building, robot technology, computer technology, instrument-making, and electronics—are simultaneously the basic catalysts of military-technical progress.[62]

He went on to stress the distinction between producing more of the same and gearing up to produce a new generation of unique weapons based on a radically different production system. On the eve of the XXVII Party Congress, he noted that the backbone of Soviet defense capabilities was the strength and vitality of the national economy and that the new challenge required more than the minor adjustment in the defense sector:

> The course to its accelerated development, intensification, and increasing efficiency objectively offer new potential for military building. The program of fundamental reconstruction of the national economy and of decisive acceleration of scientific-technical progress which has been worked out by the party, has its own defensive aspects. The priority development of machine-building, electronics, atomic industry, laser technology, information science and other areas affecting scientific-technical progress makes it possible to react promptly to the efforts of imperialist circles to break military-strategic parity to its advantage.[63]

Since 1986, the central problem is that, in spite of revised investment priorities and restructuring of the research and development system, the national economy has not responded favorably to the new requirements. Resolutions adopted at the XXIX Party Conference in 1988 state that "the processes of perestroika go contradictorily, complexly, difficultly in a confrontation between old and new." Finding a few positive tendencies in the economy, the Party had to admit that "the first results of the basic breakthrough in economic, social, and cultural development has not taken place." The source of the problem here was identified as a certain breaking mechanism that precluded a shift from extensive to intensive development. Neither the pace of scientific-technical progress nor the quality control of production had been improved. Added to the original problem were pressing consumer demands in the areas of housing and food production, which could no longer be ignored.[64] To borrow from Lenin, the Soviet Party elite has come to recognize that it cannot operate along traditional lines in the economic arena.

Some Soviet commentators have suggested that truly radical shifts in the economy, challenging a centrally planned economic order and the preeminence of the war economy, are now required. They have described such a course of general economic restructuring as the very rationale of Gorbachev's glasnost and perestroika. Academician N. N. Moiseev, a leader in Soviet systems analysis with close ties to the Soviet military, has been very pointed in his support for an interdisciplinary approach to the most fundamental problems affecting the Soviet Union's economy and society. In attacking the Soviet command economy and pleading for an expanded role for markets as a control mechanism to break down the "branch monpoly" that has stifled scientific-technical progress, Moiseev wrote:

> Otherwise it is impossible to secure economic progress or the economy's technological rearmament [*perevooruzhenie*]. Monopolism, production without competition, not only set up an inevitable dictatorship of the producer over the consumer and consequently an inevitable deficit, but also leads to stagnation, the degradation of society, for it [cannot] support the internal stimuli for the perfection of technology. And the introduction of the results of scientific-technical progress by command from above, without a need [for it] dictated by the very fact of the existence [of] this or that production cell is very difficult to do. The evidence of this is our postwar experience and our deep, unreduced technological backwardness in comparison with other developed countries.[65]

Moiseev favors the application of the target-planning method to direct the entire national economy, including the military economy (*voennaia ekonomika*). Such a forecasting method embraces the principles of balance, variability, integration, and validity, and seeks to optimize scientific-technical progress for the period under consideration. The Integrated Program of Scientific-Technical Progress of the USSR for the years 1986 to 2005 addresses science, technology, and production as subsystems of a single system.[66]

Soviet military analysts have begun to discuss the application of new methods to force planning and development. The methodology of program-target planning, which they freely acknowledge was taken from U.S. sources, has been applied to the planning of the development of the navy by Soviet naval analysts. This approach has, however, been acknowledged to be explicitly relevant to other branches of the armed forces and to the entire defense system. The method seeks to work out a balanced program of military development, taking into account "the objective law-governed patterns and mutual connections of armed struggle, politics, and the economy."[67]

The forecasting process begins with an evaluation of the state's military-political objectives and a prognosis of the development of international relations to establish "probable variants of the military-political situation in the period under consideration." It places central emphasis upon the assumed level of political confrontation as a major component of the "threat" and acknowledges that there are political as well as military means that can be employed to recast the threat environment during the forecasting period. In defining such variants, prudent forecasting takes into account the threat posing the greatest risk, the most probable risk, the widest range of potential uses, and the real capabilities of the economy to provide the required forces and means for armed struggle. The variant that most effectively takes into account all these factors is described by Soviet analysts as the "base variant."[68] This base variant guides the process of modeling force structure and modernization, taking into account the changing nature of the threat and providing an opportunity for adjustment in planning, based upon changes in the military-political situation, an assessment of the new achievements in science and technology, and the evident tendencies in the development of the armed forces of the probable opponent.[69]

Since Marshal Ogarkov's removal from his post as Chief of the General Staff in 1984, it has been commonplace to see a split between the military and civilian elites in the Soviet Union. Jeremy R. Azreal has made a strong case for seeing Ogarkov as a provocative spokesman for military views in a time of weak political leadership. In this view, Ogarkov's pressure for new military requirements with accompanying higher levels of funding violated one of the basic canons of being a good General Staff officer: to be more than you seem. Azreal sees the basic source of conflict as budgetary matters and concentrates upon a single dramatis persona in Marshal Ogarkov.[70]

Ogarkov's views reflected the deep concerns of the General Staff over the accelerating pace of scientific-technical innovation in military affairs, a pace that appeared to be assuming the character of another revolution in military affairs. They involved not just immediate budget items, but also forecasts regarding the likelihood of future war, the character of that war, and the need for fundamental changes in a manner by which the Soviet economy could sustain a scientific-technical base to support the military's modernization in the mid- and long-term. Ogarkov's writings reflected a fundamental distress with the basic proposition of the Brezhnev era: that the political-economic arrangements of "mature socialism" could resolve the problems of force development and force modernization by applying the same bureaucratic-command means that had been used in the past. What had come into question was what Soviet military analysts had called "the most universal historical achievement of developed socialism"—that is, "the military-strategic parity" between the United States and the Soviet Union.[71] To Ogarkov, the new challenge demanded a more innovative approach, reflecting the seriousness of the problem, especially in the face of the U.S. defense buildup. Strengthening Soviet defense capabilities was nothing less than "an objective, vital necessity."[72]

In fact, Ogarkov's removal was not a simple fall, but a lateral transfer to command the newly created post of Commander-in-Chief, Western TVD. Furthermore, his warnings about an emerging scientific-technical revolution in conventional warfare have persisted as a theme in the military writings of the General Staff. The dispute in the early 1980s may not have been budgetary, but profoundly political-economic instead, reflecting the General Staff's dissatisfaction with bureaucratic inertia and stagnation in dealing with the new dynamics of the arms race in a time of heightened tensions. During the last Brezhnev years, Ogarkov was certainly an open critic of the "action/reaction" approach as it affected the military and Soviet national security policy.

A careful reading of what the leaders of the Soviet General Staff have been writing since 1984 on the topic of future war and the scientific-technical revolution in military affairs makes quite clear the military's acceptance of Gorbachev's commitment to the twin pillars of perestroika: political initiatives to reduce the risks of war and de-escalate the military aspect of the East-West competition, and domestic economic rejuvenation and technological innovation to provide the basis for military power in the next century.

Colonel General M. A. Gareev, Deputy Chief of the Soviet General Staff and Chief of the Directorate for Military Science, has addressed the profound changes that were at work on the military-technical side of Soviet military doctrine when he wrote:

> Now we can speak about a turning point in the development of military science and military art. In general, a new qualitative leap in the development of military affairs, connected with the modernization of nuclear weapons and especially the appearance of new types of conventional weapons, is ripening. In connection with this [process] there has arisen the need to rethink the basic military-political and operational-strategic problems of the defense of the socialist Fatherland.[73]

Marshal Ogarkov has stressed the impact of a new generation of weapons "based on new physical principles" and called attention to the contribution of a new generation of conventional weapons to enhance warfighting capabilities, which he ascribes to U.S./NATO military doctrine, including AirLand Battle and FOFA:

> The conception proposes the surprise initiation of combat actions simultaneously by the air, naval, and ground forces with the extensive use of the latest conventional, high-accuracy means of armed struggle and of reconnaissance-strike complexes at great depth—with the objective of inflicting maximum losses on enemy troops, the achievement in the shortest possible time of an overwhelming superiority against him and a subsequent offensive for the seizure of his territory.[74]

While such a conception sounds very much like the Soviets' own "deep operations," there is a distinction to be made about the content of such operations, especially the effectiveness attributed to deep interdiction systems and the possibility of using fire to preempt enemy concentration and deployment of forces. The Soviets attribute to such systems a potential effectiveness approaching that of tactical nuclear weapons.[75]

Initial Period of War

In this context, Soviet authors have sought to address the problem of strategic defense in the initial period of war. Since the 1920s, the Soviet General Staff has carried out periodic reviews regarding the nature of the initial period of war.[76] These studies have addressed the transition from peace to war in a period of mounting threat; the role of mobilization, concentration, and deployment of forces; the role of air and naval operations; the impact of surprise, covert mobilization, and creeping up to war; and the influence of initial operations on the course and outcome of a conflict. These assessments have addressed both the political and military-technical aspects of the initial period of war. In this process, the Soviet General Staff has sought to draw lessons from the initial periods of World War I, World War II, the Great Patriotic War, and local wars.

From this past combat experience, the General Staff has sought the "law-governed patterns" (*zakonomernosti*) that have shaped and are now shaping the initial period of a future war. In 1985, Lieutenant General A. I. Evseev pointed out that the Soviet failure to draw appropriate conclusions regarding the initial period of a German-Soviet conflict prior to June 22, 1941, specifically the real leverage that an already-mobilized Wehrmacht would enjoy against a Red Army struggling to complete its mobilization, made a major contribution to German success in the initial period of the Great Patriotic War (June 22 to July 10, 1941). This advantage contributed to German successes throughout the first period of the war, until Stalingrad.

Evseev identifies the following trends affecting the initial period of war. First, there is a steady tendency toward the achievement of significant goals by the mass employment of the latest means of armed struggle. This applies to the employment of weapons systems (weapons of mass destruction and the latest conventional armaments) and to forms of combat. Second, an increasing area is affected by combat actions in the initial period of war. Third, there is a tendency toward the reduction of the length of time for the achievement of the most immediate strategic objectives during the initial period of war. Fourth, there is a tendency for the aggressor to seek to exploit surprise in all its forms to achieve his objectives. Evseev links surprise to *maskirovka* (concealment and deception) to include the use of disinformation that aims to misinform the enemy about his objectives while at the same time creating a psychological climate at home to justify his actions.[77] The result of these tendencies since World War II, Evseev stated, were quite clear:

> The most intense combat actions for the seizure of the initiative and the achievement of the most important strategic objectives have become the main content of the initial period of war. The changes of the way of entering into war has conditioned qualitative changes in the entire system of preparation of the country for war and above all in the order and time of the execution of strategic deployment of the armed forces. The urgent necessity has come into existence to conduct with the appearance of a real threat of attack the basic measures of preparation to frustrate aggression.[78]

Given this assessment of the nature of the initial period of war, Soviet military spokesmen have been very specific about how far the Soviets are currently willing to go toward embracing "defensive defense." It turns out not to be very far. Soviet military doctrine continues to embrace both offense and defense. That is to say, Soviet military doctrine accepts the need to stop an attacker and then recognizes the offense as the means by which war is terminated. Minister of Defense D. T. Yazov has stated:

> Soviet military doctrine looks upon *defense* in quality as the basic type of military actions in the repulse of aggression. It must be reliable and steadfast, stubborn and active, calculated to stop the enemy offensive, to drain it, to prevent loss of territory, to strive for the destruction of the invading enemy groupings.
> However, it is impossible to destroy the aggressor by defense alone. Therefore, after the repulse of the attack troops and naval forces must be able to mount a *decisive offensive*. The transition to this takes the form of a counteroffensive, which it will be necessary to conduct in a difficult and tense situation of confrontation with a well-armed enemy.[79]

While Yazov's theme is one of continuity in form, other Soviet authors are stressing radical changes in the content of military art. They see the combination of the application of new means, including automated systems of troop control, with new types of high-accuracy, deep-strike weapons systems as working a new revolution in military affairs. This revolution is rapidly and continuously recasting the relationship between the weapons and forms and means of military action. Military art, encompassing strategy, operational art, and tactics, is undergoing radical change.

As evidence, Soviet General Staff officers point to a changing relationship among fire, maneuver, and shock at all three levels. However, the same authors see the dominant trend in the development of military art as confirming the predominance of the offense:

> An important law-governed pattern of the evolution of military art is that the most active and decisive means of military action are developed in the first place. Preference is given to the offensive, directed toward the complete defeat and destruction of the enemy.[80]

The continuing dominance of the offense has taken the form of increasing capabilities for the maneuver of forces and means over ever-increasing areas. The key point in modern operations is to apply in continental and oceanic theaters of military actions the "further development of the theory of deep operations and the tactics of deep battle." Soviet authors emphasize the need to develop the means of maneuver by fire that will permit the most effective combination of fire, maneuver, and shock to be applied throughout the depth of the defense. "The principle of massing of the basic forces at the decisive place and at the decisive moment not only has not lost its significance, but has taken on a new qualitative content. The main [point] in this now is the massing of fire."[81]

Implications for Arms Control

The Soviet General Staff understands full well that the national economy under current conditions is not in any position to meet this "qualitative leap" that the Soviets assert is reshaping every aspect of military art. Indeed, Soviet authors acknowledge only three such leaps: the introduction of firearms, the industrialization of warfare, and the introduction of "nuclear-rocket weapons and other latest means of armed struggles." The central features of this latest qualitative leap in military affairs are its universal impact and the quickening pace of weapons introduction and obsolescence, and the increasing costs of new weapons systems. It would be equally dangerous for the USSR both to fall behind in this area and to have a more wealthy opponent seize the technological initiative and exploit it to exhaust the USSR by forcing it continually counter his weapons development.[82] The shift must be away from past quantitative indicators of military power, such as tank-heavy forces, to investment in new qualitative means.

There is no evidence that the Soviet General Staff or the intelligence organs have any quarrel with the Communist Party's assessment of the low probability of a major war in the near future. Nor is there any great Party-military dichotomy over the emphasis in the gains to be made by political-military accommodation in the European context. Furthermore, the Soviet General Staff's own analysis of the law-governed trends affecting the current revolution in military affairs makes compelling the argument for a breathing space and a restructuring of the national economy to meet the future needs of national defense. While there is certainly "ordered ferment," to use John Erickson's term to describe such discussions, it would be very wrong to see the current situation as one pitting military hawks against civilian doves. There is, of course, considerable bureaucratic inertia within the Soviet military system. Some senior military scientists associated with the General Staff, including General M. A. Gareev, have been criticized by their fellow Party members for being slow to respond to the demands of the new era.[83] Moreover, profound changes in Soviet force structure, force posture, and military art will take considerable time. By their very nature, such changes in capabilities will be ambiguous.

Given this revolution in conventional military affairs, absolute reductions in obsolescent military technologies, such as main battle tanks and conventional towed tube artillery, are likely. Meanwhile, lighter, more sophisticated armored fighting vehicles; attack helicopters; long-range, precision-guided weapons; and self-propelled artillery will be acquired. New force structure concepts (the combined arms battalions, brigade and corps innovations) may create greater diversity in Soviet force structure and permit fewer overall combat formations to conduct more effective tactical and operational maneuvers on the emerging "unconventional" conventional battlefield.[84]

To understand the political content of the current situation, the outsider could do worse than listen to the current Soviet leadership's pronouncements and their amplifications from the Soviet analysts. In his UN speech of December 7, 1988, Gorbachev presented a series of unilateral Soviet steps to reduce its armed forces by 500,000 men; cut back its armor, artillery, and attack aviation deployed in Eastern Europe; remove air assault and bridging assets from the forward area; and restructure Soviet units and formations so that they would be clearly defensive in organization. These moves were part of a political calculus designed to reduce the evident Soviet/WTO military threat and to create opportunities for political maneuver in Europe, not only in the area of military affairs and arms control, but across the spectrum of political, economic, ideological, social, and even ecological interaction.

On the military-technical side of military doctrine, the voice that matters in the end is that of the Politburo, but the General Staff shapes the terms of reference, the range of options, and the forecast of the content and nature of future war. While much of the discussion in conventional arms control talks will be about current force levels, the most important objective for the Soviets will be to manage the transition to new conventional systems, which promise to revolutionize ground, air, and naval combat. The key objectives will be to prevent the West both from seizing the technological initiative in military terms and from imposing excessive costs upon the Soviet national economy.

The Soviets are trying to fulfill their objectives by reducing the evident threat to Europe. Given the Soviet/WTO numerical advantages in manpower, tanks, and artillery, Gorbachev's unilateral reductions can test the water and create a climate for additional reductions, but these unilateral reductions will serve only as the prelude for a gradual force reduction package to be presented at the Conventional Stability Talks.[85]

Gorbachev's proposals for unilateral cuts of 500,000 troops by 1991, along with the reductions of 10,000 tanks, 8,500 artillery pieces, and 800 combat aircraft in European Russia and the removal of 5,000 tanks, 6 tank divisions, air assault troops, and river crossing troops from the groups of Soviet forces in the German Democratic Republic, Poland, and Czechoslovakia should be seen in these terms. The USSR does not intend to accept unilateral cuts as an end in and of themselves. Rather, such cuts set the stage for asymmetrical trade-offs in ground forces against NATO's advantages in strike aviation and theater naval forces. Prior to Gorbachev's UN speech, General Yazov had called for force cuts by both sides of 100,000 to 150,000 troops over a period of one or two years. While this proposal has been swept aside by events, Yazov's recommendation that subsequent reductions of ground and tactical air forces (1,000,000) should follow in the early 1990s suggests the scale of reductions that the Soviet leadership has in mind. The Soviets want to count combat-ready formations throughout the theater. They emphasize the existence of rough parity under present conditions.[86] Regarding weapons systems, the Soviets admit to a superiority in tanks and artillery, but offer trade-offs in naval and air systems. Soviet military analysts see naval and air systems as vital areas for the application of reconnaissance-strike complexes. They are at the heart of the future threat posed by "air-land" and "air-naval" operations, which the Soviets see as the long-range objective of both AirLand Battle and Maritime Strategy.[87]

Reducing numbers will not preclude technological modernization, force posture changes, or the articulation of new operational concepts, but arms control measures can slow that modernization and make the threat from long-range, precision-guided systems more manageable and less pressing while the Soviets mount their own responses. Indeed, Gorbachev's proclaimed defensive reorganization of Soviet divisions in Eastern Europe may well prove to be one of the most disputed issues in the entire force reduction package. Minister of Defense Yazov himself pointed to these concerns regarding conventional weapons modernization: "The development of conventional arms are reaching new heights in principle. Their power, accuracy, speed of employment, and range are growing."[88] A key Soviet objective in such arms control talks would be the elimination of or radical reduction in dual-capable systems (systems that can be used to deliver both nuclear and advanced conventional munitions).[89]

At the same time, the Soviets have extended arms control/confidence-building measures beyond Central Europe. Under the formula, "Atlantic to the Urals," the Soviets have brought into the calculation of NATO/Warsaw Pact forces those of France and Spain. The Soviets have also proposed to include U.S. POMCUS stocks in calculating the conventional correlation of forces. In addition, the Soviets have raised the issue of subtheater imbalances, linking it to U.S. concepts of horizontal escalation. Freezing U.S. and Soviet naval force levels in the Mediterranean has already been proposed. The Warsaw Pact has also proposed a 300-kilometer "demilitarized" zone in Central Europe, along with various nuclear/chemical-free zones. The Soviets have sought to extend confidence-building measures outside the European continent to include the Arctic and the Asian-Pacific region; the denuclearization of warships and the creation of specific regions, where no ASW operations would be conducted,[90] would be included in this proposal. The unilateral withdrawals of Soviet forces from Mongolia and Afghanistan, as well as the withdrawal of Vietnamese forces from Kampuchea, should be seen as major steps in an effort toward improved relations with the People's Republic of China. Such an improvement would not only radically recast the correlation of forces in the entire Asian-Pacific region, but it would also allow the Soviet Union to undertake a substantial redeployment or even reduction of forces.

In June 1988, A. A. Kokoshin and Lieutenant General V. V. Larionov addressed the problem of conventional force postures and their contribution to strategic stability.[91] Their article, which was an additional manifestation of the cooperation between academic analysts and military specialists for which Yakovlev had called, postulated four distinct force postures: The first variant was an offensive orientation under which both sides strive to conduct offensive operations from the initiation of hostilities and in which war termination is assumed to come with one side achieving strategic victory and imposing its terms upon the other. According to the authors, at the current high force levels and with the existing nuclear arsenals, such a posture invites the mounting of deep strikes against enemy second-echelon forces and reserves and raises the risk of uncontrolled escalation of such a conflict into global nuclear war.[92]

The second variant was a counteroffensive operational orientation, or Kursk paradigm, under which both sides deliberately reject initial offensive operations but still possess the means to mount a general counteroffensive. The objectives of such an orientation are to carry the war back into enemy territory, destroy enemy forces, and achieve war termination defined as victory in a given theater of military actions. The authors imply that the current shift in Soviet military doctrine has been toward such a posture. This implies that the intelligence systems of both sides would be able to provide sufficient information about enemy intentions and capabilities so as to negate any operational advantage that an attacker could derive from the element of surprise. This would represent nothing more or less than the acceptance of the viability of "premeditated defense" during the initial period of war.[93] Moreover, the authors note that such a posture still raised grave risks of escalation and presents numerous ambiguous aspects in force posture that could constitute offensive capabilities during the initial period of war. It is this variant that defensive sufficiency currently addresses, according to the authors.[94]

Kokoshin has stated that such a posture with regard to conventional forces is now viable because at the current time the capabilities for strategic defense by conventional means have negated offensive capabilities. However, this negation of the negation is historically conditioned, and by implication the further modernization of conventional forces carries with it the resurgence of offensive capabilites in the long run. Thus, the problem for conventional arms control and arms reduction demands both medium-range and long-term forecasts of the applicable law-governed patterns and a thorough examination of the "real dynamics of the development of new means of destruction, first of all, high-accuracy, long-range weapons." Such weapons hold out the prospect of overturning basic propositions of military art, again restoring to the offensive its dominance over the defense and thereby undermining strategic stability. "High-accuracy, long-range weapons, if they were procured in mass, will add additional instability. Their appearance will stimulate the development of new means and methods of armed struggle and make the arms race even more costly."[95]

Kokoshin also cited Colonel General Gareev's assertions about the defensive focus of Soviet operations and combat actions as "an answer . . . to the frequently raised in the West issue concerning Soviet 'operational maneuver groups.'" Such declarations in the face of the very ambiguous nature of a counteroffensive posture itself in no way lessen the very real threat posed by such deep maneuver capabilities in a theater-strategic operation, especially in the context of the prolonged and intense interest in such concepts on the part of the Soviet military. The basic issue for Western security cannot be answered by declarations of Soviet intent, but demand a prudent assessment of the potential capabilities of such forces in the initial period of a future war.

The third variant is one in which both sides are limited to mounting only an operational counterstroke. In this case, both sides possess sufficient means to defeat the attacking force and to retake lost territory, without carrying the war into enemy territory. Kokoshin and Larionov describe the Soviet-Mongolian offensive against the Kwantung Army at Khalkhin-Gol in August 1939 as such an operational counterstroke.[96] Similar limitations on offensive actions operated on a de facto basis during the final phase of the

Korean War after the intervention of the People's Liberation Army and the stabilization of the front line in the vicinity of the 38th Parallel (July 10, 1951, to June 27, 1953). That this third variant coincides with NATO's declared policy in case of aggression—to destroy the attacking force, restore the territorial integrity of the alliance member under attack, and then seek peace based upon the restoration of the status quo ante—goes unmentioned by the authors. They do, however, have some serious reservations about whether such limitation on further operations could function in a European conflict because of the disequilibrium in collateral damages inflicted upon the defenders' society.[97]

The fourth variant, which encompasses "defensive" defense, would involve mutually agreed-upon or mutually reciprocated actions leading to military postures, precluding the maintenance of forces capable of mounting offensive operations. This "strictly defensive variant" has no historical analogue, but represents a situation that could come into existence as a result of negotiations as the process of denuclearization moves ahead. This variant would limit high mobility to tactical level formations (battalion, regiment, or, at the most, division) and would require that both sides foreswear the maintenance of attack aviation, reconnaissance-strike complexes, large mobile formations, or strike forces, including tank and air-assault divisions. The remaining forces would not possess the ability to mount deep operations. "Consequently the concept of victory in this particular variant is sustained only at the tactical level. At the strategic and operational levels the concept of victory is excluded."[98]

Defensive defense would require the mutually satisfactory resolution of a host of political, military-technical, and doctrinal questions. The authors envision a multistage process that could begin with discussions among military and civilian specialists on both sides. These discussions would address qualitative and quantitative assessments of the offensive versus the defensive capabilities of major weapons systems, including, air, naval, and space strike assets in addition to ground forces. They would consider questions of military personnel and their training and preparation, including a shift of force structures to reduce standing regular cadre formations while expanding reserve components. The discussions would also seek to circumscribe the types of maneuvers and exercises that each side might conduct. Such negotiations would be unprecedented in their complexity.[99]

The path to "defensive" defense has been described by Kokoshin as a final objective at the end of a long process, which he directly associated with the denuclearization of war:

> One of the immediate tasks that today stands before military-political science [*voenno-politicheskaia nauka*] is this working out of the conditions of securing military-strategic stability in a non-nuclear world (and in the stages of movement toward that [condition], the

search for the limits of a reasonable sufficiency of military potentials, which could be determined on a mutual basis or unilaterally.[100]

The announcement of Soviet unilateral actions along these lines raises the question of whether such cuts contemplated by the Soviet leadership are ends in and of themselves, a manifestation of fiscal and economic necessity if perestroika is to have any chance of success. Two points are noteworthy here. First, in their comments about "defensive" defense, Kokoshin and Larionov called attention to Western European military specialists, especially those in the Federal Republic, who were proposing major unilateral steps in the transition to a strictly defensive operational-strategic variant on the basis that the Warsaw Pact would take corresponding actions. No unilateral process for the Soviet Union were proposed in the article itself.[101] Second, in response to NATO's call for unilateral actions to reduce the offensive capabilities of Soviet and Warsaw Pact forces deployed in Central Europe, Marshal S. Akhromeyev explicitly stated that conventional arms control and force reductions would have to be on a mutual basis. "To demand unilateral disarmament from the USSR is just a waste of time."[102] While it undercut his Chief of the General Staff, Gorbachev's announcement of unilateral cuts was timed to preempt NATO's discussion of theater-nuclear modernization.

Marshal Akhromeyev's resignation and replacement by Colonel General M. A. Moiseev suggests that Gorbachev's unilateral proposals were a matter of some debate and that Akhromeyev found himself in a situation in which he could not in good conscience oversee such reductions. Soviet spokesmen have made every effort to picture Akhromeyev's resignation as a matter of health and have stressed the fact that he will continue to serve as a senior military advisor to President Gorbachev.

In his capacity as a national security advisor to Gorbachev, Akhromeyev has again stated, "One should not think that the Soviet Union and its allies will completely unilaterally disarm while members of the North Atlantic Alliance watch without taking adequate measures themselves."[103]

Only now is the new role that the Soviet General Staff, under new and younger leadership, will play in Gorbachev's new national security apparatus becoming clear in its particulars. Recent articles by Minister of Defense Yazov, Chief of the General Staff Moiseyev, and former first Deputy Chief of the General Staff and current Chief of Staff of the Joint Forces of the Warsaw Treaty Organization, General of the Army V. N. Lobov make explicit the military-technical details of Gorbachev's unilateral cuts, the impact of force reductions, and the need to remake the Soviet Armed Forces into a high-quality force. It is not surprising that these authors have spoken of the new Party "line" (*ustanovka*) in these areas or that they have emphasized issues of morale, discipline, and training in a period of rapid change.

While conventional arms control and confidence-building measures have now emerged as key elements in East-West relations, Western policymakers must make evident the underlying reality. Soviet-U.S. political and ideological competition continues within the context of what Raymond Garthoff has labeled "competitive coexistence/controlled competition."[104] The objective remains to manage this ongoing political-ideological-military competition in such a fashion so as to enhance the security of the United States and its allies while reducing the risks of war. The Soviets have mounted a well-integrated and sophisticated campaign in an effort to reshape the international security system. Their objectives are to create such a system as will promote the goals and objectives of the Soviet Union. The demilitarization of the competition in Europe is a necessary prerequisite for perestroika's success. At the same time, this demilitarization is a form of ideological struggle.

> The most important tendency of the current era of ideological confrontation on the fundamental problem of modernity is closely interconnected with the above enumerated tendencies in the development of ideological struggle over the issues of war and at the same time would accumulate the action of all of them. Ideological struggle has entered its decisive stage [possibly, quite protracted], when the question [who will dominate whom (*kto kogo*)], which concept of war—Marxist-Leninist or bourgeois—will achieve the commanding positions in the consciousness of the majority of humanity, will be decided on a worldwide scale.[105] (Emphasis added.)

As an element for ideological struggle and a component part of the arms control process, military doctrine has become one arena of that competition. This is the challenge to be met. The West must recognize the interconnections linking political-ideological-military-economic aspects of the controlled competition. This will require a common commitment by NATO members to see arms control as one of several means to the end of enhanced security and reduced risks of war. It will demand a vigilant, realistic net assessment by the United States and its allies of conventional arms control and confidence-building proposals (both individually and collectively) as to their long-term contribution to Western security and to the improvement of strategic stability. This assessment must not only address the current balance of forces under conditions of Flexible Response, but it must also examine them in light of prospects for denuclearization and with regard to a revolution in military affairs, which is recasting general-purpose forces as it stimulates new tactical and operational concepts. Finally, this new challenge should call forth a Western response in the struggle of ideas, offering its vision of an international order that addresses the fear of nuclear war, reduces the burden of defense, promotes the evolution of the East-West competition toward nonmilitary avenues, deters aggression, and can terminate hostilities on terms favorable to the West should war be unleashed upon those free and sovereign states.

Notes

1. *Krasnaya zvezda*, December 8, 1988.

2. *Gambit* in this sense is used as a "first move" (*pervyy shag*) in chess, designed to sacrifice a minor piece or pieces to gain an advantage. However, it also carries with it the meaning of a move intended to direct a negotiating process. Gorbachev's *gambit* also carries with it the concept of *stratagem* as a clever move designed to achieve one's outcome—if not immediately, then over time. The chess context here is important because chess matches have three outcomes: victory, defeat, and draw. Grand masters play series of matches, or protracted contests; they do not expect and seldom achieve the utter annihilation of an opposing grand master.

3. The exception that proves the rule in this case is the ongoing Mutual Balanced Force Reduction Talks in Vienna, which have made little progress. Intra-allied and East-West asymmetries in force postures, force structures, and military art have frustrated efforts to enhance conventional stability by means of numerical force reductions.

4. "NSC 68" in: Thomas H. Etzold and John Lewis Gaddis, eds., *Containment: Documents on American Policy and Strategy, 1945–1950* (New York: Columbia University Press, 1978), p. 398.

5. Michael R. Gordon, "Talks on Conventional Arms to Open," *New York Times*, March 5, 1989, p. A10.

6. *Krasnaya zvezda*, December 8, 1988, p. 1, and December 15, 1988, p. 1.

7. "Akhromeyev to Serve as 'Top' Government Advisor," *TASS*, December 15, 1988, in FBIS-SOV-88-242 (December 16, 1988), p. 7.

8. *Krasnaya zvezda*, January 31, 1989, p. 2.

9. Sergei Gorshkov, ed., *Voyeno-morskoy flot: Rol', perspektivy razvitiya, ispol'zovanie* (Moscow: Voenizdat, 1988), pp. 43–89; V. N. Lobov, "Mirovomu okeanu—mir i stabil'nost'," *Krasnaya zvezda*, June 28, 1987, p. 3; and V. N. Lobov, "Kto stremitsya k prevoskhodstvu: O sootnoshenii voyenno-morskikh Sil SSSR i SShA v aziatsko-tikhookeanskom regione," *Krasnaya zvezda*, July 18, 1988, p. 3; and V. Tatarnikov, "'Resheniia v Vene vseliaiut nadezhdu," *Krasnaya zvezda*, February 4, 1989, p. 5.

For a detailed presentation of the Soviet perception of the threat posed by SLGMs and carrier aviation as part of U. S. Maritime Strategy in the Atlantic and Pacific TVDs during the initial period of war, see Iu. Lilin, "VMS SShA: Starye postulaty 'Novoi morskoi strategii," *Morskoy sbornik*, No. 2, February 1989, pp. 65–70.

10. *New York Times*, March 7, 1989, pp. A1, 6.

11. See note 10.

12. G. M. Sturua, "Bylo li neobkhodimo razvertyvaniye raket SS-20?" *SShA*, No. 12, December 1988, pp. 23–29; A. E. Bovin, "Inye varianty," *SShA*, No. 12, December 1988, pp. 29–32; L. S. Semeyko, "SS-20: Oshibka, no men'shaya chem mozhno bylo by dumat'," *SShA*, No. 12, December 1988, pp. 32–36; and S. A. Karaganov, "Eshche neskol'ko soobrazhenii," *SShA*, No. 12, December 1988, pp. 37–41.

13. Semeyko, note 12, p. 36.
14. Sturua, note 12; Bovin, note 12; Semeyko, note 12, pp. 32–37; and Karaganov, note 12.
15. Semeyko, note 12, p. 36.
16. John Borawski, "The Stockholm Conference on Confidence and Security Building Measures in Europe," *Arms Control*, VI, No. 2, September 1985, p. 115.
17. Jeffrey Simon, *Warsaw Pact Forces: Problems of Command and Control* (Boulder, CO: Westview, 1985), pp. 192–193.
18. On this topic, see the following works: C. S. Donnelly, "The Soviet Operational-Maneuver Group: A New Challenge for NATO," *Military Review*, LXIII, No. 3, March 1983, pp. 43–60; Philip A. Peterson and John G. Hines, "The Conventional Offensive in Soviet Theater Strategy," *Orbis*, XXVII, No. 3, Fall 1983, pp. 695–739; and David M. Glantz, *Deep Attack: The Soviet Conduct of Operational Manuever* (Ft. Leavenworth, KS: Soviet Army Studies Office, 1987).
19. Jacob W. Kipp, "Conventional Force Modernization and the Asymmetries of Military Doctrine: Historical Reflections on Air/Land Battle and the Operational Maneuver Group," in Carl G. Jacobsen, ed., *The Uncertain Course: New Weapons, Strategies, and Mind-Sets* (Oxford: Oxford University Press, 1987), pp. 150ff.
20. Peter Vigor, *Soviet Blitzkrieg Theory* (London: Macmillan, 1983), pp. 1ff.
21. For one such theory and paradigm of the arms race, see: Dieter Senghaas, *Ruestung und Militarismus* (Frankfurt/Main: Suhrkamp Verlag, 1972), pp. 361–364. Such analysis was heavily influenced by U.S. involvement in Vietnam.
22. Christoph Butterwegge and Heinz-Gerd Hofschen, eds., *Sozialdemokratie, Krieg und Frieden: Die Stellung der SPD zur Friedensfrage von den Anfaengen bis zur Gegenwart. Eine kommentierte Dokumentation* (Heilbronn: Distel Verlag, 1984), p. 381. See also Ronald Borkowski, "Defensive Militaerstrategie," in Werner Buckel et al., *Nachdenken statt Nachruesten: Karlsruher Wissenschaftler fuer den Frieden* (Karlsruhe, Federal Republic of Germany: Loeper Verlag, 1984), pp. 62–73. During this period in the United States, an academic school of deterrence theory, which emphasized the risks of the "cult of the offensive," emerged. Some scholars have examined the balance between offensive and defensive technologies as they emerged from the 1930s with the mechanization of warfare to confer hegemony at first on offensive systems (i. e., the armor-mechanized infantry, tactical air combination associated with blitzkrieg). John Mearsheimer has argued that since 1973 the balance between offensive and defensive systems has shifted toward the predominance of "defensive" technologies (i. e., precision-guided antitank systems over armor). Greater consideration of the role of military doctrine as a contributing factor to international stability and crisis management has also emerged as a central theme in recent scholarship. See: Jack Snyder, "Civil-Military Relations and the Cult of the Offensive," in Steven E. Miller, *Military Strategy and the Origins of the First World War* (Princeton: Princeton University Press, 1985), pp. 108–146; John J. Mearsheimer, *Conventional Deterrence* (Ithaca, NY: Cornell University Press, 1983), and Barry Posen, *The Sources of Military Doctrine: France, Britain, and Germany between the World Wars* (Ithaca, NY: Cornell University Press, 1984), pp. 1–33.
23. Alexander Yakovlev, *On the Edge of the Abyss: From Truman to*

Reagan, the Doctrines and Realities of the Nuclear Age (Moscow: Progress, 1985), p. 17.

24. Genrikh Trofimenko, *The U. S. Military Doctrine* (Moscow: Progress, 1986), p. 9.

25. The role of Soviet social scientists, natural scientists, and military specialists in the struggle against SDI has been conspicuous. To take only one example, A. A. Kokoshin, of the Institute for the Study of the United States and Canada, has played a prominent role. Kokoshin, whose major studies of the United States have addressed the role of forecasting in U.S. foreign policy, the role of information-analytical organs in the formation of U.S. foreign policy, and the role of domestic factors in shaping U.S. foreign policy in the early 1980s, was a major figure in the Soviet Scientists' Committee for the Defense of Peace Against Nuclear Threat for Disarmament and Peace, organized in May 1983 to conduct the ideological struggle against the Strategic Defense Initiative. Kokoshin took an active part in the Pugwash Conference devoted to SDI. He was one of the three editors of a work devoted to showing the technical nonfeasibility of the SDI concept applied to area defense, its limited application to enhanced protection against an enemy second-strike, and the negative impact upon deterrence and international security of a new round in the strategic arms race dominated by an interaction between offensive and defensive systems. See: Ye. Velikov, R. Sagdeyev, and A. Kokoshin, eds., *Weaponry in Space: The Dilemma of Security* (Moscow: Mir Publishers, 1986).

26. John Borawski, *From the Atlantic to the Urals: Negotiating Arms Control at the Stockholm Conference* (Washington: Pergamon-Brassey's International Defense Publishers, 1988), pp. 96–98, 107–114.

27. Kommunisticheskaia Partiia Sovetskogo Soiuza, *Materialy XXVII s'ezda Kommunistioheskoi Partii Sovetskogo Soiuza* (Moscow: Izdatel'stvo Politicheskoi Literatury, 1986), pp. 20–21, 67, 136, 177.

28. A. N. Yakovlev, "Dostizhenie kachestvenno novogo sostoianiia sovetskogo obshchestva i obshchestvennye nauki," *Vestnik Akademii Nauk SSSR*, No. 6, June 1987, p. 76.

29. A. N. Yakovlev, "Dostizhenie kachestvenno novogo sostoianiia sovetskogo obshchestva i obshchestvennye nauki," *Kommunist*, No. 8, May 1986, p. 18. Two recent works, one by an academic and the other by an officer of the General Staff, have addressed this problem of finding a common methodology for addressing the interweaving and merging of political and military problems in the nuclear space age. See V. Liashenko, "Net Nichego praktichne khoroshei metodologii," *Mezhdunarodnaia zhizn'*, No. 1, January 1988, p. 107; and M. A. Gareev, *Sovetskaia voennaia nauka* in: *Zashchita rodiny*, No. 11, November 1987.

30. In private conversations with foreigners, Gorbachev has reputedly stated that Rust's unexpected landing in Red Square enabled him to cashier twenty-eight general officers.

31. D. T. Yazov, "Perestroika v rabote voennykh kadrov," *Voenno-istoricheskii zhurnal*, No. 7, July 1987, p. 4.

32. Robert Legvold, "Gorbachev's New Approach to Conventional Arms Control," *Forum*, I, No. 1, January 1988, pp. 1–8; Gerhard Wettig, "Gorbatschows 'ausreichende Verteidigung' in der sowjetischen Sicherheitspolitik," *Berichte des Bundesinstituts fuer ostwissenschaftliche und internationale Studien*, No. 42, September 1987, pp. 1–28; Douglas Clarke, "The USSR's 'Defensive' Military Doctrine," *Radio Free Europe Research*, RAD Background Report/40 (East-West Relations), March 14, 1988, pp. 1–5; and

Albert L. Weeks, "Soviet Military Doctrine," *Global Affairs*, III, No. 1, Winter 1988, pp. 170–187.
33. K. Kozlov, "Sovetskaia voennaia doktrina," *Voennye znaniia*, No. 6, June 1986, p. 9.
34. Ole Diehl and Anton Krakau, "Die KRK-Initiativen des Warschauer Paktes im Lichte des sowjetischen Verstaendnisses von Paritaet und Defensivitaet," *Berichte des Bundesinstituts fuer ostwissenschaftliche und internationale Studien*, No. 45, 1988, pp. 21–30.
35. Sergei Akhromeyev, "The Doctrine of Averting War and Defending Peace and Socialism," *World Marxist Review*, XXX, No. 12, December 1987, pp. 40–41.
36. D. T. Yazov, *Na strazhe sotsializma i mira* (Moscow: Voenizdat, 1987), p. 23.
37. *Sovetskaia voennaia entsiklopediia* (Moscow: Voenizdat, 1976–1980), III, pp. 225–226.
38. *Voennyi entsiklopicheskii slovar'*, 2d Edition (Moscow: Voenizdat, 1986), p. 240.
39. Yazov, note 31.
40. Iu. Ia. Kirshin, V. M. Popov, and R. A. Savushkin, *Politicheskoe soderzhanie sovremennykh voin* (Moscow: Nauka, 1987), p. 253.
41. Legvold, note 32, p. 3.
42. V. Gulin and I. Kondyrev, "Oboronitel'naia napravlennost' sovetskoi voennoi doktriny," *Morskoi sbornik*, No. 2, February 1988, p. 12.
43. Iu. Ia. Kirshin, "Voennaia teoriia i effektivnost' ideologicheskoi bor'by po problemam voiny i mira," in M. M. Kir'ian et al., *Krakh blitskriga: urok militaristam i agressoram* (Moscow: Voenizdat, 1987), p. 91.
44. *Pravda*, February 17, 1987.
45. Kirshin, Popov, and Savushkin, note 40.
46. See: D. Proektor and A. Utkin, "Evropa i Klausevits," *Moskovskie vedomosti*, No. 17, April 26, 1987; B. Kanevsky and P. Shabardin, "K voprosu o sootnoshenii politiki, voiny i raketno-iadernoi katastrofy," *Mezhdunarodnaia zhizn'*, No. 10, October 1987, pp. 120–129; N. Grachev, "O raketno-iadernoi voine i ee posledstviiakh," No. 1, January 1988, pp. 102–105; V. Liashenko, "Net nichego praktichne khoroshei metodologii," *Mezhdunarodnaia zhizn'*, No. 1, January 1988, pp. 105–107; B. Tkachuk and V. Tumalar'ian, "Povod dlia razmyshlenii," *Mezhdunarodnaia zhizn'*, No. 1, January 1988, pp. 108–110; O. Bel'kov, "Pobedit' ne v voine, no voinu," *Mezhdunarodnaia zhizn'*, No. 1, January 1988, pp. 110–112; A. Dyrin and A. Savinkin, "Polnee uchutyvat' real'nosti iadernogo veka," *Mezhdunarodnaia zhizn'*, No. 1 (January 1988), pp. 112–115; and D. Proektor, "O politike, Klausevitse i pobede v iadernoi voine," *Mezhdunarodnaia zhizn'*, No. 4, April 1988, pp. 79–85.
47. Gulin and Kondyrev, note 42, p. 13.
48. S. A. Tiushkevich, *Voina i sovremennost'* (Moscow: Nauka, 1986), p. 117.
49. V. V. Zhurkin, S. A. Karaganov, and A. A. Kortunov, "Vyzovy besopastnosti—starye i novye," *Kommunist*, No. 1, January 1988, p. 43.
50. Ibid., p. 44.
51. Ibid.
52. Ibid., p. 46.
53. Ibid.
54. Ibid., pp. 48–49.
55. A. Vasil'ev and M. Gerasev, "Nekotorye itogi voenno-politicheskogo

kursa administratsii R. Reigana," *Mirovaia ekonomika i mezhdunarodnye otnosheniia*, No. 5, May 1988, pp. 43–56.

56. I. E. Shavrov and M. I. Galkin, *Metodologiia voenno-nauchnogo poznaniia* (Moscow: Voenizdat, 1977), p. 64.

57. Ibid., p. 67.

58. "Lectures from the Voroshilov General Staff Academy, Chapter One: Principles and Content of Military Strategy," *The Journal of Soviet Military Studies*, I, No. 1, April 1988, p. 32.

59. V. M. Bondarenko, "Nauka kak faktor ukrepleniia oboronosposobnosti strany," in A. S. Milovidov, *Voenno-teoreticheskoe nasledie V. I. Lenina i problemy sovremennoi voiny* (Moscow: Voenizdat, 1987), pp. 229–231.

60. Abraham S. Becker, *Ogarkov's Complaint and Gorbachev's Dilemma* (Santa Monica: Rand, 1987), p. 25.

61. Ed A. Hewett, "Gorbachev's Economic Strategy: A Preliminary Assessment," *Soviet Economy*, I, No. 4, October–December 1985, pp. 286–287.

62. M. Yasiukov, "Voennaia politika KPSS: Sushchnost', soderzhanie," *Kommunist vooruzhennykh sil*, No. 20, October 1985, p. 20.

63. M. Yasiukov, "Po glave voennogo stroitel'stva," *Krasnaia zvezda*, December 3, 1986, p. 2.

64. Kommunisticheskaia Partiia Sovetskogo Soiuza, *Materialy XIX Vsesoiuznoi konferentsii Kommunisticheskoi partii Sovetskogo Soiuza* (Moscow: Politizdat, 1988), p. 108.

65. N. Moiseev, "Moi predstavleniia o novom oblike sotsializma," *Kommunist*, No. 14, September 1988, pp. 21–22.

66. V. S. Bialkovskaia, *Programmno-tselevye metody v razvitii promyshelennosti* (Moscow: Ekonomika, 1983), pp. 15–22.

67. N. P. V'iunenko, B. N. Makeev, and V. D. Skugarev, *Voenno-morskoi flot: Rol' perspektivy razvitiia, ispol'zovaniia* (Moscow: Voenizdat, 1988), p. 66.

68. Ibid., pp. 66–69.

69. Ibid., p. 81.

70. Jeremy R. Azreal, *The Soviet Civilian Leadership and the Military High Command, 1976–1986* (Santa Monica: Rand, 1987), pp. 1ff.

71. Iu. Ia. Kirshin et al., *Sovetskie Vooruzhennye Sily v usloviiakh razvitogo sotsializma* (Moscow: Nauka, 1985), p. 127.

72. N. V. Ogarkov, *Istoriia uchit bditel'nosti* (Moscow: Voenizdat, 1985), p. 80.

73. M. A. Gareev, *M. V. Frunze—voennyi teoretik* (Moscow: Voenizdat, 1985), p. 438.

74. Ogarkov, note 72, p. 69.

75. A. A. Babakov, *Vooruzhennye Sily SSSR posle voiny (1945–1986 gg.): Istoriia stroitel'stva* (Moscow: Voenizdat, 1987), p. 241.

76. B. M. Shaposhnikov, *Mozg armii*, in B. M. Shaposhnikov, *Vospominaniia. Voenno-nauchnye trudy* (Moscow: Voenizdat, 1974), pp. 538ff; R. P. Eideman et al., "Plan zhurnala na 1929 g.," *Voina i revoliutsiia*, No. 12, December 1928, p. 2; V. K. Triandafillov, *Kharakter operatsii sovremennykh armii* (Moscow: Gosvoenizdat, 1929), pp. 51ff; V. Novitsky, "Bor'ba za kharakter budushchei voiny," *Voina i revoliutsiia*, No. 3, March 1929, pp. 3–13; A. Lapchinsky, "Deistvie aviatsii v nachal'nom periode voiny," *Voina i revoliutsiia*, No. 6, June 1929, pp. 55–66; Ia. Ia. Alksnis, "Nachal'nyi period voiny," *Voina i revoliutsiia*, No. 9, September 1929, pp.

3-22, and No. 10, 1929, pp. 3-15; V. Novitsky, "Deistviia aviatsii v nachal'nom periode voiny," *Voina i revoliutsiia*, No. 9, 1929, pp. 23-31; R. P. Eideman, "K voprosu o kharaktere nachal'nogo perioda voiny," *Voina i revoliutsiia*, No. 8, August 1931, pp. 3-12; E. Shilovsky, "Nachal'nyi period voiny," *Voina i revoliutsiia*, No. 9-10, September-October 1933, pp. 3-11; M. N. Tukhachevsky, "Kharakter pogranichnykh operatsii," in *Izbrannye proizvedeniia* (Moscow: Voenizdat, 1964), II, pp. 212-221; S. N. Krasil'nikov, "Nachal'nyi period budushchei voiny," *Pravda*, May 20, 1936, p. 2; G. Isserson, *Novye formy bor'by* (Moscow: Voenizdat, 1940); A. I. Starunin, "Operativnaia vnezapnost'," *Voennaia mysl'*, No. 3, March 1941, pp. 27-35; I. Rukhle, "O kharaktere nachal'nogo perioda v dvukh mirovykh voinakh," *Voenno-istoricheskii zhurnal*, No. 10, October 1959, pp. 3-13; A. Kolushkin and I. Bershadsky, "O nachal'nom periode minuvshei voiny (Otklik na stat'iu general-maiora Rukhle," *Voenno-istoricheskii zhurnal*, No. 8, August 1960, pp. 50-55; V. Mernov, "O soderzhanii nachal'nogo perioda mirovykh voin," *Voenno-istoricheskii zhurnal*, No. 9, September 1960, pp. 30-42; V. D. Sokolovsky, ed., *Voennaia strategiia* 1st, 2d, and 3d Editions (Moscow: Voenizdat, 1962, 1963, 1968); P. Korkodinov, "Fakty i mysli o nachal'nom periode Velikoi Otechestvennoi voiny," *Voenno-istoricheskii zhurnal*, No. 10, October 1965, pp. 26-34; V. Baskakov, "Ob osobennostiakh nachal'nogo perioda voiny," *Voenno-istoricheskii zhurnal*, No. 2, February 1966, pp. 29-34; S. V. Ivanov, ed., *Nachal'nyi period voiny (Po opytu kampanii i operatsii vtoroi mirovoi voiny)* (Moscow: Voenizdat, 1974); V. Matsulenko, "Nekotorye vyvody iz opyta nachal'nogo perioda Velikoi Otechestvennoi voiny," *Voenno-istoricheskii zhurnal*, No. 3, March 1984, pp. 35-43; A. I. Evseev, "O nekotorykh tendentsiiakh v izmenenii soderzhaniia i kharaktera nachal'nogo perioda voiny," *Voenno-istoricheskii zhurnal*, No. 11, October 1985, pp. 10-20; M. M. Kir'ian, *Problemy voennoi teorii v sovetskikh nauchno-spravochnykh izdaniiakh* (Moscow: Nauka, 1985), pp. 114-125; and M. M. Kir'ian, "Nachal'nyi period Velikoi Otechestvennoi voiny," *Voenno-istoricheskii zhurnal*, No. 6, June 1988, pp. 11-17.

77. A. I. Evseev, "O nekotorykh tendentsiiakh v izmenenii soderzhaniia i kharaktera nachal'nogo perioda voiny," *Voenno-istoricheskii zhurnal*, No. 11, October 1985, pp.10-19.

78. Ibid., p. 20.

79. Yazov, note 31, pp. 32-33.

80. V. V. Larionov et al., *Evoliutsiia voennogo iskusstva: Etapy, tendentsii, printsipy* (Moscow: Voenizdat, 1987), p. 232.

81. Ibid., p. 233.

82. V. Zhurkin, S. Karaganov, and A. Kortunov, "Razumnaia dostatochnost' ili kak razorvat' porochnyi krug," *Novoe vremia*, No. 40, 1987, pp. 13-15.

83. "Kursom obnovleniia," *Krasnaia zvezda*, December 28, 1988, p. 2.

84. David M. Glantz, "Force Structure: Meeting Contemporary Requirements," *Military Review*, Vol. LXVIII, No. 12, December 1988, pp. 58-70.

85. *New York Times*, December 8, 1988, p. 1.

86. *Krasnaia zvezda*, February 8, 1988, p. 5.

87. N. Perov, "Agressivnaia sushchnost' novykh kontseptsii SShA i NATO," *Zarubezhnoe voennoe obozrenie*, No. 2, February 1988, pp. 7-17.

88. Ibid.

89. A. A. Kokoshin and V. V. Larionov, "Protivostoianie sil obshchego naznacheniia v kontekste obespecheniia strategicheskoi stabil'nosti,"

Mirovaia ekonomika i mezhdunarodnaia otnosheniia, No. 6, June 1988, p. 24.

90. *Krasnaia zvezda*, July 14, 1988.
91. Kokoshin and Larionov, note 89, pp. 24–26.
92. Ibid.
93. It is noteworthy that the problems of strategic defense during the initial period of war (June 22 to July 10, 1941) and during the Battle of Kursk, including both defensive and counteroffensive phases (July to August 1943), were topics of papers delivered by General of the Army M. M. Kozlov, Chief of the Voroshilov Academy of the General Staff, at the conferences sponsored by the Ministry of Defense in 1981 and 1983 (*Akademiia General'nogo shtaba: Istoriia Voennoi ordenov Lenina i Suvorova I stepeni akademii General'nogo shtaba Vooruzhennykh Sil SSR imeni K. E. Voroshilova*, 2d Edition (Moscow: Voenizdat, 1987), p. 185. In 1985, Marshal Sergei Akhromeyev, Chief of the Soviet General Staff, authored an article on Kursk as the turning point in World War II; in that article, he discussed the continued relevance of the concepts "premeditated defense" and the counteroffense for Soviet military art (S. F. Akhromeyev, "Rol' Sovetskogo Soiuza i ego Vooruzhennykh Sil v dostizhenii korennogo pereloma vo vtoroi mirovoi voine i ego mezhdunarodnoe znachenie," *Voenno-istoricheskii zhurnal*, No. 2, February 1984, pp. 11–26). Major General Larionov, as a member of the faculty of the Academy, was intimately involved in this process of reassessing the evolution of military art during the war and in the postwar period.
94. Kokoshin and Larionov, note 89, p. 26; and A. A. Kokoshin and V. V. Larionov, "Kurskaia bitva v svete sovremennoi oboronitel'noi doktriny," *Mirovaia ekonomika i mezhdunarodnye otnosheniia*, No. 8, August 1987, pp. 32–41.
95. A. A. Kokoshin, "Razvitie voennogo dela i sokrashchenie vorushennykh sil i obychnykh vooruzhenii," *Mirovaia ekonomika i mezhdunarodnye otnosheniia*, No. 1, January 1988, p. 29.
96. Kokoshin and Larionov, note 89, pp. 27–28.
97. Ibid., p. 28.
98. Ibid.
99. Ibid., pp. 29–31.
100. Kokoshin, note 95.
101. Kokoshin and Larionov, note 89, p. 28.
102. S. Akhromeyev, "Chto kroetsia za briussel'skim zaiavleniem NATO," *Krasnaia zvezda*, March 20, 1988.
103. *Moscow News*, January 25, 1989.
104. Raymond L. Garthoff, *Detente and Confrontation: American-Soviet Relations from Nixon to Reagan* (Washington, D.C.: Brookings Institution, 1985), p. 1091.
105. Kirshin, Popov, and Savushkin, note 40, p. 310.

CHAPTER 6

NATO in a New Strategic Environment

EDWARD A. KOLODZIEJ

Marshal Ferdinand Foch, chief of Allied armies during World War I, reportedly opened his lectures at the French staff college with the question, "De quoi s'agit-il?" (What's the problem?). In other words, is NATO, including its existing force levels, weapons systems, and strategy, sustainable? If not, then what options are available to place NATO on a more sound footing that will effectively manage or resolve the strategic threats confronting the Western states and the United States?

The analysis that follows outlines and evaluates conflicting responses to these two questions. The first section evaluates the factors pressing for change or for the preservation of the status quo within NATO's strategic environment. It concludes that the forces of change are in the ascendancy and their eroding effects can be slowed but not arrested. Weakened is the strategic rationale on which NATO planning is based, and the political and economic underpinnings on which NATO's force posture depends.

The second section evaluates the strengths and weaknesses of three options open to the United States and NATO. The first is essentially predicated on the assumption that any change is likely to be worse for NATO and that adaptation to the forces eroding NATO's current posture should be resisted as much as possible. The second option seizes the initiative and attempts to shape forces for change in ways that affirm the current political division between East and West in Europe but place them on a security foundation that is less costly and, arguably, less risky than the current balance. A third option assumes an optimistic future in which the Soviet Union and its allies within the Warsaw Pact genuinely renounce the use of force to expand their influence in Europe and engage themselves in the construction of a new security and political framework that gradually effaces Europe's division. The security structure that would be developed to guarantee such a Europe would be created with the cooperation of the Soviet Union, and not in response to the threat that it posed to Western aims and interests.

A concluding section argues that the second option offers the best mix of shaping fundamental strategic and techno-economic forces within the international environment in ways favorable to the West. If the first option were adopted, the United States and the West risk having their security interests shaped by the Soviet Union. In contrast to option three, moreover, option two provides a means to moderate Soviet and Warsaw Pact behavior and to engage these states in the creation of new long-term strategic and diplomatic processes; these processes would depreciate reliance on force by both sides in resolving and managing differences without precipitately unraveling the security guarantees that have protected and promoted Western interests until now. The West should resist dismantling the existing system until it has confidence that a new system will work. A vigorous and visionary U.S. and NATO arms control negotiating stance, particularly with respect to the conventional arms talks in Vienna, offers a strategy calculated to test Soviet peaceful intentions and to preserve what has served well in the past with an openness to possibly fundamental and mutually advantageous change in East-West relations.

Why the Status Quo Will Not Hold

Pressures for Change

The reform movement within the Soviet Union and Eastern Europe and the fundamental political and socioeconomic changes within the West and the world environment, particularly related to the growing interdependence of states in the world economy and the increasing competitiveness of market forces, are eroding the strategic, economic, and political foundations on which current NATO forces and strategy rest.

A declining threat. The Soviet reform movement, propelled by glasnost and perestroika, diminishes the perceived and, conceivably, the real threat posed by the Soviet Union. Glasnost appears in many forms. Criticism of past failures and of Stalinist atrocities is officially condoned and encouraged. Soviet newspapers and journals are engaged in the debate over social and economic policy. Elections for some governmental officials have been introduced for the first time on a limited basis in order to permit a small but discernible measure of choice for Soviet citizens. Meanwhile, limited markets and a decentralization of economic operations have been instituted to make production and distribution more efficient and effective, with the effect of challenging the grip of the party and governmental bureaucracies on the economy. Even collectivized agriculture, a hallmark of the ruthless Stalinist pursuit of communist ideology, is under siege as a result of Gorbachev's leadership. The Soviet model of economic and political development no longer appears attractive to the Soviet Union, nor does its extension by force appear compelling to the Soviets themselves.

If reform is to succeed, Moscow must decrease spending on arms in order to release scarce resources for productive areas of the economy as a precondition for the stimulation of economic growth and technological development. In adjusting to this constraint, Moscow is pursuing an ambitious arms control and détente strategy with the West to relax the military requirements of its long-term security and foreign policy objectives, as well as to gain access to needed economic assistance from the West to propel its reform efforts.

Signs of détente are everywhere. The 1986 Communist Party document on nuclear disarmament is as much a manifesto for domestic reform as it is a diplomatic initiative to pressure the West to disarm. The unexpected Soviet withdrawal from Afghanistan, despite its damage to Soviet reliability as an ally and its staying power, appears to be in the service of domestic reform.[1] Shifts in Soviet policy toward Angola and the Middle East, where the interests of the superpowers are pitted against each other, provide reinforcing evidence of Moscow's need to cut losses and to assume a more conciliatory diplomatic stance. This stance seeks to enhance the Soviet Union's negotiating position within a global bargaining framework that relies less on force and threats than deft diplomacy. The Soviet Union's signing of the INF Treaty, which would not have been thought possible only a few years ago,[2] and its embrace of the triple-zero option reinforce its commitment to a new arms control and détente line. So does the speech that Party Secretary Mikhail Gorbachev gave to the United Nations in which he announced unilateral troop cuts of 500,000 military personnel and 5,000 tanks in Europe and Asia, as well as a corresponding redeployment of some forward-based forces to rear areas.

It will be difficult convincing NATO governments and their national populations that the Soviet threat presents a clear and present danger. Indeed, the argument may well be turned around. NATO forces and U.S. presence in Europe, as well as NATO reliance on nuclear deterrence and the possibility of first-use of these weapons, may be progressively viewed by European public opinion, particularly in West Germany, as the more imminent threat to European security interests than the Soviet Union. The almost-successful attack of the peace movement on INF deployments suggests the strength of this negative feeling regarding the presence of U.S. nuclear weapons in Europe. There is also some grounds for the belief that Moscow is turning necessity—the projection of a decreased threat through a strategy of détente and disarmament—into a virtue. Emerging Soviet arms control diplomacy alternately stimulates popular sentiment in the West to make concessions to Moscow while serving to rationalize these concessions by Western governmental officials sensitive to domestic pressures.

The Soviet antinuclear campaign is alluring. At a strategic level, it appeals to U.S. and European sentiments to decrease and even eliminate reliance on nuclear weapons. At the Reykjavik summit in 1986, even

President Reagan, who is associated with a hard line on defense, flirted with the possibility of dismantling superpower ICBMs. Many Europeans, particularly Germans, find the idea of a triple-zero option or some sort of nuclear-free zone in central Europe attractive possibilities.

Saying "no" to the Soviet "yes" to conventional and nuclear arms control and disarmament will become increasingly difficult to sustain among alliance governments and with home populations. If the West is forced to react to Soviet proposals because it has no common or coherent position, there is the risk that hasty concessions may be made to the disadvantage of Western security and diplomatic interests. Inaction or merely reaction to Soviet initiatives by the United States may also lead to unilateral moves by NATO states to reduce their contributions to NATO or to make concessions to the Soviet Union independently of their allies. The accumulation of Western concessions as a consequence of Western disarray could actually strengthen the Soviet Union and the Warsaw Pact at lower levels of forces while enabling the Soviet Union to cut military expenditures and gain increased access to the West for trade, investment, and know-how. Less may be more for the Soviet Union. The West, not the East, may be compelled to cut or redeploy its forces asymmetrically. Even if a principle of equality were invoked, the resulting balance might well favor the East in terms of geography and logistical support.

In short, barring the frustration of reform elements in the Soviet Union and the ouster of the Gorbachev regime, the West will not be able to rely on the Soviet threat to sustain, much less to spur, military spending and modernization. Nor can NATO use the Soviet danger to overcome the natural divisions of an alliance of fifteen states. It will have to adapt to a less-threatening environment in Europe that will require lower levels of forces and conceivably lower levels of military preparedness.

Changes within the West and the world environment. Quite apart from a decline in the real or perceived Soviet threat, there are forces operating within the West and the global environment that are also eroding the strategic, political, and economic support for NATO's current posture. Within this rubric, there are, first of all, the structural geopolitical differences between the United States and its European allies concerning the priority each attaches to conventional defense, nuclear deterrence, and détente. Since none of the countries wishes to be the field of battle in any superpower conflict and since their interests differ globally and regionally (such as in the Middle East), these conflicting priorities have been managed—not resolved—since the end of U.S. nuclear monopoly in the 1950s. The apparently receding Soviet threat sharpens differences again. The Europeans, with Germany in the forefront, prefer to find ways to accommodate Soviet interests and demands and to seize on Soviet peace overtures to relax tensions. If Britain and France, out of concern for their nuclear deterrents, are aligned with the United States against the denuclearization of NATO, they do not have the same policies toward conventional and tactical nuclear forces. Both will continue to favor nuclear forces over conventional ones when budgetary and strategic choices will have to be made. The result is lower Western conventional preparedness on the central front.

West Germany, of course, is the key problem, as it is the only revisionist state in the Western camp. The West German government still has a basic interest in relaxing tensions between East and West and, specifically, in fostering intra-German relations. German reunification of some sort now seems inevitable, but as the potential field of battle between the two armed blocs, Germany also has an acute interest in precluding the eruption of war and, simultaneously, in sharing the risk of war with its allies by their early commitment to battle and threatened escalation to nuclear levels as a deterrent to Soviet aggression.

Détente politics is particularly attractive to most Germans and parties, sustaining the solid gains made since the Berlin accords of 1971. These are particularly marked by closer economic and personal exchanges between the two Germanys. Détente is also best suited as a strategy to relax the division of Germany through pragmatic means, permitting increased governmental and personal contacts and economic and cultural exchange. Détente also lowers the fears among Germans across the political spectrum that Germany will serve as the battleground between East and West. It is not surprising, then, that under a conservative government, Bonn is no less interested in fostering accommodation with the East than its opponents on the Left. These have assumed the form of German interest in pursuing negotiations on a triple-zero option and in deferring the decision on Lance modernization until after the next general German elections.

Even if these geopolitical and domestic political pressures for accommodation with the Soviet Union were not present in Germany, NATO would still face the problem of finding substitutes for German soldiers now defending key sectors of NATO's forward positions. In the next decade, a major decline in the draftable age group in Germany will annually lead to shortfalls in excess of a 100,000 effectiveness. There is little interest among Germany's allies to fill in this gap with their own forces or to incur the increased costs associated with substitute measures. Cuts in Warsaw Pact forces through arms control accords appears to be an attractive alternative to efforts to sustain NATO's current conventional posture.

U.S. decline. The decline of relative U.S. economic power and competitiveness in world markets is gradually redefining long-term strategic threats to U.S. security and welfare. The popularity of Paul Kennedy's book, *The Rise and Fall of the Great Powers*,[3] which argues that big powers fall because they starve investment and economic growth—the engines of military power—suggests a gradual consensual realignment in U.S. elite opinion as to what are the major threats confronting the United States. A declining economic Soviet Union and a receding Soviet military threat—at least in perceived intention, if not in actual military capabilities—encourages a refocused interest on U.S. techno-economic growth and competitiveness. The bureaucratic war between the Departments of Commerce and Defense over the contract with Japan to collaborate in the development of an advanced fighter is symptomatic of this widening conception of external threat and of incentives to relax tensions in Europe and elsewhere in order to refocus resources and attention to the Asian economic challenge. For different but converging reasons, all of the major players in the European security environment have an interest in reducing their presence and expenditures there.

U.S. defense budget. In the short run, the United States confronts a massive federal deficit, and the Pentagon is expected to contribute its share to reducing this burden. President Bush's revision of the last Reagan defense budget provides neither for growth in the defense budget nor even for inflation. It has been estimated that currently authorized Pentagon programs, primarily for procurement and research and development, will be underfunded by $102 billion between fiscal year 1989 and fiscal year 1994, even if spending levels can keep pace with inflation. The shortfall is calculated at $236 billion if present levels are maintained, with no provision for growth or inflation.[4] One respected defense analyst estimates that by the end of the century, the Pentagon will be almost a trillion dollars in arrears if current spending levels are maintained.[5] Hard program choices regarding weapon systems, personnel levels, modernization, and preparedness and sustainability face the Pentagon. They all point to cutbacks and, correspondingly, to a reduction of NATO commitments.

As NATO's strategic, economic, and political supports weaken, its capabilities and preparedness will also inevitably erode. NATO confronts a future in which decreased numbers of troops will be available either in being or in reserve from almost all allied sources, including those of the United States. The preparedness and sustainability of these forces will also very likely decline unless heroic efforts are made to resist the temptation to spend proportionately more on procurement and research and development. Since the early 1980s, spending on support and readiness has grown at a rate that is one-third as rapid as for weapons modernization.[6]

The iron triangle of Congress, the military services, and weapons producers will impede efforts to change priorities, with the result that the armed forces, particularly the Army, risk being "hollowed out" in the service of these domestic interests. Moreover, as conventional forces decline, NATO and the United States will be compelled to rely more, not less, on nuclear deterrence and early use of nuclear weapons to prevent a conventional breakthrough by Warsaw Pact forces.

Adapting NATO to a New Strategic Environment

NATO has three options in responding to this new environment. First, it can do nothing and even attempt to resist secular decline until the trends in the world environment run their course and settle at a new equilibrium in support of NATO forces levels. This is an essentially passive or reactive strategy.

A second option would be for NATO to assume a leadership role in the Vienna conventional arms control talks in which it attempts to define the terms of the East-West military balance, as well as the security conditions vital to the protection of its collective interests. Such a stance would require not only a redefinition of NATO strategy, but also a clear statement by NATO of desirable Soviet military capabilities, deployments, and confidence-building and verification measures. Current negotiations appear predicated on static notions of the East-West military balance, with a provision for reductions on both sides, and on bean-counting exercises of categories of weapons on each side. However important these elements are to a successful arms control accord, they are secondary to some estimate by NATO of what it needs to defend its interests at presumably lower levels of current capability within a strategic framework acceptable to all of the allies, much like NATO's present forward posture has been the basis for planning since the 1950s. In other words, it will have to define what it needs to ensure against a surprise attack and against quick breakout by Soviet and Warsaw Pact forces if hostilities should erupt.

A final option would be to plan optimistically for a fundamental shift in Soviet military and foreign policy, leading to an end to the Cold War. Soviet notions of "reasonable sufficiency," "defensive defense," "asymmetrical cuts," and the military and economic interdependence of states would be accepted at face value, much like the line that German Foreign Minister Hans-Dietrich Genscher has suggested that the West adopt. In such a radically transformed setting, European security, which would include provision for the assurance of superpower interests, would be progressively defined through competitive cooperation between the East and West rather than by sustained military confrontation and arms races, the dominant pattern in Europe since World War II.

As the discussion below argues, the second option is the most persuasive immediate course. It puts the Soviet Union and the Warsaw Pact on the defensive while defining the needs of the West on its terms. It is also a strategy calculated to win domestic support and to promote allied cohesion since NATO would seize the initiative by common governmental agreement before presentation to the Soviet Union. The Soviet ability to manipulate divisions within the West as a consequence of the disparate reactions of Western capitals to Soviet proposals would be blunted. On the other hand, option three appears premature. Until there are deep cuts in offensive Soviet conventional and nuclear forces, it does not appear prudent to respond to Soviet overtures in the absence of reliable security guarantees that await hard bargaining at Vienna on conventional arms and at Geneva on superpower nuclear strategic forces.

A convincing case for option two can be best made by weighing the merits of each option in turn.

Option One: Do Nothing and Let Events Run Their Course

This option assumes that any change in NATO's posture will be for the worse. It relies on continued high allied support for NATO and the Atlantic Alliance. Public opinion polls in Europe and the United States, like those of the Chicago Council on Foreign Relations, continue to show widespread public confidence in the Western alliance.[7] Fear of neutralism, rising anti-Americanism, or what is derisively characterized as "Hollanditis" fever may be exaggerated. Until now, the discordant debate over trans-Atlantic burdensharing has been managed and its damaging effects contained. Note its absence in the presidential debates. The alleged harmful effects of U.S. budget deficits may also be alarmist since a rising GNP softens the adverse impact of the deficit, and military expenditures as a proportion of GNP are actually falling and well below levels during the Vietnam years.

The first option also assumes that Germany's political and strategic needs can be accommodated, short of a major change in NATO's strategy and force posture. Talk of a reversal of alliances or German pursuit of a mittel European strategy, which attempts to balance opponents in the East and West, does not appear to be borne out by current German policies. A former German Defense Minister now heads NATO, partly as a response to German sensitivities and allied concerns about wavering German support for NATO. The Western European Union has been revived as a European and German defense policy forum. Recent Franco-German military cooperation—joint military exercises, joint development of an assault helicopter, and the creation of a defense council—is aimed at anchoring Germany to the West. West German economic growth is tied inextricably to the European Community which, after 1992, promises to achieve an unprecedented degree of integration among the West European states, most of which are members of NATO. Furthermore, the United States, not the Soviet Union, is Germany's principal extra-European partner. The Soviet model is irrelevant to German interests. Similarly, West Germany's democratic institutions contrast with the authoritarian regimes of the East.

On a political level, option one assumes two complementary forms. On the one hand, it accepts Soviet reform efforts as genuine, but views them, if successful, as a greater long-term threat to the United States and the West than the present strategic balance. Reform is viewed as in the service of Soviet power, which has been frustrated by a strong and cohesive West.

Why, then, undermine the West's strength by improving the Soviet Union's techno-economic base on which its future military capabilities will be built? On the other hand, if the reform effort is a failure, so much the better for the West since those who will again be in the ascendancy will be those whose policies produced the current economic stagnation and the corruption of the nation's social fabric, fundamental weaknesses of the Soviet system that account for the West's current success.

At a military-strategic level, option one would have the West and the United States assume a fundamentally damage-control negotiating stance in conventional and strategic arms talks with the Soviet Union. As much of the West's military posture would be maintained in the face of the adverse trends sketched earlier, opportunities for future growth and modernization would be exploited at every turn, such as the initiatives associated with new weapons developments (smart munitions, for example). Meanwhile, in arms control negotiations, the long-term Soviet threat, based on a record of intransigence, would be emphasized. Even if one may have to concede that shifts in Soviet military doctrine and behavior, symbolized by the INF Treaty, no longer make such claims politically persuasive, guarantees against the possibility of the failure of the Gorbachev reforms would still be defined in sufficiently stiff terms to ensure the West's security interests if conventional and nuclear arms control accords are signed as a reaction to domestic and alliance political pressures.

Option Two: Assume a Leadership Role in Arms Control

Under this rubric, the secular changes emerging within NATO's security environment would be recognized as essentially irreversible. Rather than allow the vicissitudes of domestic and alliance politics, as well as Soviet initiative, to define the West's strategic interests and posture, NATO and the United States would assume a more ambitious arms control stance than they have until now. As a precondition, NATO would integrate, as equally important functions, strategic and arms control planning. Rather than negotiate from the perspective of force ratios and weapon system balances and deployments, NATO would develop a flexible strategy based on different East-West mixes of forces, all essentially implying lower levels than those existing on the central front.

These postures would define tolerable levels of East-West readiness that is primarily responsive to alliance needs, and not those of the Soviet Union. The West would be obliged to define what it meant by "reasonable sufficiency," "defensive defense," or asymmetrical cuts.[8] Specifically, the West should press the Eastern bloc to decrease its forces (especially those that shock and have offense characteristics, such as tanks, mobile armor, and artillery) and to redeploy them as far east as possible to impede their rapid mobilization for an attack on the West. What the West must prevent is surprise attack and rapid breakthrough. In addition, severe limits on conventional and tactical nuclear forces must be negotiated to preclude any unforeseen changes in current Soviet attitudes and interest in détente. The West will have to insist on appropriate verification and confidence-building measures, extending the recent progress achieved within the framework of the Conference on Security and Cooperation in Europe (CSCE) regarding military exercises and on the INF Treaty. If the Soviet Union and the Gorbachev regime are serious about glasnost and perestroika, the West is in a favorable position to define what level of Soviet military threat responds to its interests rather than have the Soviet Union define the West on its terms.

For arms control negotiations to be successful, however, the West will have to distinguish between its strategic needs and the underlying Soviet security interests in Eastern Europe. Under option two, the aim of arms control is stability, not a redefinition of inner–Warsaw Pact relations. So ambitious a negotiating agenda risks progress on arms control. Option three adopts this political transformation of Eastern Europe as its primary objective. An arms control posture goes well beyond the conservative position of the first option, but resists undermining the currently favorably arms control and détente framework by pushing for the rapid erosion of the Soviet empire—certainly not until a new security framework is in place in which both blocs have confidence. Such a fundamental transformation of Europe's security framework requires time and testing to ensure its durability before one can expect major and lasting changes in the Warsaw Pact and the internal political regimes of its members.

Under option two, the political outcomes of World War II would not be directly challenged. Europe would remain divided into two spheres of interest under the leadership of a superpower. At the same time, there would be no question that Soviet efforts to exclude the United States from Europe would be resisted. Germany would also remain divided. Each part would also be constrained from pursuing independent security and unilaterally defined security policies outside the alliance framework of which it is an integral part.

Simultaneous with the pursuit of a broad and ambitious arms control agenda with the East, NATO would also be obliged to press for greater integration of its military assets and for improved joint planning and consultation on strategic and arms control issues. In the absence of this double-pronged approach, the West risks splitting itself in bargaining with the Eastern bloc or weakening its negotiating position by internal misunderstanding and dissension. To strengthen the West under conditions of lower military capabilities, several reinforcing lines of initiative should be undertaken. First, Western European military cooperation should be encouraged within an alliance framework. Current efforts to revive the Western European Union and continuing bilateral talks and cooperative ventures between Europe's big three (West Germany, France, and the United Kingdom) should be considered welcome and long-overdue developments. Although these ties may not always match Pentagon preferences, a militarily strong Western Europe fosters long-term U.S. security interests as a buffer to and insurance against Soviet expansionism.

France has a fundamental security interest in anchoring Bonn to the West. The principal obstacles to greater bilateral cooperation remain France's attachment to national independence in nuclear and conventional planning and operations. Unless Paris relaxes its attachment to the principles of nonautomaticity and nonbelligerency in order to foster increased military cooperation between France and Germany as well as with France's other NATO allies, it risks being isolated in Europe while contributing to the eastern drift in German security and foreign policy arising from the attractions of détente politics. Bilateral planning between Paris and Bonn would not necessarily challenge French independence nor imply French submission to NATO command. Increased security ties between the two countries, already confirmed in the 1963 treaty, would essentially draw France into NATO through the back door. As suggested above, France under the Socialists and Gaullists has gradually relaxed the political and psychological prohibitions of cooperation of the de Gaulle period. If this trend can be continued, NATO would then be able to count on France for support in a crisis and, conceivably, it may be able to rely on France's military assets to bolster NATO's conventional capabilities at a time of diminished Western spending on defense.

French tactical forces present a thornier problem. They are currently distributed among the three armed services. The French Hades missile, which will replace the aging Pluton in the 1990s, still raises serious concerns in Germany. As part of France's deterrent planning, these so-called pre-strategic forces might well be used on German soil against attacking Warsaw Pact units. The absence of clear plans regarding the employment of these weapons may also lead to their precipitate use and the escalation of European conflict beyond the control of all combatants.

One approach to these dilemmas, aside from greater French-German conventional arms cooperation, would be increased British-French nuclear talks, which could possibly lead to greater coordination of their separate national modernization programs or even actual joint planning efforts. For different reasons, French-British reservations about going much further than political exchanges of viewpoints on nuclear policy are likely to remain formidable. The French government still refuses to consider any restriction on its nuclear forces, even the most tenuous arising from mere discussions. Prime Minister Margaret Thatcher has equally compelling motives to go slow. These alternately revolve around concerns regarding U.S. restrictions about sharing nuclear know-how that are tied to the Trident accord or about the tendency of the United States to dilute its commitment to European defense if European defense efforts should prove too successful. On the other hand, it would appear that Franco-American nuclear cooperation has been far more extensive than previously has been believed.[9]

U.S. and Franco-British cooperation can proceed on the common assumption that the British and French nuclear modernization programs will be completed in the 1990s. The Soviet Union has already accepted the principle of asymmetrical cuts and no longer poses an obstacle to these modernizations. Neither London nor Paris will consent to have their forces counted as part of the U.S. deterrent. Once both states are assured that their nuclear programs will not be challenged, a foundation will have been laid to coordinate their efforts as part of a new European security system. Superpower nuclear cuts would enhance the credibility of the British and French deterrents. There is also some grounds for the belief that the Socialist-dominated government is prepared to contemplate a closer merger than exists in doctrine and operations between French tactical and strategic forces. Such an evolution would narrow the gap between French and allied nuclear doctrine. Moreover, as long as U.S. troops remain on the European continent as hostage to the U.S. guarantee, the risk of conventional and nuclear confrontation with the Soviet Union will be shared. To this degree also, the West German singularization issue, real and apparent, will be addressed and German anxieties may then be lowered through the intensification of bilateral security arrangements within the alliance. Alliance nuclear policy can then become more flexible, responding to shared security concerns yet responsive to the inevitably different strategic and political and internal domestic needs of all partners.[10]

Option Three: Plan for a Fundamental Shift in Soviet Policy

This option goes well beyond the assumptions and objectives of option two. Arms control accords with the Soviet Union would be conceived not as ends in themselves to preserve the existing European order, but as a complement to a diplomatic offensive aimed at ending the division of Europe and Germany between two ideologically opposed blocs under the leadership of a superpower. Option three, if implemented, would strive for the democratization of East European regimes along Western pluralistic lines. These aims would be in the forefront of East-West negotiations. Their achievement would not be subordinated to the arms control arrangements outlined in option two. The INF Treaty would be viewed as but the first phase of negotiations, likely to be long and tough, to efface the differences between the two blocs in favor of the long-term Western preference for pluralistic political regimes, open market operations, and respect for private ownership of property and the means of production. This line of negotiation would eventually lead to the end of the military confrontation in the center of Europe and the return of national forces to home territories. It would also open the way for increased intra-German cooperation and, conceivably, to the unification of Germany

Several lines of reasoning argue for so ambitious a negotiating stance. First, it would end the Cold War on terms favorable to the West. Option two consolidates the Cold War solution for German expansion and legitimates the Soviet Union's special security interests over Eastern Europe. Option two also accepts Moscow's right to define the political regimes of this region in accord with its own political preferences. These outcomes fundamentally violate Western values and preferences, and are incompatible with Western notions of an international order that is both stable (not war prone) and legitimate.

On grounds of feasibility, a case can be made that there is a rare convergence of superpower interests to press reform in Eastern Europe. The Soviets themselves are ostensibly partisans of reform, at least with respect to those political constraints that currently inhibit their internal socioeconomic development. The Soviet Union has an interest in encouraging internal reform in Eastern Europe that is at least in step with those now underway in their own country. Moscow has already consented—even urged—political and economic reforms in Poland and Hungary. Both states are moving toward plural-party governments and the increasing adoption of market strategies to stimulate their economies. The visit of Soviet Communist Party Secretary Mikhail Gorbachev to East Germany and his subsequent announcement during a visit to Finland of the right of states to decide their domestic regimes, free from outside intervention, signal the abandonment of the Brezhnev doctrine. As the fall of the Berlin Wall and the opening of East German borders suggests, communist governments will be obliged to respond to internal demands for greater economic growth and political freedom. On the other hand, Moscow affirmed its commitment to an independent East Germany, setting limits merely as to how far the Soviet Union may be willing to go to permit full national independence in Eastern Europe. These limits can also be discerned in Moscow's resistance to demands from the Baltic states to secede from the USSR.

The liberalizing trends in Eastern Europe are nevertheless encouraging. If the European question can be resolved once and for all and if the Cold War can be essentially declared to be over, then the United States can address the serious economic problems posed by large governmental deficits and declining U.S. competitiveness abroad. Burdensharing problems between the United States and its Western European allies would be relaxed since the requirements of military preparedness would be dramatically lowered. In turn, both the United States and its allies would have incentive to compete for markets in the Soviet Union and Eastern Europe, drawing this region of the world into a global economic system based on liberal trading and investment principles.

The West is at a great advantage if the East-West confrontation shifts from military conflict to peaceful, but yet competitive, socioeconomic engagement. The attractiveness of the Stalinist model of economic development, based on centralized planning, rigid one-party control, and suffocating bureaucratic management of the economy, has faded on both sides of the European divide, in the developing world, and now in the Soviet Union. The combined GNP of the United States, Western Europe, and Japan is approximately three times that of the Soviet Union and the Warsaw bloc. Unless reforms are successful in the Soviet Union—and conceivably even if they are—the gap will continue to grow.

The outcome of this process would essentially return Europe to the vision of the Marshall Plan over the Truman doctrine. Imaginative implementation of the Marshall Plan vision, with the Soviet Union unexpectedly playing the role of demandeur, promises to be more effective in resolving the Cold War and transforming intra-European conflict than inflexible attachment to the militarized version containment. The Atlantic Alliance would be a part of the solution and not a part of the problem of resolving the Cold War. Socialist economies would be gradually liberalized and drawn into a Western capitalist global economy. European security would be built *with* the Soviet Union, and not against it.

Specifically, the Western and Eastern European states would resume their traditional cultural and economic intercourse, envisioned by the Helsinki process. In this long transition process, a greater Western European role in leading the Eastern European states to more openness guards against a precipitous challenge to Soviet hegemony that might arrest emerging détente. European economic help and influence, exercised deftly by Germany and France in assisting Spain and Portugal toward democracy and open market practices after decades of isolation, suggest that the European states and the European community are quite capable of furnishing an apt example and adequate resources to guide Eastern Europe through this transition period in a fashion that is less threatening than if it had been undertaken principally by the United States.

As recent events in Poland illustrate, with Solidarity's assumption of power and legitimacy in the political process, Eastern European groups opposed to the Soviet Union or Communist Party rule in their countries appear to be acutely aware of their effective margins of maneuverability in liberalizing their societies, short of prompting Soviet military intervention or the imposition of martial rule. One has a greater level of confidence than before, partly as a consequence of the harsh experience of the postwar period, that these states are capable of avoiding a return to the Cold War reflected in the crises of 1953 (East Germany), 1956 (Hungary), 1968 (Czechoslovakia), and Poland (1980s).

Objections to this ambitious line of negotiation are not negligible. First, it is by no means certain that the Gorbachev regime will stay in power or that the reform effort will succeed. At this writing, there are widespread reports of food shortages, rationing of basic commodities, and production breakdowns. Wildcat strikes, such as those of miners in Siberia (where food was in short supply and elemental items, like soap, unavailable), hint at the failure of the reform effort to meet the basic needs of the population, much less to establish a base for economic and technological growth. Meanwhile, conservative and chauvinistic groups, many still lodged in important governmental offices, object to cutbacks in military spending, arms control concessions to the West, and the growing national independence and socioeconomic reform in Eastern Europe.

Second, it is by no means certain that the nationalism of the Eastern European states can be contained, short of Soviet political and even military intervention to retain its hold on these states. The reforms instituted by the Gorbachev regime do not amount to an abandonment of the principle of Communist Party rule at home or to a preference for its application to Eastern Europe. Western notions of reform and those of the current Soviet leadership remain sharply at odds.

On the other hand, Western attempts to intervene in Soviet politics to foster reform have proven counterproductive. Examples include the Jackson-Vanek amendment, which prohibited extension of the most-favored-nation principle to the Soviet Union unless dissident and Jewish immigration were liberalized, as well as the human rights campaign of the Carter Administration. Both efforts failed to achieve their announced objectives. Each had the perverse effect of actually hardening Soviet-U.S. relations. This line of analysis does not imply a need to renounce U.S. and Western principles. Rather, it calls attention to the difficulties of applying these principles without considering their likely effect on eliciting favorable Soviet responses. It is premature to pressure the Soviet Union in a way that might be interpreted as an intolerable intervention in Soviet domestic affairs.

Moreover, there appears little room for optimism that the Soviets are willing to extend national independence to the Baltic republics (Latvia, Lithuania, and Estonia) or to contemplate soon the breakup of the Warsaw Pact. Centuries-old internal nationality problems would also be exacerbated if Moscow were to assume an indifferent posture to intrabloc relations within Eastern Europe. Socioeconomic reform and the political rehabilitation of Communist Party rule should not be equated with national independence in deciding alliance ties. Nor does it make sense today to press Western fortunes by deliberately utilizing these national sentiments as leverage in bargaining with Moscow. One can draw on these fissiparous tendencies without encouraging a backlash that sets back the progress in détente that has been achieved as a consequence of the internal reforms underway within the Soviet Union.

The significance of Western insistence in forcing reforms on the Soviet Union should not be exaggerated. It would appear that the example and attraction of the West's economic and social development (rather than simply its military preparedness) led to the decision of current Soviet leaders to embark on change. Option two would preserve a security framework responsive to Western security needs, and assure the Soviet Union that Communist rule would not be fundamentally undermined or that national sentiment in Eastern Europe would be manipulated by the West in ways threatening to Soviet security interests. The Soviets themselves should be permitted to redefine relations with their clients as a function of its reform needs. This trend, driven by internal Soviet concerns, has already resulted in positive benefits for the West and the rejection of the Brezhnev doctrine. The international climate favors progress in détente and resists the resorting to military threats and bombast in Eastern-Western diplomacy. To accelerate these forces for positive change beyond Moscow's control and, potentially, to risk a conservative backlash run counter to Western interests.

Conclusion

NATO is in transition. Systemic changes at work within the Eastern bloc, the Western camp, and the global political and economic environment will no longer sustain NATO forces at current levels. There appears nothing to arrest these trends. NATO will have to adapt to them. Resistance, paradoxically, may well undermine NATO's strength. Under these conditions, the Soviet Union, rather than the West, would define the West's long-term security needs. Public confidence in NATO strategy may erode if NATO does not respond to the opportunities for decreased tensions afforded by reformist-minded Soviet leaders, and if it does not adjust to the socioeconomic and demographic realities of domestic politics within the Western democracies. From these perspectives, option one does not appear to be a winning strategy that protects the West's security interests, that exploits Soviet interest in lowering military levels and political tensions in Europe and elsewhere, and that responds to internal pressures for a relaxation of the costs and risks of the Cold War and for increased welfare expenditures.

Conversely, option three appears premature. In its permissive and optimistic mode, it assumes Soviet acceptance of Western conceptions of political and economic reform. The evidence is still not conclusive that the authoritarian, one-party rule of the Communist Party has been broken throughout the Eastern bloc or in the Soviet Union. Nor is it clear that the Gorbachev regime will survive in the Soviet Union in the face of continued economic and social crisis or that the reform effort will be successful. In its aggressive mode, option three would attempt to intervene in Soviet and Eastern European domestic policies to deepen the crisis within the Soviet Union and in its empire. Such a strategy has not worked in the past. It also runs the risk that the gains made in arms control and détente under Gorbachev will be lost.

In this period of transition, option two has the most to recommend it. Unlike option one, it capitalizes on the forces for structural change within NATO and attempts to channel and define them on terms favorable to Western security interests and political aims. Lowered levels of military confrontation and threat are conceivably of mutual advantage for the East and West, and are not at the expense of either. It assumes Western initiative in defining a strategy and military posture that preclude surprise attack or quick breakout by Warsaw Pact forces. It does not leave to chance that lowered NATO and Warsaw Pact force levels on the central front as a result of negotiated reductions will necessarily spell greater Western security.

Meanwhile, under option two, the future is left open, not closed, as option one implies. Once both camps have experience in managing a security system that is less costly and threatening to each of them than the current regime, the confidence earned through this mutual testing process can be the basis to advance toward the more ambitious political goals of option three. These would efface the divisions of Europe and Germany and lead to a peaceful and stable settlement of the Cold War conflict. To move immediately to option three as an overriding priority, whether driven by optimistic or pessimistic assumptions of Soviet rule, would be to vault the preconditions needed for the successful realization of the aims of this option. Better the West and East learn to crawl, but with all deliberate speed, than to attempt to run when both have not yet learned to walk together.

Notes

1. The implications of reform on Soviet foreign and strategic behavior, with particular reference to the Third World, are examined extensively in Edward A. Kolodziej and Roger E. Kanet, eds., *The Limits of Soviet Power in the Developing World: Thermidor in the Revolutionary Struggle* (Baltimore, MD: Johns Hopkins University Press, 1989).

2. See, for example, Strobe Talbott, *Deadly Gambits* (New York: Vintage, 1985).

3. Paul Kennedy, *The Rise and Fall of the Great Powers* (New York: Random House, 1987).

4. Center on Budget and Policy Priorities, "The FY 1989 Defense Budget: Preliminary Analysis," February 22, 1989 (Washington, D.C.: Center on Budget and Policy Priorities).

5. William W. Kaufmann, "A Defense Agenda for Fiscal Years 1990–1994," in *Restructuring American Foreign Policy*, John D. Steinbruner, ed. (Washington, D.C.: Brookings Institution, 1989), p. 83.

6. Ibid., pp. 48–93.

7. Chicago Council on Foreign Relations, *American Public Opinion and U.S. Foreign Policy 1987* (Chicago: Chicago Council on Foreign Relations, 1987).

8. See recent issues of *International Affairs* (Moscow), such as Alexei Arbatov, "Parity and Reasonable Sufficiency," Vol. X, October 1988, pp. 75–97; and Alexei Izyumov and Andrei Kortunov, "The USSR in the Changing World," Vol. VIII, August 1988, pp. 46–56.

9. See, for example, Richard H. Ullman, "The Covert French Connection," *Foreign Policy*, No. 75, Summer 1989, pp. 3–33.

10. These points are elaborated in Edward A. Kolodziej, "British-French Nuclearization and European Denuclearization: Implications for U.S. Policy," in Philippe G. Le Prestre, ed., *French Security Policy in a Disarming World* (Boulder, CO: Lynne Rienner, 1989), pp. 105–146.

CHAPTER 7

Forces and Politics in Europe

ARTHUR CYR

The North Atlantic Treaty Organization (NATO), one of the oldest and most durable regional security pacts in history, is one of the most (if not the most) significant in the international system. The dominant role of the Soviet Union in the Warsaw Pact makes that formation less of a genuine *alliance*, a term that implies partnership and therefore something approximating equality (or at least reciprocity) of influence. NATO is certainly the most consequential multilateral pact for the United States. Hence, there is no surprise involved in observing that the character of the debate in this country over the *true* balance of forces between East and West has been long term. The best, and indeed only truly accurate, way to assess the balance of forces in Europe is to be as specific as possible in examining the factors that comprise military organization, and to be attentive to the wider political context. Military components, human and material, must be evaluated on their own and within the wider, more nebulous context of political and diplomatic atmosphere.[1]

In purely military terms, the NATO alliance is not in particular danger, and indeed there is some room for hope concerning the present state of affairs compared with earlier periods. The sense of crisis that animates the public and media debates on both sides of the Atlantic is not justified by the state of affairs between the two military alliances in purely military terms. However, in political terms, the picture at worst is mixed, though with features that must be altered if U.S. policy is to be successful. During much of the Reagan Administration, there were important reassuring elements in the balance between NATO and the Warsaw Pact; currently, however, important political gains have been scored and the initiative has been seized by the other side.[2]

The most important basic observation preliminary to analysis is the understanding that the NATO alliance has never been free of tensions of different sorts. Arguably, tension is positive insofar as it is one indication that the alliance is alive. In trying to understand NATO, it is useful to consider the past when viewing the present. Arguably also, the greatest political earthquake in the history of the alliance remains that which occurred more than three decades ago: the Suez crisis of 1956. This crisis drove the Americans into the arms of the Soviets in the United Nations and created the fundamental fissures between the United States and Britain, and France and Israel.[3]

Suez had a number of features that were particularly alarming in regard to the stability—and even the survival—of NATO. Three of the most important partners in the coalition were pitted against each another in very direct terms. The two European allies (Britain and France) were guilty of concealing an important planned military attack from Washington, with the hope that the United States would be forced to go along when confronted with a fait accompli. British and French collaboration with Israel in the planned attack meant the United States was also involved in crisis conflict with one of our most important allies outside the NATO area. Finally, and relatedly, the crisis in effect meant that a third area confrontation, beyond the boundaries of the regional alliance, was nevertheless threatening the viability of the organization. NATO partners have been able to avoid this sort of problem in the years since. The long-term U.S. military involvement in Indochina was generally unpopular in Europe, and led to the weakening of U.S. military units in that theater. However, the alliance was not directly undermined. Even in the case of Suez, wrenches in the domestic politics of Britain and France did not bring down the regional security pact.

The Kennedy years were perhaps the most turbulent for the NATO alliance, even while representing the high-water mark of pro-Atlanticist and pro–European Community sentiment within the United States. German Chancellor Konrad Adenauer's difficulty in relating to a younger generation in power in Washington, especially after his comfortable rapport with President Eisenhower, plus French President Charles de Gaulle's determined policy of independence within NATO and vis-à-vis Moscow, guaranteed that there would be serious friction. Yet the Kennedy Administration also can be faulted for a thrust in Atlantic area affairs that was fundamentally inconsistent. The President spoke of a partnership among Atlantic area nations that was at odds with Defense Secretary Robert McNamara's drive to centralize control of nuclear weapons in American hands. The image of cooperation among equals in the alliance structure was belied by the imagery of U.S. monopolization of the nuclear "cavalry" role while relegating the Europeans to being the conventional "infantry."[4]

The Multilateral Force (MLF) of mixed manned nuclear ships within the NATO structure, tolerated by President Kennedy and finally vetoed by President Johnson, symbolized the inconsistencies that seem to have been unavoidable for the foreign policy establishment of the time. The MLF was supported by both a State Department that was anxious to maintain rapport with allies through sharing nuclear capabilities and a Defense Department that was anxious to solidify U.S. control over those same weapons. Compared with these earlier Cold War years, more recent times have been relatively free of serious crises within the alliance.[5]

The earlier conflicts reflect more fundamental, inescapable dilemmas associated with the NATO alliance. They can be controlled and restrained, but not eliminated. First, the congruence of view between Europe and the United States in protecting the security of the former masks a fundamental divergence of sentiment resulting from the military dependence on the latter. The United States provides crucial nuclear guarantees as well as a substantial ground commitment in Europe. No matter how strong the formal commitment to NATO by all partners, there is no way that the Americans can escape feeling beleaguered and put upon, and no way that the Europeans can avoid being nervous over their comparative lack of control over their fate. The United States no longer exercises the exceptional economic leverage over Britain, France, or Western Europe as a whole that permitted the Eisenhower Administration to place extraordinary direct pressure on the partners engaged in the Suez operation in 1956. There was all the more reason, therefore, for basic tensions resulting from difference in position to grow.

Second, the growth in comparative economic strength of Western Europe in general, and the Federal Republic of Germany in particular, has brought indirect pressure to bear for change within the alliance. A set of relationships that grew out of a time of unprecedented economic dominance by the United States in the wake of the devastation of World War II has been remarkably durable, but increasingly questioned as that unique period in history recedes in time. The United States remains the largest, and in many respects still the most powerful, economy in the world. Compared with the late 1940s, however, when U.S. strength relative to other great powers surpassed even that of Britain in the nineteenth century, the sense of declining influence is inescapable. Americans are therefore particularly inclined to question whether old commitments and responsibilities are still sensible, just as Europeans argue simultaneously that greater strength implies greater influence and that they are already contributing more than enough directly (through military forces) and indirectly (through subsidy of the presence of U.S. forces in Europe) to maintain the strength and effectiveness of NATO.[6]

Most fundamentally, if a serious clash were possible even during the Eisenhower and Kennedy years, when the United States was exceptionally powerful, we should not be surprised to find conflict present also in a time of relative economic decline. Hence, the comparative passivity of the Reagan Administration in foreign policy terms through most of its tenure has been useful in avoiding clashes that would otherwise be inescapable. This point as prologue is important only because we so commonly overlook previous difficulties, preferring to focus on the past with a sort of optimistic, selective amnesia.

The Reagan Years

The Reagan Administration and, to date, the Bush Administration have been characterized by anomalous features. Defense policy assertiveness, at least during Reagan's first term, was married to a certain passivity, not only in arms control but in more general diplomatic policy areas. In purely military terms, the Reagan presidency was successful in both achieving the goal of significantly expanding defense spending and also, generally, though not completely, avoiding disruptions with European allies.

The overall approach of the Reagan Administration, activism in military spending and preparedness and basic passivity in political and diplomatic terms, has until recently been stabilizing for the alliance overall. First, the administration's priority emphasis on strengthening defense clearly was in tune with basic public sentiment in the United States, and was, overall, probably reassuring to Europe. Public opinion polls conducted by the Chicago Council on Foreign Relations in cooperation with the Gallup organization measured a massive net shift in public sentiment favoring increased defense spending in the late 1970s. The support for defense spending was linked to a clear perception that the United States was weaker and less influential than the Soviet Union. Rather than press public opinion and public policy in the direction of more defense, the actual political situation in the United States during the Reagan Administration was in fact much more dynamic, with the political leadership following clear, dramatically indicated public sentiment as much as leading a basic fresh policy initiative.[7]

Second, the administration was largely consistent, as well as effective, in policy. This was particularly important in the wake of the Carter Administration, which had been increasingly beleaguered with a reputation for both inconsistency and ineffectiveness. The Carter Administration is recent enough in time, and the press received by that President sufficiently negative, that attentive members of the public are conscious of the shortcomings of the late 1970s in a way that is not present when considering the 1950s or early 1960s. The controversy over the "neutron bomb," or enhanced radiation warhead, in the late 1970s is only one of several that might be cited. After urging West German Chancellor Helmut Schmidt to go out on a political limb by endorsing the U.S. desire to deploy this unusual, obviously controversial, weapon, Carter had second thoughts and reversed course. This solidified the hostility toward him on the part of German governmental leadership generally and Chancellor Schmidt in particular.[8]

By contrast, the Reagan Administration generally did not have to deal with serious intraalliance crises and had a lack of comprehensive ambitious goals of reform in European relations. Early in the administration, Secretary of State Alexander Haig was in constant battle with his senior colleagues in the White House and elsewhere, reflecting not just a desire to exert total control on foreign policy but also genuine policy differences. For instance, the Secretary went against others who were extremely critical of Western European plans in the early 1980s for a natural gas pipeline transmission arrangement with the Soviet Union. This is notable in part because, with few exceptions, U.S.-European relations were comparatively untroubled. After Haig's resignation and the succession of George Shultz to the post of Secretary, conflict with others on international issues waned.[9]

Third, there was flexibility in foreign policy matters in Washington that contributed to effective crisis management rather than exacerbation of tensions within the alliance. The Reagan Administration, and in particular the President, neatly reversed course on arms control policy, surprising and outflanking political and policy critics who had previously decried the lack of arms control initiatives. The reactions engendered by the 1986 Reykjavik summit disaster, in which the President's advocacy of the abolition of all nuclear weapons created both confusion and consternation within the alliance, was overshadowed in importance by the Intermediate-range Nuclear Forces Treaty that followed. The INF Treaty calls for the pull-out of weapons, specifically the 464 cruise missiles and 108 Pershing II missiles that had been designated for deployment in Europe for primarily political rather than military reasons. If the weapons were of genuine military consequence, the rationale for their addition to the European NATO arsenal would have been different. Specifically, they were a component of the NATO "two-track" decision of 1979, which declared that the alliance would simultaneously both strengthen arms capabilities and pursue energetic arms control initiatives. In symbolic terms, the new missiles were viewed mainly as a counterweight to the Soviet SS-20 mobile missiles, which at the time were causing alarm, alarm that increased seemingly in correlation with the relentless deployment of more warheads and launchers by the other side.

Several aspects of the INF Treaty are attractive. The Soviet decision to cut back approximately three times more warheads than the United States amounts to a rough form of equity, which recognized the substantial numerical superiority of the Warsaw Pact in certain selected military categories. For years, the NATO nations, led by the United States, have been urging arms reductions; the Soviets in technical terms have accommodated us. The weapons at issue on the Western side also have been particularly worrisome to the Soviets. While slow, the cruise missile is capable of the sort of complex prearranged flight plan that symbolizes the exceptional power of Western technology, always a sensitive issue to the other side. This missile is also generally comparable to the German V-1 rocket, which created extensive destruction and alarm in London during the closing months of World War II. The Pershing's exceptional accuracy and short flight time makes that weapon destabilizing in the sense that the other side would have a much enhanced incentive to strike first in a crisis.

Additionally, and much more broadly, the alliance was helped by the character of the regimes in the most important NATO nations. There have been politically conservative governments in power in London and Bonn, and the French socialists today are as reliable allies as were the European socialists of the 1950s. This national political stability has translated into a more fully integrated and more stable alliance. Both Prime Minister Margaret Thatcher of Britain and Chancellor Helmut Kohl of the Federal Republic of Germany are consistent supporters of the NATO alliance. The complexities that attend relations with Washington when the Labour Party of Britain or the Social Democratic Party of West Germany are in national power have been absent. The problems experienced historically by both of these "left" parties concerning maintenance of nuclear weapons linked to national soil, and acceptance of leadership by Washington, are avoided when conservative governments are in control.

Ironically, in the case of France, conservatives are the independents in alliance terms, dramatically under President Charles de Gaulle, and in a more muted fashion during the tenure of Giscard d'Estaing. French socialists today, as in the earlier era, have been much more reliable alliance partners, hostile to Moscow, more willing to cooperate in NATO operations, and recently taking the historic step of collaborating in a joint military brigade with the West Germans.

Finally, the Reagan Administration, an administration that was intellectually unassertive and unimaginative vis-à-vis NATO, completed the comparatively long tenure—in U.S. terms—of eight years. It was an administration that was not interested in major initiatives. This stance has been beneficial for the maintenance of stability, though not necessarily for the effectiveness of the alliance. Lack of conflict is not necessarily the same thing as solidarity. Yet efforts at drastic reform, even when well intentioned, can carry with them counterproductive consequences.

This point can be underscored by reference to the John Kennedy and Jimmy Carter presidential years. Both Presidents were foreign policy reformers, anxious to have an impact on the international system, including improvement of the state of relations in NATO. Nonetheless, the fact remains that when Kennedy and Carter attempted fresh policy departures for Western Europe, European leaders generally reacted negatively. Kennedy's emphasis on the emerging "united states" of Europe, American nuclear control, "flexible response," and the Multilateral Force was in a sense matched by Carter's efforts (through his national security advisor) conceptually to redefine the character of the East-West conflict, to consider novel new nuclear weapons systems, and to bring the allies along in tightly controlled boycotts of the Soviet Union (over the invasion of Afghanistan) and Iran. Both administrations ultimately were frustrated in their efforts to redefine international relations among the NATO partners.

On the whole, NATO operates with the most internal stability (although not necessarily most effectively in countering external challenge) in a policy environment that is inactive. The Reagan Administration, frequently criticized at home as well as abroad for its lack of assertiveness, was helpful to alliance stability for this very reason; regularity and predictability were the unappreciated consequences of Washington inertia. The style that would not have served during the challenging years of Harry Truman's tenure in the White House nevertheless did have some benefits, especially following on the turbulent, indeed in some respects revolutionary, international system of the 1960s and 1970s.

The Military Balance

The Reagan Administration was greatly assisted in an essentially passive diplomatic approach by the fact that the overall balance between the two blocs has been essentially stable and, in some respects, favorable to the West rather than the East. The media have masked the fact that the Warsaw Pact enjoys some essential superiority over the West in military terms. To be sure, the other side has built up a much-advertised advantage of approximately three-to-one in tanks, artillery, and certain other categories. Fortunately, this is neutralized by other considerations, which, again, tend to be more political than military in nature.

First, and probably most important fundamentally, is the fact that the NATO alliance does not need to maintain weaponry or manpower sufficient to balance the other side one-to-one across the board. Rather, what is required is enough to make war sufficiently unattractive so as to be deterred. In one fundamental sense, the presence of nuclear weapons, and the likelihood that any war involving the United States and the Soviet Union would become nuclear, operates as a powerful deterrent to a conventional or nuclear attack by either side. Evaluation of the conventional balance in the absence of attention to the nuclear equation, and more specifically to the reality that use of even a few nuclear weapons would be the most profound sort of human tragedy as well as diplomatic disaster, underscores why the stability of Europe has been maintained during the past forty years. This fundamental military reality pressing for stability is reinforced by a variety of more specific secondary considerations.[10]

Second, NATO's own forces profile is not particularly disadvantageous when the likely nature of any conventional war in Europe is considered. The best measure of the capacity of the alliance to counter Soviet tanks, for instance, is not the number of opposing tanks in the inventory of the West, either in total or in Europe, but rather the overall capacity of NATO to destroy Warsaw Pact tanks. Here, Alexander Haig during his years as SACEUR (Supreme Allied Commander, Europe) provided a special service by taking the initiative in importing thousands of antitank weapons, notably precision-guided munitions of the sort used effectively against Arab tanks in the 1973 Middle East war and North Vietnamese tanks in the spring 1972 offensive against South Vietnam. This weapons situation relates to the broader military consideration that the NATO alliance enjoys the advantage of not necessarily being required to conquer enemy territory—though, as argued below, that perspective is becoming increasingly significant in alliance planning—but rather to field forces sufficient to make believable the capacity to resist an offensive attack.

Third, in human terms, NATO has strong advantages in at least two senses. In any general war in Europe, reasonable people can assume that the alliance will hang together well, driven into unity by the very fact of hostile attack. Even France, already a more reliable ally under President François Mitterrand's leadership, surely would not become less so in actual combat. By contrast, the Soviet Union has to be concerned about the loyalty of a range of satellite forces, including, in particular, those from Poland, Hungary, Czechoslovakia, and East Germany, all states with geographically central locations on the Eastern front. Even more committed hard-line communist governments and military forces in the East would be given pause presumably by a war that did not directly involve defending the homeland, but rather assaulting the homelands of others.[11]

Additionally, there is in total a comparatively large amount of direct combat experience among the NATO officers and noncommissioned officers who provide the backbone of continuity in national military forces. Substantial numbers of career professional military men from the United States saw combat or combat-related action in Southeast Asia during the long Vietnam War. On a smaller scale, British and French officers and noncommissioned officers have received somewhat comparable experience off the coast of Argentina and in Africa, the Middle East, parts of Asia, and other corners of the world. The experience of Soviet forces since World War II has simply been less extensive, despite the relatively small numbers of troops (compared to the Americans in Southeast Asia) in Afghanistan during the years of direct support of the puppet government in Kabul.

Finally, the NATO alliance during General Bernard Rogers' tenure as SACEUR took a number of initiatives to try to move from a defensive to a more offensive mode in the event of military attack. The effort builds upon earlier such initiatives. General Haig emphasized organizational mechanisms and such factors as interoperability and standardization of weapons and equipment. Essentially, Rogers and his staff have engaged in much more comprehensive planning, which has updated the tenet that effective defense includes attention to the offensive. "Deep strike" has been one of several terms applied to a new emphasis on the use of precision-guided, advanced-technology weapons to break up Warsaw Pact attacks in the event of war in Europe and includes penetration into Eastern Europe to destroy crucial bridges, roads, airfields, supply depots, and troop concentrations. The approach includes a focus on brigade-level and smaller units, downplaying earlier stress on division-level control and use of firepower to hammer an enemy. The new doctrinal activity, closely linked to actual military plans, served to help revitalize NATO at a time when Washington's overall defense policies under Reagan were moving in different, less imaginative directions.[12]

One very important consideration, especially at a time when the U.S. Congress has reached the limit of support for expanded defense spending, is that the Rogers plan did not involve substantial new expenditures. As with Haig's earlier effort to counter Soviet tanks with U.S. antitank weapons, notably the TOW (Tube-launched, Optically-tracked, Wire-guided) missile, which are substantially less expensive than the tanks they are aimed to destroy, Rogers stressed doctrinal shifts that have not required enormous fresh spending on weapons or equipment. Precision-guided munitions have opened the door to the design and development of a range of new weapons that will be much less expensive than the weapons they can reliably destroy.

Present and Future Shocks

The creation and evolution of NATO over the past decades were based on the premise of a direct Soviet military threat emerging from the political and ideological confrontations between East and West. This extended to many parts of the globe. With the emergence of Gorbachev, glasnost, and perestroika, many changes are taking place that appear to be creating a more accommodating environment. In turn, these developments have important military implications for NATO and the United States.

In 1989 and 1990, historic changes were occurring in the Soviet Union and Eastern Europe. Czechoslovakia ousted its Communist government and Rumania and Bulgaria moved rapidly in that direction. The Hungarians shed the label of "People's Republic" and moved in the direction of a multiparty system. Earlier, the Polish system had moved to a multiparty structure and sought help from the West. As these changes and reforms accelerated, the government of the German Democratic Republic opened its borders to free travel for the first time since 1961. The massive exodus earlier of young East Germans through Hungary and Czechoslovakia undoubtedly made the closed borders between East and West Germany virtually irrelevant. With the opening of the border, the Berlin Wall also became irrelevant. What appeared to be as important was the German Democratic Republic's announcement that it would set into motion plans for free elections. The unraveling of the Eastern bloc was well on its way as the 1990s began.

The changes in Eastern Europe were triggered mainly by Gorbachev's efforts to reform the internal structure of the Soviet Union. Glasnost and perestroika have led to the emergence of nationalism in the Baltic states and more fiercely so in the Caucasus. Also, efforts were underway to modernize the Soviet military and reduce the defense burden on Soviet society. This was matched by the peace campaign waged by Gorbachev. In the aggregate, these efforts prompted many Europeans and Americans to see Gorbachev as a true reformer, with the Soviet Union no longer a serious and imminent military threat to the West. The INF Treaty concluded by Gorbachev and President Reagan earlier had set the stage for the momentum for arms control and a reduction of the military force structures throughout Europe.

The perceptions of a less-threatening Soviet Union and a Soviet leader seeking peace and accommodations struck a responsive chord in Europe and the United States. Not only have these perceptions changed the relationships between the East and West, but they have had a major impact on the strategic landscape. The premise upon which NATO was formed and shaped appears increasingly irrelevant in this new strategic environment. At the same time, there appeared to be a slow but sure convergence of the political and economic fortunes of Eastern and Western Europe, as well as Europe and the Soviet Union. With the planned European economic integration in 1992, this convergence appeared to be on course. In brief, European concern with the military threat was rapidly being replaced by the promise of economic and political benefits.

Yet, it is also clear that 1989 initiated a period of uncertainty regarding the political shape of Europe, uncertainty regarding the tenure of Gorbachev's leadership, and uncertainty about the political changes taking place in the Soviet Union. This uncertainty was reinforced by the transition of post–World War II Europe to a new era—whatever that might be. The dynamics of this new era extended into the security environment and military systems, with particular impact on NATO and the United States.

The shape of the strategic landscape has opened a public debate in the United States that is dominated by two contradictory themes. On the one hand, the apparent reduction of the Soviet military threat and the presumption that peace is at hand and that the Cold War has ended drive the movement to reduce military forces across Europe and in the United States. Burdensharing, the federal deficit, and a focus on domestic programs have convinced many in the United States that it is an opportune time to respond to the new European and Soviet environment. Another theme rests on the premise that the Soviet political and ideological rhetoric and changes have not been matched by real reductions in Soviet military capability or of Soviet involvement in the Third World. This view contends that this is not the time to reduce Western military strength. Regardless of the particular theme or its variations and the intensity of the public debate in the United States and Europe, it seems clear that important changes have taken place in Europe and the Soviet Union that have long-range security implications for NATO and the United States. These may require rethinking strategy and redesigning force structures, not only for Europe, but globally.

In a perceptive essay, "The End of History," Francis Fukuyama concludes, "The Soviet Union, then, is at a fork in the road: it can start down the path that was staked out by Western Europe forty-five years ago . . . or it can realize its own uniqueness and remain stuck in history."[13]

The principal challenge to the NATO alliance comes from political rather than military factors, and from the East rather than from the West. The Soviet Union possesses the policy and public relations initiative in Europe today. In Western Europe, especially West Germany, Soviet leader Mikhail Gorbachev enjoys a positive image, as does his country. In this milieu, the Soviet Union is given credit for such achievements as the INF Treaty. Indeed, the West was taken aback at the Soviet accommodation regarding asymmetrical reductions and on-site verification and inspection.

Gorbachev followed up this initiative with others. The most notable of these for the purposes of this discussion was the decision, dramatically announced in late 1988 at the General Assembly of the United Nations, to reduce troops, tanks, and artillery unilaterally in Eastern Europe. The announcement both underscored the sheer numerical advantage of the Soviet Union and highlighted the Soviet leader's capacity to maintain stage center. The speech text was as interesting for style and literary structure as for policy content. Gorbachev mentioned in passing that the Soviet Union does not claim to have a monopoly on or certain grasp of truth; this may be the first time since the Russian Revolution that a senior Soviet leader has talked this way. He quoted Ernest Hemingway's *For Whom the Bell Tolls*, a novel dealing with the Spanish Civil War, a great disaster for Soviet policy. He also managed to sound like President Eisenhower when talking about the need to work through the United Nations. In short, he turned in a masterful political performance. The speech was perhaps singular in international impact, but also symptomatic of broader public relations. It was a political success for Gorbachev.

The challenge provided by the Soviet leadership to NATO currently is overwhelmingly political rather than military, and psychological rather than substantive. Because of the nebulous and indirect nature of the threat, an appropriate response by the United States, and, more particularly, President Bush, is both urgent and difficult. To do nothing in these circumstances, or to assume that the apparently open and benign character of the Soviet leadership is not threatening, would abandon the field entirely to the other side.

There are several steps that President Bush and his administration can take to counter this threat. First, the President should be actively seen to be engaged in the foreign policy process. Regular press conferences, televised live, would be one device to establish a sense of momentum and public impact. Several major foreign policy addresses annually, designed and explicitly advertised as a mechanism to further the definition of U.S. foreign policy and assertion of U.S. international leadership, would be another.

Second, the United States can move to capture at least part of the stage in the play of dramatic gesture currently monopolized by the Soviet Union. We should reduce, if not abandon, the Strategic Defense Initiative (SDI) and take steps to bring about a new international regime outlawing chemical and biological weapons. Unilaterally destroying existing stocks of such weapons would be politically useful and, in reality, militarily inconsequential.

Third, we should highlight more strongly the human rights abuses by the Soviet Union and client states.

Fourth, we should press further the doctrinal and organizational issues implied by the Rogers' plan and other efforts of recent years to revitalize NATO. This means avoiding such politically explosive, ultimately counterproductive topics as the modernizaton of short-range missiles. On the other hand, we can try for further imaginative integrative steps along the lines of the joint French-German brigade. Opening the subject of a German SACEUR would be worthwhile as a device to reassure that particular NATO ally. The appointment of German Defense Minister Manfred Woerner as Secretary-General of NATO has already opened this subject implicitly.

Fifth, the approaching, much-discussed full economic integration of the European Community in 1992 provides many challenges, but also opportunities. Eastern Europe has special access to the European Community through East Germany, which is a de facto member of the economic organization through its special relationship with the Federal Republic of Germany. One principal initiative of the Gorbachev regime is greater decentralization of authority from Moscow. A more fully integrated, dynamic Western European regional economy should provide new opportunities to draw economic activity, and ultimately political interest, from the East.

As noted at the start, NATO is one of the oldest regional security pacts. Like many durable relationships, it is impressive that it has lasted so long. But one cannot expect it to remain the same over time, and one has to be reasonably attentive and not too neglectful if it is to survive. In short, George Bush may be the heir to Ronald Reagan, but he has neither the luck nor the opportunity for foreign policy leisure that his predecessor enjoyed.

Notes

1. The subject of present realities in the NATO alliance and its future directions is hardly a neglected one. The strongest ongoing studies of the alliance are almost certainly those carried out by the Brookings Institution in Washington and the International Institute for Strategic Studies (IISS) in London.

2. According to the IISS, the Warsaw Pact leads NATO (in the region of the Atlantic to the Urals) by 53,000 to 22,200 in main battle tanks, 36,000 to 10,600 artillery pieces, and 23,600 to 6,200 in wheeled and tracked infantry fighting vehicles with one cannon of at least 20mm caliber. See *The*

Military Balance 1988–1989 (London: The International Institute for Strategic Studies, 1988), p. 237.

3. One particularly readable as well as insightful analysis of misperceptions and miscalculations regarding Suez in 1956 is provided by Richard Neustadt, *Alliance Politics* (New York: Columbia University Press, 1970), especially Chapter 2.

4. For a durable critique of the approaches by Washington to reform Atlantic alliance relations during the 1960s is provided by Henry Kissinger: *The Troubled Partnership—A Re-appraisal of the Atlantic Alliance* (Garden City, NY: Anchor Books, Doubleday, 1965).

5. Catherine McArdle Kelleher, *Germany and the Politics of Nuclear Weapons* (New York and London: Columbia University Press, 1970), pp. 240ff. on the MLF.

6. One good discussion of the decline of the post–World War II system of international economic relations, with particular reference to the Atlantic area, is provided by Benjamin J. Cohen, "The Revolution in Atlantic Economic Relations: A Bargain Comes Unstuck," in Wolfram F. Hanreider, ed., *The United States and Western Europe* (Cambridge, MA: Winthrop, 1974), pp. 106–133.

7. John E. Rielly, ed., *American Public Opinion and U.S. Foreign Policy 1987* (The Chicago Council on Foreign Relations, 1987), especially Chapter 5.

8. Arthur Cyr, *U.S. Foreign Policy and European Security* (London and New York: Macmillan and St. Martin's, 1987), pp. 103ff.

9. Ibid., pp. 122ff.

10. The most comprehensive, elegant analysis of the strategic change wrought by nuclear weapons, with some special reference to Atlantic area relations, is provided by McGeorge Bundy, *Danger and Survival—Choices About the Bomb in the First Fifty Years* (New York: Random House, 1988), passim.

11. A stimulating discussion of the evolution of relations between Western and Eastern Europe is provided in Lincoln Gordon, ed., *Eroding Empire: Western Relations with Eastern Europe* (Washington D.C.: The Brookings Institution, 1987).

12. On the implications of new technologies and related strategies, one good analysis is provided by Andrew Pierre, Richard D. DeLaver, Francois L. Heisbourg, Andreas von Bulow, and General Sir Hugh Beach, *The Conventional Defense of Europe: New Technologies and New Strategies* (New York: Council on Foreign Relations, 1986).

13. Francis Fukuyama, "The End of History," *The National Interest*, No. 16, Summer 1989, p. 17.

CHAPTER 8

Force Structures: The United States and Europe in the Coming Decade

COL. DAVID E. SHAVER, U.S. Army

The purpose of this chapter is to stimulate ideas about force structuring the armies of NATO, including the U.S. Army, in this decade. A new U.S. administration, President Gorbachev's United Nations speech, the apparent resolution of several regional conflicts, dialogue between the United States and the Palestine Liberation Organization, conflict with Libya, and increasing U.S. domestic political pressure to reduce defense spending via allied burdensharing, arms control negotiations, base closures, and/or unilateral U.S. force reductions have produced an exceptional current world environment. The current situation presents a formidable challenge to the long-range defense planner "to determine how the strategic environment might look; identify U.S. national interests (and NATO interests); examine how the Army might best support those interests; and provide the Army leadership with the requisite options upon which to base a course of action."[1]

The Questions

Since force structuring is formulating the means to accomplish assigned tasks and execute plans in support of overall U.S. military strategic goals and objectives, we begin by asking basic questions concerning the future strategic environment for which the force structure will be required.

General Andrew Goodpaster, former Supreme Allied Commander, Europe, recently challenged the Regional Conflict Working Group of the Commission on Integrated Long-Term Strategy with these questions:[2]

1. What are our real objectives? What do we really want?
2. What concepts should guide us in pursuit of these objectives?
3. What means shall we (can we) employ to accomplish them?

What may be inferred from General Goodpaster's questions is that we need to widen the aperture of our world focus from concentrating almost exclusively on the Soviet threat to formulating new strategic concepts that respond to a variety of global threats. Of his three questions, the first one remains the most important and the most difficult to answer. In its report, *Supporting U.S. Strategy for Third World Conflict*, the Regional Conflict Working Group attempted to answer the first question:

> Survival as a free and independent nation with values and institutions, freedoms and security intact through healthy economic growth, a "threat-free" stable and secure world, continued growth of freedom, democratic institutions and free market economies (fair and open international trading system) and healthy and vigorous alliances.[3]

Stability, security, freedom, and economic growth mentioned by the Working Group seem straightforward, if somewhat oversimplified, objectives in a world in which traditional national/religious rivalries, increasing economic problems, and human rights deprivations persist. But are these the objectives we really seek in the near-term future—a future obscured by broiling arguments concerning Gorbachev's announced intentions versus the reality of existing Soviet military capabilities, arms control, U.S. domestic problems, burdensharing, trade protectionism and deficits, negative defense budget growth, and the perception of a diminishing Soviet threat?

> Most objectives are brief descriptions of aspirations that move people and organizations to exert effort cooperatively. Seldom are objectives concrete or precise. They are necessary but not sufficient guides to common effort. Containing the Soviets, deterring wars, and encouraging democratic tendencies all admit to at least two or more policies and strategies to achieve them. We should not pretend that identifying and rationalizing strategic objectives is any more than the beginning of a process of trying to know what we want of the world. Because strategic objectives are necessarily very broad in how they are stated, they leave ambiguous any sense of means to ends. Policy reduces the ambiguity but may not eliminate it, so it is important to be clear about policies, even more so than about objectives.[4]

In this chapter, the focus is not on seeking answers to General Goodpaster's three questions. Instead the focus is on assessing force structure options for the future that will comprise answers to all three questions taken as a package. By varying ends, ways, and means relative to national policies, the world and domestic U.S. environments, and national and alliance current and emerging resources and capabilities, force structure options will be developed for the long-range planner to assess that address today's pressing national security issues.

Option Development Methodology

There is only one way to formally address force planning—the military way.

> Force planning is complex and is characterized by an interrelated series of analyses to determine an affordable force. It begins by establishing the minimum risk force requirements and accepts resource and time constraints to develop the program, budget, and current forces. Throughout this process, the key consideration is how to execute successfully the national military strategy and to keep risk to a minimum. . . .[5] Force development begins with requirements for doctrine, training, organizations, and equipment derived from a concept of how-to-fight. These requirements initiate the three force development tasks: designing unit models, developing force structure, and documenting unit authorizations. . . . The resource-driven force structuring process determines the mix of units for a balanced force and how many units the Army can afford in our resource-constrained environment.[6]

The above excerpts from an Army War College text summarize what a difficult and complicated task force structuring really is. The long-range force structure planner must be aware of what other strategic planners foresee, as well as understand the predictions of those outside the military community, including academic strategic thinkers, budgeteers, and futurists. These external "visionaries" provide forecasts that stress the expected, rather than the unexpected or the catastrophic. They concentrate on relevant time periods and circumstances that can be extrapolated from the world as it is today.[7] Although these external sources all use some amount of intuition, most use logical steps to qualify their forecasts with recognized expert judgments or well-accepted assumptions.[8] The value of their contributions must be weighed by the long-range force structure planner in terms of the logic and credibility of the methodologies used.

A different methodology for developing tomorrow's force structure alternatives is offered here. The process includes the following:

1. Select the influences—"drivers" that strongly affect force structure decisions.
2. Build brief crisis scenarios within each "driver" that encompass the questions (ends, ways, and means).
3. Determine and integrate into the scenarios the issues most pertinent to the process.
4. Assess the impact of the issues upon the scenario.
5. Determine the size, composition, mission capability, and stationing variables for each force structure option.

"Drivers" strongly influence force structure decisions. For example, the military planning methodology for Army force structuring cruised along efficiently for several years without any changes in the Army's selected personnel strength ceiling of 781,000. While the rationale behind sustaining such a constant force over time is not the issue, one cannot help but be concerned by the personnel cuts in 1988. The Army was jolted by a reduction to a personnel ceiling of 772,000, brought about by congressional initiative and a responsive (to the White House) Army leadership. The defense budget process "drove" force structure to lower levels. This force structure reduction is not presented here as a case study, but as an example of an external influence that caused unplanned, internal force structuring decisions. There are a number of these influential "drivers" external to the military, and identifying them is the first step necessary in the author's option development methodology.

The Drivers

A primary assumption of this methodology is that future force structure decisions are made by external "drivers" (e.g., national policy, the environment, resources and capabilities) more so than by the formal military force structure planning process. Future force structuring is then a function of the "drivers." In this context, the following apply:

1. *National Policy* is a compilation of stated or implied policy objectives (deterrence, safeguards, assistance to friends, and reduction of Soviet influence); policy realities (the United States first, containment, freedom fighter support, human rights); and policy perceptions by others.
2. *The Environment* is framed by threat assessment (regional in structure), international economic issues (trade deficits, competition, interdependence, protectionism); international diplomacy (peace euphoria, arms control, United Nations initiatives); and psychosociological situations (human rights, drugs, failure of communism, movement to democracy).
3. *Resources* are a dominant force (in prioritization, defense vs domestic needs, deficit reduction, successful arms control response to unilateral Soviet withdrawal, and alliance burdensharing).
4. *Capabilities* include alternative choices of quantity vs quality, nuclear vs conventional; and an endless array of hi-tech advances in reconnaissance, target acquisition, accuracy, and lethality.

These "drivers" may operate independently or combine to influence force structuring decisions. A secondary assumption is that force structure can be further driven by crises in the functional areas presented above or, likewise, by the absence of crisis. As an example, witness how the U.S. military buildup from the "hollow Army" of yesterday was justified to some extent as a needed response to the Soviet invasion of Afghanistan and the Soviet conventional buildup. By varying the conditions of crisis or calm in the "drivers," plausible scenarios can be formulated that enable us to isolate a selected "driver" and determine its force structure impact.

The Issues

National security issues impact upon force structure decisions, but they are more problematic and pragmatic than drivers. Differing views between nations and NATO allies, between political factions, and between legislative and executive governmental bodies create issues that will be resolved or remain unresolved as we progress toward the next century. In this particular option development methodology, we address issues of allied burdensharing, perception of Soviet threat, national priorities, arms control, international trade, and zero to negative defense budget growth.

Burdensharing

The most complex issue facing the NATO alliance is burdensharing. It can be defined simply as sharing the risks, roles, and responsibilities among NATO partners on a "fair" basis, commensurate with each nation's ability to contribute. The issue is cyclic in nature and one that takes on added importance during periods of U.S. defense budget decline. At the heart of the issue is NATO's failure to define what constitutes a "fair share" of the alliance defense burden. Since neither the United States nor our NATO allies have been willing to systematically negotiate burdensharing standards that could be acceptable to all parties, we are deluged with a number of reports, commentaries, and articles on the subject from both sides of the Atlantic. Some highlights include the following:

1. *Report of the Defense Burdensharing Panel of the Committee on Armed Services.*[9] Called the Schroeder Report, it concludes that, based on the military expenditure percentage of Gross Domestic Product (GDP) figures, neither our NATO allies nor the Japanese are spending enough on defense and are instead still dependent upon the United States. It further suggests that since Europeans and the Japanese are world economic powers, they must break away from their regional perspectives and take a worldwide defense role.
2. *Fair Shares: Bearing the Burden of the NATO Alliance.*[10] A U.S. Defense Budget Office project, this report finds that the burdens of

the alliance are so complex that they cannot be measured by a single, simplistic formula, such as GDP figures.
3. *Pooling Allied and American Resources to Produce a Credible Collective Conventional Deterrent.*[11] Ambassador David M. Abshire calls for a rethinking of the NATO alliance by developing a new two-pillar treaty based upon U.S. nuclear deterrence.
4. *Report on Allied Contributions to the Common Defense.*[12] This annual Department of Defense report concludes that U.S. Allies contribute far more to defense than is normally recognized. The report also concludes that the alliance must do more to ensure Western security.

There is an entire cottage industry of writers contributing to the burdensharing debate. Whether this debate will be settled in time to influence force structuring decisions in the near future is doubtful, but if the issue were resolved, the results might have a dramatic impact upon U.S. and European force structure. If the burdensharing issue is not resolved, this, too, may impact on future force structures by increasing U.S. national pressure for a conventional arms control agreement and/or by increasing pressure for U.S. unilateral reductions, contributions to NATO, and/or NATO defense specialization that capitalizes on the expertise of specific NATO nations by assigning them alliance-wide responsibility for specific strategic, operational, or tactical roles and missions.[13]

Perception of the Soviet Threat

This issue is as important an issue as burdensharing and arms control. By *restricting* naval operations to near Soviet coastal waters; *hinting* at pulling out of Cam Ranh Bay; *announcing unilateral* force cuts at the United Nations; *continuing* to withdraw from Afghanistan; *encouraging* communist allies to disengage throughout the Third World; and *allowing* openness through his policies of glasnost and perestroika, Gorbachev has seized all of the "high ground" in the diplomatic arena. His political actions appear to many to raise the threshold of war.

> Since the United States and its major NATO alliance partners rely heavily on a threat-driven strategy to construct military budgets, the diminishing threat (perception) may logically lead to diminishing military budgets, which in turn lead to diminishing force structure, and the ever smaller budget spiral continues unabated as the threat continues to diminish.[14]

This issue may severely impact on U.S. and European force structures of the next decade. Yes, we will continue to be vigilant. Yes, we will caution others against irrational force structure reductions based upon Soviet policy announcements rather than completed policy implementation. But, how long can the United States sustain that position if the Soviets *do* everything they have stated they would, including implementing substantial reductions in their defense capabilities?

Although forecasting future events is problematical at best, it is important to identify strategic options available to Gorbachev. These include the withdrawal of short-range nuclear forces from Eastern Europe to the USSR in order to create a nuclear-free zone on the Soviet side of the "Iron Curtain" and prompt Western response in kind; the formal destruction of the Berlin Wall, but with measured constraint on East-West passage as a symbolic war-termination initiative to end the Cold War; and the formal abolishment of the Warsaw Treaty Organization to prompt NATO's demise and end U.S. involvement in Europe.

Plausible initiatives such as these are not studied or debated often within the U.S. military. We must "speak with one voice" on matters pertaining to national security, or at least censure discussion through document security classification procedures. But there are real, possible strategic initiatives that need to be explored, not only within the military, but in strategic think tanks, newspaper editorials, academic journals, and elsewhere to develop political strategies to retake the "high ground" of world diplomatic leadership in this decade.

National Priorities

National priorities in the United States, unlike those of European nations, do not seem to center on the "guns versus butter" debate. In the United States, Americans are blessed with strong special-interest groups that lobby long and hard for their domestic concerns and seem to fight among themselves for the market share of the "butter" budget. Most Americans and their elected representatives favor a strong national defense establishment. However, the public becomes highly critical of defense spending when cases of waste, fraud, corruption, and abuse occur, or when new weapon systems are exceedingly costly (the B-2 Bomber, for example). The current debate regarding defense expenditures focuses on high-cost, high-tech versus low-cost, low-tech approaches to national defense. Current circumstances would appear to dictate acceptance of zero to negative defense budget growth over the next several years in favor of increased domestic spending and deficit reduction. Advocates of high-cost, high-tech make a strong case that science and technology can replace costly force structure with costly, but more effective and more lethal weapon systems. Those who see this argument clearly propose that limited dollars be spent on hardware, such as aircraft carriers, submarines, strategic lift, and high-tech battlefield systems (e.g., ATACMS, TACIT RAINBOW, "competitive strategies" systems, and modern, survivable strategic missiles and bombers) because they perceive that time is the critical factor in mobilization, and there will not be enough of it to build these high-ticket items in the next war.

Those who favor low-cost, low-tech solutions see a different war tomorrow, one that will be fought in the deserts, jungles, and plains of Third World countries: low-intensity conflicts, special operations, and military assistance and training—conflicts that require soldiers and marines that are lightly but lethally equipped. These advocates are against force structure cuts as acceptable trade-offs for the high-cost, high-tech equipment.

This is not a zero-sum game. The result of debate will be a compromise that allows some level of both positions. The issue is who gets how much. Obviously, both defense arguments will impact force structure decisions, with still an outside chance that domestic priorities may severely reduce defense expenditure.

Arms Control

This complex issue has the potential of greatly influencing force structure decisions. Although negotiations at the strategic level in START seem to be the most important to the United States and its allies due to the importance of nuclear deterrence in NATO's doctrine of flexible response, conventional arms control negotiations may have a greater impact upon force structuring decisions.

At the crux of the conventional arms control issue is time. It has taken over a year to determine the wording and format for the conventional arms control talks in the recently concluded "mandate" phase. The talks will progress slowly through the "data exchange" phase to actual proposals and counterproposals. During the Mutual and Balanced Force Reductions (MBFR) talks, the data exchange between NATO and the Warsaw Pact took years to negotiate, and the MBFR talks have been ongoing for over fifteen years without reaching agreement. Although the Soviet negotiators in the new talks seem to be more flexible and results-motivated under Gorbachev's firm leadership, indications from the length of time it took to reach agreement on the mandate for the talks forecast a long process of tough, step-by-step negotiations with the Soviets and within NATO itself.

Conventional arms control is interrelated with other issues presented in this chapter. It is related directly to burdensharing because one of the difficult issues for NATO to resolve is how to allocate Western reductions. Without resolution of fair shares, there is question as to how NATO will determine which nation will receive force structure reductions, which may be interpreted as a windfall reduction in defense budget outlays. Since Gorbachev has seized the diplomatic "high ground" with his recent initiatives, threat perception in the NATO public sector has decreased and national priorities stressing strong defenses are vacillating. A successful conventional arms control agreement, which includes asymmetrical Warsaw Pact cuts that are composed of both "bean counts" of major weapons systems and various military operational and tactical capabilities (including force regeneration), may not be in the U.S. national interest. Even prior to recent CONUS base closure agreements, the U.S. military base capacity was insufficient to house any significant forces returning from Europe. Since existing military basing will not permit the restationing of large forward-deployed troop units in the United States without high capital investment in housing and facilities, stationing and mission alternatives must be found; otherwise, returning forces will be decremented from the active force strength. Without alternative mission tasks and creative stationing ideas, even with an active to reserve conversion on a one-for-one basis, readiness will suffer and mobilization requirements for strategic lift will be astronomical and cost prohibitive. Retaining these currently forward-deployed forces in the U.S. military, in the aftermath of a successful conventional arms control agreement, will require our military leadership's most creative talent and marketing skills. The Army leadership must explore alternatives for its active force structure other than in combat missions. Nation building, the antidrug war, civic actions, and other missions must receive a market share of the Pentagon's "brain trust" if reductions are to be stayed. If not, Army planners need to develop detailed plans, not only for the reductions, but for balancing the remaining risk.

Trade

The very existence of nations today depends to a large degree on trade. Trade imbalances, protectionism, and interdependence among nations have the attention of governments and publics. This overall issue may have a greater impact on force structure than any other issue. In 1992, the European Economic Community will drop its national trade barriers to form an integrated European trade structure. When the wealth of U.S. allies, as measured in Gross Domestic Product (GDP) as $7.8 trillion,[15] is compared with the U.S. GDP of $4.7 trillion, and with the concurrent rise of Japan as a leader in world trade, the United States may become outflanked. Interdependence is deemed essential in today's world; however, trading partner deficits, debtor nation status, the "buy-out" of the United States, heightened competition from emerging nations, and a continuing Soviet economic disaster may contribute to military conflict. Military alliances could fracture because of economic conflict.

In recent history, major economic powers have avoided trade wars. However, the United States is currently involved in point-counterpoint battles with Europe concerning beef exports and with Japan regarding closed markets. How these battles will be fought, who wins and loses, and the impact of economic trade war on the U.S. economy—and thus on the U.S. military budget—will have dramatic implications for military force structure.

An economic trade war may qualify for what Theodore J. Gordon has described as a "covert" war. "What is a covert war? Simply this—a war in which no nation, other than the aggressor, is a combatant. It is a war waged in secret. It is a war which can be waged in an otherwise peaceful world."[16]

It can be argued that the United States is involved in a covert war as described by Gordon. But Americans are the victims, not the aggressors. Americans need to understand how to fight such a war and must take the offensive to win. There are no college or military education courses that teach the integration of economic and military arts to win trade battles. It is understood that certain military missions would remain the same, but others, such as military assistance to the economic sector, remain unexplored. The author begs the question "how-to-fight" before a force structure can be developed. Military threat assessments only gloss over this new covert war. We need to begin our schooling in this area now, before it is too late.

Zero to Negative Defense Budget Growth

This is simply a reality for the next several administrations, until the federal deficit is finally resolved. The same future awaits many U.S. allies in Europe. This reality means that Americans have to "do more with less" (which doesn't work very well over time) or they must "do less with less" (which doesn't work very well, either). The choices are tough. Budget "enhancers," such as base closures, burdensharing, and arms control, are not national security enhancers. In such an environment, the Soviet risk must be countered by sound planning, creative ideas, and leadership judgment; in the end, however, results rest in the hands of external drivers—national policies, the environment, resources, and capabilities. Though long-range planners must be pragmatic and parochial, they should also be visionaries or be smart enough to consult with those who have a plausible view of what the future may bring.

Moving from threat-driven strategies to resource-driven ones requires great effort. This effort seems to be wasted in the formal military procedures of developing the minimum risk, planning, objective, and program forces before arriving at the resource-constrained budget and current force structure. There is a need to meld these joint service planning exercises into one effort for the President's budget and Five-Year Defense Plan (FYDP). Further, there is a need to shrink commitments that Americans make to ourselves, like protecting the world's sea lines of communication. If U.S. commitments are reduced, the void will either be filled with allied "out of area" forces, or it will not be filled at all. Zero to negative defense budget growth will precipitate headquarters consolidations, unit deactivations or conversions, and procurement stretchouts, cancellations, and postponements. On the positive side, NATO host nation support, cooperative research and development, standardization, and interoperability may flourish. Real defense budget decline may force us to return to successful U.S. business practices like lease versus buy, sale and lease back, leveraging assets, and subcontracting. When ethical business procedures are finally imposed upon the military, more defense with less money may be the result. In any event, the budget issue looms as the greatest factor in force structure planning.

The Variables

Returning to the option development methodology, the United States must next determine the variables of the force structure it seeks. Simply stated, the variables include the size, composition, mission capability, and stationing of the future force.

The size variable appears to be the easiest to address. Small, medium, large, and extra large seem to cover the full spectrum of force structure size variation. Those who forecast conditions leading to a smaller Army in the coming decades include authors of the *Army Long-Range Planning Guidance*,[17] virtually all futurists, relevant Congressmen (Nunn, Levin), the Germans, the Soviets, and a few Army long-range planners whose names shall go unmentioned to protect the innocent. Advocates of conventional force buildup appear to be reacting to decreased reliance on nuclear deterrence as a result of the INF Treaty and the potential for similar, future nuclear arms control agreements, rather than to any other justification.

The separate variable of force composition includes Active or Reserve Component mix, nuclear/conventional mix, and light versus heavy design. The mission capability variable includes mission specialization among the U.S. military services (U.S. Army light infantry versus U.S. Marine Corps objective force, for a provocative example), mission specialization within NATO (effects of burdensharing and/or successful conventional arms control agreement), and impacts of emerging technologies (modernization). Finally, the stationing variable includes strategic mobility versus forward stationing, and Europe versus the Third World focus.

Each of these variables has an imaginary "dial setting" associated with it. For example, the size variable dial setting has been explained by small, medium, and large; the force composition variable has three dials to set: active or reserve, nuclear to conventional, and light versus heavy. These variable dial settings are the "bottom line" solutions to the option development methodology. Each option selected for analysis will ultimately result in setting the variable dials.

A review of the option development methodology includes selecting a force structure driver; building a brief scenario around the driver, including crisis or calm conditions; determining the primary issues involved in the scenario; assessing the impact of the issues upon the force structure driver, including the associated threat; and selecting the variable dial settings most suited to the logical, predictable, or intuitively plausible choice of force structure in each scenario.

Six potential options are offered for force structures in the coming decade, derived from six alternative scenarios, which will provide answers to General Goodpaster's three questions: What is the objective? What concept is available to achieve it? What resources does the concept need?

The Options

For scenario development, the following are selected: driver (national policy), the condition (crisis), and the issues (conflicting national priorities, diminishing threat perception, and burdensharing).

Option 1

In this option, conflicting national priorities drive national policies, which in turn shape force structure. At the extreme, the U.S. Congress exerts pressure and threatens to legislate a unilateral withdrawal from Europe in accordance with the Mansfield amendments of 1973. These circumstances are intended to encourage increased allied defense expenditure.

Ironically, internal political pressure within the Federal Republic of Germany (FRG) for substantial troop reductions, in light of a greatly reduced European perception of the Soviet threat and demographic and environmental concerns, creates a call for the expulsion of foreign troops, labeled occupation forces. The FRG then negotiates successfully within the Western European Union (WEU) for WEU to Warsaw Pact (WP) conventional arms reductions.

It is possible that within the next few years, the United States may react to domestic and European pressures to greatly reduce U.S. influence in NATO or actually redeploy U.S. forces from Europe to the United States. These forces would then serve as NATO's strategic reserve. In this scenario, the United States would want to encourage increased allied defense expenditure. What could result is possible troop expulsion and reduced political influence in NATO. If U.S. congressional reaction directly correlates to public reaction, the United States would remove its forces from Europe, and such forces might then serve as part of NATO's strategic reserve. It is more likely that the United States would secede from the NATO alliance altogether and U.S. strategic goals would then evolve around CONUS (continental U.S.) defense in the absence of a strong alliance. The United States would then have to make difficult choices concerning its future from among the strategic options available: neoisolationism, selective engagement/disengagement, or interventionism.

Neoisolationism, the adoption of a policy orientation paralleling that of the Carter years (pre-1980), is characterized by international retrenchment and the accommodation of adversaries, involving a variety of measures. These could include a significant reduction in the defense budget in absolute terms, as well as significant reductions in conventional forces, particularly ground forces. Additionally, measures might be taken to limit any significant modernization of nuclear forces. Such measures may be reinforced by strong pressure for real reductions in existing forces if this is linked to an arms control agreement. Also, such measures can include massive reductions in European forward-based U.S. forces. A number of policy options include the rejection of military intervention as an instrument of policy, with the possible exception of Central America or in the context of rescue operations. Finally, efforts can be made to reduce other alliance security arrangements, including the severance of diplomatic relations and/or security assistance with conservative, authoritarian regimes.

Selective Engagement/Disengagement is the adoption of a policy orientation similar to that of the Nixon-Ford years, entailing more moderate actions. This could entail modest reductions in the defense budget in absolute terms, with no increase, and probable reductions, in nuclear and conventional forces. Additionally, modest reductions in other than European forward-based/forward-deployed U.S. forces could be sought, with increased reliance on air and naval general-purpose forces, relative to ground forces. Finally, there could evolve a reduced willingness to rely on direct military intervention abroad. This would go hand in hand with no expansion of formal or informal security arrangements and selective reduction in the level of U.S. involvement in other existing arrangements.

Interventionism is the adoption of a high-profile, activist, high-risk policy orientation reminiscent of the Kennedy-Johnson years and, in a somewhat muted form, the first Reagan Administration.

This policy orientation would involve an increase in the defense budget in absolute terms, with significant increases in nuclear and conventional forces of all types. It would also promote a harder-line approach and the rejection or avoidance of arms control agreements (but not necessarily negotiations) with the Soviet Union. It follows that such a policy would opt for an increase in forward-based ground and tactical air forces and forward-deployed naval and marine forces in non-European regions. Additionally, there would be a strong reaffirmation of existing non-European U.S. security commitments, coupled with the expansion of formal and informal security arrangements, including security assistance programs, basing, access, and overflight arrangements. Finally, this interventionism policy would signal an increased willingness to use force and to conduct direct military intervention in Central America, the Middle East, and Southwest Asia unilaterally or in concert with other nations.

U.S. anger, provoked by European calls for expulsion, would favor the latter national policy of interventionism. This crisis would then drive us to set the force structure variable dials to a larger, more flexible composition of forces having expanded mission capabilities and increased, diversified forward stationing. Defense spending would necessarily increase to balance the Soviet threat without reliance on the NATO alliance. The overall risk is seen as balanced, due in part to U.S. buildup in response to WEU and WP conventional arms control agreement reductions. As separate defense structures, the United States and the Western European Union still are predictable wartime allies, and peacetime rapprochement remains viable.

Option 2

The scenario here is the selected driver (the environment), condition (crisis), and the issues (trade and budget). In this scenario, a crisis in the threat or in the economic, diplomatic, or psychosociological environments may cause a larger force structure to develop. A crisis in the threat could be triggered by a number of events or actions that precipitates a higher level of readiness alert in NATO. Examples of such a threat include a revolt by Soviet conservatives who then replace the Gorbachev regime; massive deployment of the Soviet navy; reversal of announced Soviet troop withdrawals; and armed suppression of internal Soviet and Warsaw Pact dissident demonstrations. A crisis in the economic environment could be triggered by an escalating series of trade barriers among the United States, Europe, and Far East trading partners. A crisis could also be generated in the diplomatic environment by announced withdrawals of key NATO members from the alliance in favor of neutral and nonaligned status (the FRG, France, the Benelux, the UK, Greece, Turkey). Examples of crises in the psychosociological environment could be the increased escalation of drug-related crime and political corruption, the spiraling increase in AIDS-related cases and disinformation campaigning to link the source to Americans, or the spread of communist insurgencies to Mexico and the rest of Latin America.

In any of these environmental crises, selected issues will pale by comparison with the driver behind the crisis. Though the trade issue, encompassing deficits, debt, or nation status; the "buy-out" of America; or heightened competition or Soviet economic collapse could lead to armed conflict, it only enhances or detracts from the immediate national security danger when a crisis in other than the economic environment occurs. The same projection can be made of the budget issue, which currently occupies the center of the planning arena.

Regardless of which environmental crisis is selected, the strategic focus will be on restoring the stability of that environment. Concepts or means to attain this objective will require additional money, manpower, and material resources, regardless of the "ways" selected. Variable dial settings will also be set in the "more of everything" mode until the danger is alleviated or restored to a suitable level of stability. Since time will be very important, the increases in manpower and materiel necessary to carry out the restoration plan could cause a return to the drafting of men (and women), massive procurement of materiel from foreign sources, revitalization of the U.S. industrial base, or development of innovative leasing arrangements.

This option, in effect, previews U.S. preparations for war. The risk of war is dramatic should a real crisis develop in the environment described in this scenario. Perhaps the best way to negate this increased risk is by planning and testing the alternative ways to resolve the crises proposed above before they occur.

The concepts of a limited draft, massive foreign and domestic purchases in a severely time-constrained delivery schedule, and the leasing rather than purchase of one U.S. weapon system all need to be tested if the Army leadership plans to implement such concepts during national security emergencies.

Option 3

The following criteria are selected here: driver (resources), condition (crisis), and the issues (arms control, burdensharing, and budget). In this option, the scenario is constructed around a dramatic reduction in the Department of Defense budget due to increased emphasis on domestic concerns. Although such a situation is realistic, the immediate reaction of military professionals is negative; however, such a scenario may enhance and strengthen the search for realistic alternatives. Conventional arms control negotiations will become essential in such a scenario and will move to become the nation's "centerpiece of foreign policy." Significant reductions of U.S. and NATO forces in Europe will only take place within the framework of NATO's objectives; however, military concerns will be overshadowed by political necessities. Active force structure will be cut since there are inadequate basing facilities available in the United States and alternative missions have not been fully developed and marketed. The major force structure options remaining that are viable are to expand the Reserve Component and greatly expand strategic lift capabilities through bilateral agreements with non-NATO allies and other friendly trading partners (in addition to NATO agreements).

The impact of successful allied burdensharing agreements, as a result of congressional pressure on U.S. allies, will also serve to reduce U.S. active force structure forward-stationed in Europe. If these two significant issues are not addressed in consort (for purposes of this scenario), separate actions on these issues might result in consecutive reductions. Coordinating the issues by resolving the matter of burdensharing prior to concluding conventional arms control agreements will enable the United States and NATO members to restructure risks, roles, and responsibilities in preparation for NATO's ultimate force reduction regime in the Conventional

Stability Talks (Conventional Forces in Europe, or CFE, Negotiations or whatever the final, formal designation of conventional arms control talks becomes).

If the budget issue of zero to negative defense expenditure growth is added to the scenario development that also results in force structure reductions, the United States would face a triple-option attack on force structure. Advocates of low-cost, low-tech solutions will not realistically be able to defend against such an attack. If the United States slows down the current rush to arms control; reevaluates burdensharing "bludgeoning" tactics; seeks low-cost, low-tech solutions with an appropriate mix of high-cost, high-tech potential stockage; shrinks self-imposed worldwide commitments selectively; continues to consolidate headquarters; and enhances host nation support efforts and NATO cooperative research and development, this nation might limit troop reduction damage by balancing the overall risk.

In such a resource-constrained scenario, the United States may want to stabilize the risk by adopting the concepts presented above or by seeking other alternatives. In any case, the United States will most likely have less resources with which to accomplish national security objectives. The variable dials will be set at smaller, highly mobile, highly lethal active forces; increased Reserve Component forces; and balanced strategic and conventional forces, predominantly stationed within the United States and its territories, with self-imposed, reduced worldwide responsibilities.

Option 4

The criteria used here are the selected driver (capabilities), condition (crisis), and the issues (arms control and threat perception). The construct of capabilities includes quantity, quality, and high-technology relative to both nuclear and conventional forces. At one extreme, a nuclear-free Europe may evolve in the next decade as a result of a continuing series of Soviet initiatives to reduce the threat. This may increase pressure for conventional parity through arms control, high-cost, high-tech solutions, or the restructuring of forces or warfighting doctrine as possible results. In the absence of a nuclear-free Europe, less pressure for high-cost, high-tech solutions and arms control may prevail in a budget-constrained environment, again supported by a decreasing Western threat perception.

This option is driven by emerging technologies having highly lethal and accurate characteristics and whose destructive potential nearly equates to nuclear weapons. Conventional arms control negotiations may limit the fielding of emerging technologies in Europe, but not their development and production in the more prosperous nations of NATO and the WP. Resulting restrictions in the CST process may cause two distinct types of U.S. force structure to develop: NATO-assigned and continental U.S. (CONUS) forces.

CONUS forces, including both Active and Reserve Components, will be equipped and structured as necessary to accommodate the new technologies. CONUS forces will fit budgetary constraints with active forces structured in the small, highly lethal, highly mobile model. Reserve forces will be proportionally structured, with one-third reflecting the CONUS model and two-thirds maintaining a Europe-reinforcing model.

U.S. NATO forces, affected by substantial reductions in tanks, artillery, and armored troop carriers, will be compelled to initiate a lighter, less costly force design, but mission capabilities will improve due to requirements for cooperative research and development and rigid NATO rationalization, standardization, and interoperability. The NATO alliance remains strong in this scenario, but at substantially lower levels of forces. The risk is reduced by arms control agreement in Europe and by the increased lethality and accuracy of CONUS-based weaponry and the accompanying conventional deterrence enhancements. The variable dial settings include a smaller, lighter force structure in all armies—East and West, in Europe—and small active forces in CONUS, equipped with the emerging technologies. The Reserve Component grows at a one-for-one pace of Active reduction to reserve increase.

Option 5

This section uses the following criteria: selected driver (none), condition (calm, lack of crisis), and the issues (arms control and burdensharing). In the absence of a major crisis, force structuring will become evolutionary and be influenced by the successful resolution of one or more issues. In this option, NATO conventional arms control objectives are attained, reaching an agreement with the Warsaw Pact that provides NATO greater security and stability and reduces WP surprise attack capability, at lower levels and cost.[18] The U.S. reduction is significant at 25 percent of land forces stationed in Europe.[19]

An arms control agreement will have an immediate impact on resolving the burdensharing issue, particularly in mission specialization, achieving the same results if burdensharing is resolved prior to arms control agreement. Reductions of combat forces will force NATO to make some tough decisions. Elements to consider include the following:

1. Some conversion of "have not" nations and European Home Defense Brigades to combat support arms will need to be accomplished while U.S. combat support arms units are converted to combat maneuver forces;[20]

2. Air Defense and Combat Service Support (CSS) missions are candidates for partial conversions.
3. Adoption of one of the alternative defense plans collected and explained by Jonathan Dean may be initiated. Choices include the Afheldt plan, the SAS plan, Hanning's fire wall, wide area territorial defense, and civilian-based defense.[21]

The U.S. Army would also face some tough decisionmaking, particularly involving whether to take the reductions out of the force structure, as mandated, or to use the reductions to fill CONUS shortfall, staff CONUS security missions, such as supporting the antidrug war, and form nation-building units or other politically attractive alternatives.[22] The risk is assumed to be less than it is today (in this scenario) due to a successful conventional arms control agreement that achieves the NATO and CFE mandate objectives cited above (see note 18). If a conventional arms control agreement is not reached and burdensharing becomes the dominant issue, risk must be assumed to remain status quo since burdensharing only reflects the NATO side of the East-West confronting forces. Again, working burdensharing and arms control issues in consort will alleviate concerns for double jeopardy in force reductions.

The variable dial settings are turned to a smaller force structure by evolution, not crisis condition. Capabilities and composition of the force may likewise evolve; however, successful resolution of either the burdensharing or arms control issues will automatically set the forward-stationing dial to less and the strategic lift dial to more.

Option 6

In this scenario, we'll use the following: selected driver (none), condition (calm, lack of crisis), and the issues (arms control and burdensharing remain unresolved). Without consensus and resolution by NATO to address the difficult issues of burdensharing and arms control, the force will slowly evolve to find less expansive tactical, operational, and/or doctrinal solutions to the current East-West imbalance. Without an arms control agreement, the Soviets will continue to build up the quality of conventional forces, while perhaps only increasing quantity at the margins (particularly naval forces). Although there will be national reductions in NATO force structure stemming from defense budget reductions, the introduction of emerging technologies to increase "quality" may redress the force quantity imbalance. The risk will increase in this scenario, but only at the margins. Without resolution of the arms control and burdensharing issues, nations will have only limited opportunities to reduce defense expenditures. The evolutionary, year-by-year force-structuring process may find the United States and NATO possessing a suboptimal force in Europe, incapable of mounting a strong defense. The United States may want arms control and greater allied burdensharing, but in the absence of successful negotiations, it may desire to balance the marginal risk by opting for quality, high-cost, high-tech weaponry and equipment. In any event, evolutionary force-structure design will find the U.S. and European armies planning for smaller forces with increased capabilities as the major variable dial settings for the future force.

Summary and Conclusions

This chapter has examined a number of components important in considering NATO force structuring and the U.S. Army in the 1990s. The purpose has been to stimulate the study and analysis of these matters, particularly with respect to driving forces, conditions, issues, and variables. The focal point of this inquiry was based on General Goodpaster's three questions, which were examined in the aggregate: What do we really want? What concepts are available? What resources are needed to support those concepts?

Six options for the future were developed by selecting external (as opposed to formal military force planning procedures) "drivers" that press the system to unplanned decisions, creating conditions of crisis or calm, supplementing the discussion with consideration of national security issues, assessing the impacts those issues might have upon force structure, and dial-setting the structural variables of the future force in an effort to bound the debate on what the future force will look like.

A number of postulates were offered throughout this chapter, as well as a number of recommendations. In sum, these postulates include the recognition that force planning is complex and characterized by an interrelated series of analyses to determine an affordable force. It follows that force structuring is a function of national policy, the environment, resources, and capabilities in conditions of crisis or calm. In examining and analyzing force planning and structures, there is a need to recognize that identifying and rationalizing strategic objectives are merely the beginnings of a process that tries to come to grips with U.S. national interests and how these are translated into the external world.

These postulates are reinforced by a number of others, which include the following:

1. Burdensharing is the most complex issue facing the NATO alliance.
2. Soviet threat perception is the most important issue impacting force structure.
3. Arms control is a complex issue that is interrelated with the issues of burdensharing, threat perception, and budget decline.

4. Trade issues may ultimately have the greatest impact on all national security decisions.
5. Zero to negative defense budget growth is a reality for the next several U.S. administrations.
6. Long-range force-structure planners need to assess external futurist predictions.
7. Time is considered the critical path to mobilization.

A number of recommendations (and derivative assumptions) are drawn from the analysis in this chapter. On the assumptions that Gorbachev has several options that can be exercised and that his tenure in office continues concomitantly with the unraveling of the Eastern bloc, the following recommendations are in order:

1. Assign burdensharing roles and responsibilities in accordance with what each nation does best (specialization of labor concept).
2. Make the compromise decisions of low-cost, low-tech or high-cost, high-tech solutions now.
3. Resolve the burdensharing issue prior to concluding arms control agreements to produce a "consensus-driven" NATO reduction plan.
4. Explore alternatives to force inactivations other than in the combat units, including nation building, antidrug war, and civic actions.
5. Begin schooling on how to fight in a covert trade war using integrative economic and military arts.
6. Meld force-planning effort into one exercise to leverage planner time.
7. Shrink self-imposed commitments to the world.
8. Overlay solid, practical, and ethical U.S. business practices like lease versus buy, sale and lease back, and leveraging and subcontracting to buy more defense with less money.

In conclusion, regardless of the various views concerning Gorbachev's impact and the directions in Europe, it is clear that significant changes have taken place in the security environment with respect to NATO and the Warsaw Pact and between the United States and the USSR. These changes signal a transition period from the post–World War II era to the erosion of the Cold War environment and have implications beyond the European landscape. It is in the best interests of the United States to broaden its strategic vision, reach beyond a reactive posture, and seek to respond to these changes while at the same time developing a vision of the strategic landscape based on its own sense of national interest. Care must be taken to ensure that precipitous reaction to current changes is not institutionalized into a short-term, ad-hoc policy that erodes the security wherewithal needed for long-range U.S. strategic initiatives.

Notes

1. Col. John R. Rose and Lt. Col. John E. Peters, "What Will the Army Look Like in 2010?" *Army*, July 1988, p. 19.
2. *Supporting U.S. Strategy for Third World Conflicts*. Report by the Regional Conflict Working Group, submitted to the Commission on Integrated Long-Term Strategy, June 1988, p. 16.
3. Ibid., p. 17.
4. John F. Scott, "Strategic Objectives and Arms Negotiations in Europe," unpublished draft (Carlisle Barracks, PA: Strategic Studies Institute, November 3, 1988), pp. 4–8.
5. *Army Command and Management: Theory and Practice* (Carlisle Barracks, PA: U.S. Army War College, 1988–1989), pp. 10–21.
6. Ibid., pp. 11–17.
7. Lt. Col. David E. Shaver, "A Case for a Larger Army in the 21st Century," Military Studies Project (Carlisle Barracks, PA: U.S. Army War College), April 20, 1987, p. 1.
8. Theodore Gordon and Olaf Helmer, "Report on a Long-Range Forecasting Study," in Olaf Helmer, ed., *Social Technology* (New York: Basic Books, 1966), pp. 46–47.
9. U.S. House of Representatives, *Report of the Defense Burdensharing Panel of the Committee on Armed Services* (Washington, D.C.: U.S. Government Printing Office, 1988).
10. Gordon Adams and Eric Munz, *Fair Shares: Bearing the Burden of the NATO Alliance* (Washington, D.C.: Center on Budget and Policy Priorities, 1988).
11. Thomas A. Callaghan, Jr., *Pooling Allied and American Resources to Produce a Credible Collective Conventional Deterrent*. A Report for the U.S. Department of Defense, Washington, D.C., August 1988.
12. Frank C. Carlucci, *Report on the Allied Contributions to the Common Defense*. A Report to the U.S. Congress (Washington, D.C.: U.S. Department of Defense, 1989).
13. David Greenwood, *Economic Constraints and Program Choices in British Defence Planning for the 1990s*. A Contingencies Series Report for the Center for Strategic and International Studies, Washington, D.C., February 1988.
14. Strategic Studies Institute, *How to Think about Conventional Arms Control: A Framework* (Carlisle Barracks, PA: U.S. Army War College, June 24, 1988), p. 80.
15. James McCartney, "For the Common Defense, A Big Price," *The Philadelphia Inquirer*, December 18, 1988, p. 3-F.
16. Theodore J. Gordon, *The Future* (New York: St. Martin's Press, 1965), p. 56.
17. U.S. Department of the Army, *Army Long-Range Planning Guidance*, Revised Edition (Washington, D.C.: Office of the Deputy Chief of Staff for Operations and Plans, July 1988), p. 11., which states that (conditions) "are likely to result in smaller, but more effective, Army units in the future." The document was prepared for signature by John O. Marsh, Jr., Secretary of the Army, and Gen. Carl E. Vuono, Chief of Staff, U.S. Army.
18. Strategic Studies Institute, note 14, p. ix.
19. Ibid., p. 82. The authors project that a "significant agreement" of approximately 50,000 soldiers is a potential outcome of future Conventional Stability Talks (CST) in Europe.

20. During a NATO Northern Army Group (NORTHAG) "Makefast" Conference in May 1986, the author presented "Landmine Warfare in the Year 2000" to Army engineer general officers from seven NATO countries. The striking difference between "have and have not" armies influenced the author to seek ways of sharing high-tech munitions among NATO members in time of war. This concept allows the transfer of ground-emplaced Family of Scatterable Mines (FASCAM) to NATO "have not" engineers.

21. Jonathan Dean, "Alternative Defense: Answer to NATO's Central Front Problems?" *International Affairs*, Winter 1987–88, pp. 61–82:

• The Afheldt Plan "structures NATO armies unilaterally with 'light infantry commandos equipped with antitank weapons' followed behind by an artillery network, . . . (with) tanks . . . gradually eliminated."

• The Study Group on Alternative Security Planning (SAS) plan uses a "static 'web' of light infantry much like Afheldt's followed by armored formations ('spikers')."

• Hanning's fire wall proposed "an uninhabited barrier . . . saturated with fire (indirect). Behind the 'fire wall' would be antitank units equipped with precision-guided missiles."

• Wide area territorial defense "envisions a frontier defense zone 80–100 kilometers deep in which barriers and blocking units channel attacking units toward concentrations of fire."

• Civilian-based defense . . . in which cities would . . . engage in passive (nonviolent) resistance.

22. Strategic Studies Institute, note 14, p. 83.

PART 4
Beyond Europe

CHAPTER 9

Conventional Conflicts Beyond Europe

DAVID W. TARR

This chapter is devoted to an analysis of those security interests of the United States that might require U.S. deployment or employment of conventional ground forces beyond Europe. Within the context of this chapter, "conventional conflicts" refer to nonnuclear limited wars fought by conventionally armed forces. "Beyond Europe" refers to the developing nations, or Third World. Furthermore, this chapter does not address unconventional (revolutionary) conflicts, typically undertaken by guerrilla forces engaged in or countering insurgencies.

Since the 1940s the United States has maintained the capability to station land forces abroad and to deploy still more of them overseas at short notice to signal or reinforce our commitment to protect our security interests. This undertaking has become complicated by changes in the international political environment and by the trend toward increasingly sophisticated weapons possessed by the armed forces of the Third World. As the *Department of Defense Annual Report for Fiscal Year 1990* put the matter:

> Because of the variety of contingencies against which we must plan, structuring our land forces has become an increasingly difficult task, requiring sophisticated analysis of the threat and of our own capabilities. Today's structure is designed to balance the requirements for heavy, light, and special operations forces (SOF); forward-deployed forces and forces based in the continental United States (CONUS); and active and reserve forces.[1]

In order to focus our analysis, we will confine our remarks to the potential need to deploy "heavy" and "light" conventionally armed ground forces in out-of-Europe contexts. "Heavy forces provide extra mobility and firepower for operations against a mechanized foe. Light forces are rapidly deployable and are especially useful in restricted terrain."[2] The trade-off between these two values is a technical problem of great significance, but the implications of the analysis to follow is that the requirement of the light divisions has been exaggerated. Special operations are omitted here because discussing such operations leads us into unconventional or low-intensity conflict analysis. In short, we have defined our topic within the following limits: conventional, not nuclear; Third World, not First or Second; and conventional, not low-intensity.

In 1988, the Report of the Commission on Integrated Long-Term Strategy made the following observation about conflicts beyond Europe:

> Nearly all the armed conflicts of the past forty years have occurred in what is vaguely called the Third World. . . . In the same period, all the wars in which the United States was involved—either directly with its combat forces or indirectly with military assistance—occurred in the Third World. Given future trends in the diffusion of technology and military power, the United States needs a clear understanding of its interests and military role in these regions.[3]

One should not be misled by the commission's observation about past conflicts. There are few plausible Third World conventional war scenarios in which the interests of the United States would be served by direct involvement of U.S. ground forces in conventional battle. If one takes into account changes that have taken place in U.S. international and domestic political and economic environments, it is clear that while there is every prospect for continued turmoil and warfare in the Third World, U.S. security interests would seldom, if ever, be served by direct military engagement. Indeed, in most instances, military intervention by the United States would likely be counterproductive. The analysis of U.S. security interests that follows drives the conclusion that U.S. conventional war capabilities are most appropriate to, and only required for, the protection and support of this country's most important overseas interests—principally those related to the security of Western Europe, Japan, South Korea, and, for the sake of access to oil, the Persian Gulf/Middle East. For other countries and regions, such as Thailand and the Philippines, or Latin America and Africa, the issues and contexts involved are generally unsuited to conventional force applications.

More specifically, this chapter will argue that:

1. Conventional conflicts beyond Europe have *not* been a principal threat to the security of the United States, despite our involvement in several cases over the past forty years; such conflicts will be even less important to the interests of the United States in the future.
2. Those conflicts that may arise between, and most often within, Third World states will very likely *not* put our interests at such risk as to warrant conventional force intervention. In cases where our

interests are threatened, the instruments of policy will more likely be those of military assistance and possibly special forces.
3. The Soviet Union is not and will not become capable of significant application of conventional force in the Third World beyond the Eurasian continent. The USSR is a continental power capable of exerting force against any and all states on its continental periphery; that is and should be our principal concern, but not because of Soviet capabilities per se, but because of the nature of U.S. principal security interests.
4. The primary conventional conflict mission for the U.S. Army thus should be directed to the defense of NATO, Japan, and South Korea. Special considerations also dictate modest conventional force capabilities for potential conflict in the Persian Gulf/Middle East.

U.S. Security Interests

How should U.S. security interests be defined? The key to our analysis is found in the phrase "security interests," a controversial topic. We can identify at least three major schools of thought that represent fundamentally different conceptions both of the role of the United States in the world and of the nature of international politics:

1. The "Cold War internationalists,"[4] who represent the neoconservative vision of a global ideological struggle between communism and democracy and therefore favor global containment of communism;
2. The neorealists,[5] who believe that U.S. strategic interests are largely determined by geopolitics, industrial capacity, and military power balances, and therefore prefer a more restrictive or "selective" containment of the USSR;[6] and
3. The neo-idealists (world-order and liberal idealists), who regard economic factors as central and who promote international cooperation, not national security based on military power.[7]

There is no need to resolve these differing perspectives here, but simply to relate them to those military considerations that might lead to a conventional ground combat role for the U.S. Army. Briefly put, whatever the value of the Cold War internationalist perspective, military preparations for conventional conflict based on that outlook would be imprudently unlimited. Moreover, the most appropriate instruments for supporting embattled noncommunist governments in the Third World are found in more subtle and less intrusive measures. On the other hand, the neo-idealist perspective is largely irrelevant to conventional military power calculations because it tends to reject national military considerations in preference for international economic ones; it tends to see threats emanating not from states but out of problems (such as a global warming and nuclear war) that are to be resolved through international cooperation and collective action. Both perspectives play a part in the politics of national security policymaking in the United States. However, only the neorealists address the problem of conventional conflict beyond Europe in a way helpful to assessing the U.S. Army's conventional conflict role beyond Europe.

Neorealists argue correctly that geography and industrial capacity best define the basic security interests of the United States and thus shape our military requirements. The United States is a maritime power by location, and leader and ally of the industrial states of the noncommunist world by commitment. Our principal adversary is a land-bound, continental empire of lesser industrial capacity, even in combination with its satellite states. Geopolitically speaking, the principal security interest of the United States remains as George F. Kennan defined it years ago: "that no single Continental land power should come to dominate the entire Eurasian land mass."[8] The only power capable of such domination in this century has been the Soviet Union. The Soviets have therefore been our principal adversary and major security concern.

Neorealists believe this definition of geopolitical interest is no less essential today, but also that it is, fortunately, in less danger of challenge than at any time since World War II. This is so because Soviet policy and leadership are more moderate, and the industrial capacity and political strength of the industrial nations of Western Europe and Asia make them less susceptible to Soviet domination than at any time since the end of World War II. Although some neorealists have therefore concluded that the "Third World doesn't matter,"[9] that, as some have argued, U.S. strategic interests are confined to the United States, Europe, Northeast Asia, and the Persian Gulf,[10] they do so with the mistaken logic that only interests that directly affect U.S. national security do matter. Michael C. Desch properly points out that those areas beyond Europe that can be regarded as of little "intrinsic value" nevertheless can be strategically important because they have "extrinsic values" (the distinction being between those interests that directly affect U.S. national security and those that do not), such as proximity to the United States or access to military bases that optimize U.S. strategy for protecting its interests abroad.[11]

However, the analysis that follows suggests that while protection of extrinsic values in the Third World can be important to the United States, these are best supported by economic and military assistance programs and, if direct force is necessary, by air, naval, and special forces. Third World conflicts are unlikely to emerge as "conventional" land wars, but even in the event that they do so (as in the recent Iran-Iraq war), conventional ground force intervention by the United States would seldom serve to enhance U.S. national security interests—whether defined as intrinsic or extrinsic.

In short, while the realist perspective employs a definition of security interests that is sometimes too narrowly defined for U.S. grand strategy, this perspective nonetheless defines the requirements for U.S. Army conventional war strategy well, precisely because of its prudent definition of interests. So far as conventional force engagement is concerned, our principal security problem along the entire Eurasian perimeter is the military capacity of the USSR. Limits to Soviet power projection capability make it unnecessary to consider an "all theaters" approach, as former Secretary of Defense Caspar Weinberger characterized it during his tenure. As Stephen Van Evera persuasively argued in congressional testimony, the Soviets have no powerful allies, few friends, poor access to the high seas (further complicated by choke points), few secure bases beyond Eurasia, and long and insecure lines of supply beyond their own borders.[12] In other words, the Soviet capacity for power projection by means of conventional forces is tenuous at best, and under the "new thinking" of Gorbachev, may be on the decline.

Conventional Force Planning

During the first decade of the Cold War, the United States forged the diplomacy of containment, with its principal commitment to NATO and thereafter to a number of bilateral and multilateral security agreements around the globe. During the height of the Cold War, the United States was concerned that the Sino-Soviet threat might expand communist influence and control beyond Eurasia. Many in the West feared that the Soviets sought to establish enclaves in the Third World, and that the communist bloc fomented revolutionary forces to achieve these aggrandizing goals. By the early 1960s, U.S. conventional force planning was premised on the capacity to fight two and one-half wars simultaneously: one in Europe, one in Asia, and a limited war elsewhere. After it became clear that China was no longer an ally of the USSR, force planning was adjusted downward to one and one-half wars as a measure of conventional capacity. More recently, force planning criteria have been developed on the basis of a "worldwide war" or "all-theaters" strategy.[13]

None of these force planning perspectives is suitable to the contemporary strategic environment. The Soviet bloc is no longer monolithic (indeed, it never was). The robust economies of the industrial states of the Western alliance, broadly defined, are in stark contrast to the postwar weaknesses that so concerned U.S. leaders of the past. Moreover, new sectors of industrial strength in Europe and Asia have arisen to rival the capacities of the United States as well as of the communist states. In short, the balance of economic and political power has changed dramatically, disadvantaging the Soviets considerably compared to past decades, and shifted the political and economic equation such that U.S. military power beyond Europe is no longer so central to that balance. Moreover, Soviet globalist aspirations appear to be undergoing serious modification.

Changes in the Strategic Environment

There are at least seven principal changes in the strategic environment that need to be taken into account in assessing conventional force policies and capabilities.

First, U.S. economic preponderance has ended (but predictions of imminent decline miss the point). This shift is due to the economic vitality of Europe and Asia, and not to an absolute decline in U.S. economic strength.

Second, the Soviet brand of socialism is a failed enterprise and an unattractive model for development. The economic reforms among the Soviet bloc states and in China are blunt indicators of this fact as well as an obvious admission of failure. The Third World is not in danger of communist insurgency and revolution, but is seized with intractable economic problems and political issues.

Third, China is no longer our enemy, nor the enemy of the Soviet Union. Neither is it our ally. It is a player to be counted on to continue to counter Soviet influence in Asia and the Third World. The Chinese do and will pursue their own interests, of course. But China's independence from the Soviet orbit and socialism's profound economic and political failures will have enormous repercussions in the Third World.

Fourth, the Brezhnev era of military growth and influence in the USSR is over. It is unlikely to return in another guise in the foreseeable future. Whether or not Gorbachev succeeds in his reforms, the Soviets have grave economic difficulties that they may not be able to surmount.

Fifth, the interconnectivity of U.S. commitments—a key assumption of the Cold War period—is no longer self-evident and should not be a basis for policy. U.S. security commitments abroad vary in value, and the credibility of these commitments should not be measured, one against the other, as indicators of the strength of our determination everywhere else. Modifications and changes can and have been made in many instances without undue jeopardy to the symbolic meaning of U.S. resolve elsewhere.

Sixth, "wars of national liberation" are no longer matters that should unduly concern U.S. policymakers. The critical features of Third World politics are nationalism and factionalism, not communism. Those phenomena are as disruptive to any Soviet adventure as they have been to past U.S. interventions. Since our principal objective is to contain Soviet power, this factor enhances U.S. security even though our influence in the Third World may be diminished as well. The most frequent mode of conflict experienced in the Third World has been internal, not international (interstate)—cases where governments have attempted to suppress indigenous cultures (e.g., Kurds) and regional ethnic groups, or to combat rival domestic forces. Taking sides in these struggles by military means hardly ever advances our interests. In any case, these are generally not the conditions that are susceptible to conventional ground force expeditions.

However, some analysts maintain that the United States depends heavily upon raw materials from the Third World, requiring reliable access and therefore the military capacity to preserve access. Evidence for this argument rests on the large flow of imports of certain "critical" raw materials from developing countries. Stephen Walt argues persuasively that this concern is incorrect:

> Although the United States imports a large percentage of its annual consumption of certain raw materials, it does so because foreign suppliers are the least expensive, not because they are the only alternative. The magnitude of a state's imports does not determine its dependence on others; what is important is the cost of replacing existing sources of supply or doing without them entirely.[14]

In short, the case for greater U.S. capacity for intervention in the Third World because of U.S. economic dependence is seriously flawed by the tendency to equate trade with dependence.

Finally, there are indications that the United States and the Soviet Union are entering a new era of détente. The INF Treaty, the "deep cuts" agenda of the START negotiations, and the sudden progress experienced in negotiations on conventional armed forces in Europe (CFE) suggest a potentially profound change in strategic outlooks. The Cold War may not be over, but many of the assumptions associated with Cold War diplomacy and conflict may no longer apply. Furthermore, both superpowers seem inclined to be altering their respective approaches to the Third World. Under Gorbachev, Soviet "New Thinking" appears to forecast significant retrenchment in the Third World as its interest in globalism recedes or is reformulated into less intrusive and threatening modes of operation.

Much of the foregoing analysis appears to support the conclusions of those that Steven R. David calls, pejoratively, "hyper-realists"—those who argue on grounds similar to the ones set forth here that U.S. vital interests are largely confined to Europe, Japan, and the Persian Gulf and that U.S. Third World interests are peripheral at best.[15] However, the analysis presented here does not make the case that U.S. security interests do not justify intervention capabilities in the Third World. The point made here is specific to conventional force planning: that the United States does not need to generate conventional ground forces to protect its interests in the Third World (beyond the Central Command, Japan, and South Korea) because Soviet power projection capabilities are limited, large-scale intervention would be counterproductive, and better instruments of policy (e.g., economic and military assistance, air/sea power, and special forces) are available.

Changes in the Policymaking Environment in the U.S.

The American people and the opinions of our political elites have changed considerably in the past two decades. The Cold War consensus—that the Soviet Union represented the principal threat to our security, that communism needed to be contained, and that nuclear deterrence and the forward deployment of U.S. armed forces were necessary to support our foreign policies—is subject to dispute today. Elite opinion is fragmented. As a result, the policy environment is now considerably more fluid than in past decades.[16] Some of the most salient changes are as follows:

First, the foreign policy consensus among U.S. political elites is now clearly against military intervention in the Third World. This is a predisposition. It does not preclude support for such action in crisis, as the Grenada operation suggests. However, a significant coalition of political opinion is currently disposed in principle to "no more Vietnams" and to oppose U.S. engagement in Third World conflicts in general.

This predisposition against intervention is reinforced by a second major shift in political consensus. U.S. political elites are more inclined today to believe that the utility of military force has declined and that the importance of economic factors has risen. They are probably correct. While some have argued that vital resources in the Third World require U.S. intervention capabilities, this conclusion should not be taken at face value because intervention will more often beget nationalist resentment and termination of access. In any case, intervention would run against the grain of current domestic and allied political predilections.

Third, the American public is, as one wag put it, "for peace and against taxes." This is our traditional state of mind, and it is very likely to continue. Defense spending is expected to decline as a percent of GNP as well as in absolute terms (short of any significant crisis). Moreover, the cumulative political effect of substantial and continuing budget deficits makes the prospects for real cuts in defense spending the most likely trend for at least the short-run future. Thus, one should expect reductions in defense spending during the Bush Administration and beyond—probably a better than even chance.[17] For that reason alone, scarce defense dollars should be directed to supporting the Army's primary conventional defense responsibilities, and not be allocated in any substantial way to capabilities to deal with improbable and unwise Third World intervention scenarios.

Conclusions

If these assumptions are largely correct, the implications for U.S. policy in the Third World are profound. U.S. and Soviet restraint may pave the way toward opportunities for disconnecting policy from old Cold War (East-West) premises. The Soviet Union's power and influence are, after all, the principal reasons for U.S. security policy in the Third World. The Soviets do not represent a grave threat in those regions. Moreover, most important for consideration in this chapter, U.S. conventional ground force interventions in Third World conflicts will not likely enhance or protect U.S. interests; they will more likely have the opposite effect and thus should be avoided.

Regional Analysis of Third World Security Issues

If the Soviet Union represents the principal concern of the United States in the Third World, what can be said about the prospects for conflict with our superpower rival, region by region? In the first place, both superpowers have gone through a period of globalist aspirations during the Cold War, followed on each side by disillusion, reassessment, and retrenchment. Each has suffered major setbacks in the Third World (e.g., Vietnam and Iran for the United States, and Egypt and Afghanistan for the USSR), and both have found other involvements not always worth the candle in retrospect. While the United States remains far more capable of power projection in the regions beyond Eurasia, both superpowers enter the 1990s considerably chastened by past experiences. The brief discussions of each region that follow outline the reasons why the Soviet threat is likely on the decline and why U.S. Third World security requirements are consequently less demanding for conventional force planning.

The Middle East and Persian Gulf

We begin our regional survey with the principal exception to our summary conclusions. Of all the Third World nonindustrial regions, only this area represents values and issues sufficient to postulate U.S. attention to conventional force requirements. And even here, the potential for direct involvement by either side—as measured by the intractability of the issues as much as by the interests at stake—suggests cautious optimism. A prolonged and costly conventional war between Iraq and Iran, for example, failed to draw in either superpower (flagging Kuwaiti tankers notwithstanding), despite the region's geostrategic importance.

In both the Middle East and the Persian Gulf, the objective of U.S. policy is to keep the Soviets out, while the Soviets seek, equally, to retain or enhance access and influence. U.S. commitments can be summarized in two words: Israel and oil. A significant threat to the security of either one could trigger the use of U.S. military forces, although the least likely option would be the deployment of sizable U.S. ground forces. Soviet access is leveraged through the Arab states; U.S. oil logic is complicated by our commitment to Israel. Both the United States and the USSR find the Mediterranean Sea a critical waterway, which assures access for the United States and serves as a way out of its icebound rimlands for the Soviet Union. Both superpowers have lost a crucial client state in the region: the United States when the Shah fell in Iran, and the Soviets when Egyptian President Anwar Sadat switched sides.

Based on past experience, both superpowers have reasons to proceed with caution. The deployment of sizable ground forces to any country in the region by either side would be regarded by the other as destabilizing and provocative, and both sides are aware of this fact. As the 1973 DefCon alert in response to Soviet intentions to send troops to Egypt signaled, the United States is unlikely to accept a Soviet adventure of that kind in the Middle East; as the U.S. response to the Soviet invasion of Afghanistan illustrates, the United States will not involve itself directly in conflicts in Southwest Asia. On the other hand, the U.S. commitment to Pakistan is unlikely to be challenged directly by the Soviets. Moreover, as it has done in the past, the United States will surely avoid direct involvement in any conflict between Pakistan and India. Finally, U.S. ground force commitment in the event of any indirect challenge by Soviet surrogates is also very remote. Soviet intervention in the Persian Gulf area remains the only plausible scenario for direct conventional conflict. U.S. policy is designed to deter that option. Maintaining the U.S. Central Command at about its present size serves this objective well.

Africa

Africa does not enjoy high saliency in the policy circles of either Washington or Moscow. During the height of the Cold War, both powers found reasons to intervene, the Soviets going so far as to employ Cuban hired guns, while the United States, although strongly objecting to the role of Cubans and other Soviet surrogates in Africa, restricted its instruments of policy to noncombat activities and programs. However, none of these past undertakings and few imaginable future scenarios could trigger conventional force commitments by either superpower. Moreover, there is evidence in the newly arranged Namibia and Angola accords that the role of Cuban troops in the Third World will decline and, more specifically, that the Soviets will be less interested in sponsoring such interventions; indeed, it suggests a tacit spirit of cooperation between the United States and the USSR.

South Asia

Also an area of very low saliency for either superpower, this region is not seriously threatened by Soviet expansion and is not an area for which U.S. ground force commitments would likely arise. The U.S. commitment to Pakistan has already been mentioned. The United States has no interests in South Asia that would justify conventional military intervention in conflicts between India and China or between Pakistan and India. Soviet involvement in conflicts in that region are largely beyond its capabilities and interest as well. Thus, while the region has a high potential for the outbreak of conventional conflict (unlike most of the regions under discussion), as has been the case in the past, it is hardly conceivable that these conflicts would draw in the troops of either superpower.

Southeast Asia

The U.S. withdrawal from Vietnam and the Vietnam experience condition subsequent U.S. policy in this region of the world. In Vietnam, the Soviets have gained an important foothold and a valuable location for military bases, especially the naval facility at Cam Ranh Bay. Though the U.S. commitment to Thailand remains a significant one, U.S. conventional ground force intervention in Southeast Asia in the foreseeable future is virtually unthinkable. U.S. domestic constraints preclude this option. The principal unresolved problem is the issue of Cambodian independence and a possible civil war. This dispute places the Soviets and China in opposition and will be played out without a significant U.S. role in the situation.

Beyond Indochina, the primary security interest of the United States is in the Philippines. That country's constitution of 1987 requires renegotiating U.S. bases in the Philippines after 1991, for which two-thirds of the Philippines Senate is necessary for ratification. While U.S. maritime strategy requires consideration of alternative basing in the region, whatever the outcome of this issue, armed conflict of any kind arising in the Philippines, Indonesia, or any of the other island territories of the region would encompass issues and contexts unrelated to U.S. intrinsic security interests and would not justify direct U.S. military involvement.

East Asia

The most significant shift in world economic power is found in this area of the globe. The prosperity of Japan and the impressive performance of the new industrial countries (NICs) of this region, Taiwan, South Korea, Singapore, and the colony of Hong Kong are significant factors. Money, trade, and investment are transforming the political terrain of the region. The importance of U.S. security commitments to Japan and South Korea must be seen in this light, as well as U.S. relations with the new economic powers of Asia. Moreover, northeast Asia is a region of major geostrategic importance. Consider the impressive intersection of world powers: China, the Soviet Union, Japan, and the United States via our military presence in South Korea and Japan. As a result, U.S. conventional force capabilities in northeast Asia will remain an important military consideration for future planning, although the sensitivity of Japanese and South Korean domestic politics is likely to make our continuing military presence there more tenuous as time goes on. The shift from the Cold War considerations that drew our military forces into the region, to new economic and political realities, some of which may contribute to pressures to get our forces out, suggest prospective policy challenges requiring creative alternatives not yet reflected in U.S. policy initiatives.

In any case, the economic and political factors of this region demand U.S. attention and concern. Fortunately, the security of the region is not imminently threatened by any serious imbalances in forces or in prospective conflicts. However, the division of Korea and of Taiwan from China remain potential flash points for armed conflict.

Latin America

The United States has long been regarded as the hegemonic power of Latin America. While the United States is the dominant political, economic, and military force in this hemisphere, the Soviet Union established a beachhead in Castro's Cuba and was able to exercise some influence, principally (although not entirely) over revolutionary movements in the region. Thus, although it had been fundamental to U.S. foreign policy to keep foreign powers out of this hemisphere, this objective has not been completely met. Given the variety of circumstances that have elicited U.S. security concerns in Latin America and, most especially, in Central America, it is nevertheless instructive to note that there have been no conventional conflicts in this hemisphere related to Cold War issues throughout the entire Cold War period, and none is in prospect.[18] It is true, of course, that the 1962 missile crisis was a near miss, that U.S. ground troops were sent to the Dominican Republic in 1965, and U.S. forces invaded Grenada, but none of these were conventional conflicts. The 1989 invasion of Panama was a conventional conflict, but one unrelated to Cold War issues. Current concern over Nicaragua, El Salvador, and Panama continue to excite interest in U.S. conventional force requirements in the region, yet these issues also arise, not out of problems suitable to conventional military operations and capabilities, but out of unconventional ones. The only security issue for which U.S. conventional forces serve an obvious role is for the protection of the Panama Canal itself.

Even in Latin America, our chief adversary is none other than the Soviet Union. However, the Soviet Union is forced to be most circumspect in its behavior in this hemisphere, obviously in recognition of U.S. local superiority. The Soviets have, of course, exploited the advantages obtained by the unexpected access they have been given by their client state, Cuba, thanks to Fidel Castro. Cuba has thus been a willing instrument of Soviet intervention and mischief. However, under Gorbachev, Soviet policy is in retrenchment. Cuba's future role is not yet clear. Whatever develops, no future conventional conflict contingency in the region is likely to involve Soviet armed forces, and few would involve Cuban troops. A collision course over Nicaragua has been avoided thus far, and the prospects for military intervention there are even less likely as time goes on. The Soviets have clearly, if tacitly, acquiesced to the U.S. point that the United States will not accept a Soviet military base there or major equipment upgrades, such as jet fighters, in Nicaragua. The Soviets will surely not risk direct conflict with the armed forces of the United States in a region so far removed from their own territory.

In any case, throughout the Western Hemisphere, the prospects for events that would require U.S. armed intervention in conventional conflicts are extremely low. Full-scale conventional wars are unlikely in South and Central America; Soviet and Cuban forces are not expected to be used in that manner. U.S. armed forces, if used in the future, would not likely face significant conventional capabilities in the forces opposing them. The most likely events to precipitate U.S. military intervention involve rescue operations to protect U.S. citizens or to protect the Panama Canal against local intrusions. Whatever interests the United States wishes to protect in Latin America, proximity of the United States to those interests, in addition to the overwhelming U.S. military capabilities, make this region, while not the most important in terms of our national security interests, relatively easy to secure without demanding additional allocations to conventional ground force capabilities.

Summary

No conventional war scenarios beyond the current commitment of U.S. combat troops to NATO and South Korea would endanger major security interests of the United States, except possibly the Persian Gulf scenario. The Soviet Union doesn't have the reach for most of the Third World, and the United States doesn't have the interest. The issues over which we and the Soviets have in the past been engaged in the Third World are of relatively low salience today. Furthermore, the globalist aspirations of both superpowers are going through readjustment and retrenchment. That trend is likely to continue well into the 1990s.

Conclusions: The Superpower Rules of the Road in the Third World

Learning

The United States and the Soviet Union have "learned" a good deal about each other in the process of Cold War contentions over Third World issues. In earlier years, they tended to see this world and each other's relationship to it in zero-sum terms: A gain for the Soviets was a loss for the United States, and vice versa. This mutual perception often precipitated an action-reaction process, with mixed results. Over time, the high cost and intractability of the problems encountered by both countries undoubtedly contributed to modifications in policy and posture. Vietnam and Afghanistan were not the only chastening experiences, but they were the principal ones. Gorbachev's "New Thinking" with respect to the Third World apparently allows not only for the withdrawal of Soviet troops from Afghanistan, but also for more circumspect behavior elsewhere. The signals are there, although the United States should continue to hedge its bets against the actual record as it unfolds.

Rules of the Road

A macroanalysis of U.S.-Soviet Third World relations leads to some contingently optimistic assessments and conclusions. Possessing nuclear arsenals and substantial armed forces, the superpowers have been deadly adversaries for the past forty years. However, largely as a consequence of nuclear weapons and the danger they represent to both sides, informal understandings began to develop as each side found reasons to try to manage the risks and avoid loss of control.[19] These rules of the road began as conceptions of spheres of influence: the Soviets unchallenged in Eastern Europe, and the United States in Western Europe and the Western Hemisphere, which helps explain why the United States did not intervene in Hungary in 1956 and why the Soviets did nothing about U.S. intervention in Guatemala in 1954.

However, many of the Third World countries emerging from colonial control were nonaligned, and their regions appeared up for grabs. There were no rules of superpower engagement because no defined spheres of influence existed (although the U.S. vision of containment was that the Soviet and Chinese communists must be confined to the one sphere under their control and not allowed to go beyond). Indochina was thus a testing ground, as was much of Africa. Moreover, when Castro unexpectedly joined the Soviet camp, a disturbing change occurred in the Western Hemisphere, punctuated by the Cuban missile crisis of 1962. Although the Soviets were compelled to withdraw their missiles in that confrontation, we now know that in a secret agreement arranged at that time, the United States agreed not to invade

Cuba, and to withdraw its Jupiter missiles from Turkey. This quid pro quo tends to substantiate the observation that rules of the road were developing implicitly, to manage the rivalry and control the risks of superpower engagement. Yet resolution of the missile crisis left Cuba a major anomaly. Cuba's client status undermined the spheres of influence rule: The Soviets would be able to continue their military presence in Cuba; Cuba would function as a training base for guerrilla warfare; and Cubans would act as surrogates of the Soviets in more than twenty countries, ranging from the Latin American region to Angola, Vietnam, Cambodia, and the Yemens.

In retrospect, it appears that U.S. efforts to gain or block alignment of states in the Third World and then to attempt to contest and defeat "wars of liberation" climaxed in the late 1960s; similarly, the Soviets, after the U.S. withdrawal from Vietnam in the early 1970s, expanded their Third World adventurism, culminating in the Afghanistan invasion and followed by their own disillusioned retreat under Gorbachev. By the late 1980s, converging views in both capitals suggested that the superpowers had found the underdeveloped areas of the world rife with intractable problems; both seemed interested in reducing the intensity of their competition and the cost of their involvement.

This process has fed on itself to some degree, because each side had in some respects seen the other as a major reason for its own involvement in these regions—to pre-empt or counter the influence or control of the other. But it works both ways. If one side retreats, the raison d'être for the other side's vigilance may disappear. Current trends suggest this to be the case.

In any event, it is notable that a fundamental "rule" of conduct existing between the two superpowers evolved over time: Each avoided direct combat against the armed forces of the other superpower. Exceptions to this rule have involved incidents, not combat operations. The Soviets, for example, did not use troops in the Korean War, but did shoot down a U-2 during the Cuban missile crisis. Similarly, the United States steadfastly refused to escalate the Korean War to targets in the USSR or China, just as President Kennedy was extremely cautious about using force in the Cuban missile crisis that might inflict casualties on Soviet troops located there. The other aspect of this rule is reflected in the deliberate exception taken by the United States to signals of Soviet preparations to send troops to Egypt during the 1973 war, by undertaking a DefCon 3 alert: The caution to avoid direct conflict had its deterrent effect.

Disengagement

Reflecting on the intrinsic strategic value of most Third World areas, it is obvious that their worth is slight in terms of the direct security interests of the superpowers. As disinterest began to develop, both sides saw fit to cut some of their losses and reduce several of their commitments. What appears to be happening with respect to the Third World aspirations of the two superpowers is, as one political scientist expressed it, a "symmetrical disillusionment with globalism."[20]

However, to conclude that the Cold War has ended is premature. What is clear is that Soviet power, interest, and opportunity in the Third World is in significant decline. The USSR no longer offers an alternative model for economic or political development. Neither does China. The whole communist world is discredited in these respects. At the same time, the United States is less inclined toward Third World activism. It thus appears that both superpowers are tired of the Cold War, even if it may continue at a lower level of intensity.

What this means for the topic addressed in this chapter is that, whatever conflicts arise in the Third World in the near future, surely each superpower expects that a conventional war in the nonaligned world would not and should not draw in the regular armed forces of the United States and/or the Soviet Union. While we are short of agreement on this point, we are not far from it, not because we have come to like each other, but because we have learned the hard way that the effort to intervene is not worth the cost, and direct superpower conflict is not worth the risk.

On the other hand, the Eurasian perimeter is vital to the security of the United States. U.S. armed forces are deployed to maintain the security of the two most important security positions: NATO and Northeast Asia. U.S. security interests beyond Europe and the industrial sector of Asia are not significant; in any case they cannot be readily served by the introduction of conventional ground forces. Our foremost adversary remains the Soviet Union. In the future, as in the past, any U.S. strategy for dealing with Soviet conventional forces will have to take into account the nuclear shadows cast by the two sides. This restraining factor largely advantages the defender of the status quo; in virtually every case, this is the United States. Moreover, Soviet conventional forces are bottled up in a landlocked continental army posture; a principal purpose of U.S. security policy is to keep it that way.

Selective Containment

The most fundamental conclusion from this analysis is that the current deployment of U.S. ground forces is more than sufficient to support the selective containment of Soviet power because the forces are forward-deployed to protect the primary security interests of the United States abroad. The vision of a ubiquitous Soviet threat throughout the Third World comes from unrealistic assessments of Soviet power and U.S. interests. The Soviet threat is, fortunately, confined to continental Eurasia. U.S. containment policy and the conventional and nuclear forces necessary to implement that policy are best directed to the defense of NATO and northeast Asia. The irresoluteness of most of the problems of the rest of the Third World make for uninviting consequences for any nation undaunted by them.

Hedging Our Bets

Having said all this, every student of U.S. military history knows that Presidents have suddenly reversed policy and committed U.S. ground troops to combat in unexpected locations for unanticipated objectives. The current planning problem for the U.S. Army is additionally compounded by the potential progress of CFE talks in that the principal Army mission in Europe may be altered by an arms reduction agreement. Should reductions in U.S. heavy conventional forces in NATO be translated into an even smaller active duty force for the United States than currently exists? That may be a tempting outcome for politicians looking for reduced defense expenditures, but it would make it more difficult for the United States to retain a prudent military readiness posture in an always uncertain future.

Notes

1. U.S. Department of Defense, Frank C. Carlucci, *Report to Congress, FY 1990* (Washington, D.C.: U.S. Government Printing Office, 1989), p. 127.
2. Ibid.
3. *Discriminate Deterrence*, Report of the Commission on Integrated Long-Term Strategy (Washington, D.C.: U.S. Government Printing Office, January 1988), p. 13.
4. See Ole R. Holsti and James N. Rosenau, *American Leadership in World Affairs: Vietnam and the Breakdown of Consensus* (Boston: Allen & Unwin, 1984), p. 109, and passim for a similar category.
5. I use this term simply to refer to contemporary realists, although more specialized meaning often applies in the literature of political science.
6. One of their number calls this objective "finite containment." See Stephen Walt, "The Case for Finite Containment: Analyzing U.S. Grand Strategy, *International Security*, Vol. 14, No. 1, Summer 1989, pp. 5–49.
7. Michael C. Desch, "The Keys that Lock Up the World: Identifying American Interests in the Periphery," *International Security*, Vol. 14, No. 1, Summer 1989, pp. 90–97, identifies two schools, "neo-internationalism" and "neorealism." Walt, "Finite Containment," note 6, pp. 6–9, identifies six, based on their strategies: world order idealism, neo-isolationism, disengagement, finite containment, global containment, and rollback.
8. George F. Kennan, *American Diplomacy 1900–1950* (New York: The New American Library, 1951), p. 10.
9. See Stephen W. Van Evera, "American Strategic Interests: Why Europe Matters, Why the Third World Doesn't." Testimony before the Panel on Defense Burdensharing, Committee on Armed Services, U.S. House of Representatives, March 2, 1988, and Stephen M. Walt, note 6.
10. Barry R. Posen and Stephen W. Van Evera, "Defense Policy and the Reagan Administration: Departure From Containment," *International Security*, Vol. 8, No. 1, Summer 1983.

11. Desch, note 7, p. 98, footnote.
12. Van Evera, note 9.
13. For a brief review and analysis of these policy developments, see Jeffrey Record, *Revising U.S. Military Strategy: Tailoring Means to Ends* (Washington, D.C.: Pergamon-Brassey's, 1984), Part I.
14. Walt, note 6, p. 20. For a discussion of the "myth of interdependence," see Kenneth N. Waltz, *Theory of International Politics*, (Reading, MA: Addison-Wesley, 1979), Chapter 7.
15. Steven R. David, "Why the Third World Matters," *International Security*, Vol. 14, No. 1, Summer 1989, pp. 50–85.
16. See especially, Holsti and Rosenau, note 4, and Holsti and Rosenau, "Consensus Lost, Consensus Gained? Foreign Policy Beliefs of American Leaders, 1976–1980," *International Studies Quarterly*, Vol. 30, December 1986, pp. 375–409.
17. For a recent source of evidence that supports these three observations, see Roosevelt Center for American Policy Studies, "Old Doctrine vs. New Threats: Citizens Look at Defense Spending and National Security," (Washington, D.C.: Roosevelt Center for American Policy Studies), April 1989.
18. Indeed, the only conventional war was the Falkland Island conflict between Britain and Argentina.
19. Thomas C. Schelling noted in his classic, *Strategy of Conflict* (New York: Oxford University Press, 1960, footnote 5, pp. 11–12), that rivals do not have to have similar values in order to cooperate: "They may just be in the same boat together," meaning that whatever else they do, they have a shared interest "in not tipping the boat."
20. Sharam Chubin, quoted by James M. Markham in "The Idea That Democracy Pays Helps Reshape East-West Ties," *New York Times*, September 25, 1988, p. C1.

CHAPTER 10

U.S. Strategy and Unconventional Conflicts: The Elusive Goal

SAM C. SARKESIAN

As the 1990s began, it was clear to many Europeans and Americans that the strategic landscape had changed and was continuing to do so in Europe. In addition to the unraveling of the Eastern bloc under the Gorbachev regime and the policies of glasnost and perestroika, political changes were taking place inside the Soviet Union that were creating tremendous pressures on the Soviet system. Some saw serious political ferment. All of these changes have had an impact on the shape of Soviet foreign policy, with implications for the Third World.

While there are a number of conflicting assessments, it appears that the Soviet Union is seeking to reduce its presence and economic burden of maintaining outposts in Third World areas. At the same time, it appears that the Soviets do not necessarily want to withdraw completely from their established positions. A less visible and more economical strategy is likely to be put in place.

Even if visible Soviet presence is considerably reduced, it is likely that regional conflicts, particularly of an unconventional character, will continue. Some argue that ethnic rivalries, power struggles, and historical animosities will increase. A number of such conflicts in the past did not spring from the confrontations between the United States and USSR; rather, they had their roots in the dynamics of indigenous areas in the Third World. The landscape of the 1990s is likely to continue these conflict characteristics and probabilities. In critical Third World areas, these conflicts may require U.S. involvement in one form or another. One of the most challenging to the United States is unconventional conflict.

Such conflicts are the most difficult for conventionally postured forces to deal with, as even the Soviets learned in Afghanistan. For a democracy, such as the United States, designing strategy and an appropriate force posture is particularly difficult. What is even more difficult is to develop a political rationale for engaging in unconventional conflict.

In sum, the changing strategic landscape evolving out of the internal dynamics of Eastern and Western Europe and the USSR have global implications. But such implications do not necessarily result in a peace syndrome outside Europe. The period of uncertainty and transition may increase confrontations and internal struggles within a number of Third World areas. Thus, until there is a decided change in the conflict environment in a number of Third World areas, it is likely that the United States will need to be prepared to defend its vital interests, including the possibility of becoming involved in critical areas. The design of strategy and relevant force posture for unconventional conflicts poses the most difficult problem for the United States.

Complicating this period of uncertainty and transition is the fact that the Pacific Rim has become increasingly important to U.S. national interests. The issue of U.S. strategy and involvement in unconventional conflicts, therefore, must also be considered in this context, compounding the difficulties and complexities of effective response.

Historically, U.S. strategy has been shaped by a combination of geostrategic considerations, Clausewitzian notions, and self-images of the U.S. role in world affairs. This is also the case in the contemporary period, and is likely to remain so for the foreseeable future. However, with the exception of Europe (NATO), there is much truth to the view that U.S. strategy over the past two decades has been generally disjointed, incoherent, and operationally questionable. This is particularly the case with respect to unconventional conflicts and the Third World.

One of the most relevant and intriguing Clausewitzian observations in this regard is that in "strategy everything is very simple, but not on that account very easy."[1] On the one hand, there is a direct and clear link between policy and strategy, but on the other, the implementation of strategy is a complex and difficult proposition. It is this intertwining of the simple with the complex and difficult that is critical and challenging in the design of U.S. strategy for unconventional conflicts.[2] This is the frame of reference for this study.

The purpose here is to examine U.S. unconventional conflict strategy in the context of Clausewitzian logic in order to determine the following:

1. The nature and character of unconventional conflict;
2. A critique of U.S. strategy and the political-military system; and
3. What needs to be done in U.S. strategy and the political-military system.

The Nature and Character of Unconventional Conflicts

More than a decade has passed since the second U.S. counterinsurgency era began.[3] Since that time, there has been a proliferation of studies, concepts, and terms focused on unconventional conflicts, or, in official parlance, "special operations and low-intensity conflict." Even a cursory glance at published material in civilian and military publications shows the variety of views, disagreements, and confusion regarding unconventional conflicts. Differences range from weaponry and tactics to command and control structures. The crux of the matter, however, is in the way conflicts are conceptualized and defined. The importance of developing some common ground is clear. How can the United States design relevant and effective strategy if there is little agreement as to what the conflict is all about?

Concepts and Definitions

The need to clarify concepts and definitions has been a consistent theme in earlier studies of unconventional conflicts.[4] While it would appear that such matters could now be put to rest, the extent of the published literature indicates continuing problems. The scope of disagreement and the problems this creates can be reasonably inferred from the conflict labels: low-level warfare; brush-fire wars; small wars; insurgency; counterinsurgency; wars of the third kind; guerrilla war; and low-intensity, mid-intensity, and high-intensity conflicts. There is also the position that such conflicts should simply be called wars, with all this suggests about national psyche and war effort. Each of these labels has useful purposes, and there are excellent works framed around them individually and collectively. Nonetheless, these various labels and terms indicate a particular disciplinary or policy perspective that shapes the way the conflict environment is analyzed. In turn, this has a decided influence on framing the strategic response. For example, the term *insurgency* has a particular military connotation with all this suggests with respect to the "proper" response.

The concept employed in this study is based on the term *unconventional conflict*, which is used because it provides both an intellectual and strategic dimension, and a distinction that has operational utility. *Unconventional* suggests a sharp contrast to the conventional dimension and orthodoxy of the American way of war. Further, the notion of unconventional indicates nontraditional and nonconforming, reinforcing the contrast to the American way of war. The term *conflict* has a connotation not linked solely to the military dimension normally associated with *war*. Moreover, the term offers a political-social focus on confrontations, ranging from social and political turmoil to strife, hostility, and a mix of psychological and physical means to intimidate, create fear, and coerce physically.

Bernard Fall provided some clarification of these matters years ago in his study of the Indochina conflict.[5] "Just about anybody can start a 'little war' . . . even a New York street gang. . . . But all this has rarely produced the kind of revolutionary ground swell which simply swept away the existing government."[6]

Fall went on to say:

> It is . . . important to understand that guerrilla warfare is nothing but a tactical appendage of a far vaster political contest and that, no matter how expertly it is fought by competent and dedicated professionals, it cannot possibly make up for the absence of a political rationale.[7]

The "far vaster political contest" is the notion of revolution. And it is this "contest" that is driven by a strategic goal of overthrowing the existing system in order to create a revolutionary order. As Sir Robert Thompson has written, "Revolutionary war . . . is designed to reach a decisive result on its own."[8]

There is ample evidence in recent U.S. experience supporting the observations of Fall and Thompson. For example, the experience (and exploits) of Edward Lansdale based on his unorthodox views regarding fighting Marxist-Leninist revolutions are particularly instructive. "Essentially, in a revolutionary 'people's war,' the people of the country actually constitute the true battleground of the war. Whoever wins them wins the war."[9] Earlier, Lansdale had written, "We mostly sought to destroy enemy forces. The enemy sought to gain control of the people. . . . American leaders relied so heavily on military solutions in a war that begged for political solutions."[10]

Revolution and Counterrevolution

These observations are starting points for the conceptual basis of this study. The critical core of unconventional conflict is revolution and counterrevolution. The goal of revolution is to overthrow the existing system and replace it with a revolutionary one—a system that establishes a revolutionary political and social order. In the process, guerrilla war, insurgency, terror, and psychological intimidation may be used. Similarly, it is conceivable that to complete the revolution, the final stages may require the formation of conventional units to complete the defeat of the existing system. The fundamental and driving force, however, remains revolution and the revolutionary political system. There is little that is low intensity about such conflicts. They are not small wars in the eyes of the indigenous antagonists. They are conflicts over the very fundamental issue of who should rule and the nature of the political-social system. These are conflicts that in the final analysis are "wars of survival" to these participants.

In a perceptive study of the nature of "war," in contrast to insurgency, Charles Maechling, Jr., observes that in war as conceived in classical (perhaps conventional) terms,

Destruction of the opponent's entire social order has rarely been a military objective per se. By and large, the reverse has been true. . . . Implicit in the classical theory is preservation of the opponent's social order to enable a victor to enforce a viable peace. . . . The victor develops as much a stake in the stability of the loser's government as the loser.[11]

The contrast to revolution is clear. Revolutionaries are intent on destroying the existing political and social order. Indeed, even the lesser forms of unconventional conflicts, such as terror qua terror (i.e., the Japanese Red Guards), are aimed at the political-social order and are qualitatively different from war. As simple as this may appear, it is difficult to institutionalize this concept in the thinking process of political-military policymakers, strategists, and operational commanders. The driving force in assessing the nature and character of conflicts has been based on the historical experience of grand battles and interpretations of Clausewitz. What results, in brief, is the perception of conflict through conventional lenses, interpreted by mind-sets shaped by Clausewitzian notions and orthodoxy. This serves reasonably well in preparing for an adversary whose primary political-military posture is shaped by similar forces. But it does not serve well when faced with unconventional conflicts. This is not to deny that some elements of unconventional conflicts fit into a conventional pattern, more or less, but the core of such conflicts does not adhere to patterns of conventionality or orthodoxy.

The people of the indigenous area compose the true battleground. Clausewitzian notions and high-tech military capability are usually irrelevant in unconventional conflicts. Conventional military capability and the "largest" battalions rarely decide the outcome. The center of gravity is in the political-social milieu of the indigenous populace, rather than on the armed forces. Thus, it is Sun Tzu's concepts of war and success that are more appropriate, even though such principles were articulated over five hundred years before the time of Christ.[12]

Writing over twenty years ago, Hannah Arendt may well have touched the essence of the problem now facing the United States in unconventional conflict:

> Revolution, in distinction to war, will stay with us into the foreseeable future. . . . [T]hose will probably win who understand revolution, while those who still put their faith in power politics in the traditional sense of the term and, therefore, in war as the last resort of all foreign policy, may well discover in a not too distant future that they have become masters in a rather useless and obsolete trade.[13]

Complicating the problems in designing strategy and confusing the role of the military in various contingencies is the increasing attempt to categorize all conflicts outside of Europe as low-intensity conflicts. For example, in late 1989, there were calls by a variety of U.S. elected officials and others to classify everything from drug "war" to a naval force in the Persian Gulf as low-intensity conflicts, requiring mission assignments to the U.S. military. Not only does such categorization distort the concept of unconventional (low-intensity) conflicts, but it obfuscates missions and contingencies that are assigned to unconventional conflict forces. These other contingencies are best categorized as law-and-order missions, peacekeeping, or armed diplomacy. Most of these contingencies usually can be undertaken by standard elements of the military and often in support of other U.S. agencies. In such contingencies, the environment, targets, intelligence, and mission purposes usually differ from unconventional conflicts. But the attempt to include everything outside Europe as part of the unconventional conflict environment is conceptually misguided and strategically inappropriate.

In sum, U.S. strategy in unconventional conflicts has been usually ad hoc and disjointed. Much of this is a result of inconsistent policy, domestic politics, and the European battle orientation driving U.S. military posture. Most of these strategic failings stem from the difficulty of interpreting nation interests as these apply to unconventional conflicts and the Third World. In the larger sense, all of these failings evolve form the conceptual incoherency in dealing with the characteristics of unconventional conflicts.

U.S. Strategy and the Political-Military System: A Critique

Understanding the nature and character of unconventional conflicts is obviously critical in formulating relevant policy and designing appropriate strategies. Equally important, the substance and dimensions of policy and strategy must evolve directly from U.S. national interests. Acknowledging that there is some disagreement regarding the definition of national interests and their interpretation in terms of policy and strategy, the statement in the final report of the Seventieth American Assembly is offered as a useful starting point.

> It is beyond dispute that the primary obligation of Western governments must be to defend their vital interests, to maintain military balance, to protect and advance democratic and pluralist values in the world, and to seek to strengthen the international system against the chaos and violence that threaten it.[14]

From this statement, one can reasonably argue that U.S. national interests include the maintenance and perpetuation of democracy, among other things. It follows that one goal of U.S. policy includes the support of systems that are attempting to move toward openness and ruling elites whose long-term commitment is to democracy as traditionally defined.

National Interests

In this respect, U.S. national interests and policy may require, in one set of circumstances, a strategy that supports existing systems that are struggling against revolutionary forces. In other situations, strategy may involve supporting revolutionary groups against an existing system. Although there may be a body of opinion opposed to any policy and strategy requiring U.S. intervention in either set of circumstances, national interests may call for such involvement. As one expert has noted:

> A unilateral self-denying ordinance against all intervention—open or covert—is too restrictive. Some threats to American national security require responses. Some American friends in the Third World deserve support. What is imperative is to keep in mind the long-term costs of intervention for a government that is not notable for attending to long-term considerations.[15]

An important part of defining and interpreting national interests is in identifying those interests that are "vital" and those that are "important." Vital interests are directly linked to the survival of the U.S. political system and its values. These interests are associated, by and large, with the "core" areas, the U.S. mainland and its immediate contiguous areas. With some exceptions, the farther from the core areas, the less likely that U.S. national interests will be "vital." Important interests are those that can be open to compromise and negotiation, and tempered by realpolitik. These interests are primarily with "contiguous" areas (Central America) and "outer" areas, such as Black Africa. Such interests are open to a variety of policy and strategic options, in contrast to vital interests, where the use of maximum U.S. power is normally the directed strategy. These matters are discussed in detail elsewhere.[16]

In brief, there are disagreements regarding the interpretation of national interests as these may apply to the Third World and unconventional conflicts. These, in turn, are seen in policy design, strategic options, and operational guidelines. Most important, the way conflict is perceived does, in no small way, affect how U.S. national interests are interpreted and whether they are "vital" or "important." Further, the way in which conflicts are conceptualized has a decided impact on the shaping of strategy and its link to policy and national interests. And, finally, the interpretation and application of U.S. national interests into policy formulation and strategy design is tempered and shaped by democratic imperatives and the American way of war. As will be shown later, these are important constraining factors, and they provide the moral and ethical substance shaping any U.S. response to unconventional conflicts.

In the final analysis, U.S. national interests must delineate between the "vital" and "important," and policy must be designed accordingly. Further, national interests must also distinguish between Third World instability resulting from modernization and change and the instability that is part of unconventional conflicts. And, again, policy must be designed accordingly. It is in this context and with these directions that strategy must be designed and implemented.

Strategy

Returning to the Clausewitzian perspective, strategy to accomplish various policy goals in pursuit of national interests may appear simple at first glance. It follows that the United States should use all legitimate means and an appropriate intermix of instruments to achieve policy goals, including economic, political, and psychological ones, as well as appropriate military means. However, the specific mix of instruments, their operational implementation, and when they should be used are more complex and difficult to determine.

The difficulty and complexity are, in no small way, consequences of the characteristics of unconventional conflicts and the fact that most occur in a Third World environment. Thus, such conflicts tend to become enmeshed in the political and social turmoil accompanying economic development and political change. If recent history is any guide, the United States has yet to develop the necessary mechanisms, strategic sophistication, and political-military finesse to respond to the combined challenges of the Third World and unconventional conflicts. Furthermore, as pointed out earlier, U.S. political culture creates an environment that compels U.S. political-military strategy and operations to seek the moral high ground even in those conflicts in which the adversary perceives the highest morality to be success, justifying virtually any means to accomplish it. The "ends-means" relationship is an important part of the democratic imperative: Means must be in accord with democratic norms.

In addition, the U.S. body politic, including many political leaders and policymakers, has neither the patience nor the understanding to respond effectively or expeditiously to the challenges of unconventional conflicts. "The American political system is poorly suited to conduct a limited war; and the American people are lacking in two important requisites for a sound foreign policy—patience and understanding of the role that power plays in world affairs."[17]

Finally, the American way of war imposes a particular perspective on the nature of conflicts, imposing constraints and limitations on strategic options and operational guidelines. In brief, Americans tend to abide by a

"Pearl Harbor" mentality, which presume wars do not start until U.S. battleships are bombed. It follows that there is a clear distinction between war and peace and between the instruments of war and peace. Further, peace occurs when there is a formal signing of a peace treaty.

Most presume that war is characterized by the mobilization of the populace, the development of a "moral crusade," and the clear consensus that evil needs to be destroyed. Thus, expectations are that there is a clear identification of the enemy, of U.S. purposes, and of the final goal. In sum, the mission is clear and the evil is clear.

Rarely do unconventional conflicts adhere to such neatly defined distinctions or purposes. Combining these characteristics with the fact that few Americans understand the character and nature of unconventional conflicts, one can understand why the United States is placed at a distinct disadvantage in responding to such conflicts.

The Political-Military System

The creation of the First Special Operations Command in 1983, later evolving into the United States Special Operations Command, was an important step in developing a more effective operational capability for unconventional conflicts. This Command now includes units and forces from all of the military services who are trained and organized specifically for special operations and low-intensity conflict.

Special Forces were created in the early 1950s and served an important role in Vietnam. A number of Special Forces officers also served in the Korean War, conducting a variety of "special operations." Ranger units and Navy SEALs (Sea, Air, Land) evolved out of the World War II experience. All of these units, as well as Air Force Special Squadrons, have either evolved out of or have been strengthened by America's second counterinsurgency era. However, a central coordinated command structure developed only with the creation of the Special Operations Command.

Additionally, a structure was created to coordinate political-military efforts. This was mandated by Congress over the objections of many in the Department of Defense—an indication of the long-range problems associated with responding to unconventional conflicts. The position of Assistant Secretary of Defense for Special Operations and Low Intensity Conflict was created, as was the Low Intensity Conflict Board in the National Security Council. Further, Congress recommended that the President appoint a Deputy Assistant to the President for National Security Affairs for Low Intensity Conflict. A number of advisory groups and centers evolved in response to the government's apparent interests in low-intensity conflict.

There is ample evidence, however, to support the view that considerable resistance was encountered in all of these initiatives, resistance that remains today. Much of this is within the military. For example, there was a long delay in appointing an Assistant Secretary of Defense for Special Operations and Low Intensity Conflict; the Board for Low Intensity Conflict "has never met during the 2 years since its creation"; and only recently has the Special Operations Command been given the authority to develop its own budget. And as of this writing, no Deputy Assistant to the President has been appointed.[18]

In another dimension, only a handful of military professionals perceive assignments in special operations as career enhancing. The focus of most professionals remains on the European battlefield and the changes that may be required in the post INF era. In this respect, arms control, conflict limitation, strategic warfare, and conventional military trade-offs and strategies are at center stage. Much of this is a result of the changed political and policy directions of the Soviet Union and the initiatives taken by Mikhail Gorbachev.

Furthermore, most of the effort of senior service schools is shaped by concern with the Soviet Union, even though increasing weight is being given to special operations and light infantry contingencies. But this latter interest appears to subsume the concept of unconventional conflicts into a special operations mode, clearly subordinating, if not ignoring, the core of such conflicts: revolution, counterrevolution, and the terrorism evolving from them. Thus, there appears to be a much better grasp of the demands of special operations in comparison to the low-intensity conflict dimension. The operational posture of the various elements of the Special Operations Command reflect this mind-set in explicit as well as implicit ways.

For example, special operations support of theater commanders in major conflicts in the form of partisan activities against the enemy and in response to partisan activities against the United States is emerging as an integral part of the military planning for Europe. Also, considerable attention has been given to developing a counterterror capability, such as hostage rescue units and hit-and-run raids. But, as indicated earlier, these are not operations that are the core of unconventional conflict. Partisan activity is usually closely connected with supporting tactical operations of friendly conventional forces. Conversely, partisan operations also aim their primary activity against enemy armed units, extending the friendly tactical operational area.

In brief, the U.S. military appears to be better equipped mentally and organizationally to grapple with special operations than with the core of unconventional conflicts, revolution, and counterrevolution.

The problems in responding to unconventional conflicts also stem from the U.S. security assistance program. The Department of State is the lead agency that allocates resources through its Foreign Operations budget. Within this budget are a variety of military assistance programs, including foreign military sales (FMS) grants, FMS low-cost credits, international military education and training programs (IMET), and military assistance programs (MAP).[19] These are in addition to economic assistance.

The effectiveness of these programs has been criticized by a variety of analysts.[20] There is considerable imbalance in the planning and implementation of such programs. For example, there are inadequacies in the security assistance program with respect to Central and South America. Further, budget cutting has added to the problem by limiting funding.[21]

As is the case with overall strategy for unconventional conflicts, the security assistance program appears to lack central coordination and control. It appears to be designed in bits and pieces, implemented in ad hoc fashion, and disjointed in impact. All of this is exacerbated by the fact that security assistance lacks a political constituency in Congress, with the exception of that for Israel and Egypt. Many of the problems with U.S. security assistance programs may stem from the lack of understanding of the nature and character of the Third World, the process of modernization and change, and how all of these relate to unconventional conflicts.

In sum, U.S. political-military strategy for unconventional conflicts has been incoherent, ad hoc, and operationally disjointed. This can be traced to the problems of interpreting U.S. national interests in terms of unconventional conflict and their inextricability from Third World issues. This, in turn, makes it difficult to formulate coherent and realistic policy, which in turn leads to the problems of designing strategy.

U.S. Political-Military Posture: What Needs to Be Done

It is useful at this point to note that number of scholars studying unconventional conflicts, deliberately or not, confuse analysis with advocacy. Analysis and identification of effective U.S. strategies and organizations to respond to unconventional conflicts have triggered charges of policy advocacy. Yet, many of those making such charges have their own political agenda and biases. Such charges, in the main, do little to serve scholarship or serious analysis. Moreover, the perpetuation of such changes compounds the difficulty in coming to grips with unconventional conflicts.

Similarly, there are those who pejoratively place the United States in an "interventionalist" posture because of the mistaken presumption of U.S. capability and the view that the Special Operations Command reflects operational effectiveness for an interventionist policy and strategy. Those who have taken such a posture have seriously overestimated U.S. capability and effectiveness, and have ignored the essence of unconventional conflicts. Further, they have ignored the significant constraints and limitations imposed by the U.S. political system and the American people, while neglecting the countervailing forces dynamically present within the body politic. These misjudgments are exacerbated by those who equate moral equivalency with any system engaged in unconventional conflicts, regardless of the qualitative nature and ideology of the systems involved.

There is another research aspect that needs to be acknowledged. Various elements of strategy, contingencies, and operational implementation responding to unconventional conflicts may be highly classified, and therefore are not available for research and analysis. What is in the public realm and the results from observation and research may therefore neglect capabilities and directions already institutionalized. Nevertheless, inferences can be drawn and reasoned judgments made from what is available, identifying political-military patterns and experiences of the past, and developing a sense of the prevailing U.S. political-military posture and the forces driving it. It is in this context that a number of strategic and operational guidelines are addressed.

Strategy

Turning from these various research considerations to strategy guidelines, we identify seven major elements for consideration. First, U.S. strategy should be primarily nonmilitary. It must distinguish between instability inherent in the process of modernization and that which signals unconventional conflict. In the former case, security assistance and a variety of economic strategies should predominate. The extent of such assistance and the level of U.S. effort are contingent not only upon U.S. geopolitical considerations, but upon the character and political orientation of indigenous rulers and the probability that the system will move, or can be moved, toward openness.

While it is clear that the United States cannot undertake to support every system that proclaims openness, neither can it ignore the U.S. role and presence in world affairs. The nature of the international security environment, its confluence with the emerging global economy, and the outreach of U.S. business and commercial interests, among other things, has drawn the United States into a highly competitive world. For better or for worse, U.S. presence is felt in virtually every corner of the globe. One major consequence is that the scope of U.S. national interests has considerably broadened.

The United States need not necessarily pursue these interests unilaterally. Strategy can be designed to include a major effort toward cooperation with or working through "friendly" states. If involvement in unconventional conflict is absolutely necessary, it is best done by a multinational strategy.[22]

Second, strategy for unconventional conflicts must include both a defensive and offensive phase. The defensive phase refers to support of the existing system. The offensive phase is that phase that strikes at the revolutionary strategy in order to take the revolution out of the hands of the revolutionaries. The two phases are inextricable.

Third, an offensive phase also must be conceived separately in support of revolutionary groups intent on overthrowing a repressive regime. Support for such groups must be based on the conviction that they have enlightened leadership committed to democracy and are intent on establishing an open system. A variety of covert operations can be undertaken in this offensive phase. There is no reason to assume that such operations cannot be undertaken successfully within the broad framework of democratic moral and ethical imperatives. Moreover, given the oversight function of Congress and the variety of multiple power centers within the decisionmaking arena, it is difficult, but not necessarily impossible, to conceal unauthorized covert operations.

Fourth, the long-range strategic goal should be focused on creating a nonmilitary environment in the contested area. Usually a political-military capability must be first demonstrated to convince adversaries that there is little likelihood that armed conflict can succeed, even an unconventional conflict. Demonstrated political-military capability and staying power are important elements in establishing a credible deterrent capacity in unconventional conflicts. Further, such a capacity may raise the costs to adversaries contemplating engaging in unconventional conflicts.

In any case, if the conflict area can be turned into a nonmilitarized one, then the advantage can shift to the United States. Economic assistance and adequate levels of security assistance, combined with an effective political-psychological campaign and effective intelligence, are the essential elements for success in countering adversaries in unconventional conflicts.

Fifth, strategy must be seen in the context of long-term U.S. national interests. Even if certain situations are less than important to short-term national interests, it is conceivable that they are vital in the long term. Further, by themselves, some Third World states may not seriously challenge U.S. national interests, but by acting as conduits or proxies for other states, they may pose such a challenge.

Sixth, strategy must be conceived with a vision that embraces the nature of U.S. national interests and policy goals over the long term and the notions of staying power and political will. Through this combination, strategy can also develop a sense of mission that is essential in effective operational implementation. These considerations are important in strengthening the intellectual dimension of strategic thought.

Seventh, strategy to engage in unconventional conflicts must consider options for withdrawal during any particular phase in order to cut losses. The continued escalation of the conflict by expanding U.S. efforts that become increasingly visible in the indigenous area may Americanize the war. The perceived shift of the effort from the indigenous system to the United States changes the political-psychological dimension, and the United States becomes the primary adversary. The conflict may well be seen as U.S.-inspired and controlled, with all this suggests for indigenous loyalty and commitment and impact on the U.S. domestic arena.

None of these strategic guidelines is easy to institutionalize into the U.S. policymaking process, nor are these guidelines easy to incorporate into strategic thought. Yet, they are essential in designing a more effective U.S. posture for unconventional conflicts. Basic to all of this is a realistic grasp of the essence of unconventional conflicts: These are not primarily military threats, even if the military has an important role to play. They are challenges to the very nature of the political system—its legitimacy and credibility. Effective response rests primarily on the nature and character of rule.

It is our view that an important step in accomplishing the goals set forth in these strategic guidelines is a restructuring of the U.S. political-military system for unconventional conflicts and the refocusing of primary responsibility into civilian instruments.

The Political-Military System

The creation of the First Special Operations Command was a major step in strengthening U.S. capability in unconventional conflict. This is reinforced by command authority created from the Assistant Secretary of Defense to the commander of the Special Operations Command, as well as the various boards and advisory groups linked to the Joint Chiefs of Staff. As noted earlier, there has been and remains a great deal of resistance to these developments, but the more basic issue of operational capability has to do with the missions and feasibility of U.S. military personnel and units in unconventional conflicts.

In an earlier study, it was suggested that a revised structure be created out of the Special Operations Command to reflect the realities of the unconventional conflict environment.[23] This triggered a degree of criticism—criticism, it might be added, that was well founded in terms of military considerations but not always well founded in terms of the characteristics of unconventional conflict.

After a long period of analysis and research on this matter, we are now convinced that the low-intensity dimension of unconventional conflicts (revolution and counterrevolution) needs to be placed under the operational control of an instrument that is dominated by civilians, including elements of the Department of State and the Central Intelligence Agency. This can be designed in a task force configuration capable of central control and supervision of U.S. efforts in response to unconventional conflicts. The role of the military should be strictly supportive, as dictated by the task force.

The structure of such a task force can follow the patterns of specified and unified commands present in the U.S. military system. The *unified* task force is one that is aimed at the initial phases of unconventional conflicts, depending on the characteristics of the indigenous area. Thus, a civilian heads the task force with various civilian agencies, as well as some military ones, providing the necessary elements. The *specified* task force is one that is aimed at later phases of the conflict, with a particular agency taking control and specific elements from other agencies designated as inherent parts of the task force. Again, this may be particularly appropriate in the latter phases of unconventional conflicts.

Finally, the very nature of unconventional conflicts places an important and often critical role on the Central Intelligence Agency. Equally important, as emphasized in this study, the major issue is indigenous government efficiency and effectiveness. This is largely, but not exclusively, a nonmilitary dimension.

In addition to the various factors already discussed, there are a number of practical reasons why the primary efforts need to be shifted to a civilian task force concept. First, it has been extremely difficult for U.S. military planners and operators to come to terms with the political-psychological essence of unconventional conflicts, and it is not easy for them to develop the covert operations mentality and operational finesse necessary to engage successfully in such conflicts. Moreover, in light of the institutionalized resistance and career considerations, as well as the visibility of U.S. military operations, military involvement in the low-intensity dimension should be primarily in the latter phases, when it is clear that light infantry forces will be required.

Second, the center of gravity of unconventional conflicts is in the political-social milieu of the indigenous system, with all this means in terms of strategy and operational focus. Political-psychological efforts and attention to government efficiency and effectiveness are critical in successful counterrevolution, as is the development of loyalty and commitment of the populace to the system. These are primarily missions best undertaken by nonmilitary agencies and instruments, supported as required by the military, but equally important, by effective police forces.

Third, the commitment of visible U.S. military forces into a conflict environment that is contrary to the American way of war is likely to create considerable disquiet within the U.S. body politic—a disquiet that can easily expand and deepen into serious public opposition. This is likely to be reflected within the halls of Congress and elements within civilian and military policymaking circles. Even the commitment of a small, but visible contingent of U.S. military advisors can generate a degree of disquiet. Given the evolving relationship between the United States and the USSR, it will probably be increasingly difficult to convince Americans to support the commitment of U.S. military forces, even in contiguous areas, except in clear crisis situations.

Summary and Conclusions

Over the past decades, the United States has taken a number of major steps to improve its capability in what is officially termed special operations and low-intensity conflict. This second counterinsurgency era grew out of the presumed first counterinsurgency era debacle in Vietnam. Beginning with concern over the developments in Central America and the variety of conflicts in Black Africa, the second era took on a momentum of its own, nurtured by a new feeling of U.S. strength and responsibility for responding to the perceived challenges of Marxist-inspired conflicts. U.S. national interests encompassed the idea of fostering the development of open systems, including support of non-Marxists revolutionaries, such as the Nicaraguan Democratic Resistance (Contras), and UNITA in Angola, lead by Jonas Savimbi.

In this respect, a number of important steps have been taken in developing a more effective U.S. capability in special operations and low-intensity conflict. Not only is there an Assistant Secretary of Defense for Special Operations and Low Intensity Conflict, but there is an operational capacity in the United States Special Operations Command. Complementing these developments are the creation and emergence of a number of advisory groups and centers, both government and private, whose primary focus is on this "new" battlefield. Moreover, scholarly analysis and practical assessments now appear in a variety of journals, ranging from historical perspectives to modern doctrinal concerns.

Entering the decade of the 1990s, the second counterinsurgency era seems to have lost its rationale with the widespread perception that "peace is breaking out all over." The rise of Gorbachev, the massive public relations strategy undertaken by the new Soviet leadership, and the emergence of the post-INF period have been instrumental in reducing tensions and in creating a more accommodating environment in many Third World areas. For the United States, budgetary constraints have, in no small measure, contributed to the tendency to seek less-expensive policy and strategy options. All of these developments have tended to reduce the "crisis" mentality that seemed to characterize the initial part of the second counterinsurgency era.

Nonetheless, the persistence of international terrorism, drug wars, the continuing conflicts in Central America, and the underlying turmoil in many Third World states promise the potential of serious conflicts in the coming decade. Although such conflicts may not assume the dimensions of the Vietnam War or the Soviet involvement in Afghanistan, their long-range consequences may be as important. Moreover, the nature of such conflicts may be such a complex intermix of political, social, and economic issues that they defy analysis and response by prevailing strategies and instruments. Indeed, even the "lessons" of Vietnam and Afghanistan may need to be reconsidered in the emerging security environment. If history is any guide, the U.S. response to such conflicts is likely to be characterized by strategic diffusion and irrelevancy, compounded by mismatches between policy goals and capabilities.

While the second counterinsurgency era was an attempt to resolve the dilemma facing the United States in responding to unconventional conflicts, the third counterinsurgency era, which is evolving now, is characterized by "irony"—the unwarranted assumption of great effectiveness on the part of the United States in unconventional conflicts when, in reality, such capability is minimal. Indeed, there is sufficient evidence to suggest that U.S. capability has actually decreased.

In the coming decade, the United States will be faced with four basic questions. How should one define unconventional conflicts? What unconventional conflicts will be threats to U.S. national security interests? When should the United States respond? The relative simplicity of these questions belies the complexity of the answers.

For the United States, coming to grips with the issues of Vietnam was difficult enough. However, in the security environment emerging in the 1990s, the difficulty is compounded by the changed relationship between the United States and Gorbachev's Soviet Union, and by the conviction by many that peace is at hand. Underpinning these new forces is the fact that the United States has yet to come to terms with its Vietnam experience—to draw relevant lessons and design effective doctrines.

This is not to suggest that Herculean efforts have not been made by the military system, policymaking officials, and specialists in unconventional conflicts. Indeed, there are a variety of excellent studies and analyses of such conflicts that have emerged from government and nongovernment sources. Further, there have been changes in the military system that are a result of reasoned analyses of what needs to be done.

Nonetheless, no amount of institutional or force structure change or scholarly analysis can provide an effective U.S. capability in unconventional conflict without first developing a strategic insight that is germane to the political and military environment in which unconventional conflicts occur. For such an insight to emerge, political and military mind-sets must be emancipated from traditional concepts of war. In brief, the American way of war must be reshaped. This is no mean task since the way we fight wars is contingent upon our notions of the enemy, moral and ethical guidelines, and the concepts of just war and just conduct. These are not new challenges. Over a period of at least one hundred years, the "humane" way to conduct wars has been an international issue.

However, by their very nature, unconventional conflicts not only stand outside of traditional concepts of war, but they pose serious problems to a conventionally postured military. The dilemma of open systems is that they are placed in a position of relying on conventional responses to conflicts that do not adhere to conventional modes of warfare.

Moreover, there is a basic U.S. proclivity to "get on with it." There is a tendency to view unconventional conflicts—indeed, all conflicts—in terms of problems to be solved, tantamount to mathematical reasoning processes. All problems have solutions. One needs to identify the problem, determine the right solution, and then implement it.

But as one perceptive analyst has stated,

> Just solutions are elusive. Many problems have no solutions at all, not even unjust ones; at most they can be managed, prevented from getting worse or from spreading to wider areas. Other problems are

best left to simmer in benign neglect until parties are disposed to settle them. American problems may never become imminent enough to require our intervention. Finally, international problems hardly ever are solved by the sedulous pursuit of legal and moral principles, so often urged by lawyers who help shape our foreign policies.[24]

For the U.S. military, particularly ground forces, the dilemma and challenges are compounded, not only because of the responsibility to respond across the conflict spectrum, but also because national policy, strategy, and doctrine for responding to unconventional conflicts remain the most elusive and ambiguous.

In this respect, over the past several years, there has been an increasing amount of attention given to unconventional conflicts, more pointedly to a variety of subjects that include insurgency, special operations, low-intensity conflict, low-level conflict, brush-fire wars, guerrilla warfare, and terrorism. Additionally, many of these studies have suggested ways to structure the military institution, shape force postures, and develop careers in special operations. All sorts of issues have been raised regarding the role of the Air Force, Navy, and Marines in such conflicts. One result is the surfacing of a variety of recommendations, suggestions, and observations as to what should be done.

But much of this concerns the structures, command lines, equipment, training, and administrative and logistical considerations. To be sure, these are important. However, unless attention is given to the essence of conflicts and what it is the United States is supposed to respond to, much may be simply form without substance and style without meaning.

This is what leads to the major recommendation in this study. The primary efforts in unconventional conflict should be placed in the hands of a civilian task force. The military should be given a supportive role, primarily with Special Forces under the operational control of the task force. Only when the conflict is seen as a vital interest should the military be committed in the latter phases, with the deployment of light infantry forces.

In closing, we return to the primary issue raised in this study: the need to develop a realistic conceptual framework for unconventional conflicts and a strategy designed accordingly. Concepts establish the boundaries and mindsets around which the external environment is assessed and acted upon. Evolving from this is another issue: the need for a restructured political-military system capable of providing operational elements suited to unconventional conflicts—adaptable, flexible, and aimed at the essence of such conflicts. But the underlying focus is a military profession whose horizons extend beyond the immediate demands of the traditional battlefield and a political-military system that can bring to bear keen insights and a high level of sophistication in knowing when, where, and how the United States must engage in unconventional conflicts.

Notes

1. Anatol Rapoport, ed., *Clausewitz, On War* (Baltimore, MD: Penguin Books, 1968), p. 243.
2. The term *unconventional conflicts* is used rather than low-intensity conflict. The latter term suggests conflict characteristics that may not be realistic and a strategic dimension that is focused on the specifics of the conflict environment. These matters are explained in more detail later in this study. In earlier studies, the author used the term *low-intensity conflict*. See, for example, Sam C. Sarkesian, "Organizational Strategy and Low-Intensity Conflicts," in Frank R. Barnet, B. Hugh Tovar, and Richard Shultz, eds., *Special Operations in US Strategy* (Washington, D.C.: National Defense University Press, 1984). Over the past years, however, the author has revised his views on this matter, adopting the term *unconventional conflict* for a variety of reasons explained in this study.
3. The first counterinsurgency era is associated with the Kennedy presidency, the revitalization of U.S. Special Forces, and the Vietnam era. The second era is associated with the Reagan presidency and the creation of the First Special Operations Command.
4. See, for example, Sam C. Sarkesian, *America's Forgotten Wars: The Counterrevolutionary Past and Lessons for the Future* (Westport, CT: Greenwood Press, 1984).
5. Bernard Fall, *Street Without Joy: Insurgency in Indochina, 1946–63*, 3d Revised Edition (Harrisburg, PA: Stackpole Co., 1963), p. 356.
6. Ibid.
7. Ibid., p. 357.
8. Sir Robert Thompson, *Revolutionary Wars in World Strategy, 1945–1969* (New York: Taplinger, 1970), p. 17.
9. Cecil B. Currey, *Edward Lansdale: The Unquiet American* (New York: Houghton Mifflin Co., 1989), p. 279.
10. Ibid., p. 278.
11. Charles Maechling, Jr., "Insurgency and Counterinsurgency: The Role of Strategic Theory," *Parameters: Journal of the U.S. Army War College*, Vol. XIV, No. 3, Autumn 1984, p. 35.
12. Sun Tzu, *The Art of War* (New York: Oxford University Press, 1963). Translated and with an introduction by Samuel B. Griffith.
13. Hannah Arendt, *On Revolution* (New York: Viking Press, 1965), p. 8.
14. Marshall D. Shulman, ed., *East-West Tensions in the Third World* (New York: W. W. Norton and Co., 1986), p. 224.
15. Gregory F. Treverton, "Covert Action and Open Society," *Foreign Affairs*, Vol. 65, No. 5, Summer 1987, p. 1007.
16. See, for example, Sam C. Sarkesian, *U.S. National Security: Policymakers, Processes, and Politics* (Boulder, CO: Lynne Rienner, 1989), pp. 3–23.
17. Ole R. Holsti and James N. Rosenau, *American Leadership in World Affairs: Vietnam and the Breakdown of Consensus* (Boston: Allen & Unwin, 1984), p. 70.
18. Benjamin F. Schemmer, "Senate Leaders Ask Scowcroft for New White House Focus on Low-Intensity Conflict," *Armed Forces Journal International*, Vol. 126, No. 8, March 1989, p. 67.
19. For an explanation of current security assistance programs, see *United States Military Posture, FY 1989*, prepared by the Joint Staff. No other data provided.

20. See, for example, A. J. Bacevich, James D. Hallums, Richard H. White, and Thomas F. Young, *American Military Policy in Small Wars: The Case of El Salvador* (Washington, D.C.: Pergamon-Brassey's, 1988), and John G. Roos, "US Missing Chance to Win Friends, Influence in Africa," *Armed Forces Journal International*, Vol. 126, No. 8, March 1989, pp. 39–40, 42.

21. See *United States Military Posture, FY 1989*.

22. A useful exploration of this view is contained in M. Elizabeth Guran, "Challenge in the Pacific: US Basing Beyond the 1990s," *Armed Forces Journal International*, Vol. 127, No. 4, November 1989, pp. 56, 58, 60. Although the author focuses specifically on conventional force posture, she does explore the principles of multinational strategies and multinational use of bases. Equally important, the author does point out the importance of the Pacific Rim.

23. Sam C. Sarkesian, "The Myth of US Capability in Unconventional Conflicts," *Military Review*, Vol. LXVIII, No. 9, September 1989, pp. 2–17.

24. Ernest van den Haag, "The Busyness of American Foreign Policy," *Foreign Affairs*, Vol. 64, No. 1, Fall 1985, pp. 114–115.

PART 5
Naval and Air Strategies

CHAPTER 11

The Maritime Strategy in a New Security Era

JOHN ALLEN WILLIAMS

As the administration of George Bush confronts the realities of a Soviet Union that appears less threatening and the increasing pressure on the defense budget, the strategy and budget of the U.S. Navy is receiving a great deal of attention. Concerns about the proper type and level of naval forces and their employment—particularly in a conflict with the Soviet Union—are more acute in the wake of a U.S. government fiscal crisis that threatens the forces needed to make the U.S. Navy's preferred strategy work. Additionally, the wisdom of the Navy's "Maritime Strategy" is questioned by critics who feel that it is ineffective, extravagant, or dangerous.[1] The purpose of this chapter is to describe the Maritime Strategy in the Bush Administration at the time of this writing and to discuss and evaluate its strategic options. Questions of force structure will be addressed as they relate to the strategic discussion.

Several factors will pressure the administration as it plans for the future of the Navy. The widespread perception in the United States and Europe of benign intentions on the part of Mikhail Gorbachev masks the reality of Soviet naval capabilities that have yet to diminish significantly, the Soviet rhetorical offensive notwithstanding. There is great popular support for arms control agreements that would reduce the levels of both tensions and expenditures—even, perhaps, for proposals put forth by the Soviets that are fundamentally disadvantageous to the West.[2] The greatest pressure on the administration is the widely agreed-upon need to reduce the federal deficit, which could reduce force levels to such an extent so as to affect the ability of the Navy to carry out both its wartime plans and its peacetime commitments.[3] Such pressures are resisted by naval leaders, of course.[4]

President Bush inherits a Maritime Strategy that has thoroughly penetrated the Defense Department.[5] (Indeed, within the Navy, the Maritime Strategy is often referred to as "the maritime component of national military strategy.") The President also has a naval force structure that cannot be greatly expanded during his administration, given the great cost of ship construction and the long lead times required. Preferred Navy plans call for naval forces to center around fifteen aircraft carrier battle groups (CVBGs), and to include 100 attack submarines (SSNs), four battleship battle groups (BBBGs),[6] amphibious shipping for one Marine expeditionary force (MEF) and one Marine expeditionary brigade (MEB), twenty to forty or so ballistic-missile-firing submarines (SSBNs),[7] and various other vessels for protection of shipping, mine warfare, resupply, and so forth. It is now clear that the Reagan Administration's goal of a "600 ship Navy" will not be met in this century,[8] since the Navy is reluctantly downsizing—including giving up two battleships and an as yet undetermined number of aircraft carriers.

Whether these are the best naval forces to buy is not the primary concern here, nor is whether national resources might better have been spent on Army or Air Force programs, or even whether the funds should have gone to defense at all. These issues are covered extensively elsewhere, too often at the expense of serious thinking about how best to employ the Navy that is becoming available. Three questions are of principal importance: What are the most effective missions for the U.S. Navy? What is its proper geographic emphasis? What is the best peacetime deployment posture? The discussion begins with a consideration of the Maritime Strategy.

The Maritime Strategy

Background

In the early 1970s, the U.S. Navy still consisted of over a thousand ships. Many of these were of World War II vintage and were becoming both obsolete and difficult to maintain. The Chief of Naval Operations at the time, Admiral Elmo Zumwalt, decided to retire those ships that had reached the end of their service lives and replace them with a smaller number of more capable ships. Given the much greater cost of these replacements and a general tendency to minimize U.S. defense expenditures in the aftermath of the Vietnam War, the decommissioned ships could not be replaced on a one-for-one basis by the more capable ships that were entering the fleet.

The result was a Navy that was about half the size it had been in the 1960s, and one that was tightly stretched to meet even its peacetime commitments. Such a Navy was tolerable to the Carter Administration, which focused defense resources on forces immediately useful on the Central Front of NATO. The Navy found itself relegated to a secondary position in national military strategy, which primarily envisioned a defensive sea control mission for it. Given the state of naval forces, a more ambitious orientation was not then feasible.

Not surprisingly, naval leaders were dissatisfied with this state of affairs. The Chief of Naval Operations (CNO) who bridged the Carter and Reagan Administrations, Admiral Thomas Hayward, set the course in 1979 from which the Maritime Strategy emerged.[9] He argued the need for offensive actions against Soviet forces in the event of war, even near the Soviet Union, and set his staff the task of developing a strategy that would incorporate these views. The efforts of his Strategic Concepts Group (OP-603) in the Pentagon and the Strategic Studies Group (SSG) at the Naval War College resulted in a classified briefing on the Maritime Strategy, which is still revised periodically and distributed in "hard copy" around the Pentagon. Hayward's ideas found a receptive audience in the Reagan Administration, particularly in the person of Navy Secretary John Lehman, Jr., who shared the Admiral's strategic priorities. Lehman added the political connections and bureaucratic skills necessary to sell the evolving Maritime Strategy, which became the basis of the 600-ship Navy.

Hayward's successor as CNO, Admiral James Watkins, published an unclassified version of this strategy in a January 1986 supplement to the semiofficial *Proceedings* of the U.S. Naval Institute.[10] In fact, the details of the strategy were already available to anyone willing to wade through congressional testimony.[11] The current CNO, Admiral Carlisle A. H. Trost, has stated his support for the Maritime Strategy and its continued development. As he noted in an early posture statement, "By continually examining and challenging its assumptions, we will continue to ensure its vitality and utility."[12]

Options

Technically, the Maritime Strategy is a "CNO's Program Advisory Memorandum" (or "CPAM"), and its accomplishment is the goal that justifies force acquisition. As such, it is the planning element of the planning, programming, and budgeting system (PPBS).[13] It is also the baseline strategy outlining how a conventional war with the Soviet Union might be fought. Although the Maritime Strategy does not dictate the timing of operations or even the specific operations that are required (a much-misunderstood point among both supporters and critics of the strategy), it is clear on the need for forward operations, rather than the passive ones, which Lehman stated display "a lack of understanding of the fundamental mechanics of war at sea" and are "defeatist."[14] Admiral Trost summarized the Maritime Strategy as "forward, offensive naval operations, in a conventional environment and in concert with available allies."[15]

The Maritime Strategy emphasizes that any conflict with the Soviet Union will be global in character, if only because it is in the interest of the United States to make it so to take the pressure off Central Europe. Very importantly, the Maritime Strategy relies on the contributions U.S. allies will make to its implementation, particularly in the provision of diesel submarines, escort ships, patrol aircraft, and mine warfare capabilities. As former Navy Secretary Lehman noted, "we count among our friends all of the world's great navies, save one."[16]

The Maritime Strategy can best be viewed as a "bundle of options" from which operational commanders and their civilian leaders can choose when planning campaigns. It is strategy, not tactics or a campaign plan, and it is not "a cookbook on employment of forces."[17] Possible actions include the following, which the next section will evaluate in more detail:

1. *Sea Control*: ensuring that the seas are available for use as necessary by U.S. and allied forces, and denying the use of the seas to hostile forces.
2. *Horizontal Escalation*: a phrase that has gone out of favor, but still a good one to describe war-widening options that attempt to tie down hostile forces and to fight in areas of U.S. advantage.
3. *Defense of the NATO Flanks*: ensuring that the Soviets cannot turn the NATO flanks by neutralizing or occupying such areas as Norway, Denmark, and the Aegean.
4. *Direct Participation*: contributing directly to the battle on the Central Front, a very demanding proposition for naval forces, as will be seen.
5. *Anti-SSBN Operations*: attempting to alter the correlation of nuclear forces by using conventional weapons against Soviet SSBNs.
6. *Third World Operations*: actions in the Third World not necessarily directly related to the U.S.-Soviet rivalry.

Evaluation of Maritime Strategy Options

Several options for maritime campaigns are within the scope of the Maritime Strategy. Some analysts believe that all of these are feasible and should be attempted in the event of a NATO–Warsaw Pact war; others would limit the Navy to the defensive form of sea control and forego the other options.

Sea Control

Military analysts are in wide agreement that sea control is vital for the success of allied forces in a land war in Europe. No one wants to confront a U.S. President with the choice of escalating to nuclear weapons or watching West Germany be overrun because allied forces were running out of supplies. Former Defense Secretary Frank C. Carlucci noted in his fiscal year 1990/91 posture statement, "Control of the sea lines of communication (SLOC) . . . is vital to our peacetime commerce and critical to the defense of U.S. interests and those of our allies in time of war."[18]

There is less agreement over the kind of sea control that is necessary for success in this effort. One can still strongly support the need for sea control to ensure the maintenance of the "Atlantic bridge" to Europe, yet oppose the most aggressive and forward options of the Maritime Strategy.

Sea control has several logical variants, although the Navy has preferred to discuss it as if it were not possible to disaggregate its components analytically. Clear thinking about campaign choices requires that this be done, however. In an earlier work, the author discussed defensive and offensive sea control,[19] and now proposes a third alternative: forward area sea control.

Defensive sea control. This is the defense of the part of the seas one wants to use. Given the wide expanse of the seas and the capabilities of modern weapons systems, this close-in defense could actually occur some distance from the force to be defended, whether this be a carrier battle group (CVBG), an underway replenishment group, an amphibious assault force, or a convoy of merchant ships. For example, defensive sea control operations to protect merchant ships resupplying Europe during a NATO–Warsaw Pact war could include setting up a barrier along the line from Greenland and Iceland to Norway (the "GIN Gap") or the United Kingdom (the "GIUK Gap") to prevent Soviet submarines from infesting the sea-lanes, but would not envision missions north of that line into the North Atlantic or the Norwegian Sea. Of course, more forward variants of defensive sea control are also possible, in which the defensive perimeter would be drawn even farther north (for example, between Norway's North Cape and Svalbard Island). Wherever the line is drawn, a barrier defense, composed of mines and allied antisubmarine warfare (ASW) forces, such as SSNs and, if possible, ASW aircraft, would be augmented by surface ships and other forces closer to the sea-lanes to detect and attack any hostile forces that slipped through the barrier.

Whether these activities would be sufficient to protect the sea-lanes is a matter of professional judgment. The U.S. Navy contends that defensive sea control alone is inadequate.[20]

Offensive sea control. This is the preferred Navy sea control mission, and writings by Navy and non-Navy officials sometimes make it seem as if this were the only form of sea control possible. Offensive sea control includes all of the activities of defensive sea control, but adds to them forward operations of surface and subsurface forces above the defense perimeter, strikes against hostile bases in the Soviet homeland, and a campaign of attrition against Soviet ballistic missile firing submarines (SSBNs) in their "bastions" near the Soviet Union and under the Arctic ice.[21] It could also include air strikes behind the forward edge of troops in a NATO–Warsaw Pact war, amphibious raids to secure forward bases, and the mining of harbors. This is a far more demanding mission, and one that requires the greatest number of the most sophisticated forces available for its completion. Critics allege that such missions are required to justify a large Navy building program, but even if this were correct, it does not necessarily follow that the strategic rationale underlying the buildup is invalid.

Proponents of offensive sea control argue that its emphasis on forward operations and even direct strikes on Soviet bases is effective militarily, and has the additional advantage of putting the Soviets on the defensive early in a war—regardless of the situation in Central Europe. From a military standpoint, it is certainly better to attack enemy forces before they can strike one's own, if it is possible to do so without undue risks. Opponents point out several of these, however: First, attacks on the Soviet homeland run the severe risk of retaliation against the United States itself, and perhaps also of escalation to nuclear war. Second, such attacks by naval forces require the positioning of aircraft carrier battle groups far forward. This puts at tremendous risk irreplaceable assets that would be more useful later in a war and would be indispensable for the defense of the Western Hemisphere and the Pacific basin if the land war in Europe should be lost. In addition, the close approach of these nuclear-capable forces to the Soviet Union make them more likely targets for preemptive attack.[22]

Forward area sea control. This is a middle ground between defensive and offensive sea control. It recognizes that the former may be inadequate by itself, and that the latter may be both overly ambitious and unnecessarily escalatory. Forward area sea control includes all of the defensive sea control options, plus the offensive sea control operations that do not include the movement of surface forces far forward (that is, near the Soviet Union), attacks on the Soviet homeland, or a concentrated anti-SSBN campaign. Some SSBNs would likely be destroyed anyway, but only incidentally as part of an overall campaign whose purpose is to destroy the Soviet SSNs that pose the greatest threat to the sea-lanes.[23]

This mission is consistent with the U.S. Navy judgment that operations purely in defense of the sea-lanes must involve the movement of forces as far north as possible, a point made forcefully by the current U.S. Commander in Chief, Atlantic (and NATO Supreme Allied Commander, Atlantic), Admiral Lee Baggett, Jr.: "The battle for the Atlantic is dependent upon the battle for the Norwegian Sea and the reinforcement and air support necessary to defend Norway and Iceland."[24] Attack submarines (SSNs) would tie down Soviet forces that could otherwise be much further south attacking reinforcement shipping for Europe.

Forward area sea control may also involve the movement of surface forces as necessary to secure and maintain forward bases in Norway and the Aegean. It does not envision attacks on Soviet territory or the positioning of carrier battle forces with this objective. If such attacks are deemed necessary by national command authorities, and if it is further decided that the U.S.

Navy should carry them out, they would be undertaken as part of the offensive sea control or horizontal escalation options.

The author supports this third alternative. It still permits forward operations of surface forces, although not for the purpose of attacks against targets in the Soviet Union. These are unwise, at least early in a conflict, for reasons put forth by critics of offensive sea control. Nevertheless, forward operations for the purpose of driving Soviet naval forces as far into their bastions as possible are useful and necessary to reduce the risk that they will be able to cut the sea-lanes further south. In a sense, these forward forces can be seen as a "cork in the bottle." In addition, they will seek to destroy as much of the Soviet fleet as possible—although Soviet SSBNs are a special case that will be addressed separately below. These forward operations are less escalatory than those of offensive sea control, but still put the Soviets on the defensive and deplete Soviet naval forces. They also permit additional operations, even offensive sea control options, if they should become necessary later in a war.

Horizontal Escalation

Supporters of this option argue that the best way to deter Soviet adventurism is to make it clear to them that the resulting war will not necessarily be confined to areas of Soviet choosing and Soviet advantage, but will spread to areas of comparative advantage for the United States and its allies. Admiral Trost noted, "It allows the full weight of Western capability to face the Soviets and removes their preferred option of a short, single-front war."[25] Insofar as the Soviets believe this could happen and are concerned about it, it could have a significant deterrent effect.

On the other hand, unless the area to which the war might be spread has a direct impact on the course of the war on the Central Front, or is an area of great importance to the Soviets, such a threat is unlikely to overcome the strong momentum that would be required to inspire them to consider such a war in the first place. Put differently, the Soviets are unlikely to begin a war in Europe without the perception of a great opportunity or, much more likely, the fear of a great loss—such as would be the case if they expected NATO to initiate a war or if a war were deemed necessary to prevent their society from crumbling. Since the Soviets would not initiate such a war for other than grave reasons, only the threat of serious consequences could dissuade them once the situation had developed to the point where war was imminent.

Proponents of horizontal escalation need to indicate clearly what the pressure points are, and how they might dissuade the Soviets from attacking once they had determined it was otherwise in their interest to do so. If the Soviets had decided to attack West Germany, for example, and were prepared to face the certainty of NATO resistance and the uncertainty of possible escalation to nuclear war, would they really be turned aside by the possibility that the United States would attack Cuba, Vietnam, or, for that matter, the Siberian coast of the Soviet Union? The element of uncertainty inherent in the existence of flexible, powerful naval forces might give them pause, but the linkages between horizontal escalation and conventional deterrence need to be more carefully drawn.

Once war commenced, however, some of these attacks might well be considered by the United States for their contribution to the war effort or to a postwar balance of power. These attacks need not be against the Soviet Union itself, and could be directed at Soviet client states. Cuba, of all countries, should reflect on its position in the event war breaks out. Even if it did not assist the Soviets in their war effort, it would be in Cuba's interest to become more friendly to the United States regardless of the outcome of a European war. Whatever the final position of their ground forces, the Soviets are going to finish a war without the bulk of their naval forces and without the ability to come to the aid of distant allies. If the Soviets lose the war, they will have enough troubles close to home to occupy them; if they win, it will be even more important for the United States not to have Soviet client states in the Western Hemisphere. The same line of reasoning would apply to any other client state as well.

Defense of the NATO Flanks

It is sometimes forgotten that the NATO alliance is not just for the defense of West Germany, although that is the place where there has been the most concern about a large-scale ground attack. On the European continent, NATO stretches from Norway to the Aegean. The countries on the northern and southern flanks of NATO should be defended, not only to meet NATO treaty obligations, but because of their importance for victory on the Central Front.

Defense of Norway, for example, is vital for the successful defense of the sea-lanes. The Soviet occupation of airfields in northern Norway would have serious consequences for the forward area sea control operations needed to keep the Soviet fleet in its bastions. The loss of Denmark greatly complicates the air defense problem of Great Britain. Control of the Aegean is necessary for the safe operation of naval forces in the Eastern Mediterranean and to threaten attacking Warsaw Pact forces from the south. Maritime forces are crucial for the defense of these regions, contributing significantly to the war on the Central Front. Similarly, the defense of other nations on the Soviet periphery, such as Japan and South Korea, helps to keep them allied with the United States, gives the United States continued access to vital manufactured goods, and complicates Soviet warfighting plans.

Direct Participation

Given the distances between probable operating areas for carrier battle groups and the forward edge of troops on the Central Front, opportunities for direct participation by naval forces in that area are limited. This is not to minimize the contribution these forces make to the battle there by other actions, such as maintaining the sea-lanes and preventing the Soviets from turning the NATO flanks. At least in the early stages of a war, before Soviet forces have been attrited by NATO actions, the contribution of naval forces will be indirect, but still important.[26]

Anti-SSBN Operations

A previous Chief of Naval Operations, Admiral James Watkins, called for "an aggressive campaign against all Soviet submarines, including ballistic missile submarines," as part of the Maritime Strategy. The rationale was "reducing the attractiveness of nuclear escalation by changing the nuclear balance in our favor."[27] This was not disputed at the time by then–Navy Secretary Lehman, although he now states that such a campaign is "not something the Maritime Strategy would normally do, because that would subtract SSNs from the primary conventional maritime tasks of the strategy."[28] In the event that a conventional war escalated to the strategic nuclear level, the successful completion of this mission would also assist in damage limitation.

Critics allege that this mission would be likely to provoke the Soviets into a nuclear response. This is a possibility, but it is probably more remote than the likelihood of such a response if carrier forces were to attack the Soviet Union itself. There also seems little doubt that the Soviets would sink U.S. SSBNs if the opportunity presented itself.

However, this mission is one that may not be in the U.S. interest to accomplish, even if it were possible to do so. SSBNs compose a large proportion of the Soviet nuclear strategic reserve forces, and their elimination puts a high premium on avoiding a first strike on their more vulnerable ICBMs. This vulnerability increases with the deployment of U.S. M-X "Peacekeeper" ICBMs and new Trident D-5 SLBMs. As a result, the Soviets may feel themselves forced to move to a hair-trigger "launch on warning" posture for their ICBMs, thereby lowering the nuclear threshold for these incredibly destructive forces. This latter possibility will be reduced to the extent that the Soviets deploy new, mobile land-based missiles. With a greater proportion of survivable retaliatory forces on land, especially the mobile SS-24s and SS-25s, the Soviets need not feel that they must "use or lose" their submarine-launched ballistic missiles (SLBMs), or move to the very destabilizing "launch on warning" posture for their ICBMs. It also means that the strategic leverage hoped for by the anti-SSBN mission is reduced as the relative importance to the Soviets of their sea-based deterrent is lessened.

The importance of naval forces is clear, both for conventional deterrence and for warfighting if deterrence should fail. At the same time, one must weigh carefully the costs involved in overly aggressive operations, particularly those involving direct attacks on the Soviet Union or on Soviet strategic reserve forces. The leverage these operations gain comes at the expense of increased nuclear instability.

Naval Forces in the Third World

The main focus of the Maritime Strategy is in the context of a global conventional war with the Soviet Union, but many of the activities involved in conventional warfighting could also apply to operations in the Third World. How appropriate Navy plans and forces are for these supposedly "lesser included contingencies" is a point of dispute. The issue is particularly important as the likelihood of a NATO–Warsaw Pact war grows increasingly remote in the wake of the dramatic changes sweeping Eastern Europe and the Soviet Union.

Navy officials say that recent operations, particularly in the Persian Gulf, demonstrate that the right choices have been made. The Chief of Naval Operations, Admiral Trost, asserted, "Our force structure is the right one if we are to remain militarily viable throughout all the possible levels of conflict in a geographically unlimited global arena."[29]

Yet Third World operations may have their own unique political and military requirements that are not prepared for adequately even if the demanding anti-Soviet preparations are made. This question is particularly important given the unlikelihood of global war and the virtual certainty of future Third World conflicts that will involve the United States.

Regional Priorities

The U.S. Navy plans to assign seven of its projected fifteen carrier battle groups to the Pacific in the event of war, in addition to two of its four battleship surface action groups and five of its ten underway replenishment groups. Peacetime deployments call for the same assignments, although with a different distribution between the eastern and western Pacific.[30] In effect, half the U.S. Navy is in the Pacific. The question arises whether this is the optimal force distribution in view of the requirements of a global war centered in Europe, the driving scenario of the Maritime Strategy.

If there is a sufficient number of ships, the need for strategic choices is less acute. With the force reductions of the 1970s, however, the Navy was left with forces inadequate to deal even with Atlantic needs, let alone those of the Pacific and the Indian Ocean. The result was a "swing" strategy, in which a substantial number of forces would move from the Pacific to reinforce the Atlantic in the event of war. If this were not accomplished in a timely fashion, there would be a period during the crucial early stages of a conflict when the carrier battle groups, unable to squeeze through the Panama Canal, were out of action as they sailed around South America. This was entirely unacceptable to most of the U.S. Navy. As Secretary Lehman noted in his fiscal year 1987 posture statement, "We cannot abandon one theater in order to deal with the other." In his opinion, the swing strategy was "rendered obsolete by trade, geopolitics, and the growth of the Soviet Navy."[31]

Navy preferences notwithstanding, it may be time to revisit the issue of the proper force distribution between the Atlantic and the Pacific/Indian oceans. Several factors determine this distribution, not all of them strategically sound:

Precedent

Since the Spanish-American War, the U.S. Navy has had a strong interest in the Pacific, soon demonstrated by the 1907 cruise of the Great White Fleet. World War I saw negligible Pacific actions. In the interwar period, though, the Navy conducted extensive war games at the Naval War College in anticipation of war in the Pacific with "Orange" (Japan), and designed the long-range submarines and aircraft carriers that would be necessary for such a conflict. This planning was so thorough that after World War II, Admiral Nimitz was able to say that nothing the Japanese did after Pearl Harbor was a surprise, except for the kamikaze attacks.[32]

During World War II, the Navy sought to shift strategic priorities in favor of actions in the Pacific, particularly in the assignment of scarce shipping needed for amphibious operations. The strategic culture of the Navy is still shaped by World War II actions in the Pacific. These operations powerfully influence the way in which current naval leaders think about the Navy and its role in the future, and form the basis of much of today's strategic thinking.

Regional Importance

A sounder justification for the size of the Pacific Fleet is the size and significance of the area, combined with commitments made by the United States to the countries in the region. This importance is illustrated by trade considerations: Thirty percent of U.S. trade was with Asia in 1983, and U.S. trade with East Asia alone was 24 percent greater than with Europe.[33] The sea lines of communiction with this region must be maintained, irrespective of the immediate importance of Pacific actions for the Central Front.

Deployable U.S. military power, particularly the Seventh Fleet, is a vital factor in promoting regional stability. Given the relative military weakness of most friendly nations in the area, the degree of increased military capability represented by the U.S. Navy is particularly significant.

Wartime Needs

These should be the most important determinant of force distribution decisions. The precise effect of Pacific operations may be unanswerable short of war, and much of the relevant evidence is unobtainable in an unclassified context. However, the burden of justifying the assignment of half the U.S. Navy to the Pacific is on those arguing for it. Strictly from the perspective of a conventional war with the Soviet Union, the forces would make a more direct contribution if they were repositioned nearer the strategic center—even operating on the NATO flanks. The linkage between the Pacific forces and global war needs to be made more carefully to strengthen the case for keeping so many forces there. On the other hand, it is certainly true that the Pacific is important in and of itself, global war scenarios notwithstanding.

U.S. plans cannot be made in a vacuum; they must be related to the projected threat and the forces necessary to counter it. In fact, the Soviet Pacific Ocean Fleet is formidable. In number of ships, it is their largest, and in striking power it is second only to their Northern Fleet.[34] A number of Soviet ships are likely to be operating out of the former U.S. base at Cam Ranh Bay, Vietnam.[35]

The most crucial need is to provide the level of deterrence that prevents such a war from occurring in the first place. Navy spokesmen have repeatedly stated that this is the intention of the Maritime Strategy. Rear Admiral William Pendley, then Director of the Strategy, Plans, and Policy Division of the Office of the CNO (OP-60), emphasized this priority, continuing that if deterrence fails, the United States intends to "seize the initiative, establish maritime superiority, and carry the fight to the enemy."[36] This latter action could involve early strikes against Soviet territory.[37]

If Pacific forces were thought able to inflict a high level of punishment on the Soviet Union, they could have a deterrent effect. More difficult to prove is the argument that military actions in the Pacific would divert Soviet forces that might otherwise go to the Central Front of Europe, where allied forces are relatively weaker. Since the Soviets are not great risk-takers, a decision for war in the West would likely be based on issues they consider of vital importance to the survival of the Soviet state. They may be quite willing to incur temporary losses in the Far East in order to prevail in the West.

Postwar Stability

In the event of a large-scale conventional war, it is reasonable to ask what one would like the Pacific region to look like when it is over. (Were such a war to go nuclear, it is difficult to imagine what the postwar situation might be anywhere.) No matter what the outcome of a war centered in Europe, it is vital for U.S. interests to remain a strong Pacific power. Indeed, if the war ended with Soviet military and/or political hegemony over Western Europe, it would be more important than ever for the United States to have access to the resources and economies of the Pacific basin.

If the U.S. Navy bases its Pacific force distribution on the global conventional war scenario of the Maritime Strategy, it weakens its case for maintaining such a large proportion of its forces there. The case for a direct impact of Pacific actions on the war on the Central Front is difficult to make, for reasons noted earlier. In fact, from the U.S. perspective, it may be best if the war in the Pacific remained defensive, so long as the United States was able to maintain access to the undamaged economies of its Pacific allies. Although the rationale for forward SSN operations in the North Atlantic applies to the Pacific as well, it may not be in the U.S. interest to go on the offensive in the Pacific at all. Actions there may be on a different time line than in the Atlantic, with the most important missions being defensive in nature.

The best justifications for the Pacific emphasis are the intrinsic importance of the region and the need for the United States to remain a Pacific power whatever the outcome of a war in Europe. This requires that a large number of forces, including aircraft carrier battle groups, survive that war. They should not be risked unnecessarily in either theater. In this view, Pacific forces are deterrent and defensive, forming a strategic naval reserve for use later in the war or for postwar leverage.

Peacetime Deployment Postures

An additional question to be considered is the peacetime force deployment pattern, regardless of wartime assignments. The issue is particularly timely now due to a November 1988 memorandum to then-President-Elect Bush from current National Security Advisor Brent Scowcroft and former Undersecretary of the Navy James Woolsey, arguing that forward carrier deployments should be reduced to save operating costs. They argued that some of the loss in responsiveness could be compensated for by other surface ships and submarines carrying cruise missiles.[38]

Forward Deployments

These require a substantial percentage of U.S. Navy forces to operate in forward areas, far from their home ports. This is the Navy's preferred policy,[39] and has resulted in an operating tempo (OPTEMPO) higher than that during the Vietnam War. In practice, about one-third of the Navy is forward deployed during "normal" periods, with the rest of the force in or near home ports, performing maintenance or out on local operations conducting training in preparation for deployment.

This high OPTEMPO has exacted a cost in men and materiel. Aside from the higher costs involved with increased operations, there is considerable wear and tear on equipment subjected to almost continuous operations,[40] and personnel retention is hurt by the family separations and arduous conditions of long deployments.

A good case can be made for these deployments, however. Sailors train nearer the locations in which they might have to fight, and gain experience in working with allied navies. Potential opponents have a visible reminder of U.S. commitments as the Navy carries out its peacetime presence mission. Given the tendency of U.S. Presidents to use maritime forces to show resolve in crises, these forward deployments also mean that forces are available on relatively short notice near potential problem areas.

Surge Deployments

Surge deployments are already contemplated in the event of a major crisis. In such a case, naval forces able to get underway (that is, those not in shipyards undergoing overhauls) could be sent anywhere in the world on relatively short notice to bolster forces already on station. Moving to a surge deployment posture for a large proportion of the Navy, however, would mean that a far smaller percentage of ships would be forward deployed on a regular basis. Remaining forces would be closer to home, but in a condition to deploy quickly if necessary.

The advantages of this posture would be a decrease in the costs of forward deployments and a reduction in personnel hardship. Additionally, when it did become necessary for a surge deployment, the political impact of sending forces forward that are not routinely present would arguably be much greater. The trade-offs would be significant, however: Forces would be farther from potential trouble spots, and both allies and opponents could draw the conclusion that the United States had undertaken a strategic withdrawal from the forward regions. Indeed, this conclusion could become a reality if the American people concluded that the "fleet in being" was not being used and was therefore unnecessary.

Conclusion

The evidence available to naval strategists does not generally lead to agreed-upon conclusions. The only real test of these would occur in the war everyone hopes will not happen.[41] Nevertheless, decisions must be made with imperfect information, and the following conclusions seem reasonable.

First, if the U.S. Navy is to have a decisive role in a war against the Soviet Union, it must have the ability to conduct forward operations with a high probability of success. This capability is necessary for deterrence and for warfighting if deterrence should fail. It means that a large number of highly capable weapons platforms must be maintained in readiness. In the case of the Navy, it may be that fifteen carrier battle groups are necessary, even if the operations of offensive sea control are not undertaken. The tasks of forward area sea control will be rigorous enough. One cannot say in advance what the lower limit of carrier numbers could be and still permit the Navy to carry out its essential missions, but the former Chairman of the Joint Chiefs of Staff, Admiral William Crowe, has stated that even with fifteen carriers, the margin for success is thin.[42]

Second, certain forward operations are likely to be unwise, including attacks on the Soviet Union itself and campaigns of attrition against Soviet SSBNs.[43] Later in a war, both missions may become necessary, but the risks to U.S. forces and the probability of undesirable escalation are too great to assume that such operations should be undertaken during any particular phase of a conflict.

Third, the contribution of naval forces to a war on the Central Front is significant, particularly in the areas of sea control and flank protection, but it is not immediate. There is very little direct assistance such forces can provide immediately once a war has broken out.

Fourth, U.S. planners need to consider the need for force conservation. Carrier battle groups can be very effective later in a war when land-based forces have been attrited; they would also be of vital importance to protect the interests of a United States forced to fall back upon the Western Hemisphere and the Pacific basin. They are therefore too valuable to be put at undue risk.

Fifth, the role of the Pacific theater must be carefully considered. If actions there do not contribute to the success of a European war, the rationale for keeping half the U.S. Navy there needs to be reviewed. Granted that the area is important in itself without regard to a war in Europe, the justification for maintaining such a large naval presence there needs more work to be convincing.

Sixth, moving from a forward deployment to a surge deployment posture should be considered, at least for some areas of the world. This option becomes more sensible if the Soviet naval threat truly recedes significantly. Even with fifteen carrier battle groups, the Navy is not large enough to cover the entire globe—especially since carriers are far more effective when they work together rather than separately.

The conclusions reached here emphasize the importance of forward operations, even in peacetime. At the same time, certain overly aggressive forward operations are unwise, such as an early campaign of attrition against Soviet SSBNs or an early movement of surface forces near Soviet home waters. Although these actions are consistent with the Maritime Strategy, they are not required by it. At the same time, the U.S. Navy should rethink the role of Pacific naval forces and be more selective in the areas in which forward presence is thought to be continuously necessary.

It is likely that a combination of domestic budgetary concerns and European disengagement between the superpowers will generate pressure for significant cutbacks in U.S. military expenditures. Some of these are unavoidable, and, on balance, they will be for the best; there are many unmet domestic needs in the United States that should be addressed, ranging from education to homelessness.

Nevertheless, as defense reductions are apportioned, the unique strategic role of the U.S. Navy in the post-INF era should be considered. With a reduced foreign base structure, a greatly diminished U.S. presence in Europe and, eventually, in Korea, the need for strategic mobility and the ability to project power from the seas will be even more important than it is now. If the bulk of the U.S. Army should be taken out of Europe, the difficulty of reinforcing NATO will increase exponentially. The ability to return to Europe in force, if necessary, would serve as a deterrent to a post-Gorbachev Soviet Union and a reassurance to our European allies that the United States stands ready to meet its treaty obligations.

In sum, important issues remain to be resolved by the Bush Administration. These include the appropriate level of naval spending and the proper balance of expenditures among the military forces, and between defense and important nondefense priorities. These decisions will be more sound if they are based on an appreciation of the important role of naval forces in national defense. It is an important development that the U.S. Navy is now thinking in terms of how to win a conventional war and, by extension, how to keep it conventional, rather than how to hang on with declining force levels and reduced capabilities.

Notes

I am grateful to my friend and colleague, Capt. Peter M. Swartz, U.S. Navy, for helping to clarify my thinking on these matters. The conclusions are, of course, my responsibility.

1. The basic issues are well debated in John J. Mearsheimer, "A Strategic Misstep: The Maritime Strategy and Deterrence in Europe," *International Security*, Vol. 11, No. 2, Fall 1986; pp. 3–57, and the response of Linton F. Brooks, "Naval Power and National Security: The Case for the Maritime Strategy," pp. 58–88 of the same issue.

2. The Director of Naval Intelligence noted in recent testimony that the Soviets have offered to trade marginally useful capabilities for U.S. concessions that are crucial for our defense. An example of this is the Soviet offer to scrap one hundred submarines "which they probably intend to scrap in the near term anyway" for five to seven U.S. aircraft carriers. See Rear Adm.

Thomas A. Brooks, USN, "Statement Before the Seapower, Strategic, and Critical Materials Subcommittee of the House Armed Services Committee," February 22, 1989.

3. The Congressional Budget Office has developed several proposals which, if adopted, could affect the Navy's ability to operate in accordance with its current strategy. These include reducing the number of deployable aircraft carrier battle groups to thirteen by retiring the USS *Midway* and USS *Coral Sea* in 1990, retiring the USS *Enterprise* in 1992 (avoiding a costly refueling of its eight reactors), and slowing the procurement of the V-22 "tilt rotor" vertical takeoff and landing aircraft and the DDG-51 *Arleigh Burke* class guided-missile destroyers (DDGs). Congressional Budget Office, *Reducing the Deficit: Spending and Revenue Options* (Washington, D.C.: U.S. Government Printing Office, February 1989).

4. Adm. Carlisle A. H. Trost, USN, "This Era and the Next: American Security Interests and the U.S. Navy." Address at the Naval War College, Newport, RI, January 10, 1989 (Washington, D.C.: Navy Internal Relations Activity, 1989). Trost strongly supports the current force structure, based around fifteen aircraft carrier battle groups.

5. The final report of President Reagan's Secretary of Defense is fully consistent with the Maritime Strategy. For example, "Of primary importance is our ability to operate effectively in forward areas against determined Soviet opposition. . . . Toward that end, our maritime strategy emphasizes offensive operations employing qualitatively superior forces." Frank C. Carlucci, *Annual Report to the Congress, FY 1990/1991*, January 9, 1989, p. 141. Navy Secretary William L. Ball, Jr., has also indicated his support for the forward options of the strategy. See William L. Ball, Jr., "Pivotal in Sustaining Adequate Deterrence," *Naval Forces*, Vol. IX, No. 5, 1988, pp. 24–26.

6. These were formerly called battleship surface action groups (BB SAGs), as carrier enthusiasts tried to reserve the phrase "battle group" for the CVBGs.

7. The final number has not been determined, and will depend at least in part on arms control agreements.

8. Carlucci, note 5, pp. 141–142. Carlucci expects that the number of battle force-capable ships "will vary between about 570 and 590 for the next eight years."

9. See, for example, Adm. Thomas B. Hayward, USN, "The Future of U.S. Sea Power," U.S. Naval Institute *Proceedings*, Vol. 105, No. 5, May 1979, pp. 66–71.

10. Ibid.

11. Senate Armed Services Committee, *Department of Defense Authorization for Appropriations for FY 1985*, Part 8 (Sea Power and Force Projection), 98th Congress, 2d session (Washington, D.C.: U.S. Government Printing Office, March 14, 1984), pp. 3851–3900.

12. Adm. Carlisle A. H. Trost, USN, *Report to the Congress, Fiscal Year 1988* (Arlington, VA: Navy Internal Relations Activity, 1987), p. 55.

13. Capt. T. M. Daly, USN, "Maritime Strategy and Long Range Planning." Presentation to the First Annual Long Range Planners' Conference of the Chief of Naval Operations, September 17–18, 1985, in Washington, D.C., p. 26.

14. John F. Lehman, Jr., "The 600-Ship Navy." Supplement to the U.S. Naval Institute *Proceedings*, January 1986, p. 37.

15. Adm. Carlisle A. H. Trost, USN, "Strategic Options: Bringing Down

the Bird of Thought." Address to the Current Strategy Forum, Naval War College, June 18, 1987, p. 3.

16. Lehman, note 14, p. 33.

17. Trost, note 15, p. 2.

18. Carlucci, note 5, p. 27.

19. John Allen Williams, "U.S. Navy Missions and Force Structure: A Critical Reappraisal," *Armed Forces and Society*, Vol. 7, No. 4, Summer 1981, pp. 501–508.

20. This position was well elaborated publicly in Adm. James D. Watkins, USN, "The Maritime Strategy." Supplement to the U.S. Naval Institute *Proceedings*, January 1986, pp. 3–17.

21. See Carlucci, note 5, pp. 22, 47, and 146, for examples of his strong support for operations discussed here as part of offensive sea control and for the horizontal escalation option to be discussed below. The position of Defense Secretary Richard Cheney on these issues is not yet clear. Certainly, these operations are strongly urged by the CNO, Adm. Trost. See Adm. Carlisle A. H. Trost, USN, *Report to the Congress, Fiscal Year 1989* (Arlington, VA: Navy Internal Relations Activity, 1988), pp. 22–31.

22. For a fuller elaboration of this position, see Barry R. Posen, "Inadvertent Nuclear War? Escalation and NATO's Northern Flank," *International Security*, Vol. 7, No. 2, Fall 1982, pp. 28–54.

23. The Soviets must surely expect some of their SSBNs to be lost during such operations, even without a campaign of attrition against them. This could reinforce their tendency to draw back into defensive bastions and stay out of the SLOCs.

24. Adm. Lee Baggett, Jr., USN, "NATO at Sea: Future Maritime Power," *RUSI Journal*, Autumn 1988, p. 7. Emphasizing the need for early forward movement of forces, he continues, "With the Soviet Fleet loose in the North Atlantic our ability to provide needed reinforcement and re-supply to SACEUR [Supreme Allied Commander, Europe] would be gravely at risk."

25. Trost, note 21, pp. 22–23.

26. For a contrary view, see George G. Weickhardt, "U.S. Maritime Strategy and Continental Options," *Strategic Review*, Fall 1988, pp. 36–44. Weickhardt argues for an early sortie of U.S. carrier battle group and amphibious forces into the North Sea for a direct contribution to the war on the Central Front. In the author's view, this would be a strategic error: The battle for the Atlantic could thereby be lost at the expense of the rapid destruction of the naval forces thus maldeployed, and with minimal effect on the Central Front.

27. Watkins, note 20, pp. 11, 13.

28. John F. Lehman, Jr., *Command of the Seas* (New York: Scribner's, 1988), p. 149. Although the author hopes Dr. Lehman is correct, this is in clear contradiction to the statements of Adm. Watkins. As a submarine officer, Adm. Watkins may have been partial to the anti-SSBN options of the strategy, and John Lehman the aviator more friendly to the land attack options.

29. Adm. Carlisle A. H. Trost, USN, "Navy's Strategic Victory in Gulf," the *New York Times*, October 8, 1988, p. 26. See also Trost, note 4, p. 7: "[I]t became fashionable to say that we had built the wrong Navy, that big ships and high-tech systems couldn't cope with the lower threats. As it became clear that our operations in the Persian Gulf were succeeding, we heard fewer of such assertions."

30. Carlucci, note 5, p. 143. John F. Lehman, Jr., *Report to the Congress, Fiscal Year 1988* (Washington, D.C.: Navy Internal Relations

Activity, 1987), p. 10. Indian Ocean requirements are included in these numbers.

31. John F. Lehman, Jr., *Report to the Congress, Fiscal Year 1987* (Washington, D.C.: Navy Internal Relations Activity, 1986), p. 7.

32. Battleship admirals slowed this process somewhat, but significant segments of the Navy were aware of the strategic utility of naval aviation long before Pearl Harbor, and they planned carefully how to use it.

33. Donald C. Daniel and Gael D. Tarlton, "The U.S. Navy in the Western Pacific: The View from the Mid-1980s," Society for the Advancement of Education, *USA Today*, May 1985, p. 12.

34. Carlucci, note 5, p. 22.

35. James H. Webb, Jr., remarks to the Current Strategy Forum, Naval War College, Newport, RI, June 16, 1987.

36. Carlucci, note 5, p. 22.

37. Senate Armed Services Committee, note 11, passim.

38. John D. Morrocco, "Shifting Economic, Political Tides Force Reevaluation of Navy's Strategic Role," *Aviation Week and Space Technology*, Vol. 129, No. 9, February 27, 1989, p. 44. See also "Trost Girding for Major Carrier Force Debate, Triggers Roles/Missions Study," *Inside the Navy*, December 12, 1989, p. 1.

39. Adm. Carlisle A. H. Trost, USN, interview, *Sea Power*, Vol. 31, No. 10, October 1988, pp. 13ff.

40. Of course, from 30 to 50 percent of the time deployed is actually spent in port. Were it otherwise, the costs would be even higher.

41. Even wars may not settle such disputes, as is evident from the contradictory conclusions concerning the vulnerability of surface naval forces drawn from the 1982 war in the Falklands/Malvinas.

42. Morrocco, note 38, p. 44.

43. Some Soviet SSBNs would be lost during U.S. forward area sea control operations, as the Soviets must surely expect. Some losses could reinforce the Soviet tendency to draw back into defensive bastions and stay out of the SLOCs.

CHAPTER 12

New Dimensions in Air Strategy

LT. COL. DAVID MacISAAC, U.S. Air Force (Ret.)

This is a more than normally difficult time to speculate on the future directions that war in the air might take. While one might attempt to do so on a purely theoretical level—expounding on various emerging capabilities, limitations, and the like—the usefulness of such an effort is less than apparent. The recent pace and scope of events in Europe in particular have been breathtaking. Such events will undoubtedly lead to budget and force reductions that will drive strategy in ways and directions that will have official strategists climbing the walls.

Except among a few lonely idealists, airmen over the years have pretty much come to live with the role played by technology in driving capabilities—from which strategies tend to be derived. The idea that strategy should drive both the budget and the directions of technology is an ideal construct, and seems likely to remain so under our system, incapable of attainment.[1] But when budget limitations replace technology, let alone strategy, as the driving factor governing capabilities (as was the case, for example, between 1946 and 1950), airmen are faced with truly Solomonic decisions regarding what to keep, what to drop, and what to develop. In this respect, of course, they get all kinds of help from highly placed but essentially nonprofessional sources. (My own favorite example dates from June 4, 1964, when the Secretary of Defense is said to have opined that "in the context of modern aerial warfare, the idea of a fighter being equipped with a gun is as archaic as warfare with bow and arrow."[2])

When the difficulties alluded to are wedded, as they are in early 1990, with an unpredictable international security environment, no one can hope to be very precise in predicting the nature of emerging air strategies. Still, we can suggest areas of emphasis that need attention, beginning with the overall strategic context.

Air Strategy

At the level of strategic nuclear confrontation between or among the major powers, the level of threat appears to be lessening, at least as regards the numbers of weapons and platforms that have to be taken into account. If present trends continue, we can expect reductions in force levels that range from the moderate to the drastic. For the strategist, this will force a thorough re-thinking of the Single Integrated Operational Plan (SIOP) for nuclear war and its attendant force structure. Indeed, the time may have arrived when the strategy of assured destruction is called upon to consider alternate theories of finite deterrence—as was the case, briefly, in 1957.

Nuclear Proliferation

Regardless of what arrangements can be worked out between the United States and the USSR, nuclear proliferation remains an unsolved problem, and it could conceivably become a much more complex one in the relations between these two nations. It is one thing to defend against known quantities and something altogether different when one does not know who the enemy might turn out to be, let alone be aware of his intentions or capabilities. Nuclear proliferation, however, is only one part of the problem; equally dangerous is the rapidly increasing proliferation of high-tech conventional, biological, and chemical weapons. In these respects, the proliferation of ballistic missiles, however armed, is especially worrisome. The U.S. Arms Control and Disarmament Agency reports that at least sixteen Third World countries either possess ballistic missiles or are striving to develop them, and that by the year 2000 at least fifteen developing countries will be producing their own ballistic missiles. ACDA's comments on these developments are sobering:

> Nations that possess ballistic missiles can fire large, destructive warheads deep into one another's territory with assurance that defenses have little likelihood of stopping an attack. The very presence of these weapons in conflict-prone regions of the world aggravates instability. The potential for accidental launch, takeover of launch facilities by subnational groups, or use of missiles to intimidate neighbors or pursue territorial ambitions is significantly higher in the Third World than it is among the traditional missile states [for several reasons]: disputes are more volatile and wars more common in these regions, the stability of Third World governments is often fragile, and the high value ascribed to a limited number of missiles is likely to heighten a "use them or lose them" attitude. To make matters worse, missile proliferation is occurring at a time when many of the countries involved are also proceeding apace with nuclear and chemical weapons development programs.[3]

The rapid proliferation of other types of missiles—especially shoulder-fired, surface-to-air missiles (SAMs), but also cruise missiles of all types—is no secret to air strategists, even if solutions to the problems they present are evasive. But the ballistic surface-to-surface missile threat and the means to counter it become more worthy of close attention as time goes on.

Conventional Conflict

At levels below the nuclear threshold, the prospects of a full-scale NATO–Warsaw Pact battle, for years the principal focus of U.S. air strategists, has quite simply evaporated (if, indeed, it was ever a realistic prospect). It is in this regard that the USAF in particular will face its most trying conceptual and force structure conundrums. The new situation is in some ways reminiscent of the early 1960s, when the USAF's front line "fighters"—the early Century series, minus the F-102—had been optimized for the nuclear delivery role and found themselves tasked to fight in a nonnuclear jungle war. Today's F-15s, F-16s, and F-111s (of various sorts), optimized to fight a high-tech air war from an elaborate base structure, may well find themselves called to unfamiliar theaters where the necessary base, runway, and other supporting requirements cannot simply be assumed.[4]

For at least a decade now, lonely voices in the USAF wilderness have been worrying about the question of the "high-low" mix.[5] Generally, this has taken the form of arguing that the service should seriously consider buying larger numbers of less-capable aircraft, thereby reducing both dollar costs per platform and support requirements—especially long, smooth, clean runways. To do so, however, would run too many risks, most notably that of surrendering in advance any technological edge to the enemy. For the European scenario, such a choice had no chance of acceptance among pilots as a group, let alone the Air Staff. The question today would seem to be whether the traditional approach, to focus on attaining maximum capability between wheels up and wheels down, is sufficient in itself.

Unpredictable Elements

To conclude these remarks on changing contexts for the air strategist to consider, there are a number of elements that are unpredictable. These include, but are not limited to, the role of nationalism, ethnic minorities, and religious fervor as events in Europe unfold. Also, no matter what happens in Europe, we may not yet have come to the end of the age of ideology, especially in Asia and the Middle East, especially when religious fanaticism and terrorism are added to the mix. Nor can the strategist forget for a moment that economic competition is likely to increase in more ways than Americans will feel comfortable with; after all, Japan, Taiwan, and Korea already present problems. After 1992, the European Economic Community (EEC) could appear to be more of a rival than an ally. Where Eastern Europe will fit in the overall equation is anyone's guess, as, at this moment, is the future of economic relations with the USSR. All this would be less worrisome if we could convince ourselves that economic competition in the "modern, interdependent world economy" can no longer lead to armed conflict. Not very likely!

Components of Air Strategy

Given the contexts alluded to above, what should be the principal concerns of today's air strategist? First and foremost, he or she will favor neither hasty nor wholesale reductions in present air and space force structures and capabilities. In this respect, the U.S. Air Force would seem to be in a better position than, say, the U.S. Army. Air power's characteristics of speed, range, lethality, and responsiveness allow it to deploy and concentrate military power within hours, and also to attack from any point on the compass rose, with only passing regard for the limitations imposed by terrain in the target area (jungles and deep forests excepted). Given continuing advances in precision, and above all selectivity, "air power [can] be a ubiquitous arm of the first hour, and thus escape the need to be employed as a weapon of last resort."[6] Various Defense Department cost-sharing imperatives, not to mention the Congress, may not agree. Certainly, *some* reductions *will* occur, but it would help if the strategist could have equal time with the budgeteer and the programmer.

Second (though first on most such lists), we must continue to deter nuclear war, which will require a credible nuclear strike force backed up by reconnaissance and surveillance capabilities second to none. As suggested earlier, the nuclear-armed attack force will be considered among the prime targets for reductions; among these, land-based missiles will probably be first in line. That this will "greatly complicate the targeting problem" (as they say in Omaha) goes without saying, and the strategists (and numerologists) of the Joint Strategic Target Planning Staff (JSTPS) have their work cut out for them.

Third, we must remain capable of fighting highly intense, localized conflicts, however generated (by civil war, border disputes, insurrection, or ideology), but we must also improve our current capability to do so in unfamiliar theaters under conditions of reduced on-scene support-structures.

Finally, we must dramatically improve our capabilities to launch preemptive, retaliatory, demonstration, punitive, or rescue operations—"peacetime contingency operations" in LICspeak. In this respect, counterterrorism requirements are obvious but hardly inclusive.

Capabilities

In a more than normally uncertain political environment, today's air strategist is driven inevitably toward generalization, and hence toward specific capabilities (rather than specific plans for action). In the context of the components of air strategy, a number of specific capabilities need to be examined.

First, intelligence capabilities should lead the list. The recent USAF decision to retire the SR-71 will give the strategist pause. The assumption that satellites can do the necessary work in the same time frames and with equal precision may or may not be correct. In this instance, the strategist would err on the side of caution, especially at a time of international confusion. The modern tendency toward relying extensively on various forms of signals and electronic intelligence (SIGINT and ELINT) at the expense of so-called HUMINT (human intelligence, as in spies, plants, and moles) is worrisome. Our various space-based reconnaissance and surveillance assets should always be looked upon as *supplementary* sources rather than primary ones. After all, the U.S. record is, in part, one of all too many surprises; even the shortest list would have to include Pearl Harbor, the Ardennes in 1944, Czechoslovakia in 1948 (and 1968 and 1989), the Berlin blockade, the Soviet A-bomb the following year, Korea in 1950 (*twice*, first in June and again in November) and—to leap forward into the satellite age—Tet in 1968, Iran in 1978, Afghanistan in 1979, and Beirut in 1983 (and that's the *short* list). The 1990s demand intelligence systems and techniques that are innovative and imaginative, unburdened as much as possible from the peacetime routinization of "collecting data day to day and filing same in routine reports," as an experienced friend puts it.[7]

Second, the organizational structure of the USAF fighting forces needs to be revised. The present arrangement into major air commands like the Strategic and Tactical Air Commands (SAC and TAC) provides unarguable peacetime efficiencies by basing aircraft in homogeneous wings and squadrons. Maintenance, logistic, and assignment of personnel considerations, all of which are very expensive, are greatly eased in this way. What is not made easy is the requirement to meld disparate forces into the kinds of force packages that have proven necessary in the age of electronic warfare. Since at least the early 1970s (Linebacker II, the October War, and on to the Bekaa Valley in 1982 and the Libyan raid of April 1986), air strike forces have had to be cobbled together to include a multitude of capabilities and aircraft types: reconnaissance, escort, strike aircraft, jammers, tankers, and defense suppression (or SEAD) aircraft. Some air assets—notably strategic nuclear forces, long-range airlift, AWACs, and the tanker force—would still have to be concentrated in much the same manner as they are now. But others, particularly the fighter and fighter-bomber forces, along with conventionally armed bombers and special operations forces (SOF), could be formed into operational units that would, in effect, become prefabricated force packages and that would be based together and trained together. Any attempt to arrange such composite air strike forces will be doubly difficult in a period of overall reductions; therefore, the planner given the task, even if only in "study format," should take heed of Machiavelli's observation to the effect that "there is nothing more difficult to carry out, nor more doubtful of success, nor more dangerous to handle, than to initiate a new order of things."

The third consideration is the almost perennial stepchild status of the USAF special operations forces, or SOF. One Air Force observer has put the matter starkly:

> The U.S. Air Force remains poorly postured institutionally, materially, and psychologically to operate effectively in low-intensity conflict. Although there are numerous reasons for this lack of capability, the overriding factor has been the Air Force's inability to fully comprehend the threat or to develop a clear set of priorities so it can respond to the threat with confidence.[8]

This same observer spells out in detail the kind of SOF he feels is needed and includes very specifically how it should be organized, trained, and equipped. It should be added that the need for the SOF is likely to go beyond the requirements of so-called low-intensity conflict. Despite earnest efforts by some air analysts, we remain unconvinced that the USAF, as presently constituted, is capable of carrying out special operations in multiple remote areas simultaneously. In today's and tomorrow's world, the air strategist has no reason to assume that the USAF will be required to operate in only one theater at a time. And yet, the numbers and types of platforms available remain quite small.

Fourth, in a period of declining resources, a course must be charted for the directions that research and development should take. Here the risks of being wrong run high, especially if some opportunities have to be shunted aside in favor of others. This is, of course, widely recognized, and most writers who address evolving air strategies do well to concentrate in this area. The high-tech battlefield, whether upon or above the surface, grows more complex with every passing day. Even the shortest list of rapidly advancing technology would have to include electronic warfare in all its forms, stealth technology, payload improvements, AWACs capabilities, vertical/short takeoff and landing (V/STOL) aircraft development, and unforeseen advances in microcomputerology. The difficulty will come not so much in identifying promising opportunities, but in deciding which ones to support with the funds made available. In these respects, much insight has been provided over the past decade by a number of senior British officers, now referred to by some as "the RAF School." These include, but are not limited to, Air Vice-Marshal R. A. Mason, Air Chief Marshal Sir Michael

Armitage, Air Vice-Marshal J. W. Walker, Group Captain Timothy Garden, Group Captain A.G.B. Vallance, Air Commodore G. R. Profit, and Air Commodore M. A. Harvey.[9] The thinking that such officers (and their many civilian counterparts) have offered will be helpful in arriving at what promise to be some closely run decisions, but the final decisions affecting the U.S. air forces (all four of them) will have to be fought out in Washington.

Two areas of technological development that could use more emphasis are V/STOL capabilities and aerial refueling equipment. Both are related to the concern expressed earlier regarding the likely future availability of bases, whether owned, rented, borrowed, or conquered. Despite an apparent decision by the U.S. Marine Corps to concentrate future aircraft developments on V/STOL-capable platforms,[10] the USAF has remained lukewarm to the topic. The concern seems to be that such aircraft will lack the "legs" (range), maneuverability, and payload capacity seen to be required, to say nothing about the logistical problems associated with dispersed basing. Some V/STOL advocates have pointed to the Falklands campaign where, to the surprise of many, carrier-based Harriers proved effective in an air superiority role against the Argentinians. But this example, like so many of the past decade or so (Osiraq in 1981, Bekaa Valley in 1982, and Libya in 1986), was fleeting and transitory in nature; it is thereby unlikely to inspire widespread confidence among decisionmakers regarding any lessons to be learned from this instance.

With regard to aerial refueling capabilities, more needs to be done to retrofit the force with *both* the boom and receptacle system (for USAF aircraft) *and* the probe and drouge system (for most U.S. Navy aircraft). Some steps have recently been taken in this respect for the KC-10 fleet, but not for the much larger KC-135 fleet.[11]

Concepts and Problems

The areas singled out for special attention by air strategists—intelligence, organization, special operations, and technical improvements related to basing considerations, especially V/STOL and aerial refueling—reflect a concern that the USAF is more likely to be called upon to perform in roles and theaters in which it has not concentrated over the past few decades. Others might stress much more forcibly the need to move ahead on all elements of the technological front, including stealth (or low-observable) technology; unmanned aerial vehicles; electronic counter-countermeasures; and commercial, control, communications, and intelligence (C^3I) in all its variants. Doing so could well be correct (and surely will be so in at least some particulars). If such is the case, we can hope, as a laconic colleague observes, that they find "some stealthy money somewhere."

There are a number of tendencies and problems that have led some air strategists into difficulties. These include:

1. A prevailing tendency to magnify expected capabilities derived from designs still on the drawing boards;
2. A tendency to confuse destruction with control, which can lead in turn to an emphasis on the firepower role of air power at the expense of its other attributes;
3. A difficulty in accepting the idea that air combat engagements, no matter how successful, *can* prove irrelevant to broader outcomes depending on the nature of the conflict; and
4. A continuing tendency to emphasize the unique aspects of war in and from the air while neglecting the elements of continuity that mark all warfare.[12]

In this last respect, Air Vice-Marshal Tony Mason has provided some pointed reminders that include the following:

1. Every offensive weapon or tactic will in time stimulate an effective defense response.
2. Identifying the enemy's center of gravity is a prerequisite for offensive action.
3. Neutralizing an opponent's military strength does not *necessarily* call for its destruction.
4. Preliminary division of strength is not incompatible with concentration of force at the decisive point.
5. "War is the province of uncertainty." [Clausewitz, again]
6. Accurate and timely intelligence of any enemy's intentions, direction, and deployment is the greatest force multiplier.[13]

Conclusion

As the century draws to a close, one of the troubling aspects facing air strategists and airmen in general is that they might well be forced by circumstances to give up their long-cherished hope for the establishment of an outlook, along with an attendant vocabulary, that will allow for some measure of purity in the concept of "air power" or "war in the third dimension." Today's advancing technology enables all kinds of weapons to strike targets from long distances, thereby blurring the former distinctions between land, sea, and air power. The *real* strategic questions of tomorrow might well become the following: What should be attacked to fulfill the purpose of the war? From what platform—air, sea, space, or land—can this be accomplished with the greatest effectiveness, efficiency, and prospects for success?

Aside from these strategic dimensions, the U.S. Air Force must seriously consider its role in support of other services, particularly the U.S. Army. Operation "Just Cause," which took place in Panama in 1989, showed the importance of the Air Force in such a role, not only in providing support to tactical units, but in providing strategic mobility to the U.S. Army. It is also the case that air support must be available for a number of contingencies engaged in by the U.S. Navy, regardless of the capability of U.S. naval air squadrons. Thus, the U.S. Air Force is not only faced with rethinking its strategy and revising its organizational structure, but it must maintain and expand its supportive role to other military services. All of this is particularly important in the new security environment. How well this will be done is not only contingent upon the keen insights and analyses of air strategists, but also on the recognition by policymakers that the new environment does not presage a reduced role for the U.S. Air Force. Indeed, the opposite is true.

Notes

The views expressed in this chapter are exclusively those of the author and carry no official sanction whatsoever. The author is indebted to two long-time friends and colleagues for many of the ideas expressed in this essay. His thanks go to Lt. Col. Price T. Bingham, USAF, and Lt. Col. Philip S. Melinger, USAF, both widely published and energetic thinkers.

1. For an excellent single-page summary of the reasons, see Paul Mann's editorial, "The Strategy Morass," *Aviation Week & Space Technology*, April 24, 1989, p. 9.

2. Cited in *USAF Fighter Weapons Review*, Fall 1989, p. 32.

3. *Defense & Economy World Report* (Washington, D.C.: Government Business Worldwide Reports, November 1, 1989) pp. 6499f.

4. Lt. Col. Price T. Bingham, USAF, "Operational Art and Aircraft Runway Requirements," *AirPower Journal*, Vol. 2, 3, Fall 1988, pp. 52–69. (Reprinted as a CADRE Paper, Air University Report No. AU-ARI-CP-89-4, December 1989).

5. The "high-low mix" question is sometimes referred to as the "quality/quantity/costs issue." See Col. [now Maj. Gen.] Walter Kross, USAF, *Military Reform: The High-Technology Debate in Tactical Air Forces* (Washington, D.C.: National Defense University Press, 1985); and, for the broader context, F. D. Margiotta and R. Sanders, eds., *Technology, Strategy, and National Security* (Washington, D.C.: National Defense University Press, 1985), especially pp. 43–76. For the issue/problem in its even broader context, see my chapter entitled "The Development of Air Power since 1945," in R. A. Mason, ed., *War in the Third Dimension* (London: Brassey's, 1986), pp. 11–31.

6. M. J. Armitage and R. A. Mason, *Air Power in the Nuclear Age* (Urbana: University of Illinois Press, 1983), p. 257.

7. Former Chairman of the Joint Chiefs of Staff, Adm. William J. Crowe, in one of his final reports to the Secretary of Defense, agreed with this view. See "Crowe Calls for Review of Military Intelligence," *Aviation Week & Space Technology*, November 20, 1989, p. 31.

8. Maj. Kenneth M. Page, USAF, "US Air Force Special Operations: Charting a Course for the Future," *AirPower Journal*, Vol. 1, 2, Fall 1987, pp. 58–69; quotation from p. 58.

9. For some examples, see Armitage and Mason, note 6, and its 2d Edition, same publisher, 1985, especially the concluding chapter, "Challenge and Opportunities," pp. 244–279; Air Vice-Marshal R. A. Mason, "The Decade of Opportunity: Air Power in the 1990s," *AirPower Journal*, Vol. 1, 2, Fall 1987, pp. 4–15; Timothy Garden, *The Technology Trap: Science and the Military* (London: Brassey's, 1989), especially pp. 32–43, 111–137; Air Chief Marshal Sir Michael Armitage, *Unmanned Aircraft* (London: Brassey's, 1988); and Air Vice-Marshal J. W. Walker, *Air Superiority Operations* (London: Brassey's, 1989).

10. Robert R. Ropelewski, "Marines Shun Runways in Future Fighter Plans," *Armed Forces Journal International*, August 1989, pp. 57, 60.

11. "Air Force to Retrofit KC-10s with Air Refueling Pods," *Aviation Week and Space Technology*, November 13, 1989, pp. 29–30. For background information regarding this problem, see Maj. Marck R. Cobb's excellent CADRE Paper, "Aerial Refueling: The Need for a Multipoint, Dual-System Capability," Air University Report No. AU-ARI-CP-87-3 (Montgomery, AL: Air University, July 1987).

12. For a fuller discussion of these points, see my essay in *War in the Third Dimension*, note 5, especially pp. 25–31.

13. Mason's complete list concludes his *AirPower Journal* article, note 9.

PART 6

Education and Training of the U.S. Army

CHAPTER 13

Education of U.S. Army Officers

LT. GEN. HOWARD D. GRAVES, U.S. Army

The U.S. Army's philosophy of officer education can be stated quite simply. It is the need to create competent, confident officers who are able to exploit the full potential of U.S. soldiers, military forces, and doctrine in joint and combined operations across the full spectrum of conflict. The U.S. Army's program for implementing that philosophy provides progressive and comprehensive professional education, with appropriate attention to the major facets of military competence.

One major facet of competence for U.S. officers is a thorough understanding of the societal context in which the Army operates. Officers must understand the role of military leaders in a democratic society. Civilian control of the military, as established in the Constitution, which every officer is sworn to uphold, is virtually never questioned in practice. The principle of civilian ascendancy must be constantly reinforced throughout the military educational system, however, in anticipation of those inevitable periods of frustration that arise in the face of adverse resource decisions by the civilian leadership or the deleterious impacts of legislative-executive power struggles regarding national military effectiveness. The U.S. governmental principle of checks and balances among the branches of government may not always appear to produce the most efficient or effective security or resourcing policy, but the process is absolutely fundamental to the U.S. way of government. Army officers must understand this context to fulfill their own role as military leaders.

A second important facet of military competence, particularly for senior officers, is the proper role in the policy process of the military adviser in regard to elected and appointed civilian officials. Uniformed advisers can play an important role in assisting in the development of national security policy and in transmitting that policy to the military for execution. Competent advisers can provide unique insights into what military forces can and cannot do, as well as the costs of military conflict in terms of human and material resources. It is important that officers in advisory positions understand from their military education the difference between advice and advocacy and know that advocacy is an abuse of the military adviser's position.

The third facet of competence for military officers at all levels and ranks is disciplined proficiency in leading forces in combat, should they be directed to do so. This is the fundamental competency that the United States expects from its military leaders. This is mentioned last only because the first two facets provide the context for true understanding of the warfighting and leader skills composing this third facet. These skills differ, of course, at the various levels of military endeavor. The Army hierarchy of schools attempts to provide progressive understanding through sequential education at appropriate points in an officer's career. Figure 13.1 depicts the three levels at which planning for and conduct of war takes place, the activities associated with those levels, and the military education courses that address the knowledge and abilities required.

Incidentally, the formal schools that every Army officer attends are but one of the three pillars of the officer education system. The two other important pillars are the education, training, and experience obtained by officers while serving in their units, and the self-development each officer is expected to pursue throughout his or her career.

A Decade of Reviews and Studies

Since 1978, four major reviews of the Army commissioned officer education system have been conducted. They were the 1978 U.S. Army Review of Education and Training for Officers (RETO), the 1985 U.S. Army Professional Development of Officers Study (PDOS), the 1987–1988 House Armed Services Committee Panel (Skelton Panel) Review of Professional Military Education, and the 1988 U.S. Army Leader Development Study (LDS).

Many initiatives have resulted from these studies. First, increased emphasis on the informal educational pillars (experience in units and personal self-development) is underway. A uniform set of Military Qualification Standards (Tier I) for precommissioning (ROTC, USMA, OCS) training and self-development is in final revision. This will be followed by similar efforts to produce Tier II for lieutenants and captains. Eventually, a Tier III may be developed for field grade officers. The objective is to provide a carefully thought-out and doctrinally correct set of standards at each major phase of an officer's progression. These will be accompanied by instructional literature and support materials necessary to execute appropriate officer training in units and to guide self-development.

Second, the Combined Arms and Services Staff School (CAS3) was opened in 1981 to respond to the need for more competent young staff officers at the battalion, brigade, and division levels. All captains now attend CAS3 at some point following their branch Advanced Course.

Figure 13.1 Military Education Related to the Levels of War Planning and Conduct

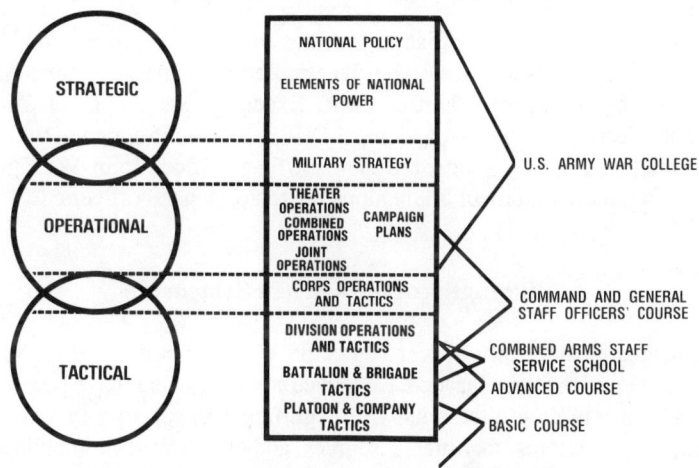

Third, the School of Advanced Military Studies (SAMS) was initiated in 1983. A one-year extension of the Command and General Staff Officer Course, it is designed to produce a modest number (forty-six per year) of carefully selected graduates who are more intensively educated in military theory, tactics, the operational art, and theater strategy. These SAMS graduates are sent immediately to key field assignments to capitalize on their special talents and training. Feedback from field commanders indicates that both CAS3 and SAMS have been highly successful.

Fourth, precommand courses for officers designated to command battalions (lieutenant colonels), brigades (colonels), and larger units (general officers) have been developed. They provide concentrated reviews of current policies and issues to these leaders immediately prior to the assumption of command. Each course contains a series of short (three days to two weeks) instructional units tailored to the specific needs of a particular command. A short (six to twelve weeks) language course may also be included for officers being assigned overseas.

Fifth, improved computer-assisted war games have been introduced for unit training and in formal schools. The Army family of computer-assisted games is much more complete at the tactical level than at the operational and strategic levels, but progress is being made in joint and combined war games.

Sixth, the 1986 Goldwater-Nichols defense reform legislation mandated revisions in Professional Joint Education, affecting both student selection and the curricula of our schools. There is a new emphasis on jointness for all officers, as well as courses tailored specially for joint specialists and general officers.

Seventh, a final major initiative provides for General Officer Continuing Education, which includes general officer conferences and war games hosted and taught by the Army Chief of Staff; Executive Development Courses taught at selected universities; a General Officer Update Program at the Army War College; a jointly sponsored General/Flag Officer Joint Warfighting Course; and interassignment orientations for senior general officers.

Strengths of the Current System

The changes to the Army officer education system resulting from the four major studies of the past decade have served it well. Several have pointed the Army in entirely new directions, with significant impacts on its personnel system, career patterns, facilities, resources, and officer education philosophy itself. Certainly, the renewed emphasis upon both self-development and in-unit development has expanded the vision of the total cluster of educational forces that shape Army officers. From commissioning onward, each officer is now expected to accept his or her personal role in self-development. Unit commanders are expected to teach subordinates and nourish an organizational climate that will sustain their education and provide for growth of character. Unit commander responsibilities extend far beyond specific training for the achievement of short-term successes and now include participation in the long-term professional growth of the unit's officers.

While some unit commanders have maintained excellent officer professional development programs, there has been little coordination thus far among units and among the three pillars of officer education. The next challenge is to coordinate the requirements of the three pillars so all development programs can progress in a mutually reinforcing manner. The Military Qualification Standards system alluded to earlier will assist in this endeavor.

A notable strength of the current Army system is that it synchronizes the growth in an officer's intellect and character with the increase in his or her rank and responsibilities. It makes great sense to increase the level of the officer's professional challenges in step with rank and education. Such adjustments enable the Army to capitalize on growth and avoid the psychological stultification that would otherwise result as officers outgrow their jobs.

Another strength is the joint and combined orientation that is now beginning to take hold throughout the Army educational system. At the Army War College, for example, 80 percent of the curriculum is joint, national, or combined in thrust. Although proficiency in the skills of one's service is the foundation for a successful joint officer, these are developed in the context of joint and combined studies, particularly for field grade and general officers.

Another Army strength is the increasing availability and acceptability of nonresident options for the various Army courses. This flexibility in instructional methods has proven helpful to both the Army and selected officer students. Unfortunately, Title IV provisions in the Goldwater-Nichols legislation do not currently accept such courses as a means to fulfill the mandated Professional Joint Education requirement, but we shall continue to pursue joint accreditation for these important and rigorous nonresident options.

Army support and sponsorship for graduate-level civilian education remains a strength. The Army Educational Requirements System provides a mechanism by which Army major commands and agencies validate needs for graduate degrees by discipline in specific Army positions. These validated requirements become the basis for Army funding to send officers to obtain graduate degrees at major civilian colleges and universities. In addition, the Army provides opportunities for officers to obtain advanced degrees on their own time; for example, as a corollary to an ROTC assignment or concurrent with attendance at a staff or senior service college.

Finally, the Army is continuing to tailor the choice of school and the choice of courses within schools to accommodate individual officer strengths, experience, and professional needs. There are now almost a dozen different options for the staff college experience, some in residence and some by correspondence. At the Army War College, the number of elective advanced courses available and the proportion of total curricular time devoted to them have increased. This initiative allows our senior officer students to focus more effort toward areas in which they either lack background or need more depth of understanding.

Thus, we see an Army officer education system today that is thorough, rigorous, and effective. Many allied officers have commented with some envy about the opportunities for formal schooling, the resources, and the institutional commitment of the U.S. Army to training and educating its officer corps.

The Challenges Before Us

Many of the strengths of the Army educational system are traditional. Others are the results of the current dynamic environment and recent studies. Many of the challenges before us involve the continual enhancement of our strengths. Others involve more complex issues arising from a serious commitment to officer education.

The major challenge is to create an understanding throughout the Army that professional education is a process that continues throughout an officer's entire career. Education, in contradistinction to training, implies a long-term process. In the long term, we need to produce officers of solid, irreproachable character. Not only is it important to do things right, which we learn from training, but it is perhaps even more important to do the right thing, which we learn from education. The ability to deal with ethical dilemmas (or even to recognize them) and the strength and quality of character to act appropriately in the face of such dilemmas are at the core of the lifelong process of the Army officer's education, commencing in his or her precommissioning preparation and extending through senior officer continuing education.

One persistent tendency in the Army system that must be overcome is the fixation on narrowly based prepping for the next assignment rather than laying the enduring groundwork for extended creative service. One would, of course, expect this tendency to be more prevalent in the hard-skill, task-oriented courses for junior officers than in, say, senior service colleges where higher levels of abstraction are emphasized. Yet, even in basic and advanced courses, we must provide our junior officers a solid basis for long-term growth in addition to teaching the obviously essential small-unit skills and proficiencies. Major General E. B. Atkeson, U.S. Army War College Deputy Commandant in 1976, portrays this tension between assignment preparation and career preparation as the competition between the traditionalists and the progressives. In his 1988 book, *The Final Argument of Kings*, he tells us:

> The traditionalist holds that the ideal product of an Army school is an officer who can immediately step into a position in a military unit or departmental bureau and perform at a high level of efficiency. This product is not expected to be a theorist; he needs to be a well-rounded executor of policy and orders.[1]

Even though the traditionalist view has merit, it has moved us too far toward training at the expense of education, process at the expense of principles, and rigidity of thought at the expense of creative, innovative thinking. It is precisely these neglected dimensions (education, principles, and innovation) that the progressives most highly espouse. Atkeson puts it this way:

> To the progressive, principles and theory merit greater attention than do standing operating procedures. He tends to be somewhat less interested in how a task is accomplished under present circumstances, and more interested in why it is done, and what alternatives there may be for its execution.[2]

As a practical matter, officer schools will always be torn to some degree between these two divergent impulses, but all should agree with the general proposition that Army schools should broaden, not narrow, an officer's intellectual horizons as he or she advances up the ladder of rank and responsibility.

The Army school system and the Army as a whole still place insufficient priority on providing opportunities for reflection about the profession of arms. The Army does not provide sufficient institutional incentives to reward its young thinkers, nor does it provide sufficient time, either in units or in school curricula, for serious thought and professional writing. This is less a problem at entry-level schools, where the appropriate emphasis is on training in defined techniques, but it becomes a serious shortcoming at the intermediate and senior-level schools, where problems are more cerebral and abstract and where a greater premium should be placed accordingly upon seeking creative alternatives. The temptation is to fill the academic schedule with mandatory class attendances and to keep each day fully structured. This is less and less appropriate at higher-level schools because the environment in which senior officers operate becomes progressively less structured, the problems they face in peace or war become less amenable to solution by textbook methods, and useful solutions become products of independent creative thought. Fortunately, the Army is making progress in this area, but more needs to be done.

The Army, as well as the other services, will continue to face the challenge of overcoming isolation from American society. While the all-volunteer system has provided excellent and educated soldiers, they are not a true cross-section of U.S. youth. As environmental and economic factors constrain Army activities to relatively remote posts and training areas, and as fewer members of our population experience military service, the profession faces the dangers of professional insularity and of having its members become outsiders to the majority of Americans. The officer education system should do more to reach out to civilians by encouraging fertile contacts between camp and community. At the Army War College, for example, the student Current Affairs Panel continues to visit some thirty university campuses annually. An outreach program is also being developed that encourages cross-fertilization between officers and civilian educators around the nation. The workshop at Loyola University of Chicago, reflected in this book, is an outgrowth of just such an initiative. But more must be done, and we must involve more students and faculty at all levels of our Army educational system in interactions with the American public.

The Army continues to suffer a shortage of officers who are masters of communications skills. This challenge is not helped by the current trend toward lower standards of literacy in many of the nation's high schools and colleges. The Army must apply the resources necessary to reach a consistently high standard of writing and speaking throughout the officer education system. In all areas and at every level of officer education, we need to demand more writing, more oral presentations, more critiques, and more evaluation against appropriate standards.

Senior schools in all services need more rigor and less structure. Rigor results from establishing and articulating clear, high standards and evaluating student progress against those standards. Less structure provides time for students to think about and prepare submissions. At the Army War College, there are increasing requirements for students to prepare papers, give oral reports and presentations, and participate in case studies, exercises, reviews, analyses, war games, and other forms of active learning. The emphasis is on developing creative alternatives. At the same time, constructive feedback is continuously provided by faculty evaluations as part of the learning process. Formal periodic reviews with faculty advisers are conducted throughout the year. The focus of the evaluation system is to improve students through feedback, not ranking students within a competitive scheme. The increased emphasis on critical analysis and creative thinking is designed to encourage the professional reflection that many of our students have neglected over the years.

Selection procedures for students attending staff and senior service colleges present a challenge to Army personnel managers. The current system is a flexible mix that is based on individual merit and branch equity, a system we can afford no longer. While there must be workable alternatives to provide for the professional development of all officers regardless of branch or specialty, the Army must develop procedures for selecting senior service college attendees whose branch and specialty will enable them to capitalize upon the strategic and operational orientation of the senior service college curricula. To do otherwise is a waste. Plans are currently underway to increase the accuracy of assignment procedures for staff and senior service college graduates, as well as to select student populations to match requirements. The new system does not prevent all members of any branch or skill from attendance at the senior institutions, but should improve the match between Army requirements and graduate proficiencies.

Another critical challenge is to improve the way Army school faculties are selected, and to change the perception in the field regarding the desirability of faculty assignments. In the competition for the best and brightest officers, a decade-old trend has seen operational assignments win out over assignments to Army school faculties. While the Army has not deliberately minimized the importance of education assignments, it is clear to Army officers that greater recognition goes with operating than with educating. Faculty tours are not considered as career enhancing as unit assignments or prestigious staff billets. This results in fewer of the best and brightest officers seeking faculty positions at all, much less recurring faculty assignments. Officers chosen to fill Army faculty billets often go reluctantly. These attitudes must be turned around if top-quality faculties in the Army school system are to be maintained. The track to higher rank and responsibility simply must include way stations for faculty duty, where outstanding officers can recharge their intellectual batteries and pass the fruits of their experience to successive generations. Promotion and selection boards must understand this goal and be instructed accordingly.

Finally, the Army must integrate its reserve components into its educational programs. This process must be sufficiently flexible to accommodate the erratic availability patterns of Army Reserve and National Guard officers and the differences in their educational requirements. Resources for curriculum support, facilities, and faculty must be built in. The Reserve Component mission is equal in importance to that of the Active Component for our overall national security. Therefore, educational provisions for both components deserve equal attention.

To Conclude

The Army education system has many traditional strengths, and these have been enhanced by initiatives of more recent origin. The underlying philosophy has remained constant over the years, serving to guide the new initiatives generated by both internal and external reviews. There are many challenges before the military profession. The dynamic nature of the Army, American society, and the international context in the post-INF era demand that we be alert to the need for change as it develops, and then direct our energy toward the implementation of appropriate adjustments.

The Army, quite clearly, is energetically pursuing high-quality professional education for all of its officers. Great strides forward have been made, and the Army will advance even more rapidly under its current leadership. Critics who maintain that "the Army is a fundamentally anti-intellectual organization"[3] are out of date. They need to visit the Army schools and units and see what is being done today.

Notes

I am grateful to Col. E. J. Glabus, R. H. Goldsmith, and Col. L. J. Matthews for many of the ideas reflected in this chapter.

1. Maj. Gen. Edward B. Atkeson, USA, Retired, *The Final Argument of Kings* (Fairfax, VA.: Hero Books, 1988), p. 24.

2. Ibid., p. 25.

3. Christopher Bassford, *The Spit-Shine Syndrome* (New York: Greenwood Press, 1988), p. 147.

CHAPTER 14

Challenges of U.S. Army Reserve Force Readiness

LT. GEN. FREDERIC J. BROWN, U.S. Army (Ret.)
COL. AUBREY R. MERRILL, JR., U.S. Army (Ret.)

Agreements concerning incremental reductions in nuclear and conventional capability in Europe have profound implications for the U.S. Army as conventional forces assume changing responsibilities. Military force planners will need to reassess warfighting plans, doctrine, and forces to sustain warwinning—and therefore deterring—capabilities to prevail in conventional coalition conflicts. This is a difficult challenge, particularly when potential changes in the underlying rationale generating ground force capability are combined with declining resources. Past notable successes over forty years of peace in Europe may be at risk if emerging realities in Army total force readiness are not addressed thoughtfully and realistically.

This chapter addresses a key element in building a credible deterrent force, particularly the land power component. That element is the Reserve Component (RC) force, which supplements our national military capability in increasing measure. With growing reliance on conventional capability and expanding discussion in the United States and in Europe by our allies (particularly the Federal Republic of Germany) regarding the use of reserves to provide increased conventional capability, thoughtful surveyors of the military scene need to know more about the role of Reserve Components. This chapter presents some implications for evolving national security requirements, explains RC strengths that our national defense can exploit, and explores challenges to our reserve capability that must be minimized if the capability is to be credible. Lastly, this chapter offers some thoughts about major directions that could be taken to sustain and, in fact, improve total force readiness.

The key to deterrence and defense in a post-INF, conventional posture will continue to be a landpower force that is ready to fight and accomplish assigned missions. Current conventional force asymmetry and imbalance between the respective NATO and Warsaw Pact alliances are significant factors to consider when assessing post-INF force structure, doctrine, and training. A must for U.S. and allied planning will be cross-alliance actions to develop credible forces (sustainable in the face of a threat changing in reality and in perception), limited growth, and, quite probably, declining resources as perceptions of increased security divert resources to resolve other social and economic problems. We describe a military force that must integrate successfully both active and reserve forces across the alliance if it is to be credible.

In sum, while it is hoped that purposeful negotiation will moderate NATO–Warsaw Pact force imbalances, recognition of significant shifts in the rationale that has justified the military capability of NATO for forty years does mandate that national security planners find force multipliers to continue the stable correlation of military capability that has sustained a free Western Europe and that can nurture increased freedom in Eastern Europe in the future. The force multiplier of choice for the 1990s appears to be the reserve forces, and it behooves us all to become more knowledgeable in this area.

Increasing Reliance on Reserves in NATO

On both sides of the Atlantic, there is increasing discussion as to how defenses might be restructured as NATO–Warsaw Pact force reductions are carefully negotiated. European alliance colleagues propose that NATO defense initiatives incorporate a significantly greater role for reserve, home guard, or territorial forces, particularly in the Federal Republic of Germany.[1] While the active strength of NATO member armed forces decreased from 1.59 to 1.54 million in strength between 1980 and 1985, their reserve forces increased from 2.05 to 2.18 million members. In the Federal Republic, fully 60 percent of the Corps, 55 percent of the Divisions, and 80 percent of the Territorial Army strengths are in the RC at present, with every prospect of increase in the future.

During the last two decades, our alliance partners have invested to upgrade the capability of their reserve forces, and increased their force structure to provide more cadres to train such units. The basic U.S. decision to transfer an increasing share of fundamental responsibilities to the Reserve Components was made in the 1970s. This decision has been affirmed in subsequent congressional authorizations across administrations. Now, with a changing threat and declining budget, this decision appears virtually irreversible.

The U.S. Army expects the full integration of the RC into operational plans and missions, and has provided the requisite staffing, equipping, and training of RC forces. In many cases, the schedule for deployment in various contingency plans deploys some Army Reserve and Army National Guard units with or ahead of their active duty counterparts.[2] The RC will be "over there" early in time of crisis; that has become a given in both joint and combined contingency operational planning. Prudent national security planners must seek to employ best the advantages and special characteristics of the RC.

260 Education and Training of the U.S. Army

Table 14.1 Relative Manpower Standing of NATO Countries, 1960, 1970, 1980, 1985

Country	Active Force Strength (in thousands)				Reserves (in thousands)	
	1960	1970	1980	1985	1980	1985
West Germany	330.0	467.0	495.0	478.0	750.0	770.0
France	1009.0	501.0	494.0	476.6	342.0	393.0
United Kingdom	454.0	380.9	329.0	327.1	265.5	294.4
Belgium	110.0	96.5	87.9	91.6	115.5	178.5
Netherlands	142.0	116.5	115.0	105.9	171.0	176.3
Denmark	43.0	40.5	35.1	29.6	154.5	162.2
Norway	37.0	35.9	37.0	37.0	247.0	201.0
NATO Europe Total	2125.0	1638.8	1593.9	1545.8	2045.5	2175.4
United States	2606.0	2699.0	1545.8	2151.6	817.9	1212.3
NATO Total	4731.0	4337.8	3643.9	3697.4	2863.4	3387.7

Figure 14.1 Active and Reserve Components of the Federal Republic of Germany

Manpower	Corps	Divisions	TA BDE/RGMT	36 Brigades
	40% Active	45% Active	20% Active	90% Active
	60% Reserve	55% Reserve	80% Reserve	(18%) Training
				10% Reserve

The Reserve Components: A Center of Gravity

Army Field Manual 100-5, *Operations*, discusses the concept of "center of gravity," noting that any joint or combined operation is a complex organism whose effective operation depends not merely on the performance of each constituent part, but also on the smoothness with which the parts interact. Some component parts are more vital than others because their absence would unbalance the entire structure, producing inefficiency and accelerating deterioration of capability. The center of gravity refers to those special sources of strength or balance.[3] The RC, the militia if you will, may in fact have become such a center of gravity to our national military capability, particularly with respect to our NATO alliance obligations. A central premise of this chapter is that, by virtue of the significant increase in reliance on reserve forces in the West in general and particularly the landpower capability of the U.S. Army, RC readiness has become *a*, if not *the*, center of gravity for the highest priority landpower missions for the United States.

As a result of this increased import, a critical challenge for the national security decisionmaker is to understand the strengths and weaknesses of U.S. Army reserve forces in order to achieve maximum capability from these reserve forces in a post-INF environment. Simply stated, our reliance is such that we must maximize RC strengths and minimize their weaknesses if the United States is to remain credible as a land power.

To understand this new reliance on the RC, one should look at the sources of their rise to more significant responsibilities, their strengths, and their potential weaknesses. The recent growth in the RC is generally traced to decisions made by then–Secretary of Defense Melvin Laird. The force mix in 1973, 800,000 in the active Army compared to just over 230,000 in the U.S. Army Reserve and 386,000 in the Army National Guard, seemed inappropriate to the long-term defense structure after Vietnam. Secretary Laird sought to bond a "Total Force" of Active and Reserve Components (the National Guard and U.S. Army Reserve) by dramatically increasing the responsibility given the RC. His vision has reached maturity over time. In today's force structure, reliance on the RC is significant, and continuing to increase steadily. At the end of fiscal year 1988, the combined strength of the Army National Guard and Army Reserve was approximately 768,000, compared to 772,000 personnel in active Army strength. In 1989, the reserves became the majority of total force units, and the clear preponderance if the individual replacement pool of reservists is included.

Unfortunately, this new reality is not generally understood by most Americans—those concerned with national security issues as well as the general public. Few realize how totally integrated the force has become and how little capability to sustain land warfare would exist were mobilization of the Reserve and National Guard not to occur.

Today's National Guard and Army Reserve

The Reserve Component of the Army today is made up of citizen soldiers in the Army Reserve and the National Guard who meet each month at over four thousand reserve centers or armories. Until mobilization, the National Guard is commanded by the Governor of each state, through the state Adjutant General, and trains for both federal and state missions, especially state disaster relief responsibilities. The active force has the constitutional role of providing advice to each state Adjutant General and assesses the readiness of its units.[4] These state forces represent a significant portion of U.S. combat power: almost 32 percent of the Army's total strength, 36 percent of its combat divisions, and 67 percent of its separate brigades. In fact, the Army National Guard has more maneuver battalions than does the active Army.

In terms of sheer strength, it alone is the world's eleventh largest army today.[5]

The active force directly commands the USAR through five regionally distributed continental armies. The USAR represents more than 30 percent of the Army's organized structure, and provided 51 percent of all deployable units in fiscal year 1988/89. The selected reserve includes nearly 300,000 soldiers in almost 2,000 units worldwide who train every month and attend annual training for two weeks. The Individual Ready Reserve has a like number, 300,000, who have completed their active service or wish to continue reserve service but are not assigned to a specific training unit. These soldiers would likely become individual replacements and the cadre of newly organized units in the event of mobilization.[6]

The capability of any force, and its attendant deterrent value, is directly related to the quality of its personnel. Fortunately, RC quality has improved dramatically over the last decades. Figure 14.2 shows the remarkable increase in quality of new soldiers entering the USAR during the 1980s. These statistics mirror the quality increase in the National Guard units of the various states.

Today's RC soldiers are extraordinary, with over 90 percent high school graduates and nearly two-thirds scoring in the top half of vocational tests based on national norms. Every indicator shows these to be the best soldiers in recent military history. They want to accomplish their unit mission, they expect challenges to develop their potential, and they want to be technically and tactically proficient.

What Do the Reserve Components Mean to U.S. Defense?

It is important to keep reliance on the reserves in perspective. The Army strength of U.S. Forces Command, the line troops in the Continental United States, is 48 percent Active Component (AC) and 52 percent RC. Of the eighteen active force divisions, six have RC roundout brigades. For example, Fourth Army's 205th Infantry Brigade, a USAR unit, rounds out the 6th Infantry Division in Alaska; that is, this reserve brigade would become an integral part of the 6th Infantry Division in time of war. In fact, 60 percent of the deploying combat power of the total Army comes from the RC, a percentage that is increasing annually. Fully two-thirds of the infantry battalions, nearly half the armored and mechanized infantry battalions, more than half the field artillery battalions, two-thirds of the combat engineers, and half of the total Army aviation exists in the RC. Sixty percent of the Army's special operations assets are in the RC.

That high percentage of RC combat power mirrors the reliance on the RC for combat support and combat service support. Fully 60 percent of the Army's capability to sustain itself is found in the RC. 68 percent of all fuel

Figure 14.2 Manpower Quality of U.S. Army Reserve Components

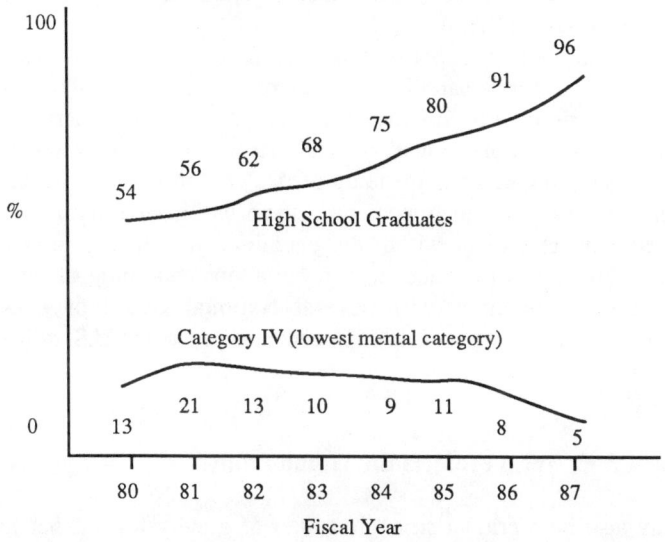

storage and distribution, 54 percent of all ammunition handling, 62 percent of all hospitals, and 82 percent of the nurses in the total Army are in the RC. These units have challenging missions. For example, Fourth Army's 103d Corps Support Command (COSCOM), located in Des Moines, Iowa, has the mission of sustaining the 250,000 soldiers of Fifth Corps, who in wartime would be in Europe astride the Fulda Gap.

Battlefield sustainment, in this case accomplished by the 103d COSCOM, *must* be present in a timely manner if defense is to be credible—one criterion for successful deterrence. Yet for such deterrence to be credible, there must be a strategic lift capable of relocating these reserve forces to a troubled location, preferably at such a pace that there is a timely credible U.S. land force on the ground. The total Army remains a strategic force that is critically dependent on the mobility capability of the other military services. In this area, the Active Army and the Reserves are equally dependent and vulnerable.

First to Fight, First to Be Equipped

The total force concept has meant that all units (active or reserve) are issued the most modern equipment based on the sequence of deployment. For example, M1 Abrams tanks are being issued to reserve armor units early in the deployment sequence while active armored forces later in the sequence have older M60A3 tanks. Similar equipping has taken place with other new equipment, such as the Bradley Fighting Vehicle, the High Mobility

Multipurpose Vehicle (HUMMV), the Apache helicopter, and the Multiple Launch Rocket System (MLRS).

Many combat service support units are multicomponent—that is, Active, Guard, or Reserve battalion headquarters may have subordinate companies from one or more of the other components. For example, in Fourth Army, 75 percent of the reserve units that would deploy in wartime will consist of subordinate units made up of Active Army, Army Reserve, and National Guard units. Ninety percent of them will have at least two of the three components present within the battalion. Specifically, it is not uncommon to find combat service support battalions consisting of one or two active force companies with several National Guard or USAR companies; this level of integration is unprecedented in modern U.S. military history.

Who Protects the Home Front?

The RC may also be a critical strategic center of gravity for another less obvious reason. Their presence within the United States may well be essential in preserving both public consensus and physical capability to execute contingency deployments. RC units, particularly the National Guard of the various states, provide the base for militia to protect the industrial and mobilization base, as well as to become the core from which force reconstitution can take place. One often overlooks the extent of the potential challenge to the domestic security of the United States. There is an absolute requirement to protect the infrastructure of the nation. As one assesses potential threats, there are serious problems that could occur even in the area that most Americans would think of as being least threatened: the Midwest. Significant delays in lake shipping of war materials occurred during World War II as a result of the accidental blockage of the Soo locks in the upper Midwest. Recent metropolitan area summer "brownouts" foretell what could occur if the fragile U.S. power grid were somehow imperiled. In 1987, there were serious interruptions to commerce and communication in Chicago, the Midwest, and, to some extent, on a national level that were caused by a relatively small fire at a switching station in a Chicago suburb. Saboteurs, terrorists, or special operations forces could threaten such essential utility or mass communications sites. If successful, their actions could impugn the credibility of that state government's ability to protect its people, as well as their expected support services and security, to the point where Governors could request the national command authority to divert National Guard or Army Reserve forces for home defense. Few Governors would enthusiastically endorse the rapid departure overseas of "their Guard" in the face of extensive local public concern about interruptions in the power, communications, or transportation systems—particularly if regional service support capability (police, fire, transit, schools, and hospitals) were reduced due to the loss of deploying mobilized reservists.

As a U.S. specified command, the U.S. Forces Command has the mission of protecting key and essential facilities as a part of the land defense of the continental United States. This responsibility is accomplished on a regional basis with such forces as may remain while the Army deploys to a theater of operations.

Figure 14.3 displays the areas of geographic responsibility for each Continental U.S. Army (CONUSA), which becomes a Joint Defense Command in wartime. For example, Fourth Army executes that regional mission in the upper Midwest. At the state level, the Adjutant General is charged with organizing a joint state area command to protect critical assets. The primary security responsibility, of course, rests with local authorities, with specific arrangements varying from jurisdiction to jurisdiction.

Existing reserve forces must deploy if the United States is to fulfill its treaty obligations. Such forces are an integral part of the alliance commitment. Home guards or militias would have to be the primary execution forces for the residual national protection missions, as they have been in the past. These forces do not presently exist in many states. Efforts are being undertaken to develop contingency plans to create, equip, and train them before or during mobilization, but this is, by and large, a paper capability.[7]

This less obvious, but very important, responsibility to protect the U.S. homeland should be planned for and resourced prior to mobilization if there is to be effective, and credible, protection of the home front. This is equally important for the preservation of deployment for recently mobilized forces critically necessary to meet alliance commitments. The focus for this essential regional and local planning rests with the leadership of U.S. reserve forces.

Why So Large an Active Force?

At a time of budget constraints, it is reasonable to question why the United States needs to have such a substantial active force if these RC forces are so affordable and so capable. Clearly, the RC is important, and it does cost less per soldier. While composing some 24 percent of the total Army structure, the USAR absorbs only slightly more than 4 percent of the total Army budget. In general terms, it costs three times as much in operating cost for an active force unit than it does for a like unit in the reserve force. It is certainly reasonable for a concerned citizen to ask why the United States has as large an active force as it does.

First and foremost, RC credibility is linked closely to AC capabilities and limitations. The AC is the skeleton and nervous system on which the tissue and muscle—the RC—must be placed to have genuine capability. The AC provides virtually immediate response to national security threats—the

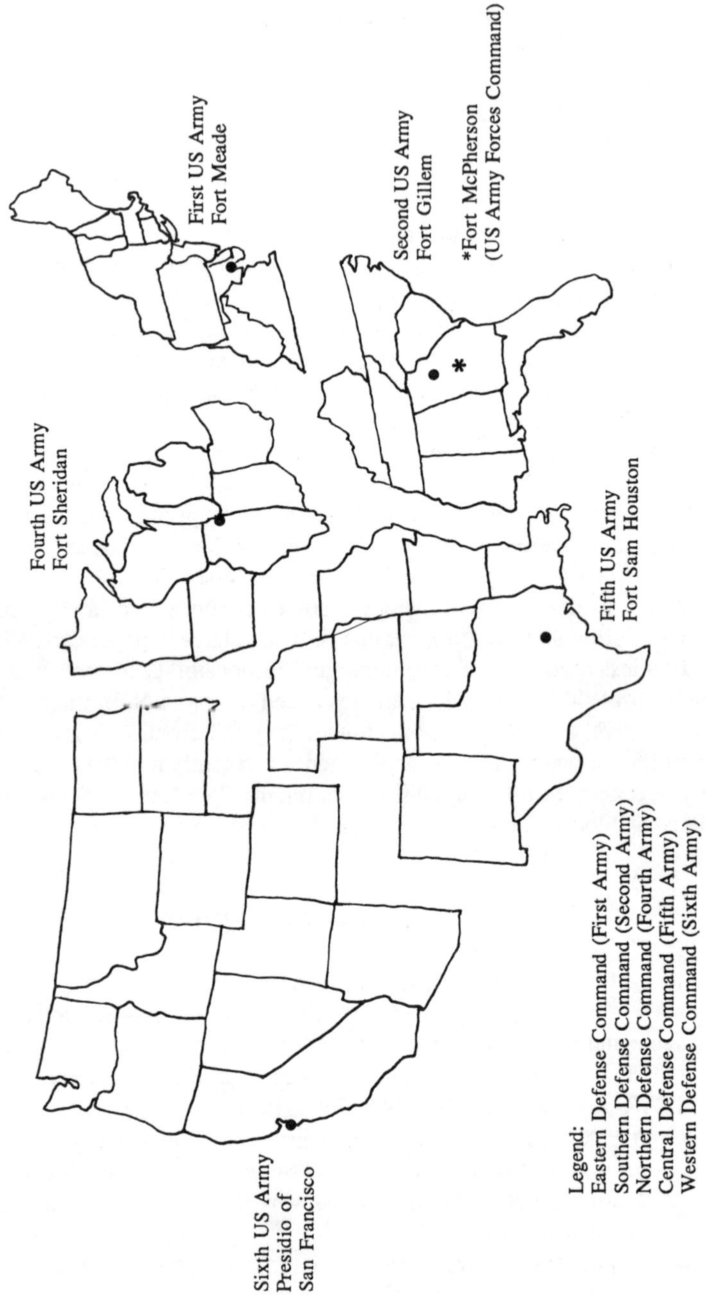

Figure 14.3 U.S. Army Defense Commands

quick response that can arrest a deteriorating situation. To be effective in countering international adventurism, the United States must clearly communicate its resolve and capability to support friendly nations in vital regions and safeguard specific interests. For example, the military action by the United States and the members of the Organization of Eastern Caribbean States in Grenada in October 1983 closed a base of operations intended to destabilize the Caribbean Basin. Forces were brought from a standing start directly into a close combat situation in sufficient strength and within such a short period of time that reinforcement by Cuba was impossible.

Second, a global power must possess the capability to project power in support of national and international commitments. Examples include the 1987 deployment to the Persian Gulf, or a land power example, Operation Golden Pheasant in March of 1988, the highly successful show of force by battalions of the 7th Infantry Division and 82d Airborne Division in Honduras. The two operations clearly demonstrated U.S. resolve in Southwest Asia and Central America. Such actions require a ready Active Force—a strategic force—since the import of readiness on today's battlefield or scene of international tension is measured in hours (which the active force can meet) rather than in days (which is the time that reserve forces require to mobilize and deploy).[8]

Third, the United States shares in worldwide coalition combined operations with its allies, and it must have professionals capable of joint and coalition planning. There is a compelling need to ensure continuing officer expertise in those and critical joint operations skills, a requirement acknowledged by the National Defense Act of 1986. The training ground for these important duties usually involves service with other U.S. services, foreign armies, or alliance staffs, and can only take place efficiently in the AC. Every day, there are active duty officers serving on the staffs of the North Atlantic Treaty Organization, Allied Forces Central Europe, and United Nations Command in Korea. Liaison officers serve with the armies of Australia, Canada, the United Kingdom, and the Federal Republic of Germany. And, within the national command structure, Army officers and noncommissioned officers serve on the staff of the Department of Defense as well as in joint commands, such as United States Central Command.

Fourth, the active force runs daily Army operations, planning and coordinating the role of land forces in international deterrence and security assistance. For example, Army officers on the staff of U.S. Southern Command assist in the planning of security assistance throughout Central and South America, and coordinate joint land power training opportunities with various host nations.

Fifth, commanders and planners in the AC set and enforce tough and professional standards that assure credibility. Credible forces exist because professional soldiers and leaders proof and validate the effectiveness of professional training. Doctrinal development must take place from a standard base that offers complementary development of both soldiers and staffs. Leaders and professional staffs are required to review what training is to take place and to what level of proficiency. Explicit, quantifiable skills of the soldier must be established and quality control measurement must take place, whether developing physical fitness standards or determining the best possible system for marksmanship training. Creating effective and efficient battle command staff training with evolving doctrine, equipment, and organization to challenge leaders and staffs is the province of the active professional force.

Finally, the regular force accomplishes research, development and procurement of tomorrow's weapons, and support systems even while managing the acquisition of today's Battlefield Operating Systems (BOS) components. Providing the wherewithal for today's Army is big business indeed. In fiscal year 1988, the Army spent 8.2 billion dollars to procure aircraft, missiles, weapons, and tracked vehicle systems. The Army's Tank Automotive Command alone, for example, would be number eight on the Fortune 500 list this year. The need for full-time presence and sustained competence is obvious. Less obvious is how this overhead should be charged off against the cost of sustaining reserve forces.

What Should the AC/RC Balance Be?

Each and all of these tasks require dedicated active forces to meet daily challenges. But there is a caution: One can no longer simply measure the AC overhead by the number of soldiers. Instead, the shifts in relative roles from active forces to reserves will mean changes in how one measures effectiveness, and how one will make subsequent force structure determinations.

When determining the cost of the RC, one normally sees a price-per-soldier cost that is noticeably less than for the AC soldier. There are, however, hidden investment costs benefiting the RC that are borne in the infrastructure of the active force. Therefore, much of the RC cost effectiveness is derived from the overhead cost sustained by the AC.

For example, the cost to maintain a National Guard tank battalion may be less than its AC counterpart until one amortizes the cost of research and development, procurement, and maintenance of a sophisticated training base that is used by both the active and reserve tank forces but funded only by the active force. Economies exist when a percentage of the force is largely AC, but when the RC is greater than half the size of the total force, those economies may no longer exist, and overall investment will be necessary. Savings by transfer to the RC may not be realized to the level that conventional wisdom presumes.

Looking at policy development and program execution, one needs to recognize that more and more functions have migrated from the active force to the reserve force, along with the forces that would execute the mission in sustained conflict. Prisoner of war (PW) doctrine is formulated in the reserves because the only PW capability exists in the RC. The management of the rear battle in the division, corps, and echelons above corps is accomplished by Rear Area Operations Centers (RAOC), all of which are either in the USAR or National Guard. Some skills that have migrated are required in any contingency: low-intensity conflict (LIC) or conventional protracted conflict. Psychological operations, civil-military operations units, and even graves registration resources required to support operations exist in the RC, and provided their functions during the Grenada operations.

Increasingly, it is becoming apparent that the process of reducing the "tail" to increase the "tooth" has meant that there is simply insufficient combat support and combat service support in the active force to sustain deployable forces without at least partial callup of the reserve sustaining base. This becomes a critical national policy issue as planners assess how much capability is needed. At what point in a destabilizing situation could such a partial callup to sustain a tailored force send a signal of mobilization with a "provocative" message of escalation? Does the United States, as a global power, need or want to have to face such a decision point very early in a developing crisis?

To Be Credible, We Must Be Capable

Another vital assessment element for the national security policymaker must be judging the credibility of reserve forces. To accomplish the RC deterrence mission, they must not only *be* capable, they must *look* capable. To be capable to potential adversaries, that is *to deter*, there must be clear, public demonstration of warfighting proficiency with soldier and unit competency in unilateral and allied readiness exercises worldwide. The dramatic and highly visible increase in RC overseas deployment training, such as REFORGER, Team Spirit, and Fuertas Caminos, has enhanced total force credibility to the world audience.

The reserves have done much to increase their credibility as full partners in defense. Nearly 200,000 reservists have trained overseas since 1980. Soldier participation has steadily increased from 12 units in fiscal year 1976 to 400 units in fiscal year 1980 and 3,700 units by fiscal year 1987. Nearly 48,000 soldiers in the Army Guard and Reserve trained in other countries during 1988. The Illinois Army National Guard, for example, has had soldiers train in twenty-three countries between 1986 and 1989. Rotations at the National Training Center and the Joint Readiness Training Center now routinely include National Guard and USAR soldiers and units, and every major Joint Chiefs of Staff exercise depends on significant RC participation.[9]

Special RC Advantages

To best understand the profound importance of credible reserve components, consider other, perhaps less obvious, advantages they offer, including continuity, availability of special skills, creation of a national defense constituency based on personal knowledge and experience (particularly useful in LIC), and provision of a source for high-tech support to allies. A complete picture should also assess potential challenges to increased RC warfighting capability, including time management, training requirements, realistic expectations, and the essentiality of public support. Just as the active force offers special strengths, the RC also represents unique capabilities. Five specific advantages are characteristic of the RC.[10]

First, RC soldiers offer a special continuity in warplanning and coordination with the host nation staffs and home guards with which they deal. Over the long term, this offers stability and friendships that are just not possible with the personnel turnover in the active force. This stability is especially valuable in the combat support and combat service support areas. For example, noncommissioned officers concerned with logistics movements for overseas deployment of heavy division forces may well deal with the same counterpart host nation harbormaster and port off-load personnel for more than a decade, seeing them not only at exercises but also at intermittent planning conferences as well. Units with an area signal center responsibility may well develop special shared facility arrangements with their home guard counterparts who are working with local national long-haul communications facilities.

Second, some RC soldiers bring extraordinary skills from their civilian employment to the Army, with no associated cost for the professional training they possess. Their stability also allows experienced soldiers to deal with allied counterparts over a period of many years. This investment is often not feasible in the AC. There are numerous examples in the Fourth Army. One unit, the 416th Engineer Command, with a wartime theater engineer responsibility, has among its ranks many certified civil engineers whose civilian professions deal with national and international contractors, and who face issues similar to those they can expect in wartime. They are able to assimilate lessons learned from their daily occupation into wartime planning. Other examples are seasoned police detectives who are assigned to Criminal Investigation detachments in the RC. Their special skills and detailed knowledge, often acquired at public expense from a city or state, are directly applicable to their wartime mission. Of course, these talents may depart at time of local crisis—a challenge discussed above.

Third, the RC also offers a ready source for special-purpose units that can be structured innovatively for specific contingencies. They could be used for special support to a host nation, either in NATO or under a bilateral treaty; to provide highly technical skills rapidly, such as as specialized, effective, and costly target acquisition, firepower, command, and control communication to selected allies; and to augment deterrence and demonstrate capability (such as multiple-launch rocket systems or attack helicopter units) not possessed by an allied nation's military. Units of citizen soldiers also may focus more intently on a particular area of operations because of their long-term stability. For example, RC units in the northern United States already have a natural proficiency in cold weather and mountain operations, and are therefore specializing in them.

Fourth, there is a special national value gained from the RC. Its membership creates a national, regionally distributed constituency that is vitally interested in national defense matters, and assures local cognizance of such important issues. While many of the states in the East and South have land power forces present at highly visible active Army posts, there are many areas of the nation in which there is no active force visibility. In the Midwest and other parts of the country, there are few active posts. What the citizens in those areas know of the Army, the military, or defense issues may come to them from informed RC leaders.

Finally, positive and informed citizen soldiers can influence attitudes overseas as well as within the United States. Through participation in humanitarian aid and overseas deployment training, such as Blazing Trails and Fuertas Caminos, RC soldiers show a healthy image to the people in emergent low-intensity conflicts. Such populations can see Americans as both citizens and soldiers, offering their personal commitment to helping less-fortunate neighbors. This image often contrasts with that of the professional military, which they may have grown to fear or distrust.

In fact, participation by these soldiers directly supports national security objectives established to combat unconventional warfare and low-intensity conflict. These reservists present to impoverished people a reassuring image of the United States and its citizens. Two stated U.S. interests are advancing the cause of democracy, freedom, and human rights throughout the world, and aiding the stability of friendly governments and institutions to combat insurgencies, state-sponsored terrorism, and international trafficking in illicit drugs.[11]

While this participation by citizen soldiers gains confidence and friendship in foreign lands, it also serves to gain the confidence of their friends and neighbors back in the States. In simplest terms, to Americans from the heartland, lofty generalized policy goals described by Washington often are met with highly skeptical, if not critical, comment. On the other hand, personal experiences of neighbors or business colleagues who have been abroad and who describe the conditions facing the people they helped overseas have proven eloquent. That freely offered testimony from men and women of the USAR and National Guard across the nation, following their two-week training experience, has gained considerable grass-root understanding and support for vital national security programs related to Central and South America.

Potential RC Weaknesses

The significant advantages just presented are matched by four specific challenges facing the RC: time management, training needs, expectations, and the need for public support. How these challenges are addressed will greatly affect U.S. warfighting readiness and consequent credibility as a capable land power force as the nation searches for more effective, efficient ways to preserve the land power military component of U.S. national security.

In mission and force decisions, the constituent parts of the capability equation are people, resources, and time. Normally, if there are insufficient numbers of people or dollars to accomplish the mission during peacetime, time is expended to complete the task at hand. This reasoning process is the normal case within the AC. In the reserves, however, every decision concerning military mission accomplishment is predicated on the single most critical commodity: time. What is three months' planning time for the active force translates into six days (that is, three weekends of command planning time) for the reservist. All are working hard to conduct every drill and the two-week annual training period more efficiently and effectively.

Special initiatives are taking place to reduce administrative burdens at the company level so that attention may focus on warfighting readiness. This initiative is necessary because of the basic law of opportunity cost: Every minute consumed by administrative reporting or record keeping is at the expense of what unit, leader, staff, or individual training could have been accomplished. For an active force commander, finding time for an X-ray, AIDS testing, or other administrative tasking is distracting, but, basically, it is not a difficult task. For the reserve commander, a day spent sending soldiers some distance to a medical facility for such testing consumes half a month's available training time, and probably half the previous month's training time to plan and coordinate the trip.

Consequently, much work is being done to improve the ability to train the RC force to standard in limited periods of time. General Carl Vuono, the Army Chief of Staff, has said, "Tough, realistic training to standard is the heart of the Army's ability to execute its missions now and in the future."[12]

Such demanding, satisfying training bonds the soldier to mission, unit, and equipment. To fulfill this need for reserve force training that is at once efficient, tough, and realistic, leaders have developed specialized training to challenge soldiers, their leaders, and the staffs of higher headquarters.

New concepts of training are being introduced that apply equally to active and reserve forces and involve entire units, ranging from the leaders down to the individual soldier. Soldiers and their leaders are expected to train simultaneously to develop efficiently a highly effective team. These new techniques especially target the best RC training opportunity, the two-week annual training period. During that time the entire force—individual soldiers, units from squad to company size, and their headquarters staffs—trains within a common framework and set of standards.

At the individual level, soldiers perform a specific skill until they gain proficiency at the required level. Their units also perform set tasks to a standard in a training lane that is designed to replicate the combat mission of the unit. Like the soldier who performs the task until he or she gets it right, the squad, platoon, or company will train through the lane in repetition. If the unit correctly accomplishes the mission, then progressively more challenging tasks are added; otherwise, the training is repeated until the task is completed satisfactorily. Each of these training sessions is accompanied by prompt feedback and performance assessment so that the soldiers and unit leadership learn their strong points and weak areas. And while the units are undergoing this training, their battalion and brigade headquarters execute battle command training programs to exercise their command and control capabilities.

Paralleling structured training initiatives is a significant potential improvement in the RC training of individuals. Leaders are becoming more proficient tactically and technically because they are now required to attend various Army schools in order to acquire necessary skills that they then take back to the unit and share with their soldiers. This long-term investment in upgrading leader quality is helping to increase the quality of training at the unit level in the RC. That high-quality training, in turn, is beginning to improve the retention of today's trained force and the recruitment of the citizen soldiers of tomorrow.

The emerging success of these new programs shows a genuine commitment of the active Army to RC training improvements. Part of that continued investment must include special training and simulation modules that need to be developed to address the unique challenges of RC training and missions. Placing sophisticated simulations at the AC schoolhouse provides great advantage to the active soldier in his preparation for warfighting. Unfortunately, that advantage has virtually no application for the RC officer or NCO who attends monthly training far away from that facility.

The Army needs to find ways to bring these highly technical devices to the RC. Since the cost to place such devices at every center or armory may be prohibitive, an efficient solution would be to centrally locate such AC-developed exportable training packages at facilities convenient to large numbers of soldiers with a particular specialty. Modern training technology clearly provides needed answers to improved RC combat readiness, but the solutions will be expensive—perhaps more expensive to train the RC than the active Army.

Yet, as one develops an increased appreciation of the RC soldiers and how they are being prepared for their mission, it is important to keep expectations of RC soldier skill level realistic. Performance standards must be uniform, yet should consider the differences between AC and RC training environments. The practical realities facing the RC officer and NCO should be the foundation from which professional competency goals are built.

It is unrealistic to presume that an RC soldier who trains thirty-nine days a year will be able to accomplish the aggregate number of tasks accomplished to standard that an AC counterpart would be proficient in after year-round training. Instead, because of this time limitation, the tasks must be clearly focused on contingency mission accomplishment. That focusing process requires the unit commander to review guidance received from the warfighting Commander-in-Chief under which the unit will serve in wartime and then to develop a training program that assures mission-essential tasks can be performed well. This clarity of purpose gives order and sequencing to the unit training plan and establishes clear soldier performance goals.

The key is for soldiers to do the most important tasks well, and for the unit to be able to do mission-essential tasks competently and confidently. Succeeding in a few vital tasks, soldiers can become genuinely proficient and gain valuable self-confidence. If they try to do too much, they're likely to fail—and will be neither competent nor confident. The bad news is that the reserves never have enough time to train; the good news is that innovations in Army training policy and programs portend revolutionary improvements in the efficiency and effectiveness of RC training.

The Need for Public Support

There is another very important challenge facing today's RC. For any military force to be credible, there must be informed and obvious public support. U.S. soldiers, nationally distributed in the RC, uniquely represent society at large. If they are to remain ready to fulfill their important missions, RC units must be led by a representative cross-section of capable men and women. There is a serious problem keeping these quality people because of time demands. Of those soldiers choosing to conclude their reserve service, the two reasons given most often were pressure from spouse and pressure from employer.[13] The American public must become more familiar with the essential contributions of the RC so that there can be greater tolerance and support of the extraordinary demands placed on the citizen soldier.

The Department of Defense sponsors an organization to get these messages to the American people. In each state, there is an employer support to the Guard and Reserve chapter, with representatives throughout the state who assist RC soldiers and their employers, and who inform centers of influence about the criticality of the RC.[14]

One of the most important messages that these chapters can present is just how much time is freely given by citizen soldiers. Conventional understanding is that a reservist or guardsman spends 39 days a year, but those are only the normal training days for which the soldier is reimbursed. A recent precommand course survey with Fourth Army showed that the average colonel spent 92 days for the Army, a lieutenant colonel spent 100, and a major spent 102, with a high of 160 days, working for the Army on weekends and holidays, away from families. Their sacrifice must be supported by supervisors, family, and friends if they are to remain active participants in the nation's defense. It is hard for an upwardly mobile DuPont, IBM, or GM executive to remain a mobilization-day (M-day) citizen soldier given the pressures of his or her corporate and Army positions. Seeking and keeping the best is not a race or gender issue, but one of gaining access to a necessary cross section of business and professional leaders for the RC so that citizen soldiers on whom the country increasingly relies do in fact represent national leadership.

Regional Representation, Regional Concerns

Another important issue of national importance is how reserve forces are distributed regionally. The rich cultural diversity of the United States is an essential component of the active and reserve forces. In some regions of the nation, there have been significant recruiting challenges, while in other areas there is a history of units being overstrength.[15] Special attention may have to be directed to recruiting and retention incentives to reduce regional losses and consequent underrepresentation in the force. In many cases, success in recruiting and retention is directly related to the proximity of active force installations, where a rewarding training program is much easier to maintain. The opposite is true in those areas where there is no real visibility, where there is little public reinforcement, or where quality training is difficult to arrange because of a long distance to training facilities. There is a genuine need for force planners to address regional distribution issues, with a view to intensively managing lest regional diversity be lost.

Lastly, there are significant practical differences between national-federal and regional-local based forces. This may appear self-evident, yet these differences are often overlooked in a busy federal bureaucracy—the Department of the Army. Conscious decisions must be made on which issues should be resolved at a *national* level or resolved instead at a *regional* level.

There are subtle issues in regional application (in the RC) of national policies (of the AC). For example, individual professional development assumes assignment mobility nationwide for the AC, but there is substantially less mobility in the RC. What should be the RC professional development pattern? Often, national military leadership, nurtured in a bureaucracy with absolute national mobility and serving frequently overseas, finds it difficult to respond to the regional orientation and requirements of most citizen soldiers.

Another example of potential AC/RC mismatch is in equipment storage and maintenance. Most Army maintenance guidance is based on an AC commander's ability to perform daily maintenance in a nearby unit motor pool. This varies greatly from the availability of immediate equipment maintenance in armories or at reserve centers. AC maintenance policies and procedures need to become more cognizant of diverse regional solutions. One solution would be the development of additional equipment concentration sites. This can be particularly appropriate for highly capital-intensive equipment. Such initiatives offer real improvements in maintenance and consequent enhanced readiness.

Recent initiatives by an RC training study and subsequent funding support clearly demonstrate greater attention by the Department of the Army to the specific needs of RC soldiers and units. An issue of concern to planners and schedulers as they build better programs involves training special soldier skills in the AC institutional training base. Such course participation is effective and efficient, but the length of such schooling often impairs attendance by RC soldiers seeking advancement. Regional RC schools with specially tailored courses have been set up in some locations. There is a clear need to find more ways for RC soldiers to progress professionally by developing regional training policies, simulations, and classes tailored to their needs and Military Occupational Specialty (MOS) densities.

Because of RC unit time constraints, RC commanders find it absolutely essential to focus their efforts. Army-wide personnel, administrative, logistics, and operational procedures written for the AC frequently consume excessive RC training time. Regional tailoring of these policies and procedures can help relieve pressures on the RC company commander. Recent studies have been initiated to determine where reports could be eliminated, what information could be obtained from existing data bases without asking subordinate commanders for a report, and whether residual redundancies held over from years ago still remain. In each of these cases, regional initiatives have been able to begin the process of relieving the administrative load from the company commander. Greater latitude should be made available to the regional commander to permit such efficiencies. Such latitude would be analogous to the Department of Defense Model Installation Program, which has brought about significant economies and progress within the active force. Many actions are underway to address these challenges. Their importance mandates continuing review.

RC Readiness Issues Merit Study

Other implications could be considered usefully in pondering post-INF land power military readiness issues. Defense policy advisors should understand that acceptance of the increased RC role means acceptance of a potential "brittleness" of the force. Whereas active force units, such as the 101st Airborne Division (Air Assault), train year-round to deploy anywhere in the world at a moment's notice, their reserve counterparts are not as capable for varied missions. RC units under the Capstone program train for a very specific purpose now, in contrast to former programs in which RC units were given a mission of General Support, Reinforcing.[16] An example is the 73d Separate Infantry Brigade, a National Guard unit from Ohio with an early deployment date, which has a very precise mission critical to national defense. The brigade commander has a specific mission and location from which to derive his task list for training. He has received guidance from his wartime Commander-in-Chief and knows the mission, enemy, terrain, troops available, and likely conditions of combat—and he trains in his objective area frequently. This enables the 73d commander to establish a carefully reasoned training program that is keyed to a wartime mission. As a consequence, the 73d is genuinely ready now to perform its mission.

However, this missioning and resultant training results in important complexities that affect planning and force structuring. If a higher headquarters alters an active force mission on very short notice, it can respond—essentially anywhere, anytime, to fight if necessary, and win. This was the case with 7th Infantry Division units, which moved from the National Training Center at Fort Irwin, to home station at Fort Ord, and on to full deployment in Honduras (Operation Golden Pheasant) within forty-eight hours. If such a diversion happens to the 73d during mobilization, the unit's readiness is significantly altered. When a reserve or guard unit is assigned to other than its Capstone location and mission, the unit may require extensive training time and re-equipping before it can fully perform its combat mission. Special effort to rationalize and systematize mission requirements is essential so that RC units can continue to train effectively so as to perform a relatively immutable mission. And, of course, national security planners need to factor the resultant decrease in mission flexibility of the total force into contingency planning.

As national defense planners contemplate continually expanding reliance on reserve forces, they should also review the organization for combat and other structural changes that may be appropriate. There is a need to review the balance of combat, combat support, and combat service support in both components. At issue is a real challenge to determine what kinds of contingencies U.S. land power should be able to respond to without resorting to mobilization, and the messages such an action sends to the world. Current combat support (CS) and combat service support (CSS) structuring actually limit AC unit sustainability without mobilization. The CS and CSS capabilities across components should be balanced. How will the Army of the future recognize these realities amid budget constraints and possible changes in alliance relationships?

In their efforts to transfer missions from the AC to the RC, analysts must define where "critical mass" will occur. They must find the point where the force, if it became any smaller, could not withstand the attack of a hostile force in a particular location should there be a lack of national consensus on full mobilization. The Bataan March would be an unacceptable provocation in the nuclear age. Would the United States tolerate a "Dunkirk"? Thoughtful study should assess how the United States can gain and sustain "critical mass" if it should occur that too many missions have migrated from the AC to the RC. A corollary issue is what dedicated intertheater transport means to critical mass. Would added airlift and sealift allow more missions to be transferred to the RC, and should there be more direct linkage between the two concerns? Issues such as these should be considered when assessing post-INF total force structure.

Need for a Healthy Discussion of the RC

The intent of this chapter has been to stimulate thinking about the critically vital national defense resource provided by the RC, especially the land power represented in the National Guard and Army Reserve. The active force provides immediate response and participates in joint, combined, and coalition operations. It is the AC role to train, maintain, and support the total force while preserving the future through responsible research and development.

That active force, however, cannot be sustained for long without the combat, combat support, and combat service support capabilities of the RC that make up more than 60 percent of a deploying force. The RC provides competence at a reduced cost, offers special skills and continuity, and provides a national constituency for defense matters.[17] How great the reliance on these citizen soldiers will be in future planning is an essential issue.

The force imbalance in conventional forces that has been the focus of so much recent international dialogue needs to be addressed, and part of the answer to that situation seems certain to be reliance on reserve forces. Enhanced credibility of the United States and its worldwide alliance commitments clearly calls for powerful, trained, and ready conventional forces, both active and reserve. It is hoped that a spirited and informed public discussion of these issues will evolve as the long-range implications of post-INF international relationships and alliance planning are considered, and appropriate strategies designed.

Notes

1. This issue is addressed in International Institute for Strategic Studies, *The Military Balance* (London: The International Institute for Strategic Studies, 1961–1962, 1971–1972, 1980–1981, and 1985–1986).

2. For additional description, see "National Security Strategy of the United States," a White House White Paper prepared in January 1987.

3. A definition and discussion of "center of gravity" is found in *Field Manual 100-5: Operations* (Washington, D.C.: Headquarters, Department of the Army, May 1986), Appendix B, "Key Concepts in Operational Design."

4. The issue of authority is an important one. The overwhelming reliance on the combat force in the Army National Guard and the extraordinary linking of the total force—Active, National Guard, and Army Reserve—mean that units must train together as they will fight. Planners seek the best opportunities where such training can take place, often in an overseas location. Recently, a few state Governors have taken issue with when and where National Guard units could train. The Montgomery amendment to the 1987 Defense Authorization Act prohibits state and territorial Governors from withholding their consent to active-duty training for their National Guard units based upon objections to the location, purpose, type, or schedule of the active-duty training. Some Governors have challenged the validity of the Montgomery amendment. A U.S. District Court decided that the Montgomery amendment was a valid exercise of the power of Congress under the Armies Clause and does not violate the Militia Clause. That decision is under appeal in the First and Eighth U.S. Circuit Courts of Appeals. The First and Eighth Circuit Courts of Appeals have affirmed the decision. The eventual outcome of the case will undoubtedly have an effect on future planning for the integration of the total force.

5. Relative size is even more pronounced with the Air National Guard, which is the seventh-largest air force in the world.

6. Table 14.2, on page 280, reflects the age and rank distribution of soldiers in the Individual Ready Reserve.

7. Of the fifty states, thirty-three have authorized a state defense force or militia. Only twenty-three of the fifty states have appropriated funds for such forces. In Fourth Army's area, for example, all seven states have existing statutes authorizing the establishment of a state defense force. Michigan was the most recent, with legislation enacted in July 1988. Of the seven states, however, only Ohio and Indiana have active cadres for a militia, and Michigan intends to move to an active cadre.

8. The great wars of the past involved lengthy periods of mobilization. In the Russo-Japanese War (1904–1905), it took the Russian army nearly a year to move existing standing forces to Manchuria and Korea. Historians feel that delay cost the Russians any chance for success. In World War I, it took a year for the United States to mobilize 54 divisions, of which 41 went to France. And in World War II, it was not until 1944 that the United States could field the full 90-division force needed to fight and win a two-front war. In today's spectrum of threat, with immediacy of communication and rapid transportation, an explosive situation could be ignited and a region destabilized in a matter of days or weeks. Legislation providing for a 200,000 person reserve callup and partial mobilization has given U.S. leaders a capability to use necessary demonstration of force promptly to meet immediate threats. The ability to call up specific units or individuals selectively would seem particularly critical.

9. This is described in the *Army Posture Statement* for fiscal year 1989, presented to the 100th Congress by Secretary of the Army John O. Marsh, Jr., and Army Chief of Staff Gen. Carl E. Vuono.

10. There are clear essential roles for the U.S. military, and specifically for the reserve forces (the National Guard of the various states) in domestic

Table 14.2 Profile of U.S. Army Officers and Enlisted Personnel

	18 - 19	20 - 24	25 - 29	30 - 34	35 - 39	40 - 44	45 - 49	50 - 54	55 - 59	60	61	OVER 61	TOTAL
E-1	1,111	10,810	2,541	509	126	17	1	45	1	0	0	0	15,289
E-2	1,351	35,923	12,918	2,884	912	329	112	128	6	0	0	0	34,564
E-3	307	21,089	10,104	2,552	895	221	61	129	5	0	0	0	35,364
E-4	47	53,202	23,835	8,834	2,903	1,078	297	437	23	2	0	3	100,482
E-5	2	5,773	12,585	7,369	3,588	1,947	746	424	113	12	7	4	32,571
E-6	0	48	1,793	3,239	2,583	2,019	1,003	596	315	28	14	7	11,645
E-7	0	5	156	1,022	2,056	2,229	1,367	1,018	662	86	36	24	8,651
E-8	0	0	0	26	261	660	592	632	633	75	34	41	2,954
E-9	0	1	0	0	9	38	144	263	461	77	24	23	1,088
WO1	0	10	32	60	17	63	44	10	1	0	0	0	294
CW2	0	10	306	464	574	883	308	142	33	2	1	1	2,324
CW3	0	0	5	79	268	377	103	130	94	4	5	2	1,133
CW4	0	0	0	2	115	242	115	180	258	44	16	17	987
2LT	1	2,264	2,004	901	390	112	10	88	1	2	0	0	5,863
1LT	0	166	3,992	2,216	1,174	458	41	23	0	0	0	1	8,072
CPT	0	4	2,092	7,300	5,826	2,833	443	111	2	1	0	1	18,414
MAJ	0	0	1	417	3,665	8,955	1,763	308	29	2	1	0	12,155
LTC	0	2	2	7	51	365	2,928	1,179	58	4	4	11	8,114
COL	0	0	1	1	1	92	530	1,069	328	28	14	19	2,081

drug suppression. At this writing, these responsibilities were still evolving and are therefore not discussed.

11. See note 2.

12. This issue was the subject of discussion in the 100th Congress during an appearance by Gen. Vuono before the Subcommittee on Defense, House Appropriations Committee.

13. A detailed analysis of why reserve soldiers did not continue their service was assessed in Section VI, "The Influence of the Family, Employer, and Other Factors," of a Rand Corporation report on the Selected Reenlistment Bonus Test presented in April 1982.

14. The National Committee for Employer Support to the Guard and Reserve (ESGR) is located in Washington, D.C. Interested parties may call (800) 336–4590 to receive additional information or to locate their nearest ESGR representative.

15. Shifts in national economic and demographic trends during the 1980s have affected RC recruiting. In fiscal year 1980, 49 percent of all armed forces RC recruiting came from twenty-one states east of the Mississippi and Ohio rivers and the Great Lakes; in fiscal year 1988, the figure for these states dropped to 37 percent. In fiscal year 1980, 50 percent of armed forces RC recruitments were from north central and northeastern states; in fiscal year 1988, that figure dropped to 40 percent.

16. Capstone provides wartime mission alignment for all Active Guard and Army Reserve units within U.S. Forces Command. This allows them to plan and train in peacetime so as to be truly prepared to accomplish specific wartime missions. Capstone alignments also influence Army priorities to ensure that units receive support (personnel, equipment, force modernization) based on order of deployment.

17. There are clear economies associated with RC forces, as many reserve operating costs are "charged off" to the active forces. As discussed, these economies may no longer prevail as the reserve forces become increasingly the preponderance of the total force.

PART 7
Conclusions

CHAPTER 15

Challenges and Requirements for the Future

JOHN ALLEN WILLIAMS

Knowing what we do about human nature, it is too much to hope that the dramatic events unfolding in 1989 and 1990 presage a world without war. As the Soviet reins are loosening in Eastern Europe, it becomes apparent that the bipolar conflict known as the Cold War was superimposed over a myriad of other conflicts that can now come to the fore. These range from irredentist claims for territory lost decades or centuries ago to serious ethnic friction, including an anti-Semitism that had generally remained latent since 1945. Indeed, Eastern Europe may not even be the best example of these conflicts. The Iran-Iraq war probably claimed more lives than any other war of this century, except for the two world wars. The potential for violent outbreaks is widely shared around the world, from Korea to South Asia to southern Africa to Central America.

This book attempts to address the major implications of these changes for U.S. national security policy, particularly the role of the U.S. Army in the new era. The contributors come from a variety of backgrounds and are far from homogeneous politically. Although there would be differences with respect to specific recommendations, there is a great deal of agreement among them as to the contours of the new strategic landscape. This final chapter revisits the most important areas of concern, concluding with some assessments concerning the U.S. Army, the U.S. military generally, and U.S. society.

Changes in the Strategic Environment

Underlying a reevaluation of U.S. national security policies are several fundamental changes in the strategic environment. These include a reduction in the threat (or at least the perceived threat) from the Soviet Union, an increased challenge to the United States from the Third World, and a shrinking pool of resources likely to be devoted to defense.

Decrease in the Soviet Threat

The end of the Cold War. Although it would not be useful for national leaders to trumpet the fact too widely, it is not too much to say that the Cold War is moving to a resolution, and the West has won it. With the demise of the Brezhnev doctrine of fraternal mutual interference among socialist states in order to prevent one another from falling from the socialist camp, the possibility of peaceful political and economic evolution in Eastern Europe (and in the Soviet Union as well) is a real one.[1]

It should be noted, however, that a noncommunist Soviet Union or, more likely, a nominally communist Soviet Union whose international agenda is determined by Soviet national interests traditionally defined rather than by ideology would still pose a major challenge to the United States as the Soviets seek to become a global power. The Soviets will be the primary adversary of the United States for the foreseeable future, although the conflict may become increasingly demilitarized. The good news of early 1990 seems to be that Soviet leaders will permit a good deal of democratization in Eastern Europe, thereby reducing the likelihood of military clashes in an area in which they have a vital interest.

Reduced Soviet military threat. Although it is clear that East-West rhetoric has cooled considerably, there has not been unanimous agreement as to whether the change in tone reflects an actual reduction in military threat. Certainly, it is remarkable that the political evolution leading to the effective elimination of the Berlin Wall[2] was tolerated, and even encouraged, by the leader of the Soviet Union. This is particularly noteworthy since the result is the weakening or elimination of that country's East European (actually, Central European) buffer zone. Whatever the preferences of current or future leaders, the Soviet Union can no longer depend, if it ever could, on the political reliability of Warsaw Pact allies in a military conflict with the West.

Possibility of arms control. The likelihood of a major clash in Europe will be further reduced by arms control initiatives in the offing. Limitations on strategic nuclear delivery systems are likely in the wake of the agreement on intermediate-range nuclear forces. Most stabilizing of all would be agreements that greatly reduce the conventional force imbalance in favor of the Warsaw Pact, together with a reduction and subsequent elimination of short-range nuclear systems in the region.[3] Certain unilateral Soviet initiatives, such as reducing the number of tanks and bridge-crossing units in the area, also reduce the level of threat, but the imbalance is such that the Soviets will have to make far deeper cuts than do the NATO nations in order to achieve parity.

Unfortunately, the foregoing events do not mean an end to the threat of

Soviet repression, particularly as that government tries to counteract the centrifugal forces of Soviet society. Another opportunity for repression would be if the Soviets were faced with the collapse of civil authority in a Warsaw Pact state.

Increased Challenge from the Third World[4]

At the same time that the threat from the Soviet Union appears to be diminishing, the threat (or at least the challenge) from the Third World is increasing. This challenge is fourfold: military, political, economic, and social. The discussion to follow is presented from the perspective of U.S. interests, which may or may not coincide with those of particular Third World countries. It might be useful to consider how to evaluate clashes of interests in terms of morality and long- versus short-range U.S. interests, but it is beyond the scope of this brief chapter to do so in any systematic way.

Military. Despite U.S. preoccupation with the bipolar balance with the Soviet Union, it is important to remember that the major engagements involving the loss of American lives since World War II occurred in the Third World, particularly Korea and Vietnam. The limits of U.S. power and political will were sorely tested there, so it would not be correct to say that U.S. policymakers have just discovered the Third World. However, the developments of the last few years have made events in the Third World even more crucial for U.S. interests.

Militarily, the capacity to inflict massive damage upon an opponent has become decentralized. The gravest concerns have been expressed concerning the proliferation of nuclear weapons to Third World countries, but other weapons of mass destruction need to be considered as well. Foremost among these are the chemical weapons that are so easy to make, even without detection, and the possible use of biological weapons in the future. Almost any country with chemists and a fertilizer plant can manufacture chemical weapons if it decides to do so.

The Falklands/Malvinas conflict in 1982 demonstrated the extent of the spread of sophisticated weapons, including precision-guided munitions (PGMs) capable of sinking British warships. The British were able to prevail, with considerable indirect help from the United States, but Argentina demonstrated that Third World nations can make such interventions costly, and with a different set of circumstances might have won. Additionally, some Third World nations, such as Brazil, have thriving defense industries, producing increasingly sophisticated products for export that range from armored vehicles and tanks to cruise and ballistic missiles.

As a result of these trends, the relative differential in power between the United States and certain Third World countries has diminished significantly, particularly since the United States would be most unlikely to use its nuclear weapons in all but the gravest circumstances. Also, military engagements with Third World countries would likely be on or near their territory, further complicating the problem of intervention.

Political. A consistent trend since the era of decolonization has been a growing reluctance of Third World countries to follow the political lead of the superpowers. The United States discovered this in the United Nations beginning in the 1960s, but there are other manifestations of this phenomenon. Some have ranked the 1973 oil boycott of the United States by OPEC as a watershed event in postwar international relations, marking as it does a significant gesture of political independence and economic power on the part of the nations participating in it. It also reminded Americans that, while they would not wait in line for bananas, they would do so for gasoline, and their economic well-being is due in no small measure to U.S. economic penetration of the Third World.

Third World attitudes favoring political independence from the major powers may also be increased by a "successor generation" of leaders and citizens who have only a dim memory of colonial times and no ties to old, "foreign" institutions. This generational gap makes it more difficult for the United States to influence Third World nations, and could have a decided effect on U.S. options there. Even nominally friendly elites will have to consider grass-roots pressures before becoming too closely identified with the United States. For example, President Corazon Aquino was severely criticized for accepting U.S. aid in repulsing the December 1989 coup attempt by elements in the Philippines armed forces.[5]

Economic. The Cold War was not all bad for the Third World, at least insofar as the superpower rivalry sometimes resulted in aid to poor economies. As the attention of governmental and business leaders shifts to the opportunities presented by the breakup of the Eastern bloc, the needs of the Third World may suffer. Western governments seeking political influence and businesses seeking a higher return on their investments are likely to channel more development aid to Eastern Europe. Meanwhile, the world's poorest states are increasingly desperate, despite the remarkable progress of newly industrialized states, such as South Korea, Malaysia, and Singapore.

Additionally, the developmental needs of Third World nations may conflict with the interests of highly developed states, particularly in the desire of the former for higher prices for the products and raw materials that they export. Brazilians criticized for the destruction of their rainforest note with some justification the hypocrisy of highly developed states that initially built their own wealth in a similar manner. Other significant problems include the crushing debt burden of many Third World states and the adverse reaction of the United States and others when Third World countries do develop high-technology exports and compete with the developed nations in that arena.

Social. Demographic pressures in many Third World nations hold the promise of greatly increased instability in the societies affected. They also have an impact on First World nations by virtue of the effect governmental instability has on international relations and the fact that the developed nations represent a decreasing percentage of the world's population. Subsequent pressures for economic redistribution will be resisted, but will increase. It is in the clear interest of developed and developing nations alike to control birth rates that are not economically sustainable. In the long run, it is a national security issue of the first magnitude. Waiting for increased prosperity to reduce birth rates (as it seems to, eventually) is a short-sighted substitute for a sensible policy in this area.

Demographic pressures combine with economic problems to increase the attractiveness of the United States as an object of emigration, legally or otherwise. This problem will increase, as will the problem of illegal drug trafficking.[6] The situation of Colombia is instructive as its government wages war on narco-terrorists in order to deal with a problem rooted in the unwillingness or inability of U.S. drug users to curb their habits. With the Colombian example before them, other nations with illegal drug industries may be less willing to support U.S. policy in this area.

In sum, the United States faces a large and growing challenge from the Third World, and the solutions to the problems emanating from there are not primarily military. Nevertheless, military force is often necessary to provide the time necessary for other instruments of policy to ameliorate the underlying problems. How the United States should structure its forces to best influence events in the Third World is a question of increasing interest and importance. It is not clear that forces designed for war with the Soviet Union are the best ones for use elsewhere, since Third World actions are not necessarily "lesser included contingencies" that are met if the Soviet threat is provided for.

Increased Competition for Revenues

A major complicating factor affecting defense allocation decisions in the United States in the coming years is that the halcyon days of greatly increased defense spending are not only over, but are almost surely going to be reversed. This will cause painful choices along several dimensions.

Public versus private purposes. The basic question remains, what level of resources will be devoted to public purposes of all kinds? Some argue against government taxation they consider excessive, and are countered by those pointing out important problems not likely to be met by private action.

Civilian versus military public purposes. Consensus on the amount of the gross national product that the government should spend does not necessarily translate into agreement on the objects of those expenditures. Unlike the early years of the Reagan presidency, the pendulum is swinging back toward more spending for civilian purposes. Even staunch supporters of a strong defense realize that such a defense is predicated on a strong and healthy economy. Both defense and prosperity also depend on scientific research and innovations to keep the United States in the forefront of technology.

Competition among military services. Alternative weapons systems from different services sometimes compete with one another directly, as the B-36 did with the supercarrier after World War II. Usually, however, the relationship is not so direct. Reductions in a particular weapons program do not necessarily mean increases in another. Nevertheless, there is an upper limit to the total amount of resources likely to be earmarked for defense. Although this limit will vary with the state of the economy and the public's sense of urgency in regard to defense matters, the limit is quite real. It is not surprising that other services looked upon the success of Navy Secretary John Lehman in building toward a 600-ship Navy with a mixture of envy and annoyance. Future reductions in defense spending will sharpen interservice differences and increase the importance to the services of defining politically attractive missions for themselves.

Competition within military services. Competition within each service for scarce resources is also well established. Army planners are wrestling with the role of light versus heavy divisions and Active versus Reserve Component forces. The Navy is divided into surface, subsurface, and aviation officers. Although all agree in principle with the need for a "balanced" force structure, each branch is convinced that it represents the future of the Navy. The Marine Corps is well used to integrated operations (operating as it does as Marine air-ground task forces, or MAGTFs), but flying and walking Marine officers can have different opinions as to the relative importance of their specialty. The Air Force also has several communities, including the Tactical Air Command, the Military Airlift Command, and the Strategic Air Command—the latter being further fragmented by bomber pilots and missileers.

Somewhere off to the side are other missions, crucial for warfare, but not central to the self-conception of service leaders. Unconventional warfare capabilities are an example of this, as noted earlier by Sam Sarkesian. These needs are likely to get lost in the scramble for resources if they are not represented by outside political or bureaucratic actors.

Uncertainties

Before making specific recommendations, it is necessary to discuss several uncertainties that qualify them. They are a caution against simple projections of current trends without analyzing other possibilities. After all, the hopeful developments now underway in Eastern Europe could lead to chaos before they lead to economic prosperity and political freedom—and the Soviet reaction to chaos on its borders is not likely to be one we would wish.[7]

Success of Gorbachev

The primary uncertainty affecting the conclusions of this chapter is the degree of success Gorbachev has with perestroika and glasnost. A major assumption underlying the judgments about a diminished Soviet threat is that the Soviet disengagement from Eastern Europe will continue and that the countries there will be permitted to find their own way economically and politically. In the long term, Gorbachev's reforms, if successful, could result in a Soviet Union of greatly increased power. Freed from the distraction of a perceived threat from NATO, the Soviets could emerge as a truly global power, able to challenge U.S. interests far from the Soviet borders in a way that is not now possible.

But Gorbachev may not succeed. The emergence of alternative leaders, or even noncommunist centers of power, in the Soviet Union cannot be ruled out, and future Soviet leaders may have a different opinion about the need for intervention on their periphery. Given Soviet history, and Russian history before that, it is likely that a successor regime would be strongly authoritarian in nature. It is much too early to tell whether democratic institutions will take root on Soviet soil; with or without Gorbachev, the degree of additional liberalization to be seen by Soviet society in the foreseeable future is most unclear.

Limits to Soviet Forbearance

It has become clear that Soviet leaders are willing to permit and even encourage a degree of independence and liberalization in Eastern Europe that would have seemed unthinkable just a short time ago. Events moved swiftly there once the people realized that their governments, which had subjected them to over forty years of corruption, economic mismanagement, and political suppression, were no longer propped up by Soviet bayonets. What is not so clear is the amount of change the Soviets are willing to permit without trying to intervene (however effectively). More critically, what would the Soviet response be to massive unrest in its western border, in an area adjacent to a still-powerful NATO? One possible future is for an increasingly prosperous and free Eastern Europe that will leave its former masters far behind both economically and politically. Would the country that pressured Czechoslovakia not to participate in the Marshall Plan (even before the coup) and that invaded that same country in 1968 partly in response to prospective West German economic penetration permit its former satellites to integrate their economies with the West?

A more immediate question concerns the Soviet government's response to more frequent assertions of ethnic nationalism. Whatever one may foresee for Eastern Europe, for example, it is harder to imagine Soviet leaders permitting the de facto secession of the Baltic republics, however illegal their 1940 incorporation into the Soviet Union.

The State of the U.S. Economy

Another uncertainty is the state of the U.S. economy. Despite continuing economic strength, a growing federal deficit and the need for large infusions of capital into basic infrastructure raise questions about the long-term ability of the United States to sustain military expenditures at the level most in the military would prefer. Analysis of the U.S. economy and its impact on national defense is important, and planners cannot be indifferent to economic considerations. But strategies and force structures must be driven primarily by long- and short-range threats to national security. The need to reconcile strategic imperatives with budgetary constraints will be a persistent challenge to both military and civilian leaders in the years ahead.

Public Support for Military Actions

As Sam Sarkesian has pointed out, the "American way of war" presupposes, among other things, a clearly defined enemy—preferably in a situation that can be seen as good versus evil, with the United States on the side of the good. Unfortunately, the conflicts on the horizon are ambiguous struggles in the Third World, where the issues are not as sharply defined, the threat to U.S. national interests is usually indirect and long term, and the means of fighting are problematic to some. Indeed, many Americans would consider U.S. intervention in the Third World to be morally objectionable, for a variety of reasons. Americans tend to side with David, not Goliath, and the relationship between U.S. intervention and meeting some well-defined threat would have to be clear. Certainly, a national leader wishing to invade a Third World country, for example, would have to consider the effect on domestic tranquility of such an action. But the U.S. public will support intervention in the Third World if it is not too costly or protracted, as the high degree of public support for the Panama invasion shows.

It is not only U.S. attitudes toward the military and military intervention that must be considered, but those of our allies and potential adversaries as well. Political movements in European NATO countries could result in more rapid developments in disarmament than would be desirable, although this is not yet clear. Of equal importance, public opinion in the non-Soviet Warsaw Pact countries, and probably in their militaries as well, makes their participation in an aggressive war in Europe increasingly unlikely.

Assessments

The foregoing considerations lead to several assessments for the U.S. Army, the U.S. military, and U.S. society.

For the U.S. Army Specifically

The U.S. Army is the service most directly affected by the factors discussed above. It is also the most likely one to be adversely affected by developments, if adversity is defined in budgetary terms. Given the changes in the strategic landscape that have been the subject of this book, the primary task facing the Army is intellectual: The U.S. Army needs to rethink its strategic rationale. This means that Army leaders need to articulate a convincing version of U.S. military strategy and define the role of the Army in that strategy. This is precisely what the U.S. Navy did beginning in the late 1970s when, faced with an administration that did not appreciate the role of the Navy, it developed the Maritime Strategy to justify its preferred roles and missions.

The task confronting the Army is more difficult. First, the Navy's Maritime Strategy was fully consistent with traditional Navy roles and missions, and responded to an agreed-upon strategic threat. Both of these factors made it easier to develop and "sell" the strategy within the Navy. The Army must devise a rationale for missions and forces that are not themselves agreed upon.

Second, although the Army contains a number of first-rate strategic analysts, the Army itself has not thought in global terms. (The contribution of the Army Chief of Staff to this book is a noteworthy exception to this, and may presage a renaissance of strategic thought in the Army similar to that which occurred in the Navy in the late 1970s.) AirLand Battle, which outlines the Army's preferred concepts for land combat in Europe, is a campaign plan, not a strategy—certainly not a global one.

Several questions will need to be addressed in the course of this strategic reevaluation. If significant numbers of forces are to be removed from Europe, they must either be housed (requiring military construction) or demobilized (requiring a transfer of responsibility to the reserves—the Army Reserve and the National Guard), or there must be a willingness to accept a higher level of risk in the face of diminished military capability.

The future holds a diminished role for forward-deployed forces, especially those requiring a large overseas infrastructure. What will be the deployment posture of the Army after a significant European withdrawal? Will the Army become a global intervention force, perhaps consisting of light infantry, based in the continental United States (CONUS)? If so, how will it differ from the U.S. Marine Corps, which is essentially a highly mobile light infantry with an integrated air arm? How can heavy divisions be reconstituted and moved to areas of need,[8] especially given the serious shortfalls in strategic airlift and sealift that exist even now? What emphasis will be placed on its unconventional warfare capability, and how will it be organized and directed?

A final question relates to the educational investment the Army makes in its officers. How should the Army educate its officers to prepare today's majors to be tomorrow's general officers? A curriculum limited to Clausewitz and a review of major wars will not suffice now, if it ever did. In the future, more than ever, officers must not only be able to deal with international ambiguity, but they must be able to participate in the national security decisionmaking process effectively—not as political partisans, but as national security experts able to explain the strategic rationale behind alternative military forces and missions. In this connection, the investment the Army makes in its War College and its program of graduate education at civilian institutions seems particularly well founded.

For the U.S. Military Generally

Many of these recommendations for the military generally have been foreshadowed earlier. Clearly, the military must refocus its strategy, doctrine, and training on U.S. global interests—not because it will result in more budget dollars, but because that is where the national interest lies. Such a consideration will underscore the importance of strategic airlift and sealift if U.S. forces are to arrive at crisis points in time and with sufficient forces to affect events.

The military will also have to accept an increased role in mission areas previously thought peripheral to their raison d'être. These include, but are not limited to, arms control agreement monitoring, peacekeeping, border control, drug enforcement, and public works. It is also possible that the Army in particular will become a vehicle for wider civic socialization following an adoption of some form of compulsory national service.

Unilateral military intervention by the United States will sometimes be necessary, although the United States will find it increasingly necessary to behave as an ally rather than as a global hegemonic power. Such interventions will need to be clearly related to U.S. interests and be short in duration if they are to maintain public support.

A final problem is the need to remember that the primary purpose of the military is to apply whatever violence is necessary to prevail in a conflict. For this, there must be a critical mass of officers and enlisted personnel who have retained something of the warrior ethic.[9] Military managers are necessary, as are soldier/scholars but, in the final analysis, someone has to be ready to do the fighting.[10]

For U.S. Society

U.S. society must also make certain adjustments if U.S. interests are to be protected in the new security era. Above all, Americans must have an awareness of the U.S. role as a world power, and have confidence in the civilian and military governmental institutions responsible for shaping and executing policies to preserve global U.S. interests.

At a minimum, there must be at least a rough consensus concerning the relative priority of U.S. interests and the balance of military and nonmilitary instruments to be used in their achievement. Never again must U.S. forces be sent to fight without public support in a protracted conflict with no reasonable hope of a satisfactory conclusion.

Conclusion

Even though the millennium is not yet upon us, the cause of peace has been greatly strengthened by events of the last few years, particularly the incipient emergence of Eastern Europe from the dead hand of communism. So even though we do not soon anticipate a world without war, there is hope that there may be a world without the Cold War. What the precise course of events in Eastern Europe will be is impossible to predict at this early date, but things can never return to the way they were under Brezhnev—let alone under Stalin.

There is no certainty where the changes that have framed the discussions in this book will lead. But the U.S. military—and the U.S. Army in particular—cannot wait for events to unfold completely before designing appropriate strategies and force postures.

This period of transition is, in many ways, a dangerous one. Unsure of the evolution of Soviet military strategy and capability, uncertain as to how all these changes will affect the Third World, and faced with differing views among U.S. political and policymaking figures regarding the direction of U.S. policy, the U.S. Army must maintain the capability to respond to a wide range of potential contingencies. To do this effectively will require sophisticated strategic analysis, keen intellectual insight, and unprecedented adaptability on the part of Army leadership. It will also require a Congress, an administration, and—most importantly—a public sensitive to the complexities of the changing strategic landscape and unwilling to draw hasty conclusions about an era that is just beginning.

Notes

1. The author has long considered that the most dangerous flash point for central war between the United States and the Soviet Union would be in the context of the dissolution of the East European buffer zone created by Stalin in the aftermath of World War II. The assumption was that Soviet leaders could not possibly permit that kind of evolution. It now appears that Mikhail Gorbachev has even gone so far as to encourage it, at least in Eastern Europe.

2. This was foreseen by Col. David Shaver in an earlier draft of his chapter in this book.

3. Short-range nuclear systems are arguably destabilizing since they are most likely to be overrun by a rapid conventional assault and to confront leaders (and/or soldiers, presuming there is no permissive action link that would physically prevent unauthorized nuclear release) with a "use 'em or lose 'em" dilemma. East and West Germans are particularly interested in such reductions since the most likely place for nuclear use is in Germany. Ironically, the existence of longer-range nuclear weapons, such as those eliminated by the INF Treaty, can be stabilizing since the extreme uncertainties of possible nuclear escalation upset the calculation of a potential aggressor's correlation of forces.

4. I am indebted to my colleagues Sam C. Sarkesian and Cynthia Watson for many insights in this section. They should not be held accountable for my conclusions, however.

5. See Samuel P. Huntington, "The Goal of Development," in Myron Weiner and Samuel P. Huntington, eds., *Understanding Political Development* (Boston: Little, Brown and Co., 1987), pp. 3–32, for an interesting discussion of several aspects of this phenomenon.

6. Brazil, the largest South American country and one that shares borders with both Peru and Colombia, will likely become the number one illicit drug exporting country in the not too distant future.

7. For that matter, the Soviets may have to deal with chaos *within* their own borders, as ethnic frictions interact with desires for greater autonomy (or even independence, as in the case of the Baltic states and in the Ukraine) and with economic shortages, thereby increasing civil unrest. We should expect the reaction of any Soviet leader to be quite harsh in this eventuality.

8. The ability of the U.S. Army to return to Europe in force in time to affect military events there would serve as an important hedge against a reversal of present Soviet policies of military disengagement without also posing the kind of military threat to the Soviet Union that would justify a more belligerent military posture on its part. European knowledge of this capability would be reassuring and would help to preserve the Atlantic alliance even after large-scale U.S. military withdrawals.

9. Most Army officers will remember the embarrassment over the

recruiting slogan, "The U.S. Army Wants to Join You," at the same time the Marine Corps was advertising, "We Never Promised You a Rose Garden." The subsequent Army slogan, "Be All You Can Be," was much more acceptable, and compared more favorably with other slogans, such as the Navy's "It's Not Just a Job, It's an Adventure." The Air Force's invitation to "Join the Aerospace Team" was uninspired, but otherwise unobjectionable.

10. This is not intended to deny the possibility that an individual could be a manager or scholar while retaining his (or, eventually, her) abilities as a combat leader. See John Allen Williams, "Interpersonal Influence and the Bases of Military Leadership," *Military Review*, Vol. 62, No. 12 (December 1982), pp. 56–65.

About the Contributors

Lt. Gen. Frederic J. Brown, U.S. Army (Ret.), recently retired as Commanding General, Fourth U.S. Army, commanding Active and Reserve Component soldiers and advising the National Guard of seven states. He earlier commanded a readiness group of Active Component advisors to Reserve Components, and as Chief of Armor at Fort Knox, Kentucky, he supported armor and cavalry units in the National Guard and Army Reserve.

Arthur Cyr is Vice-President and Program Director of the Chicago Council on Foreign Relations and is affiliated with the University of Illinois at Chicago. His publications include *U.S. Foreign Policy and European Security* (1987) and *Liberal Politics in Britain* (2d edition, 1988). He is a member of the Council of the Inter-University Seminar on Armed Forces and Society.

Lt. Gen. Howard Graves, U.S. Army, is Assistant to the Chairman, Joint Chiefs of Staff, Washington, D.C. Gen. Graves' command assignments include Company, Battalion, Brigade, and Assistant Division Commander. He has served on the faculty of the U.S. Military Academy; as Military Assistant to the Secretary of Defense; as Deputy Director of Strategy, Plans, and Policy on the Army Staff; as Vice-Director, Joint Staff, Organization of the Joint Chiefs of Staff; and as Commandant of the U.S. Army War College.

Robert F. Hale is the Assistant Director in charge of the National Security Division at the Congressional Budget Office. During his more than thirteen years at the CBO, he has been the Deputy Assistant Director for National Security; prior to holding that position, he worked as a principal analyst responsible primarily for defense manpower issues. He also served three years as an officer with the U.S. Naval Security Group.

Douglas Kinnard is a Secretary of the Navy Senior Research Fellow at the U.S. Naval War College. He graduated from West Point in 1944 and served in combat in World War II (Europe), the Korean War, and twice in Vietnam. He retired from the U.S. Army with the rank of Brigadier General. He is the author of *President Eisenhower and Strategy Management, The War Managers*, and *The Secretary of Defense*. He is Professor Emeritus of Political Science, University of Vermont.

Jacob W. Kipp is a Senior Analyst for the Soviet Army Studies Office, U.S. Army Combined Center, Fort Leavenworth, Kansas. He taught at Kansas State University from 1971 until 1986, and served as Associate Editor of *Military Affairs* from 1979 to 1983. He has published extensively on Russian and Soviet military and naval history and currently holds the rank of Adjunct Professor at the University of Kansas.

Edward A. Kolodziej is Research Professor of Political Science and Director of the European Arms Control Project at the University of Illinois, Urbana-Champaign. A frequent contributor to professional journals, he is the author of *The Uncommon Defense and Congress: 1945–1963* (1966); *French International Policy Under DeGaulle and Pompidou: The Politics of Grandeur* (1974), and *Making and Marketing Arms: The French Experience and Its Implications for the International System* (1987). He is currently working on a manuscript on comparative nuclear deterrence systems.

Lt. Col. David MacIsaac, U.S. Air Force (Ret.), is Associate Director for Research, Air Power Research Institute, Center for Aerospace Doctrine, Research, and Education at Air University, Maxwell Air Force Base, Alabama, where he is also Professor of Military History. He has taught military history and strategy at the U.S. Air Force Academy, the Naval War College, and the Air War College. His publications include *Strategic Bombing in World War II: The Story of the U.S. Strategic Bombing Survey* (1976).

Col. Aubrey R. Merrill, Jr., U.S. Army (Ret.), recently retired as Chief of Public Affairs, Fourth U.S. Army, where he developed programs to describe the essentiality of Reserve Component units. Earlier, as doctrine developer, he trained and supported Active and Reserve Component Army Military Police Units and Rear Area Operations Centers and Air Force Security Police Air Base Ground Defense Squadrons.

Sam C. Sarkesian is Professor of Political Science at Loyola University Chicago. He is immediate past Chairman of the Inter-University Seminar on Armed Forces and Society and is currently Chair of the Research Committee on Armed Forces and Society of the International Political Science

Association. He is a member of the International Institute for Strategic Studies (London) and the Chicago Council on Foreign Relations, and chairs the Research Committee of the National Strategy Forum. He has published numerous books and articles on unconventional conflicts, U.S. national strategy, and the U.S. military profession. Two of his most recent books are *U.S. National Security: Policymakers, Processes, and Politics* and *The New Battlefield: The United States and Unconventional Conflicts*. He served for over twenty years as an enlisted man and an officer in the U.S. Army.

Col. David E. Shaver, U.S. Army, is a Strategic Research Analyst with the Strategic Studies Institute, U.S. Army War College. His previous assignments have included command of combat engineer battalions in the 1st and 8th Infantry Divisions; Chief, Military Engineering and Topography divisions, USAREUR; and S-3, 937th Engineer Group. In Vietnam, he served as a unit commander and staff officer in the 62d Engineer Battalion (Land Clearing). He is a coauthor of *Conventional Arms Control in Europe: Army Perspectives*, *How to Think About Conventional Arms Control: A Framework*, and *Burdensharing and Mission Specialization in NATO*.

David W. Tarr is Professor of Political Science at the University of Wisconsin-Madison. He is currently Director of the Center for International Cooperation and Security Studies and serves on the executive committee of the Midwest Consortium for International Security Studies. He is author of a number of publications, including *American Strategy in the Nuclear Age* (1966) and *Modules in Strategy* (1974). A book provisionally titled *The Nuclear Debate: Disarming Alternatives* is scheduled for publication in 1990.

Gen. Carl E. Vuono assumed the duties of Army Chief of Staff in June 1987. Before that, he was the Commanding General of Training and Doctrine Command. His recent assignments include: Deputy Chief of Staff for Operations; Commanding General, 8th Infantry Division (Mechanized); and Commanding General, Combined Arms Center. He also served as Assistant Division Commander, 1st Infantry Division; and Commander, 82d Airborne Division Artillery. During the Vietnam War, he commanded two artillery battalions in the 1st Cavalry Division.

John Allen Williams is Associate Professor, Graduate Program Director, and Chairman designate of the Department of Political Science at Loyola University Chicago. He is a Fellow, Vice-Chairman, and Executive Director of the Inter-University Seminar on Armed Forces and Society. A member of the International Security Studies and Peace Studies Sections of the International Studies Association, he is Vice-Chairman of the International Security and Arms Control Section of the American Political Science Association. A captain (selectee) in the U.S. Naval Reserve, his duties have included service at the U.S. Naval Academy, the Naval War College, and the staffs of the Chief of Naval Operations (OP-06) and the Chairman, Joint Chiefs of Staff (J-5). His publications include works on U.S. and Soviet naval forces and missions, strategic nuclear policy, military leadership, and defense organization.

Index

Abshire, Ambassador David M., 157
Abt Associates, 79n
Acquired Immune Deficiency Syndrome (AIDS), 165, 272
Adams, Gordon, 172n
Adenauer, Chancellor Konrad, 140
Aegean Sea: importance for defense of Eastern Mediterranean, 224
Afghanistan, 62, 156, 186, 210; Soviet Union and, 98, 157, 185, 189; unconventional conflict in, 195
Africa: Cuban intervention, 186, 191; U.S. interests, 201; U.S.-Soviet rivalry, 186, 190
Air and sea lift (U.S.), 28
Air Force Magazine, 78n
Air power: characteristics, 239; in Third World, 184
Air strategy, xi, 236–245; problems of, 243; unpredictable elements, 238
Air University: CADRE, 244–245n, 299
AirLand Battle; future initiative, 28. *See also* U.S. Army
Akhromeyev, Marshal Sergei, 4, 112; resignation of, 84; Stockholm Conference and, 90; 117n; 120n
Alcala, Col. Raul H., xi
Allard, Lt. Col. Kenneth, xi
Almond, Peter, 17n
America: major concerns and, 13; moral issues and, 13; postwar economic hegemony, 41
American Political Science Association: International Security and Arms Control Section, 300
American public opinion, xii: defense spending, 62; elite opinions, 184; Gorbachev on 44; military strength and, 61; Third World intervention and, 292–293; threat perceptions, 61
"American way of war," 197, 209, 292; democratic imperatives, 201; need to reshape, 211; operational constraints caused by, 202–203

Americans Talk Security, 78n
Americans Talk Security project, 49n, 50n
Angola, 186: Soviet Union and, 98; UNITA, 209
Aquino, Corazon, 288
Arendt, Hannah, 199, 213n
Armed diplomacy, 200
Armitage, Air Chief Marshal Sir Michael, 241–242, 244–245n
Arms control, ix, 65; as strategic issue, 159; basis for success, 130; conventional, 159–160, 166–171; disadvantageous proposals for U.S., 217, 232–233n; mission specialization and, 162; NATO and U.S., 122; nuclear, 162; public opinion and, 44; SSBNs, 233n; U.S. budget and, 161; Warsaw Pact reductions, 165. *See* specific agreements and talks
Aspin, Congressman Les, 57; 79n
Atkeson, Maj. Gen E.B., 254, 257n
Atlantic Alliance, 134
Azreal, Jeremy R., 102, 118n

Babakov, A.A., 118n
Bacevich, A.J., 214n
Baggett, Adm. Lee, Jr., 222, 234n
Balanced Budget and Emergency Deficit Control Reaffirmation Act of 1987 (Gramm-Rudman-Hollings), 52
Ball, William L., Jr., 233n
Baltimore Evening Sun, 78n
Baltic republics, 135, 292, 296n. *See also* Soviet Union
Barnett, Frank R., 213n
Base closures, 160–161
Bassford, Christopher, 257n
Becker, Abraham, S., 100, 118n
Bedard, Paul, 77n
Berlin accords, 1971, 125
Berlin Wall, 133, 286
Bialer, Seweryn, 17n
Bialkovskaia, V.S., 118n
Biennial budgeting, 57

Bingham, Lt. Col. Price T., 244n
Bondarenko, V.M., 99, 118n
Borawski, John, 115n, 116n
Bovin, A.E., 114n, 115n
Brezhnev era, 102
Brezhnev Doctrine, 136, 286. *See also* Gorbachev, Mikhail
Brezhnev, Leonid I., 182, 295
British-French nuclear talks, 131
Brooks, Capt. Linton F., 232n
Brooks, Rear Adm. Thomas A., 232–233n
Brown, Lt. Gen. Frederic J., 258, 298
Brown, Harold, 59
Budan, P.J., 17n
Budapest: Warsaw Pact and, 89
Budget: nondefense spending, 63
Budget and Impoundment Control Act of 1974, 40
Burdensharing, 133; conventional arms control and, 159, 169, 171; "fair share," 156; Japanese, 156; mission specialization and, 162, 168; national security issue, 156–157; NATO, 156–157; U.S. budget and, 166–167, 170
Bush administration: new security environment, 41–42
Bush, President George, 46, 150, 217, 229; arms control and, 65; Congress and, 47, 48; conventional arms agreement and, 72; defense budget, 126; response options, 149
Butterwegge, Christoph, 115n

Callahan, Thomas A., Jr., 172n
Cambodia, 187
Carlucci, Frank C., 172n, 193n, 220, 233–235n
Carney, Admiral Robert B., 36
Carter administration, 135; defense inconsistency, 142; neutron bomb controversy, 142
Carter, President Jimmy, 163, 218: NATO and Soviet Union, 144
Castro, Fidel, 189
CBS/*New York Times*, 80n
Center on Budget and Policy Priorities, 137n
Center for Strategic and International Studies (CSIS), 78n, 172n
Central America: conflicts in, 209–210, 285; U.S. interests in, 188, 201; U.S. intervention, 164
Central Intelligence Agency: and unconventional conflicts, 208
Cheney, Richard, 234n
Chicago Council on Foreign Relations, 128, 142, 80n, 137n, 298, 300–

Chief of Naval Operations, Office of the (OPNAV), 301: Strategic Studies Group (OP-603), 219; Strategy, Plans and Policy Division (OP-60), 228
Chiles, Senator Lawton, 60
China: *See* People's Republic of China and Republic of China (Taiwan)
Chubin, Sharam, 194n
Clarke, Douglas, 116n
Clausewitz, Carl von, 94, 196, 199, 202, 243, 294
Cobb, Maj. Mark R., 245n
Cold War, 16, 133, 285; end of, 148, 188, 192, 286; erosion of consensus on premises, 184–185, 188
"Cold War Internationalists," 179–180
Combat power: Warsaw Treaty Organization (WTO) and NATO, 85
Commission on Integrated Long-Term Strategy, 75, 79n, 80n. 152, 172n, 178, 193n: competetitive strategies, 158
Communist Party (USSR): on nuclear disarmament, 123; Soviet economic reforms and, 135
Commander-in-Chief, Western TVD (USSR). *See* Orgakov, Marshal
Communism; failure of, 155, 182; in Latin America, 165
Competetive Strategies, 158. *See also* Commission on Integrated Long-Term Strategy
Conference on Security and Cooperation in Europe (CSCE), 130
Congress (U.S.): allocation of budget resources, 60; authorization and appropriations, 54; biennial budgeting, 57; budget workload, 54; concurrent budget resolution, 54; defense budget (1960), 37; defense budget, xi, 53; defense budget committee focus, 59; defense budget process (figure), 54; defense budget reform, 55; interservice rivalry and, 37; limited multiyear budgeting, 58; micromanagement and, 55; on national defense, 60–61; national security policy process and, 40; "new look" strategy and, 36; procedural issues, 60; restructuring of, 59; Roosevelt presidency and, 39; staff enlargement, 40
Congressional Budget Office (CBO), 78n, 79n, 80n, 233n, 298: aircraft cost studies, 74; federal deficit and, 63; weapons deployment and, 73
Congressional budget process: instability in defense planning, 54
Congressional Record, 77n
Containment, 23, 181; priorities for, 192

Conventional Arms Talks, 85; impact on NATO/Warsaw Pact, 72; U.S. defense spending, 72. *See also* arms control and specific agreements and talks
Conventional conflicts, 177–194
Conventional deterrence, 87–88
Conventional Forces in Europe (CFE) talks, 166–167; 169; 183, 193
Conventional Stability Talks (CST), 166–168, 172n
Counterinsurgency; first U.S. counterinsurgency era, 209, 213n; second U.S. counterinsurgency era, 196, 203, 209–210, 213n; third U.S. counterinsurgency era, 210. *See also* unconventional conflicts
Croft, Stuart, 17n
Crowe, Admiral William, 11, 231, 244n
Cruise missiles, 143
Cuba; missile crisis, 188, 190–191; position after European war, 224; Soviet involvement in, 188–189; Soviet surrogate activities, 186, 191
Currey, Cecil B., 213n
Cyr, Arthur, 139, 151n, 298

d'Estaing, Giscard, 144
Daly, Capt. Thomas N., 233n
Daniel, Donald C., 235n
David, Steven R., 183, 194n
de Gaulle, President Charles, 131, 140, 144
De Luca, Donald, 79n
Dean, Jonathan, 169, 173n
Defense Budget (U.S.): appropriation legislation, 52; as strategic issue, 161–162, 171; authorizing legislation, 52; basis for annual budget, 57; concurrent resolution, 52; Congress and, 51; domestic context (hypothesis two), 46–47; force structure planning and, 162; late budgets. 53; national security policy formulation (hypothesis one), 46; process, 51. *See also* Eisenhower Presidency
Defense Budget process: biennial budgeting, 56; impact of changes, 75; multiyear budgeting, 56
Defense spending: Arms control and, 152; Army conventional capabilities and, 184; as percentage of GDP (chart), 68; base closures, 152; burdensharing and, 152; decrease in, 71, 184, 285, 289; domestic pressures and, 152; economic growth and, 62, 70; Gallup Poll and, 72; likely futures, 72; moderate growth projection, 71; new military programs and, 73; NATO cutbacks and, 126; pressures for reductions and increases, 61, 62; Soviet Union and, 72; unilateral reductions, 152; zero growth, 72
Defense Week, 78n
Defensive defense (USSR), 111
Democracy: Spain and Portugal, 134; U.S. support of, 200–201
Democratic Leadership Council, 79n
Denmark: and British air defense, 224
Department of Defense: *Annual Report*, 78n; budget plan (1989), 73; operating and support costs, 1957–1987, 74; Soviet military strength and, 61
Desch, Michael C., 180, 193–194n
Dessert, Col. Rolland, xi
Developing world: challenges to U.S., 24; regional conflicts, 24; weapons proliferation and, 24
Dickinson, Congressman Bill, 59
Diehl, Ole, 117n
Dominican Republic: U.S. invasion of, 188
Dominici, Senator Pete, 59, 60
Drug trafficking, 26

East Asia: U.S.-Soviet rivalry and, 187–188
Eastern Europe, ix: crises (1953,1956, 1968, 1980s), 134; democratization, 132; changes, 147; German economic penetration of, 292; liberalizing trends and cold war, 133; nationalism and, 135; reforms, 122; unraveling, 147
East-West: levels of military readiness, 129
Economic assistance: in Third World, 180, 184; in unconventional conflicts, 207
Economic issues: as part of policy environment, 155; increased importance of, 184
Economic strength: Japan and the West, 134
Egypt: as Soviet setback, 185; 1973 war, 186, 191
Eisenhower administration, 34; Suez operation and, 141. *See also* Eisenhower presidency and Eisenhower, President Dwight D.
Eisenhower presidency: hypotheses on national security policy process, 45–46
Eisenhower, President Dwight D., 48n, 140; defense budget (1956 and 1959), 37; defense budget process and, 39; leadership style, 38; National Security Council, 38; national security policy, 39, 47; on strategy, 35; powerbase, 38; relations with Joint Chiefs, 38
El Salvador: and U.S. force requirements, 188

Electronic Industries Association, 80n; defense budget forecast, 73
Ellsworth, Robert F., 17n
Employer Support of the Guard and Reserve (ESGR), 281n
Erickson, John, 107
Ethnic rivalry, 285, 195
Etzold, Thomas H., 114n
Eurasia: perimeter vital to U.S. security, 192
Europe: accommodation of Soviet interests and, 124; Big Three, 131; nationalism, 8; new security landscape and, 5; nuclear-free zone and, 124; public opinion polls and, 6; tensions with U.S., 141; uncertain shape, 148; U.S. military operations and, 7
European community, 150, 160, 238–239
European Economic Entity, 7
European economic integration, 148
European security: Britain and France, 124–125
Evseev, General-Lieutenant A.I., 104–105, 119n
Executive power (U.S.): Vietnam War and, 39

Falklands/Malvinas conflict, 194n
Fall, Bernard, 197–198, 213n
Federal deficit, 57; defense spending and, 63, 70; methods to reduce, 63; need to reduce, 217, 232; percent of GNP (graph), 64
Federal Republic of Germany: economic penetration of Eastern Europe, 292; possible nuclear battlefield, 296n; possibility of Soviet attack on, 223–224; reliance on reserves, 258–259, 260 (chart), 267; research in, 66
Foch, Marshal Ferdinand, 121
Force mix: U.S. Army force packages, 26
Force reduction (U.S.): defense spending and, 73
Ford, President Gerald, 164
Forward deployment (U.S.): ground forces, 27, 177; naval forces, 229–231, 234n
Fourth U.S. Army, 263, 270, 298–299
Founding Fathers: role of Congress in foreign and national security policy, 39
France: arms control proposals, 89; Bonn and the West and, 131; defense spending, 66; tactical forces, 131; Warsaw Pact and, 131
Franco-German military cooperation, 128, 131
Fukuyama, Francis, 148–149, 16n, 151n

Galkin, Colonel M.I., 98, 118n
Gallup Poll: American public on defense spending, 67. See also American public opinion
The Gallup Report, 78n
Garden, Group Captain Timothy, 242, 245n
Gareev, Colonel General M.A., 103, 107, 110, 118n
Garthoff, Raymond, L., 113, 120n
Geopolitics: Europe and the U.S., 124
Geneva talks, 128
Genscher, Foreign Minister Dietrich, 127
Geolhoed, E. Bruce, 49n
George Washington University, x: Institute for Technology and Strategic Reserch, xi
Gerasev, M., 117n
German Democratic Republic: exodus from, 147
Germany: critique of U.S. military-industrial complex, 88; demographic problem, 125; reunification, 8, 15; detente and, 125; Soviet conflict-Great Patriotic War, 104; European security and, 88; NATO policy and, 128, uncertainty and, ix. See also Federal Republic of Germany and German Democratic Republic
Glabus, Col. E.J., 257n
Glantz, David M., 119n
Glasnost, ix, 1–2, 122, 157, 195. See also Gorbachev, Mikhail, perestroika, and Soviet Union
Global warming, 180
Goldsmith, R.H., 257n
Goldwater-Nichols legislation, 251–253
Goodpaster, Gen. Andrew, 152–153, 163, 170
Gorbachev, Mikhail, ix, xi, 4, 41–42, 112, 152–153, 159, 182, 191, 195, 204, 210–211, 296; American public opinion and, 44, 217; arms control and, 65; build-down proposals and, 90; Brezhnev doctrine and, 133; changes in Soviet Union; 44; critic of Soviet military doctrine, 94; glasnost and perestroika, 147; image in West, 123; impact on Eastern Europe, 147; impact of failure, 129; internal Soviet problems and, 135; leadership, 2, 4; longevity, 134, 105, 232, 291; new thinking and security issues, 90, 181, 183, 190; nuclear weapons elimination, 89; options of, 171; peace campaign and, 148; reformer, 148; retrenchment and, 189; Soviet reforms and, 122, 135; speech at United Nations, 149; unilateral reductions and, 83, 84, 107
Gorbachev regime. See Gorbachev, Mikhail

Gordon, Michael R., 114n
Gordon, Theodore J., 161, 172n
Gorshkov, Sergei, 114n
Government outlays (U.S.): percent of GNP (graph), 65
Graber, Doris A., 48n
Graves, Lt. Gen. Howard D., 249, 298
Great Russian population, 3
Greenwood, David, 172n
Grenada, 188, 267
Guatemala: 1954 U.S. intervention in, 190
Gulin, V., 117n
Guran, M. Elizabeth, 214n

Haig, Gen. Alexander, 142–143, 145, 146
Hale, Robert F., 51, 79n, 298
Hallums, James D., 214n
Hardt, John P., 17n
Harris survey: Allies defense spending, 66. *See also* American public opinion
Harris Survey Press Release, 80n
Harvey, Air Commodore M.A., 242
Hayward, Adm. Thomas, 218, 233n
Hearing of the Temporary Committee to Study the Senate Committee System, 78n
Helmer, Olaf, 172n
Helsinki process, 134
Hemingway, Ernest, 149
Herspring, Dale, 17n
Hewett, Ed A., 118n
Hofschen, Heinz-Gerd, 115n
Holsti, Ole R., 193–194n, 213n
Hong Kong, 187
House Committees: biennial budgeting, 57; on Armed Services, 77n; on International Relations, 49n
House of Representatives: new generation of, 40
Holloway, David, 16n
Human rights: part of external environment, 155; U.S. policy objective, 155
Hungary, 147: U.S. nonintervention in 1956. *See also* Eastern Europe
Huntington, Samuel P., 296n

Ideological blocs: East-West, 113, 132
India: India-Pakistan conflict, 186–187
Indochina, 139, 197–198
Industrial capacity: as U.S. security interest, 180
Integrated Program of Scientific-Technical Progress, USSR, 101
Intelligence: human versus electronic, 240
Inter-University Seminar on Armed Forces and Society (IUS), x–xi, 298–300

Intermediate-range Nuclear Forces (INF) treaty, ix, 6, 9, 23, 86, 93, 123, 132, 143, 148, 183, 286, 296n
International Affairs (Moscow), 138n
International Institute for Strategic Studies (IISS), 278n
International order: changed, 1
International Political Science Association: Research Committee on Armed Forces and Society, 299–300
International Studies Association: International Security Studies Section, 300; Peace Studies Section, 300
Iran, 185
Iran-Iraq War, 24, 180, 185, 285

Jackson-Vanek Amendment, 135
Japan: advanced fighter development, 126; prosperity of, 187; Red Guards, 199; research in, 66; U.S. commitment and, 224; U.S. military presence, 188
Jaruzelski, General Woijiech, 93
Johnson, President Lyndon B., 140, 164; as Senator, 38
Joint Chiefs of Staff: Eisenhower administration and, 36; the Joint Staff, 298, 301. *See also* U.S. Army and U.S. Military
Joint Strategic Target Planning Staff (JSTPS), 239
Judy, Richard W., 17n

Kaaganov, S., 114n, 115n, 119n
Karpov, Deputy Foreign Minister Viktor, 84
Kaufmann, William W., 137n
Kelleher, Catherine McArdle, 151n
Kennan, George F., 180, 193n
Kennedy, President John F., 140, 144, 164, 191, 213n; NATO and, 140
Kennedy, Paul, 125, 79n, 137n
Kinnard, Brig. Gen. Douglas, 33, 48–49n, 298
Kipp, Jacob W., 83, 115n, 298
Kirshin, Major General Iv. Ia., 94, 117n, 118n, 120n
Koch, Petr, 17n
Kohl, Chancellor Helmut, 144
Kolodziej, Edward A., 121, 138n, 299
Kokoshin, A.A., 109, 110, 111,. 112, 119n, 120n
Kommunist, 90
Kondyrev, I., 117n
Korean War, 287: U.S.-Soviet restraint in, 191
Kortunov, A.A., 117n, 119n
Kozlov, K., 117n
Krakau, Anton, 117n
Krasnaya zvezda, 114n, 119n, 120n

Kross, Maj. Gen. Walter, 244n
Kursk paradigm, 109

Labour Party (Britain), 144
Lansdale, Edward, 198, 213n
Lapidus, Gail W., 16n
Larionov, Lieutenant General V.V., 109, 110, 112, 119n, 120n
Larrabee, F. Stephen, 16n
Latin America: U.S.-Soviet rivalry, 188–189
Law and order missions, 200
Legvold, Robert, 116n, 117n
Lehman, John F., Jr., 219, 225, 227, 233–235n
Lenin: on Clausewitz, 94
LePrestre, Philippe G., 138n
Levin, Senator Carl, 162
Libya, 152, 242
Lobov, General V.N., 112
Lollis, Brent L., Jr., 17n
Lott, Senator Trent, 53, 77n
Low-Intensity Conflict, 25, 197, 200, 213n, 239: Assistant Secretary of Defense for Unconventional Conflicts, 203–204; civilian control of, 208, 212; Deputy Assistant to the President for Low-Intensity Conflict, 203–204; Low-Intensity Conflict Board, 203–204; reserve participation in, 270
Loyola University Chicago, 255, 299, 300

Machiavelli, Niccolo, 241
MacIsaac, Lt. Col. David, 236, 299
Maechling, Charles, Jr., 198, 213n
Makeev, B.N., 118n
Mann, David, 244n
Margiotti, Col. Franklin D., 244n
Maritime Power: in Third World, 184; U.S. as a maritime power, 180
Maritime Strategy (U.S.), xi, 217–235, 293: anti-SSBN operations, 220, 225–226; as deterrent, 228, 231; as weak basis for Pacific force levels, 229; classified briefing on (OP-603), 219; contributions of allies to, 219; criticisms of, 217; defense of NATO flanks, 220, 224–225; horizontal escalation, 220, 223–224; options of, 220–226
Markham, James M., 194n
Marsh, John O., Jr., 172n, 279n
Marshall, Charles Burton, 13, 18n
Marshall Plan, 134
Marxist-Leninist ideology, 4, 5
Mason, Air Vice Marshal R.A., 241, 243, 244–245n
Matthews, Col. L.J., 257n

Mattingly, Richard Thomas, Jr., 18n
McCartney, James, 172n
McElroy, Secretary of Defense Neil, 37
McNamara, Secretary of Defense Robert, 140
Mearsheimer, John J., 232n
Media: Warsaw Pact and, 145
Melinger, Lt. Col. Philip S., 244
Mellman, Mark, 79n
Merrill, Col. Aubrey R., 258, 299
Meyer, Edward C, 17n
Middle East: U.S. commitments, 185; U.S.-Soviet rivalry in, 185–186
Middle East War, 1973, 146
Midwest Consortium for International Security Studies, 300
Milestone budgeting, 58. See also Congress, Congressional budget process
Military art: Marxism-Leninism and, 98
Military assistance, 184
Military conscription, 166
Military contingencies, 19; U.S. Army role, 19–20
Military doctrine: arms control and, 84; as ideological battleground, 89; Soviet/Warsaw pact and, 93. See also Soviet military
Military force: force planning methodology and development, 154–155; utility of, 289, 295
Military strategy: uncertain environment, 76
Military-technical revolution: arms control and, 84
Milovidov, A.S., 118n
Minister of Defense (USSR): new leadership, 91
Mobilization: importance of time, 159
Moiseyev, Colonel General N.A., 84, 101, 112, 118n
"Moral equivalency," 205
Morrocco, John D., 235n
Moscow: arms control and, 123; decentralization, 150. See also Soviet Union; Gorbachev, Mikhail
Moscow News, 120n
Moskos, Charles C., xi
Multilateral force (MLF), 140
Multiyear budgeting: advantages, 58; stability in defense planning, 58; support for, 56
Munz, Eric, 172n
Mutual and Balanced Force Reduction (MBFR) talks, 85, 159

Namibia, 186
National defense budget authority (graph), 64
National Defense University, 14, 244n

National Guard. *See* Reserve Component (RC) forces
National Science Foundation, 66
National security: public opinion and, 42. *See also* various subjects under U.S. military and U.S. Army
National Security Council, 36; "new look" (NSC-162/2), 36; Eisenhower administration in, 35
National security policy process, 34; Congress and the public, 40–41; President as prime mover (hypothesis three), 47; public and, 35. *See also* Eisenhower, President Dwight D.
National Strategy Forum, x–xi, 300
Naval missions, 218: defensive sea control, 221; forward area sea control, 222–223; offensive sea control, 221–222, 231, 234n; Third World operations, 226
"Neo-idealists": definition, 179; implications of, 179–180; world order and liberal idealists, 179
"Neorealists": definition, 179; implications of, 179–181
New Look: Congress and, 36
"New Thinking" (USSR): conflict within systems and, 98. *See also* glasnost, perestroika, and Gorbachev, Mikhail
New York Times, 38, 50n, 114n, 119n
Nicaragua: Nicaraguan Democratic Resistance (Contras), 209; Soviet involvement in, 189
Nixon administration: sufficient deterrence and, 92
Nixon, President Richard M., 40, 164
North Atlantic Alliance, 112
North Atlantic Treaty Organization (NATO), 3–4, 7; alarmist views, 128; arms reduction and, 143; burdensharing, 67, 156–157; Central Front and, 218, 223–225, 227–228, 231, 234n; challenges by Soviets, 149; changes in, 136, 165; changes irreversible, 129; changing strategic environment and, 41–42; combat experienced personnel, 146; conventional arms control, 113; conventional balance, 145; declining threat and, 122ff; decline of U.S. economic power and, 125; deep strike and, 146; defense of flanks, 220, 224–225, 231; defense specialization in, 157; deterrence capability, 145; diminished Soviet threat and, 123; eroding support for, 124, 293; flexible response and, 93, 113; force redeployment and, 163; force reductions and, 93, 166–171; force structure and, 152–173; forward posture, 127; France and Germany in, 131; human dimensions and, 146; impact of changes in West, 124; impact of changes in world environment, 124; impact of Gorbachev, 147; initiative, 127; internal stability in, 144; internal tensions, 139; irrelevant basis, 148; need for change, 121, 122, 124; new strategic environment, 127; option one, 128–129; option two, 129–132; option three, 132–136; Pershing II and GLCM, 86; principal challenge, 149; post–World War II strategy and, 22, 23; public confidence in, 136; reserve forces in, 259, 267; response to Soviet conventional capability, 88; significance of, 139; Soviet and Warsaw Pact behavior and, 122; Soviet forces in Europe and, 84; Soviet threat and, 147; strategy, 87–88; three response options, 127; two-track decision (1979), 143; U.S. interests, 189, 192; Warsaw Pact force asymmetries, 258–259; Warsaw Pact conflict and, 220–221, 226, 238; weakened support for, 126
Northeast Asia: as vital U.S. concern, 192
Norway: critical importance for sea control, 224
Nuclear deterrence, 157, 239
Nuclear war: Soviet view, 94
Nuclear weapons: destabilizing short range systems, 296n; proliferation of, 237–238; restraining factor, 192
Nunn, Senator, Sam, 55, 56, 57, 59, 60, 162

Ogarkov, Marshal N.V., 102, 103, 118n
Open systems: dilemmas of, 211
Opinion polls. *See* Gallup Poll, Harris Survey, and American Public Opinion
Organization of Petroleum Exporting Countries (OPEC), 288
Owen, Henry, 17n

Pacific: importance to U.S., 196, 214n, U.S. naval force deployments in, 226–229, 231–232
Packard Commission, 61
Page, Maj. Kenneth M., 245n
Pakistan: India-Pakistan conflict, 186–187; U.S. commitment to, 186–187
Palestine Liberation Organization (PLO), 152
Panama: canal, 188–189, 227; U.S. invasion of, x, 188, 293
Party Conference (USSR), 19th: perestroika and, 100
Party Congress (USSR), 27th, 100;

Gorbachev and, 89
Peacekeeping, 200
Pendley, Rear Adm. William, 228
Pentagon: defense budget instability and, 54; procurement, research and development, 126; trade-off-weapons and force size, 76; waste and, 69
People's Republic of China: Cambodian dispute and, 187; position vis à vis the U.S. and the Soviet Union; Third World and, 182
Perestroika, ix, 1–2, 157, 195. *See also* glasnost and Gorbachev, Mikhail
Perov, N., 119n
Pershing missiles, 143. *See also* various subjects under NATO
Persian Gulf: U.S. naval operations in, 226, 234n, 267
Peters, Lt. Col. John E., 172n
Philippines: U.S. bases in, 187
Planning, programming, and budgeting system (PPBS), 219
Poland, 134. *See also* Eastern Europe
Politburo, 100. *See also* Communist Party (USSR)
Political will: importance of, 207
Popov, V.M., 117n, 120n
Posen, Barry R., 193n, 234n
Pravda, 117n
President: Congress and, 34. *See also* various subjects under Congress
Presidential campaign (1952), 35
Presidential-Pentagon relations: Eisenhower administration, 39. *See also* Eisenhower, President Dwight D.
Proektor, D., 94
Profit, Air Commander G.R., 242
Public attitudes: towards defense spending (chart), 70
Public opinion: chance of world war (chart), 68; confidence in western alliance, 128; defense spending and, 76; defense spending and the media, 69; Europe, 123; impact on defense spending, 67; support for defense and (Reagan administration), 142; U.S. national security and, 143; views of allies and, 43; view of USSR, 44–45. *See also* American public opinion

Quayle, Senator Dan, 55
Quest for Excellence: Final Report by the President's Blue Ribbon Commission on Defense Management, 78n. *See also* Packard Commission

Radford, Admiral Arthur W., 36, 37
Rand corporation, 281n
Rapoport, Anatol, 213n
Raw materials: not all critical, 183
Reagan administration, 139, 141; alliance stability and, 145; arms control and, 143; defense build-up, 46, 47; defense policy, 142; defense spending, 43, 142; NATO and, 144; shift of U.S. policy and, 97;
Reagan, President Ronald, 10, 53, 63, 124, 164, 213n, 234n. *See also* Reagan administration
Record, Jeffrey, 17n, 194n
Regional conflict, 185–193
Republic of China (Taiwan), 187, 238
Reserve Component (RC) forces, 21, 26, 258–281: age and rank distribution, 280 (chart); Air National Guard size, 279n; "Capstone" program, 277, 281n; combat support (CS) and combat service support (CSS) structuring, 277–278; cost effectiveness of, 268, 281n; doctrinal development, 267–268; domestic security threat, 264–265; equipping of, 263; force multiplier, 259–261; growth of, 261; home guards (militias), 264, 279n; in NATO, 259, 260 (chart); links with Active Component (AC), 265–269; low-intensity conflict, 270; missions, 261–263, 269, 271n; mobilization time, 279; need for educational resources, 257; overseas training, 209; potential weaknesses, 272–274; public information value, 271; quality improvements, 262, 263 (chart); RC/AC balance, 268–269, 278, 294; regional representation, 275, 281n
Reykjavik Summit, 123–124, 143
Ridgway, General Matthew B., 36
Rielly, John E., 151n
RisCassi, General Robert W., 18n
Rivkin, David B., Jr., 17n
Roesler, Rolf, 17n
Rogers, General Bernard, 146, 147: Follow-on Forces Attack (FOFA) and, 87
Rogers Plan, 150. *See also* Rogers, General Bernard
Roosevelt Center for American Policy Studies, 194n
Ropelewski, Robert R., 245n
Rose, Col. John R., 172n
Rosefielde, Steven, 16n
Rosenau, James N., 193–194n, 213n
Russett, Bruce, 79n
Rust Affair: consequences, 91
Roos, John G., 17n

Sanders, R, 244n
Sarkesian, Sam C., xii, 195, 213–214n,

290–292, 296n, 299–300
Savimbi, Jonas, 209
Savushkin, R.A., 117n, 120n
Schelling, Thomas C., 194n
Schemmer, Benjamin F., 213n
Schick, Allen, 77n
Schlesinger, James, 59
Schemmer, Benjamin F., 18n
Schmidt, Chancellor Helmut, 142
Schroeder, Representative Pat, 156
Scott, John F., 172n
Scowcroft, Lt. Gen. Brent, 229
Security assistance (U.S.): effectiveness, 205, 207; problems, 205; types, 204
Shaver, Col. David E., 152, 172n, 296n, 300
Shulman, Marshall D., 213n
Shultz, Richard, 213n
Shultz, Secretary of State George, 143
Single Integrated Operational Plan (SIOP): need to rethink, 237
Semeyko, Lev, 86, 115n
Senate Armed Services Committee, 37, 77n, 233n, 235n. *See also* Congress
Shavrov, Colonel General I.E., 98, 99, 118n
Simon, Jeffrey, 115n
Skugarev, V.D., 118n
Smoke, Richard, 49n, 50n
Snow, Donald M., 17n
Social Democratic Party (SPD), 144; party conferences, 88
Socialist Party (France), 144
South Asia: U.S.-Soviet rivalry and, 187
South Korea, 238, 267, 285: division of Korea as security problem, 188; economic performance, 187, 288; U.S. commitment, 188–189, 224, 232
Southeast Asia: U.S.-Soviet rivalry and, 187
Sovetskai voenna entsiklopediia, 117n
Soviet economic problems. *See* Soviet Union and Gorbachev, Mikhail
Soviet forces: unilateral withdrawals, 109. *See also* Gorbachev, Mikhail
Soviet General Staff, 102; Communist Party Assessment of war, 106–107; future war and, 103; military art and, 106; new role, 112; perestroika and, 103; "qualitative" leap and, 106; review of war, 104; views on present era, 98
Soviet military: combat experience, 146; combat readiness, 92; Gorbachev and, 3–4; landlocked, 192; military posture, 5; modernization of, 147; Operational Military Group, 87; quality of, 23; threat to NATO, 87; Zapad-81 (military excerise), 87
Soviet military art, 105–106

Soviet military doctrine, 83, 105, 109; dilemmas, 95; dominance of offense, 106; new approach, 92; new doctrine, 91; new thinking, 91; political context, 95; premeditated defense, 110. *See also* Soviet General Staff and Soviet military
Soviet military officers: military science and, 99
Soviet military policy, 123, 127
Soviet military threat: confined to continental Eurasia, 192; Europe and, 5–6; force structure and, 170; perception of, ix, 157
Soviet-Mongolian offensive (1939), 110
Soviet nationalities problem. *See* Soviet Union
Soviet Navy, 165, 227–228, 231: capabilities still high, 217; SSBNs, 221–222, 231, 234–235n; wartime missions, 222
Soviet party elite, 101. *See also* Communist Party
Soviet Union, ix–xi, 164: acceptance of conventional forces, 84; aid to Nicaragua and Kabul, 9; arms control concessions, 87; arms proposals in Vienna, 85; assessment of U.S. defense capabilities, 97; asymmetry, 132; "Atlantic to the Urals", 109; Baltic republics and, 292, 296n; challenge of noncommunist Soviet Union to U.S., 286; confidence building measures, 109; conventional stability talks, 108; criticism of U.S. nuclear strategy, 92; delinking U.S. from Europe, 96; denuclearization of war, 111; deterrence and war-fighting capabilities, 99; dissent and repression, 165, 287; easing of threat, 62, Eastern Europe, 2, 133; economic and military decline, 126; economy, 101, 160, 239; efforts to isolate U.S., 130; force trade-offs with West, 108; gap between rhetoric and reality, 148; historic changes, 147, 195; internal problems, 2–3, 23; less threatening, 148; military sufficiency, 96; new political system and, 4; nuclear parity, 41; placed on defensive, 127; potential for reversal, 23; potential military action, 23; program-target planning, 101–102; reaction to chaos on borders, 292–292, 296n; reforms, 128; regional conflict and, 97–98; relative military invulnerability, 95; rethinking Western Europe security and, 96, 181; revolution in military affairs, 107; Sputnik, 37; strategic options, 158; Third World and, 8–9, 97, 195;

threat in Europe, 84; threat reduction and breathing space, 97, 286; U.S. competitive strategies and, 97; U.S. Maritime Strategy and, 219; Warsaw Pact and, 65, 139
Soviet/WTO: conventional forces Europe and, 84–85; military threat, 107. *See also* Soviet Union and Warsaw Pact
Special forces, 177, 179–180, 184: Air Force Special Squadrons, 203; civilian task force and, 212; military career and, 204; origins and history, 203; ranger units, 203; SEALs, 203. *See also* special operations and unconventional conflicts
Special operations, 164, 178: role in Europe. 204; Special Operations Command, 203–205, 208, 210, 213n; U.S. Air Force and, 203, 240–241; U.S. capabilities, 210. *See also* special forces and unconventional conflicts
Spurlock, Delbert L., Jr., 17n
SS-20s (USSR), 86, 143
Staff Report to the Senate Armed Services Committee on Defense Organization: *The Need for Change*, 78n
Stalin, Joseph, 295, 296n
Stalinist model, 134
Stanley, Timothy W., 17n
Stans, Maurice, 37
State Department (U.S.): and unconventional conflicts, 208
Steinbrunner, John D., 137n
Stennis, Senator John, 57
Stevens, Senator Ted, 59
Stockholm Conference: (Confidence and Security Building Measures in Europe), 87, 89; verification issues and, 90
Strategic Arms Limitation Talks (SALT) I, 86
Strategic Arms Reduction Talks (START), 93, 159, 183
Strategic Defense Initiative (SDI), 89, 150. *See also* Defense spending
Strategic landscape, x–xi, 14, 152, 285, 296; contradictory themes, 148
Sturua, G.M., 114n, 115n
Suez crisis (1956), 140
Summers, Harry G., 18n
Sun Tzu, 213n: concepts of war and success, 199
Superpowers, 130, 132
Supreme Allied Commander Europe (SACEUR), 145–146, 150, 234n. *See also* Rogers, Gen. Bernard and Haig, Gen. Alexander
Supreme Soviet, 4
Swartz, Capt. Peter M., 232n
Symington, Senator Stuart, 37

Tarlton, Gael D., 235n
Tarr, David W., 177, 300
TASS, 114n
Taylor, Gen. Maxwell D., 38
Technology: high versus low technology weapons, 158–159, 167, 169, 171, 238; quality versus quantity, 169–170, 244n; reserve training and, 273; SDI and, 29; strategy and, 236; U.S. Air Force, 241–242; U.S. Army, 29
Terrorism, 25. *See also* Unconventional conflicts
Thailand: U.S. commitment, 187
Thatcher, Prime Minister Margaret, 131, 144
Third World: causes of instability, 202; communist disengagement, 157; conventional conflict, 177–194; economic problems, 288–289; ethnic groups, 183; future wars, 159; increased challenge to U.S., xii, 285, 287–289; internal struggles, 196; Maritime Strategy and, 220; military threats from, 287–288; nationalism in, 182; Soviet presence in, 181–182, 195, 210; sophisticated weapons, 177; U.S. elite attitudes on intervention, 184; U.S. interests in, 185, 190, 192, 195–196, 201, 207; U.S. and Soviet setbacks in, 185; U.S. strategy disjointed, 196; wars of national liberation, 182; weapons proliferation, 237
Thompson, Sir Robert, 198, 213n
Threat perceptions: public opinion and, 43
Thucydides, 46–47
Tiushkevich, S.A., 94, 117n
Tonkin Gulf Resolution, 39–40
Tovar, B. Hugh, 213n
Tower, Senator John, 59
Trade, 165: Asia, 227; effect on national security decisions, 171; European Economic Community, 160; Japan, 160; national security issue, 160–161; trade war, 161, 171
Treverton, Gregory F., 213n
Trident Accord, 131
Trofimenko, Genrikh, 89, 116n
Trost, Adm. Carlisle A.H., 223, 233–234n: and Maritime Strategy, 219
Truman Doctrine, 134
Truman, President Harry, 145
Turkey: U.S. Jupiter missiles in, 190–191
Twining, General Nathan, 38

Ullman, Richard H., 138n
Unconventional conflicts, xi, 14–15; Afghanistan, 195; concepts and definitions, 197–198, 213n; force structure needed, 196; guerrilla war and,

198; intellegence and, 207; offensive versus defensive, 206; "people's wars," 198; political context, 195, 198–200; problems for research, 205; require patience, 203; revolution and counterrevolution, 198–200; security assistance, 207; U.S. capabilities in, 210–211; U.S. military needs and, 15; U.S. strategy and, 195–214. *See also* United States military
United Kingdom: defense spending, 66
United Nations, 149, 155, 157
United States: alliance relations and coalition strategy, 22; decline of economic power, 125, 141, 182; Franco-British cooperation and, 132; force posture, 14; federal deficit, 126; Germany and, 128; "guns versus butter," 158; industrial base, 166; iron triangle impact on military, 126; NATO fair share and, 67; objectives, 152–153, 155; security interests, 178–183; strategic reserve, 19; strategy, 9–10, 163–165; vital versus important interests, 200–202. *See also* various subjects beginning with United States
United States Air Force, xi: B-2 bomber, 74; capabilities needed, 240–242; force structure, 238; internal competition, 290; organizational structure, 240; recruiting, 297n; research and development needs, 241; support of other services, 244, unconventional conflicts,212. *See also* Defense spending
United States Arms Control and Disarmament Agency (ACDA): report on missile proliferation, 237
United States Army, ix–xi: Airborne and Ranger forces, 28; AirLand Battle doctrine, 20; basis for lethality, 28; Army Educational Requirements System, 253; budget constraints and, 29; Combat Training Centers, 21, 30; Combined Center, 299; education assignments and career path, 256–257; education hierarchy (chart) 251; Europe, 232, 296n; force structure, 25, 26, 152–173, 193, 238; forward Area Defense system (Follow-on Forces Attack: FOFA), 73–74; forward deployed forces, 27; future and, 20; graduate education in civilian universities, 253; isolation from society, 255; jointness, 251–253; leader development, 21–22; "hollow Army," 156; light infantry, 204, 209, 212, 294; mix of forces, 21; modernization, 21, 28; officer education, 249–257; people oriented, 30; personnel strength, 155; quality, 20; Reserve Component (RC) forces, 258–281; security assistance and, 27; security environment (1990s) and, 25; size reduction, 30; societal context, 249; strategic lift and, 28; strategic rationale, 293–296; sustainability and, 26; traditionalists versus progressives, 254–255; training, 21; Training and Doctrine Command (TRADOC), 300; training versus education, 254–255; versatility and, 26; volunteer force, 27
United States Army Command and General Staff College (C&GSC): Combined Arms and Services Staff School (CAS3), 250–251; School of Advanced Military Studies (SAMS), 251
United States Army Reserve. *See* Reserve Component (RC) forces
United States Army War College, 154, 172n, 213n, 253, 294, 298, 300: active learning emphasis, 256; Current Affairs Panel, 255; General Officer Update Program, 252; Strategic Studies Institute, 172–173n
United States Central Command, 186, 267
United States Constitution, 249
United States domestic environment: three major problems, 10
United States economic growth, 62; public opinion polls, 42–43
United States Forces Command: continental U.S. Army areas of responsibility, 266 (chart); reliance on reserves, 262
United States Marine Corps: integrated operations, 290; internal competition, 290, recruiting, 297n; role, 294; unconventional conflicts, 212
United States Military: advisors, 249–250; bases, 180; budget constraints, 14, 236; civilian control, 249–250; force planning premises, 181; force structure, 168–169, 177–178; human needs and, 11; intellectual needs and, 12; low-intensity conflict and, 25, 195–214; missions, 160, 162, 169, 171, 294; mobilization, 171; need to reduce commitments, 161, 167, 171; professional education and, 15; purpose of, 295; readiness and defense budgets, 75; secondary contingencies and, 15; society and, 12; Soviet criticism of, 93–94; strategic lift, 169; strategic mobility, 162; strategy, 11, 158; understanding of, 16
United States Military Academy, 250, 299
United States Naval Academy, 301
United States Naval Institute, 219, 233–

234n
United States Naval War College, 219, 233n, 235n, 299, 301: interwar planning against "Orange," 227; Strategic Studies Group, 219
United States Navy: air refueling, 242; aircraft carriers, 218, 221–222, 231, 233–234n; battleships, 218–219, 233n, 235n; budget, 217; internal competition, 290; operating tempo (OPTEMPO), 229–230, 235n; preferred force structure, 218; recruiting, 297n; Seawolf Attack Submarine (SSN-21), 74; six hundred ship Navy, 218, 290; SSNs, 222; surge deployments, 230–231; unconventional conflicts, 212. *See also* Maritime Strategy and naval missions
United States strategic planning, 14
United States Total Force, 12, 15
United States-USSR: competitive coexistence/controlled competition, 113; relations and national security, 44, 45; "rules of the road," 190–191
University of Illinois: at Chicago, 298; at Urbana-Champaign, 299
University of Kansas, 299
University of Vermont, 299
USSR: *See* Soviet Union

Vallance, Group Captain A.G.B., 242
van den Haag, Ernest, 214n
Van Evera, Stephen, 181, 193–194n
Vasil'ev, A., 117n
Vienna: arms talks, 84, 122, 127, 128
Vietnam, 224: Cam Ranh Bay, 157, 187, 228; U.S.-Soviet rivalry, 187
Vietnam War, 146, 185, 190, 210–211, 229, 287; counterinsurgency in, 209; defense spending and, 62. *See also* Vietnam and Weyand, Gen. Fred
Vigor, Peter, 115n
V'iunenko, N.P., 118n
Visco, Eugene P., xi
Vitas, Robert L., xi
Voennyi entsiklopicheskii slovar', 117n
Voroshilov Academy, 99
Vuono, Gen. Carl E., ix, xi, 19, 172n, 272, 279n, 281n, 300

Walker, Air Vice Marshal J.W., 242, 245n
Walker, Wallace Earl, 18n
Walt, Stephen, 193n
War Powers Resolution(1973), 40
Warner, III, Edward L., 17n
Warsaw Pact, 23–24, 65, 135; conventional arms reductions, 163; demilitarized zone, 109; emerging technologies, 167; political reliability, 286, 293. *See also* Soviet Union,

Warsaw Treaty Organization (WTO)
Warsaw Treaty Organization (WTO), 83; Political Consultative Committee-Berlin formula, 91. *See also* Warsaw Pact
Watkins, Adm. James, 225, 234n
Watson, Cynthia, 296n
Weapons cost: defense spending and, 73; impact on United States military services, 74–75. *See also* Defense spending
Weapons modernization: budget constraints and, 74. *See also* Defense spending
Weapons proliferation, 237–238: in developing world, 24
Webb, James H., Jr., 234
Weeks, Albert L., 17n, 117n
Weickhardt, George G., 234n
Weinberger, Secretary of Defense Casper, 54, 56
Weiner, Myron, 296n
Welch, General Larry D., 47
West: new defense posture, 129; verification and confidence building measures, 130. *See also* various subjects under United States, United States military, Western Europe
Western allies: defense spending and, 66
Western European Union, 128, 163, 165
West Germany: key within Europe, 125; economic growth and European Entity, 128. *See also* Germany, Western Europe
Wettig, Gerhard, 92, 116n
Weyand, General Fred, 13, 16, 18n
White, Richard H., 214n
Williams, John Allen, xii, 217, 234n, 285, 297n, 300–301
Willis, Grant, 18n
Wilson, Secretary of Defense, Charles, 36, 37
Woerner, Defense Minister Manfred, 150
Woolsey, James, 229

Yakovlev, A.N., 93, 109, 114n, 115n; critique of U.S. security policy, 88–89; military sufficiency and, 90–91; mutual trust security system, 90; USSR military doctrine and, 91
Yankelovich, Daniel, 49n, 50n
Yasiukov, Major General M., 100 118n
Yazov, Minister of Defense D.T., 105, 108, 112, 116n, 117n, 119n; Berlin formula and perestroika, 91; USSR military strategy and, 92
Young, Thomas F., 214n

Zhurkin, V.V., 117n, 119n
Zumwalt, Adm. Elmo, 218

About the Book

Grappling with the constraints and opportunities the U.S. Army faces designing policy and strategic options for the post–INF era, a select group of scholars, military officers, and policymakers outline the current strategic posture of the army, the challenges of the future, and the steps needed to meet those challenges.

The book is the outgrowth of a workshop held to address issues raised by the U.S. Army Chief of Staff. In its final form, it presents a cohesive picture of those issues, discussing the changing European security environment, public attitudes in the U.S. legislative and budgetary concerns, the status of the U.S. reserve forces and the education of military officers, conflicts outside of Europe, and the implications of maritime and air strategy for the army's strategic posture.